D1359204

WITHDRAWN

07 / 13 / 20 22

SAINT LOUIS UNIVERSITY

A to Z Handbook
of Child and Adolescent Issues

A to Z Handbook
of Child
and Adolescent Issues

Amy Beth Taublieb, Ph.D.

Ref.
BF
721
.T38
2000

Allyn and Bacon

Boston ■ London ■ Toronto ■ Sydney ■ Tokyo ■ Singapore

Series editor: *Becky Pascal*
Series editorial assistant: *Susan Hutchinson*
Marketing manager: *Joyce Nilsen*

Copyright © 2000 by Allyn & Bacon
A Pearson Education Company
Needham Heights, MA 02494

Internet: www.abacon.com

All rights reserved. No part of the material protected by this copyright notice may be reproduced or utilized in any form or by any means, electronic or mechanical, including photocopying, recording, or by any information storage and retrieval system, without written permission from the copyright owner.

Many of the designations used by manufacturers and sellers to distinguish their products are claimed as trademarks. Where those designations appear in this book, and Allyn and Bacon was aware of a trademark claim, the designations have been printed in initial or all caps.

Library of Congress Cataloging-in-Publication Data

Taublieb, Amy Beth.
    A to Z handbook of child and adolescent
 issues / Amy Beth Taublieb.
        p.   cm.
    Includes bibliographical references and index.
    ISBN 0-205-28327-6
    1. Child psychology—Encyclopedias.   2. Adolescent psychology—
Encyclopedias.   I. Title.
BF721.T38   2000
155.4'03—dc21   99-31600
                                                                        CIP

Printed in the United States of America

10 9 8 7 6 5 4 3 2 1   04 03 02 01 00 99

*To Dad and Aunt Aliece, who gave so much of themselves to parent me,
and to Mom, who continues to do so.*

CONTENTS

PREFACE

Many years, and literally thousands of hours, spent working with parents, children, adolescents, and families have taught me more than all of my years of formalized schooling combined. The most important lesson learned from these hundreds of people who paid me the honor of sharing their deepest family trials and tribulations in my office was as follows: As sure as every parent wants to do his or her best with respect to parenting, every parent also has a multitude of questions in terms of what is the "right" way to proceed. Some of these questions often extend to concerns about the child's behavior—as to whether it is "normal." Frequently, these queries are presented rather timidly, as if the adult is convinced that the rest of the parenting world certainly knows the answers to these questions and, indeed, it is only the parent's inadequacy that necessitates the question.

It is for all those adults with whom I have had the privilege of interacting and for all of you with whom I have not spoken directly that this book is written. This book is designed for anyone and everyone who has contact with children and adolescents and, at some point, has wondered about the young person's behavior. Parents, caseworkers, babysitters, child care workers, teachers, guidance counselors, pediatricians, social workers, attorneys.... In sum, all of us who are students of child and adolescent psychology through our encounters with this young population will find our questions answered in this book. How can I be so confident? Because it is the questions and issues posed to me by such individuals that formulated the contents of the text.

Modeled after the increasingly common medical desk references, this book is intended to be unique in both its completeness and content. Written in language that is user-friendly to the layperson, it is truly encyclopedic in scope as it covers hundreds of issues dealing with the psychology of children and adolescents. With entries ranging from the most common (e.g., thumb sucking, arguing between siblings) to those more clinical in nature (e.g., school phobia, childhood depression), each entry contains an extensive definition in nontechnical language, real-life examples of the topic being discussed, as well as information on distinguishing those situations that require professional interventions from those that do not. For those issues that are problematic in nature, the reader is provided with information relevant to the theories regarding causality, frequency of occurrence, and typical symptom presentation. Also provided are practical suggestions for parent/teacher/adult response. In those cases in which professional intervention is indicated, the reader is given specific guidelines in terms of what to look for and to expect from the treatment experience.

Even as the final manuscript is being assembled, ideas for additional entries are making themselves evident. Toward that end, I look to you the reader for suggestions in terms of improvement for subsequent editions. Whether it be entries that should be included but are not, or entries that should not appear; whether it be a request for more information on a given topic, or more abbreviated coverage for another topic; whether it be a specific question you would like addressed or a more general issue you would like covered in the book, please let me know (via Allyn & Bacon or e-mail at abtaublieb@aol.com). A book such as this is only as valuable as it is useful, and it is my goal to make this text a *true* guide for parents and professionals in every sense of the word!

Acknowledgments

The credit due for any major project such as this rightfully belongs to many—certainly not to just the author. I would like to take this opportunity to pay homage to the several people who have contributed to making *A to Z Handbook of Child and Adolescent Issues* a reality:

- to the publisher's reviewers who were willing to look at the text well before the point it reached its final stages and were able to see beyond the omissions and errors, to make valuable suggestions that resulted in this final product: Dewey J. Bayer, Canisius College; Judith M. Ferrara, Consultant, Worcester, MA; Linda M. Groat, Lockport High School, Kenmore, NY; and Suzette Stringer, Child and Adolescent Treatment Services, Buffalo, NY
- to Carla Daves, acquisitions editor, who helped metamorphose a prospectus into a publishing project
- to Sue Hutchinson, editorial assistant, who patiently answered all my questions (sometimes more than once!) and provided reassurance and an organizational competence beyond any reasonable expectation
- to Rabbi Robert J. Eisen, whose wisdom extended well beyond suggestions for the title and dedication to much more important things
- and, finally, to all of the special people mentioned in the Preface who entered my office for therapy and actually gave *me* so very much.

ABOUT THE AUTHOR

Amy Beth Taublieb is a licensed psychologist with an active private practice specializing in assessment, diagnosis, and treatment of children, adolescents, and their families. With extensive experience in addressing family and parenting issues with professionals and laypeople alike, Dr. Taublieb has offered various lectures, workshops, and training experiences to different groups. She is also a frequent guest on local and national radio and television shows discussing a myriad of psychological topics of general interest. In addition, Dr. Taublieb is the author of a weekly newspaper column ("Ask Dr. Amy"), has taught numerous undergraduate psychology courses, provides clinical supervision for advanced-level psychology graduate students, and is the author of the textbook *The Psychopathology of Childhood and Adolescence* (Addison Wesley Longman, 1997) along with its accompanying *Instructor's Manual.*

A to Z Handbook
of Child and Adolescent Issues

A Academic Skill Disorders–Avoidant Personality Disorder

Academic Skill Disorders

In earlier diagnostic systems, the term *academic skill disorders* was used for the classification of disorders currently referred to as **Learning Disorders.** Included in this category are the diagnoses of **Reading Disorder** (formerly referred to as developmental reading disorder), **Mathematics Disorder** (formerly referred to as developmental arithmetic disorder), **Disorder of Written Expression** (formerly referred to as developmental expressive writing disorder), and **Learning Disorder Not Otherwise Specified.**

SUPPLEMENTAL RESOURCES

Cutler, B. C. (1993). *You, your child, and special ed: A guide to making the system work.* New York: Paul H. Brookes.

Davis, R. D., & Braun, E. M. (1994). *The gift of dyslexia.* New York: Barkley.

Featherstone, H. (1981). *A difference in the family: Living with a disabled child.* New York: Penguin.

Fisher, G., & Cummings, R. (1990). *The survival guide for kids with learning disabilities.* Minneapolis, MN: Free Spirit.

Fisher, G., & Cummings, R. (1995). *When your child has LD (learning differences).* Minneapolis, MN: Free Spirit.

Gehret, J. (1996). *The don't-give-up kid and learning differences.* Fairport, NY: Verbal Images Press.

Hamaguachi, P. M. (1995). *Childhood speech, language, and listening problems: What every parent should know.* New York: John Wiley.

Mandel, H. P., & Marcus, S. I. (1995). *Could do better.* New York: John Wiley.

McNamara, B. E., & McNamara, F. J. (1995). *Keys to parenting a child with a learning disability.* New York: Barrons.

Meyer, D., & Vadasy, P. (1996). *Living with a brother or sister with special needs: A book for siblings.* Seattle: University of Washington Press.

Miller, W. H. (1993). *Complete reading disability handbook.* West Nyack, NY: Simon & Schuster.

Rosner, J. (1993). *Helping children overcome learning difficulties.* New York: Walker.

Smith, S. L. (1991). *Succeeding against the odds.* New York: Putnam Press.

Smith, S. L. (1995). *No easy answers: The learning disabled child at home and at school.* New York: Bantam.

Trainer, M. (1991). *Differences in common.* Rockville, MD: Woodbine House.

Unger, H. G. (1998). *The learning disabilities trap: How to save your child from the perils of special education.* Chicago: Contemporary.

Acute

Acute is an adjective used to describe the nature of one or more symptoms or of the onset of a specific disorder. When a symptom or disorder is described as being acute, the implication is that the onset had a definite point and that, in most cases, this onset was relatively recent. Furthermore, characterizing a symptom or disorder as acute makes a statement regarding the clinical intensity, that is, it implies that a symptom or disorder is at (or close to) the peak of its severity.

Acute Stress Disorder

This is a relatively new diagnosis, presented for the first time in the newest edition of the *DSM,* published in 1994. It refers to a constellation of symptoms resulting from the experience of a traumatic event. However, unlike the diagnosis of **Post-Traumatic Stress Disorder,** symptoms of acute stress disorder, by definition, are short-term, and occur shortly after the actual traumatic experience. Specifically, for a diagnosis of acute stress disorder to be applied, the symptoms need to have occurred within 4 weeks of the traumatic event, and to last for a maximum duration of 4 weeks. Should the symptoms exceed these time guidelines in duration or onset of occurrence, it is likely that the diagnosis of post-traumatic stress disorder would be applied.

The type of trauma that can trigger symptoms of acute stress disorder varies extensively. For children and adolescents, these traumas include (but are certainly not limited to) experiencing a traumatic event (e.g., inappropriate sexual activities), witnessing a traumatic event (e.g., observing a family member or pet get seriously injured), or hearing/learning about a traumatic event that happened to someone else (e.g., finding out that a classmate was run over by a school bus). As a reaction to this traumatic occurrence, the child/adolescent experiences various symptoms of intense fear, hopelessness or horror, with these symptoms impacting upon the young person's ability to function. The symptoms of acute stress disorder fall into four major categories: (1) **Dissociative,** (2) reexperiencing, (3) avoidance, and (4) anxiety.

Dissociative symptoms refer to symptoms in which the young person feels dissociated, or separated, from his or her environment. Such symptoms can take the form of feeling numb or emotionally detached, feeling as if parts of the surroundings are not real, feeling as if he or she is not actually participating in life activities but rather is acting as an observer and/or is unable to remember specific parts of the traumatic event.

> *Example:* Eight-year-old Anastasia was sexually molested by her grandmother's second husband. However, she has not told anybody about this yet because he told her that the sexual activity was a special part of their relationship and that other people may be jealous and not understand. Whenever Anastasia goes to her grandmother's house, she seems

to "space out" and does not feel a part of what is going on. Sometimes, the child feels as if she is not really there but, rather, is observing what is transpiring around her as if she is watching a movie or a television program.

The phenomenon of reexperiencing the trauma is one of the most common and most characteristic of acute stress disorder. Feeling as if the traumatic event is being repeatedly relived takes various forms. For some individuals, there are repeated flashbacks that are most vivid in detail—seeming almost real. In other cases, this reexperiencing takes the form of intrusive thoughts/images, dreams, or actual illusions. Finally, in yet other cases, being in contact with people, objects, or situations that trigger a memory of the traumatic occurrence can be enough to bring on reactions similar to those when the event was actually occurring.

Example: A couple of weeks ago, 8-year-old Nadine was in a rather serious car accident. Although she was not hurt badly, she did observe her older brother being thrust through the windshield. Now, when Nadine rides in a car, she is perfectly fine for the first 5 minutes or so. Then, sometime during the ride, she will scream her brother's name in terror saying, "Mommy, save him…save him."

Example: Ten days ago, 13-year-old Jason was alone in the house with his infant sister when there was an electrical fire. When he smelled the smoke, he managed to get himself, his sister, and the family dog out of the house safely. They took shelter at the home of a nearby neighbor, who called the fire department immediately. However, the home itself was destroyed. The family is now living at a relative's home until they can locate a more permanent residence. However, whenever someone cooks something in the microwave oven and the beeper goes off, indicating that the cooking is complete, Jason exhibits a startled response and requires 5 to 10 minutes to return to normal.

Often, avoidance is another component of the symptom profile of acute stress disorder. Closely resembling phobic symptomatology, the individual who suffers from acute stress disorder may come to phobically avoid situations identical or similar to the traumatic event. In other situations, the acute stress disorder sufferer will show this same avoidance behavior in response to situations that do not appear to others to be associated with the traumatic event but which, nonetheless, evoke associations to the traumatic event for the sufferer. Thus, the situation that is avoided may not necessarily have an obvious relationship to the traumatic event but, rather, may evoke an association to the sufferer—the source of which is not blatantly obvious to others.

Example: Fourteen-year-old Marsalla was mugged on the way home from doing a grocery errand for her mother. The thug not only robbed her of the groceries and money but also punched her in the stomach and face several times. Since that incident, Marsalla refuses to ride the school bus and, instead, opts to wake up one hour earlier so that she can walk to school. Her behavior was difficult for her mother to understand until Marsalla explained that there is a boy who rides the school bus who reminds her of the man who mugged her.

When there is a visible anxiety component to the symptom profile of acute stress disorder, its form can assume anything from an appearance of nervousness to a full-blown presentation of any of the **Anxiety Disorders.** In some cases, the sufferer of the acute stress disorder simply gives the impression of being a bit more jumpy or nervous than usual. Yet, in other situations, the person will manifest full-blown symptoms of **Generalized Anxiety Disorder, Phobic Disorders, Obsessive-Compulsive Disorder,** or **Separation Anxiety Disorder.** In these latter situations, the symptomatic behavior observed is virtually identical to that seen in any of the above disorders, but is brought on by the trauma of the stressful event.

When to Seek Professional Help

A child or adolescent's demonstrating a reaction to a traumatic experience, in and of itself, is certainly not justification for seeking professional help. However, there are situations in which a young person has experienced a traumatic situation and the psychological results and ramifications of this experience significantly interfere with his or her day-to-day functioning. Further, in certain such cases, the intensity of the interference is such that parents and teachers are perplexed as to how to intervene optimally with the youngster.

Indeed, the decision as to whether to seek professional assistance after a young person experiences a traumatic event is a difficult one, in many cases perhaps even more so than in cases of adult sufferers. Especially since young people cannot always be depended upon to be able or willing to express their feelings regarding a traumatic event, the determination of its impact can come to resemble an investigation. Oftentimes, concerned adults cannot determine if indeed the child is emotionally distraught and he or she is hiding distress, or, if in reality, no significant emotional distress is being experienced. Then, if it is concluded that the latter situation is the case, there is often concern as to why such a traumatic occurrence is not more bothersome! Once again, concerned adults are placed in the uncomfortable situation of not wanting to overreact, but not wanting to ignore important clinical signs.

Clinicians are trained in distinguishing so-called normal reactions to traumatic events from those that are less usual and require professional attention. In general, concerned adults who observe any of the above signs and symptoms for an extended period of time (i.e., over two to three weeks) are encouraged to seek professional consultation for their child/adolescent. Even if the result of the consultation is simply being reassured of the normalcy of the reactions, that in and of itself is often sufficient to assuage fears and anxieties. It is important to note that, in addition to the discomfort of the actual symptoms, the young person himself or herself is probably quite worried as to the meaning and implications of the symptoms. Thus, having the symptoms explained, as well as being assured that the reactions are normal and to be expected, is often itself curative.

If indeed the young person is actually experiencing clinically significant reactions to the traumatic event, it is important to note that well-established, effective treatments exist for **Post-Traumatic Stress Disorder.** Such treatment approaches have been modified for use in the treatment of acute stress disorder. For a detailed explanation of such treatments, refer to entry **Post-Traumatic Stress Disorder.**

SUPPLEMENTAL RESOURCES

Bean, B., & Bennett, S. (1993). *The me nobody knows: A guide for teen survivors.* New York: Lexington Books.

Flannery, R. B. (1998). *PTSD: The victim's guide to healing and recovery.* New York: Crossroads.

Adolescent Depression

As normal adolescence has become associated with rather dramatic mood swings (refer to the entry **Adolescent Mood Swings**), it has similarly come to be assumed that depression is simply an expected part of this developmental stage. In reality, however, recent research supports adolescent emotional turmoil as being neither unavoidable nor as having a causal relationship with clinical depression during adolescence. Nonetheless, it can be difficult to distinguish between the expected mood variations of this developmental stage and true clinical depression. For that reason, depression in adolescents is significantly underdiagnosed, with clinical symptoms often being dismissed as a phase typical of this age group. This is most unfortunate in that adolescent depression clearly demands as much (if not more) clinical attention as does depression occurring in any of the other phases of life.

The actual psychology of adolescence itself also contributes to the difficulty in recognizing this clinical syndrome in adolescents. Indeed, the commonly observed tendency of adolescents to emotionally withdraw from adults can yield impediments in communication resulting in situations in which the depression becomes either mislabeled or entirely overlooked. The adolescent's tendency to employ denial—as well as that to behaviorally act out feelings rather than express them verbally—all contribute to adolescent depression being perceived by others as something entirely different from what it actually is. For example, it would be especially easy for a parent to dismiss a 16-year-old's sullen behavior as adolescent moodiness when he repeatedly responds "nothing" to being asked what is bothering him. Similarly, when a 14-year-old's school and home behavior deteriorates to the extent that there is frequent physical fighting with peers, it is often difficult to recognize this aggressive acting out as being symptomatic of depression. Thus, in cases such as these, the situation is often not viewed as being a result of a depressive disorder, and, unfortunately, is not addressed accordingly.

In reality, depression most often does have its first onset during adolescence and early adulthood. However, clinical literature indicates that adolescent depression is actually a continuation of a depressive process that began at an earlier time. Thus, reflective of the developmental process, the symptoms of adolescent depression can be viewed as being a combination of those observed in depressed children and those observed in depressed adults.

Depressed adolescents usually manifest symptoms that can be classified as the usual emotional turmoil of adolescence—only to a greater intensity. The actual symptom profile does indeed vary, incorporating a combination of both physical and emotional, as well as behavioral symptoms. In addition to complaints of various aches, pains, and other maladies, physical symptoms of adolescent depression also include a change in eating patterns (often resulting in a dramatic weight gain or loss), a delay in the progression of pubertal changes, **Enuresis,** compulsive behaviors (such as **Nail Biting**), fatigue, and/or disturbed sleep patterns. Adolescent depressive symptoms that are more emotional in nature include low self-esteem, an increase in the frequency and intensity of emotional outbursts and rebellious outbursts, and an intensification of the usual adolescent mood swings. More behavioral expressions of adolescent depression can be expressed as excessive risk-taking behavior, withdrawal from peers and usual activities, problems with concentration/attention, **Antisocial** behavior (often expressed as an open disregard for societal and familial rules and regulations), as well as a preoccupation with the topic of death.

When depression occurs in adolescents with no preexisting psychopathology, it is referred to as **Primary.** However, when the depressive symptoms are believed to be in some way associated with another psychological or psychiatric diagnosis, the depression is referred to as **Secondary.** Secondary depression is common when the adolescent is suffering from a psychological (or physical) disorder, and somehow coping with this disorder results in the adolescent feeling depressed. (For example, a 13-year-old who is suffering from a **Social Phobia** feels depressed as a result of the limitations placed upon her social life stemming from her avoidance.) This distinction between primary and secondary adolescent depression is an especially important one, as the clinical literature reports that those adolescents suffering from secondary depression tend to manifest symptoms of aggression, irritability, and **Somatic Preoccupation** more frequently than do adolescents suffering from primary depression.

Closely related to the issue of secondary depression in adolescence is the fact that adolescent depression is often seen in conjunction with other psychological/psychiatric diagnoses—which occurs more frequently than in cases of adult depression. This **Comorbidity** tendency has adolescent depression often coexisting with **Anxiety Disorders,** disruptive behavior disorders, impaired peer relationships, problems with academic performance/achievement, and substance abuse disorders. As would be expected, implications for treatment become more complicated as other psychological issues become involved. Indeed, no longer is it just the depressive symptoms that need to be addressed in treatment. Further, research has shown that thoughts of suicide as well as of self-injurious behavior in general are more prevalent when there are comorbid symptoms presenting with the adolescent depression.

A relatively recent study (Rosenberg, Wright, & Gershon, 1992) compared the major depressive signs and symptoms in adolescents with those in children who have not reached puberty. It is interesting to note that these researchers found that adolescents report more symptoms of **Anhedonia** and verbalize more feelings of hopelessness. As opposed to the younger age group (which tends to exhibit problems in sleeping when depressed), adolescents are more likely to exhibit a hypersomnia (i.e., more frequent and extended periods of sleeping). Also, the physical appearance of depressed adolescents is less remarkable than is that of the prepubertal group and there are similarly less physical complaints, phobic symptoms, and **Hallucinations.** However, suicide attempts made by depressed adolescents tend to be more severe (with increased incidence of lethality) than those made by the younger children.

Similar to adults, adolescents experience major depression more frequently than they do the less severe diagnosis of **Dysthymic Disorder.** In actuality, although prevalence data are not entirely conclusive, there is evidence that depression occurs as least as often (if not more frequently) in adolescence as in adulthood. The variation in prevalence estimates seems to be a function of the actual criteria used to define adolescent depression, as well as of the sample of adolescents being evaluated. Thus, whereas actual figures range anywhere from under 10% to approximating 50%, the currently accepted estimate of the number of adolescents whose depression is severe enough to require treatment is 20%. However, again, considering the tendency for this age group to mask the depression, this may very well be an estimate that is inaccurately low.

SUPPLEMENTAL RESOURCES

Canfield, J., Hansen, M. V., & Kirberger, K. (1996). *Chicken soup for the teenage soul.* Deerfield Beach, FL: Health Communications.

Capacchone, L. (1992). *The creative journal for teens: Making friends with yourself.* North Hollywood, CA: New Castle.

Cobain, B. (1998). *When nothing matters anymore: A survival guide for depressed teens.* Minneapolis, MN: Free Spirit.

Elkind, D. (1988). *All grown up and no place to go: Teenagers in crisis.* Reading, MA: Addison Wesley.

Fassler, D. G., & Dumans, L. J. (1998). *Help me, I'm sad: Recognizing, treating and preventing childhood and adolescent depression.* New York: Penguin Books.

Fenwick, E., & Smith, T. (1996). *Adolescence—The survival guide for parents and teens.* New York: DK Publishing.

Real, T. (1997). *I don't want to talk about it: Overcoming the secret legacy of male depression.* New York: Scribner.

Adolescent Mood Swings

As their child approaches adolescence, many parents give each other a pleading sigh—jokingly implying that perhaps the other parent could take over for the next

4 years or so until the awful stage of adolescence passes. Although there are multiple reasons behind the dreaded anticipation of this developmental stage, many parents look to the emotional turmoil of adolescence with the most anxiety. Indeed, folklore and clinical experience as well as the actual experiences of parents confirm the pervasiveness of the developmental phenomenon known as the adolescent mood swing.

Whereas some of the dramatic mood swings of adolescence may be accurately attributed to biological factors (in terms of hormonal fluctuations), much of the explanation of adolescent moodiness transcends the physiological. A basic premise to keep in mind is that adolescence is first and foremost a time of major transition. The adolescent is no longer a child, nor, is he or she a full-fledged adult. Rather, the adolescent is experimenting with various adult roles in interpersonal interactions (socially, academically, and in the family situation). As would be expected, success at these endeavors is mixed. Thus, to add to the confusion regarding the developmental role (i.e., adult or child?), the adolescent is faced with periodic assaults to self-esteem when his/her performance in situations is perceived (by both self and others) as less than optimal.

Combining these psychological factors with the biological changes, it is certainly no wonder that adolescents often appear to be on an emotional roller coaster. Further, it is often difficult for parents and other family members to resist being influenced to join the adolescent on the ride. Specifically, it is not at all uncommon for adolescents to manifest one, several, or all of the following:

> *Affective Lability:* Parents of adolescents often (accurately) comment that the adolescent can be in a fine mood at one point and, at almost the next moment, without any identifiable precipitating event, the adolescent will be absolutely distraught or furious. What is remarkable about these occurrences is the rapidity with which the emotional state changes, the apparent absence of any clearly identifiable cause for the change in emotional status, and (as described below) the intensity of the emotions demonstrated.

> *Exaggerated emotional intensity:* Commonly, the intensity of emotion expressed by adolescents seems dramatically out of proportion to what the situation actually demands. At times, those in the immediate surroundings are even unable to identify what the situation actually is. Indeed, in many cases, *dramatic* seems to be the operative word as the intensity of emotion expressed by some adolescents can appear virtually theatrical. Parents will often complain that, for their adolescent, every issue is major and is reacted to accordingly.

> *Emotional explosiveness:* Closely related to the exaggerated intensity of emotional expression and the affective lability described above, emotional explosiveness results in the adolescent being emotionally fragile and explosive. Sadness, anger, and frustration seem to be among the emotions that are the most frequently featured. Beyond being exaggerated, these emotions tend to be expressed in a loud, explosive fashion.

Often accompanying the exaggerated intensity described above is emotional and/or physical explosiveness—even in those adolescents for whom, prior to this stage of life, such behavior would be entirely uncharacteristic.

Emotional/psychological withdrawal: The adolescent's increased demand/described need for privacy often translates into a situation in which he or she emotionally isolates himself or herself from parents, teachers, and other family members. Peer support seems to be all that is allowed, and, that only to a limited degree and at certain times. The result of this isolation, in combination with the affective lability, emotional explosiveness, and the exaggerated emotional intensity just described combine to create an anxiety-provoking experience for parents. The adolescent is acting in an unfamiliar, unexplainable manner, and, to make matters worse, refuses to talk and/or to explain what is going on.

Because of the upsetting nature of adolescent mood swings, it is often helpful for parents to have the ability to normalize what their adolescent is experiencing. Recognizing and acknowledging the virtual universality of the phenomenon of adolescent mood swings is useful for both parents and adolescents themselves in terms of assuaging fears (on the part of all parties) that the adolescent indeed may be experiencing some clinically significant psychological or psychiatric difficulty. Thus, it is often reassuring for parents to remind each other as well as to remind the adolescent of the commonality of this experience. Of course, it is important that this parental reassurance to the adolescent is done in a respectful manner that does not trivialize what the adolescent is experiencing.

How should parents react to these adolescent mood swings? Does awareness of the dynamics behind these mood swings necessarily imply unequivocal acceptance? Whereas overreaction is not the ideal, it is important for parents to reach an agreement between themselves (and when appropriate, convey this information to the adolescent) in terms of what will be tolerated and what will not be tolerated. Although mood swings are indeed characteristic of this developmental stage, merely being an adolescent does not give one carte blanche in terms of emotional expression and behavior, in general. Further, giving the adolescent the message that he or she can act as he or she desires without any ramifications, or, that the adolescent is not responsible for his or her actions by virtue of developmental stage is certainly not doing anybody any favors!

Parents need to establish and then articulate boundaries and limits in terms of what will be deemed acceptable behavior and what will not. In addition, it is important that contingency plans are in place to be employed if or when the adolescent is unable to—or chooses not to—behave within the confines of these limits. These limits are best established while keeping in mind the general expectations of society, the expectations of the family, and the overall impact of the behavior upon others in the immediate environment. For example, whereas anger in and of itself should not be punished and should be recognized as a normal human emotion, physical violence, verbal abuse, and/or emotional abuse are best immediately identified as such and should not be tolerated under any circumstances.

When to Seek Professional Help

Although every family (with or without adolescent members) experiences times when things appear to be out of control, such events should be the exception as opposed to the norm. If the latter is the case, it is wise to seek the help of a professional in bringing the family back to the status quo. Unless the parents strongly suspect some form of significant clinical problem with the adolescent, it is recommended that this treatment take the form of either parent therapy or **Family Therapy.** It is important that the adolescent is not forced into the role of the "sick one," and that the adolescent is not given the impression that his or her behavior can disrupt the entire family's functioning. An initial telephone contact with a family therapist or an initial session in which the parents attend without the adolescent (and without the rest of the family) should provide the parents with some guidance as to the precise modality of therapy (i.e., who should attend sessions) that would be most appropriate to the specific situation.

It is important to note, however, that there are situations in which it is more appropriate for the adolescent to be seen alone (at least for some of the sessions or a portion of some of the sessions). In some cases, the adolescent is motivated to discuss his or her issues with a professional (and may even initiate the idea). Embarrassment, privacy issues, shame, as well as the desire to feel more like an adult can all potentially contribute to an adolescent's desire to have individual sessions with the clinician. For the most part, these wishes should be accommodated with the clinician making the decision when and to what extent the other family members should be brought into the therapeutic process.

Questions to Ask the Clinician

- What is your experience in working with adolescents and their families?
- What members of the family do you want to see first and why?
- Will there be any change in terms of which family members will be attending?
- Is there anything you would recommend that we as parents do or not do?
- At what point in treatment can we expect to see some changes?
- What type of changes can we expect to see (positive and negative) as treatment progresses?

For a list of questions parents should be expected to be prepared to answer, please refer to the entry **Therapist: What to Expect on the First Visit.**

SUPPLEMENTAL RESOURCES

Baynard, R. T., & Baynard, J. (1981). *How to deal with your acting up teenager.* New York: M. Evans.

Bodenhamer, G. (1995). *Parent in control.* New York: Fireside.

Cappachcone, L. (1992). *The creative journal for teens: Making friends with yourself.* North Hollywood, CA: New Castle.

Carter, W. L. (1995). *The angry teenager.* Nashville, TN: Thomas Nelson.

Creighton, A. (1992). *Helping teens stop violence.* Alameda, CA: Hunting House.

Fenwick, E., & Smith, T. (1996). *Adolescence: The survival guide for parents and teenagers.* New York: DK Publishing.

Newcomer, P. L. (1993). *Understanding and teaching emotionally disturbed children and adolescents.* Austin, TX: ProEd.

Packer, A. J. (1992). *Bringing up parents: The teenager's handbook.* Minneapolis, MN: Free Spirit.

Pasick, P. (1998). *Almost grown: Launching your child from high school to college.* Binghamton, NY: Haworth Press.

Steinberg, L., & Levine, A. (1997). *You and your adolescent: A parent's guide for ages 10–20.* New York: HarperCollins.

Wolf, A. E. (1991). *Get out of my life—But first could you drive me and Cheryl to the mall?* New York: HarperCollins.

Adolescent Rebellion

As with **Adolescent Mood Swings,** the rebellious aspects of adolescence have come to be considered as characteristic of adolescence as any other aspect. Similarly, the dread and anxiety associated with anticipating this rebellion also have come to be virtually universal. Folklore seems to convey that once a child reaches adolescence, he or she becomes a dramatically changed person, with the general assumption that these changes are certainly not for the better! Whereas there is certainly an element of reality-based truth to this anxious anticipation (i.e., rebellion is a normal, expected aspect of adolescence), in the large majority of cases, this does not have to be a disastrous time—either for the adolescent or for those in the immediate environment.

First and foremost, it is important to remember that a rebellious component is an integral part of adolescent development. Being in a rather transitional situation, adolescents fit neither into the world of the child nor into the world of the adult. Nonetheless, a major component of this transition is the adolescent's struggle to assume more of an adultlike demeanor and role in day-to-day life. Because of the insecurities inherent in assuming this more mature role, the adolescent will frequently attempt to emphasize a more mature status by expressing negative feelings and/or rejecting opinions, rules, activities and overall values of parental or other authority figures.

Despite the annoyance this type of behavior may bring to parents and other authority figures, such behavior allows the adolescent the opportunity to try out what he or she perceives as adultlike behavior, and, in a subtle way, allows him or her to make a statement that the expectations and rules of childhood should no longer apply. In many circumstances, this is expressed in terms of demanding more freedom, questioning of rules/values, or simply movement toward more independence. As is true with most behaviors of adolescents, these mannerisms are necessary rites of passage, if you will, into the adult world. However, the intensity of disruption associated with these behaviors is largely a function of the manner in which the parental figures react.

It is crucial, then, that the parent accept some degree of rebellion as a necessary evil of parenting at this developmental stage. Indeed, some theorists believe that if an individual has an adolescence that is too calm (i.e., without involving any rebellious activities), the chances are high that he or he will engage in rebellious behavior later in life—when the stakes may be higher and potentially more dangerous. The key approach here is for the parents to choose their battles carefully. This is in no way meant to imply that parents should allow their adolescent offspring to behave without regard to rules, regulations, and limits and not experience any consequences. However, by recognizing rebellion as necessary, the parent(s) needs to determine what will be tolerated as acceptable rebellious behavior and what is simply unacceptable. Of course, this will vary from adolescent to adolescent and, similarly, from family to family.

What is most crucial in this regard is that the adolescent experiences the opportunity to rebel and that the parents react with appropriate distaste. In most cases, it is not the actual act of rebellion but rather the dynamic behind the act (i.e., going against established norms) that is important to the adolescent's development. Thus, if parental figures are too rigid and attempt to prevent any form of deviation from established norms, the adolescent will fulfill the need to rebel in a more serious, potentially dangerous manner. For that reason, then, trivial acts of rebellion (i.e., those that parents would prefer to avoid but are really relatively harmless) should be allowed to transpire so that the ante is not upped to a potentially dangerous degree. For example, allowing a blond, 15-year-old boy to dye his hair a dark black could conceivably prevent him from ingesting the 2 six-packs of beer from his parents' refrigerator.

SUPPLEMENTAL RESOURCES

Baynard, R. T., & Baynard, J. (1981). *How to deal with your acting out teenager.* New York: M. Evans.
Bender, P. S. (1997). *How to keep your kids from driving you crazy.* New York: Wiley.
Bodenhamer, G. (1995). *Parent in control.* New York: Fireside.
Carter, W. L. (1995). *The angry teenager.* Nashville, TN: Thomas Nelson.
Creighton, A. (1992). *Helping teens stop violence.* Alameda, CA: Hunting House.
Fenwick, E., & Smith, T. (1996). *Adolescence—The survival guide for parents and teens.* New York: DK Publishing.
Goldstein, A. P., & McGinnis, E. (1995). *Skillstreaming the adolescent: New strategies and perspectives for teaching prosocial skills.* Champaign, IL: Research Press.
Holladay, R. (1994). *What preteens want their parents to know.* New York: Multi Media.
Packer, A. J. (1992). *Bringing up parents: The teenager's handbook.* Minneapolis, MN: Free Spirit.
Packer, A. J. (1997). *How rude—The teenager's guide to good manners, proper behavior, and not grossing people out.* Minneapolis, MN: Free Spirit.
Riera, M. (1995). *Uncommon sense for parents with teenagers.* Berkeley, CA: Celestial Arts.
Steinberg, L., & Levine, A. (1997). *You and your adolescent: A parent's guide for ages 10–20.* New York: HarperCollins.
Swets, P. W. (1995). *The art of talking with your teenager.* Holbrooke, MA: Adams Media.
Wolf, A. E. (1991). *Get out of my life—But first could you drive me and Cheryl to the mall?* New York: HarperCollins.

Adolescent Sexuality

The initial recognition of oneself as a sexual being is yet another major developmental step that occurs during adolescence. As with most major developmental milestones, the psychological components are equally (if not more) as significant as those that are more physiological in nature. In the case of adolescent sexuality, there are both physical and psychological issues to contend with. Further, issues of embarrassment, limited knowledge base, familial morals/values, and self-esteem all combine to complicate this situation for the adolescent and his or her family.

Embarrassment plays an all-too-important role in adolescent sexual development. Since sexuality remains a difficult topic for many people (adults included!) to discuss, and, since there is considerable adolescent self-esteem associated with acting as if one has a sound knowledge base regarding the subject, it is quite common for adolescents to proceed through this phase in ignorance, and to be reluctant to seek out information from reliable sources. Further complicating matters is the fact that the people to whom adolescents tend to turn for information about sexuality typically are members of their own peer group and do not have valid information to provide. Whereas parents may be better sources of information on this subject, adolescents may be less likely to turn to parental figures because of fear of parental questioning of the adolescents themselves (i.e.,"Why are you asking these questions?"), a perceived need to maintain privacy about such matters, a notion that the parents wouldn't know the answers anyway, and/or a general embarrassment about discussing the topic at all.

The most important aspect of adolescents and sexuality is that they receive information from a source with whom they feel comfortable, and from a source who is capable of providing valid information. In addition to the validity of information, however, it is also important for the information to be consistent with the values that the parents wish to convey. Indeed, whereas there is no guarantee that adolescents will accept parental values around this issue (or around any issue, for that matter), it is good for them to be at least exposed to familial norms around this issue so that they can have the opportunity to make their own decisions, using parental values as a foundation.

Despite the value component inherent in any and all talks about sexuality, the overall message conveyed to the adolescent best be as nonpunishing and as nonjudgmental as possible. Of course, the appropriate message to be conveyed is not that anything and everything is okay, but rather that sexuality in its proper form, place, and perspective is a natural and normal part of the human existence. Similarly, sexual feelings and fantasies are nothing to be ashamed of and are normal as well. The difference to be emphasized is between thoughts/fantasies and actual behaviors. Indeed, for many adolescents (and adults as well, for that matter), fantasy is actually preferable to behavioral action as it is physically, psychologically, and emotionally safer.

Although each and every person is unique, there is a core of sexual topics/issues that tends to be prominent among the concerns of adolescents. The physical and psychological changes accompanying **Puberty** (see also entry on **Adolescent Mood Swings**), sexual feelings, **Masturbation,** popularity/attractiveness with peers, dating, **Homosexuality,** contraception, sexual fantasy, and **Pornography** are all among issues that are of common concern and interest to adolescents and their parents.

SUPPLEMENTAL RESOURCES

Basso, M. J. (1997). *The underground guide to teenage sexuality.* Minneapolis, MN: Fairview Press.

Hyde, M. O. (1988). *Teen sex.* Philadelphia: Westminster Press.

Jukes, M. (1996). *It's a girl thing.* New York: Knopf.

Madaras, L. (1988). *The what's happening to my body book for boys.* New York: Newmarket.

Madaras, L. (1988). *The what's happening to my body book for girls.* New York: Newmarket.

Mathes, P. G., & Irby, B. J. (1996). *Teen pregnancy and parenting handbook.* Champaign, IL: Research Press.

Packer, A. J. (1992). *Bringing up parents: The teenager's handbook.* Minneapolis, MN: Free Spirit.

Solin, S. (1996). *The* Seventeen *guide to sex and your body.* New York: Simon & Schuster.

Stone, B., & Palmer, M. (1990). *The dating dilemma: Handling sexual pressures.* Grand Rapids, MI: Baker Book House.

Stoppard, M. (1997). *Sex ed: Growing up, relationships and sex.* New York: DK Publishers.

Adolescent Suicide

With the frequency of adolescent suicides in the United States greatly on the increase over the past two decades or so, it is commonly acknowledged that suicide is the second leading cause of death in teenagers. Further, it is important to note that many experts believe that a large proportion of accidents (deemed to be the number one cause of death among this age group) are actually intentional, and are to be more accurately conceptualized as suicides. In addition, issues of shame and stigma result in many adolescent suicides being misclassified or reported as due to other factors. Thus, the actual frequency of suicides in this population is likely to be much greater than the statistics imply.

Generally, it is acknowledged that, whereas females attempt suicide more often than do males, males actually kill themselves more frequently than do females (with ratios ranging from 3:1 to 10:1). The most common method in completed suicides (for both males and females) is the use of some type of firearm or explosive—a relatively lethal modality. In contrast, the most common method used in suicide attempts overall is some type of poisoning, usually by drug or prescription medication overdose—a considerably less lethal modality. As would be expected, the incidence of attempted suicides (or **Parasuicide**) is much higher than that of completed suicides. Indeed, estimates of the ratio of attempted suicides to completed suicides in the adolescent population are as high as 312:1. Again, when considering the psychological issues that could result in the underreporting of this phenomenon, the actual numbers relevant to the attempted to completed ratio are most likely considerably higher. Especially in this population, there are a goodly number of silent or secret attempts that are confided only to the adolescent's closest friends—if to anyone at all.

What prompts an adolescent to decide to commit such a dramatic act as the ending of his or her life? Whereas every case is certainly unique (and each adolescent, in particular, takes considerable pride in the uniqueness of his or her situation), ten commonalities of adolescent suicide have been delineated (Schneidman,

1986). Research has indicated that virtually all completed adolescent suicides share the following characteristics:

1. *Common purpose of seeking a solution:* The adolescent feels as if his or her life is full of problems. Further, previously effective coping strategies are no longer useful in dealing with the current stressors. Thus, at this time, suicide is viewed as the sole means of solving life difficulties.
2. *Common goal of cessation of consciousness:* Simply living life is a pain-ridden experience. Suicide, then, is viewed as a relief from this pain by terminating conscious awareness.
3. *Common stimulus of intolerable psychological pain:* The pain of life is intolerably intense. Suicide is seen as a way to alleviate the intensity of the psychological discomfort.
4. *Common stressor of frustrated psychological needs:* The adolescent feels as if major psychological requirements (i.e., love, comfort, security, self-esteem, etc.) are, and always will be, unattainable. Since these are believed to be necessary for living, perceiving them as being forever unreachable serves as a motivator for suicidal behavior.
5. *Common emotion of hopelessness–helplessness:* Not only is life perceived as unbearable, the adolescent views this situation as permanent in that he or she sees no way for things to improve and has no sense of how/if things could change things for the better.
6. *Common state of ambivalence:* In all cases of adolescent suicide, there is a considerable amount of uncertainty as to whether suicide is indeed the optimal way to proceed. Oftentimes, this ambivalence is utilized in therapeutic relationships as a means to prevent the act from actually occurring.
7. *Common perceptual state of constriction:* As is characteristic of the majority of individuals who are depressed, the suicidal adolescent's outlook is distorted and there is a restricted focus on the negative aspects of life.
8. *Common action of egression:* Egression (escape from that which is distressing) is a primary dynamic underlying adolescent suicide. The suicidal act is perceived as a means (often the only means) by which the psychological pain of life can be avoided.
9. *Common interpersonal act of communication of intention:* At some point prior to the actual suicidal act, the adolescent somehow communicates his or her intention to somebody. Further, some experts interpret any self-injurious behavior in and of itself as being a communication of intention.
10. *Common consistency of lifelong coping patterns:* An inability to cope adaptively with life stressors is typically not a new characteristic that develops in adolescence. Rather, suicidal behavior is usually seen in individuals who have always exhibited difficulties in dealing with life issues.

Whereas these ten items may not actually all be present in each and every case of adolescent suicide, their presence is indeed consistent enough to be viewed as regular indications which, when present in any combination, should be considered significant in their implications.

Similarly, certain risk factors have been identified as influential in affecting the frequency of adolescent suicidal behavior. Again, whereas the presence of one or more is certainly not sufficient evidence to confidently predict suicidal behavior, it is useful to view these phenomena as (at the very least) significant warning signs. These risk factors have been divided into those related to historical and developmental factors, situational factors, and psychological factors.

> *Historical and developmental factors:* medical problems; parental psychiatric/psychological illness; family history of suicide; dysfunction in the family system; an incomplete understanding of the impact of death and its consequences
>
> *Situational factors:* impact of perceived inadequacy relevant to school, sports, and others in personal situations; general life stress; increasing family problems and/or disorganization; changes in social/cultural role expectations; impact of the media's depiction of death, as well as other pertinent life events
>
> *Psychological factors:* various psychological diagnoses such as depression, **Eating Disorders, Personality Disorders,** substance abuse, **Gender Identity Disorder,** as well as experiences of a recent loss perceived to be significant in the adolescent's life

It is a misconception to think of adolescent suicide as being the natural endpoint of a depressive episode. Research and clinical experience indicate that the actual self-destructive act (whether a completed suicide or a parasuicide) is the result of an almost stepwise progression of psychological trauma, which, if allowed to progress unaddressed, results in suicidal behavior. Jacobs (1971) proposed a five-step developmental model delineating the stages through which a potentially suicidal adolescent typically proceeds. Stages along this process, if recognized early enough, can be addressed in order to prevent development to subsequent steps, and consequent self-injurious behaviors.

The first stage according to this model is a general history of problems. Oftentimes, these are problems that have begun as far back as early childhood, or may have begun or intensified in the recent past. Problems that fit into this classification include family stressors (such as parental marital problems, substance abuse in one or both of the parents, etc.), school problems, and general environmental changes. Research subsequent to Jacob's original paper (e.g., Weiner, 1992) indicates that it is not the particular life events that are crucial in this model, but, rather, the adolescent's perception of lack of support during these events.

Closely related to the general history of problems focused upon during the first stage is the escalation of problems, which marks the beginning of the second stage of this model. The source of this intensification of problems can be purely environmental, or it could be more a function of the developmental maturity occurring with adolescence. More specifically in these latter cases, the problems either seem to be worse as a function of the adolescent's perception, or actually become more intense as a function of the developmental changes accompanying this life stage. In either case, this escalation is typically marked by symptoms characteristic of adolescent depression such as mood changes, behavior problems, social withdrawal, and the like.

The third stage in this model is characterized by an overall failure or inability to cope with the problems of the first two stages. It is during this third period that the young person recognizes that previously employed methods to attempt to confront the psychological difficulties have not been useful. This third phase is marked by a sense of frustration and helplessness based upon a realization that what one thought would be a helpful coping mechanism is not.

It is only natural that this third phase eventually results in the fourth phase, characterized by an overall loss of hope. Perceiving previously effective psychological coping mechanisms to be far less than optimal results in the adolescent's feeling out of options, unable to cope with the stressors and problems of life. Thus, during this phase, the young person begins to disengage from life in general. A withdrawal from social contacts and previously enjoyable activities, a lack of interest in academic matters, and an increase in self-destructive behaviors (i.e., high-risk behaviors, alcoholism, substance abuse, etc.) characterize this presuicidal phase.

The fifth and final phase is marked by the complete loss of hope. It at this time, with hope more or less completely gone, that the adolescent moves into the justification phase. At this point, the adolescent believes that he or she is completely justified in deciding to engage in the suicidal act. As a result of the culmination of feelings accumulated during the first four stages, the adolescent is now convinced that death is the only solution to the dismal life situation. Sometimes, there is a single event (e.g., fight with a parent, a bad grade on an exam, a breakup with a boyfriend or girlfriend, etc.) that is perceived by the adolescent as the justification for the action. However, this act of justification is really the final step of a process that has been transpiring for a prolonged period of time.

Whereas Jacob's model focuses primarily on internal, more psychologically oriented factors, there are indeed models of adolescent suicide that place more of an emphasis on external, environmental factors. One example of such an approach would be those theorists who question the impact of peer suicidal behavior on adolescents. Often referred to as the *contagion effect,* or *copycat suicide,* it has been observed that awareness of the suicidal behavior of a peer can serve as somewhat of a permission-giving mechanism for an adolescent who was contemplating suicide anyway. This is especially prevalent among adolescents who are particularly suggestible—eager to look to others as models—and therefore vulnerable to being affected by their behaviors.

Closely related to this contagion effect are those situations in which adolescents react to the media coverage of suicidal events by engaging in self-destructive behavior themselves. The publicity brought about by such coverage as well as what is perceived by some adolescents as an opportunity for fame or self aggrandizement all contribute to what can be viewed as the "glory" of suicide. Again, for those adolescents whose self-esteem is somewhat fragile, they may perceive a self-destructive act as their only means of achieving recognition and/or acknowledgment as a valid, important person.

It is partially for this reason that the experience of a recent loss (or the simple awareness of the death of a peer) is considered one of the warning signs of suicide of which parents should be aware. Along these lines, it is especially important to recognize that what may be considered a trivial occurrence from the adult's perspective may indeed be conceptualized as a major loss from the perspective of the adolescent. Consider, for example, the breakup with a first boyfriend or girlfriend. Whereas the adult perspective on such an event may recognize the short-term impact in the grand scheme of things, this breakup may truly seem of exorbitant proportions to the adolescent involved.

Other warning signs of potentially suicidal behavior include previous suicide attempts, talk of suicide or death, noticeable changes in personality or mood, changes in sleeping patterns, changes in eating patterns, withdrawal from involvement with friends and other previously pleasurable activities, an increase in the amount and intensity of risk-taking behavior, involvement in alcohol or other substance abuse, making final arrangements (such as writing one's own eulogy, making funeral plans, etc.), giving away of prized possessions, and tying up of loose ends (Martin & Colbert, 1997).

SUPPLEMENTAL RESOURCES

Cobain, B. (1998). *When nothing matters anymore: A survival guide for depressed teens.* Minneapolis, MN: Free Spirit.

Fassler, D. G., & Dumans, L. J. (1998). *Help me, I'm sad: Recognizing, treating and preventing childhood and adolescent depression.* New York: Penguin Books.

Garfinkel, B., & Northrup, G. (1990). *Adolescent suicide.* Binghamton, NY: Haworth Press.

Kirk, W. G. (1993). *Adolescent suicide.* Champaign, IL: Research Press.

Marcus, E. (1996). *Why suicide?* New York: HarperCollins.

Steinberg, L., & Levine, A. (1997). *You and your adolescent: A parent's guide for ages 10–20.* New York: Harper Perennial.

Affect

Affect is a term used to describe a person's emotional state. Closely related to the concept of mood, affect is used to describe the observable aspects of a person's emotions. Specifically, characteristics of a person's body posture, facial expression, and tone of voice all contribute to a description of affect. At times, a person's affect matches what the person is actually feeling inside. This is referred to as **Congruent Affect.** For example, a child who is excited about going to pick up her new puppy from the pet store is smiling or giggling joyously. Or, a young boy who was just told that he cannot watch television for three days because his school work has been unsatisfactory stamps his feet and utters some angry words. In other situations, however, a person's affect is not consistent with what the person is really feeling (referred to as **Incongruent Affect** or *inappropriate affect*). Consider, for example the teenager who is extremely nervous about her first prom, and ends up laughing uncontrollably during most of the first part of the evening. In this case, the actual affect superficially reveals happiness, however, her true feelings are closer to anxiety. Incongruent or inappropriate affect can be a sign of something as simple as someone wanting to be socially appropriate and not hurt the feelings of another or wishing to disguise or to otherwise hide one's on true feelings; or it can be as severe as being a symptom of a schizophrenic disorder. For that reason, incongruent affect (as with any type of behavior) must be evaluated within the context of the person's presentation prior to conceptualizing it as indicative of some serious problem.

Affection, Expression of

The expression of affection in a child or adolescent is influenced by several factors, not all appropriately classified as being either healthy or pathological. Indeed, an identical manner of expression of affection could rightfully be deemed appropriate and healthy in one situation, but clearly pathological in another. Factors that influence the manner in which a young person expresses affectionate feelings include (but are certainly not limited to) the developmental stage of the child/adolescent (oftentimes, young children are more free and open in expressing affectionate feelings than are adolescents, for example); familial norms around the expression of affection (in certain families, and in certain cultures/ethnicities, physical expression of affection is more common than in others, which are more emotionally controlled); the gender of the child/adolescent (in the majority of American cultures, it is more universally acceptable and expected, therefore more common, for females to be more openly affectionate than males); and the specific object of the affectionate feelings in question (an emotionally reserved adolescent, for example, may feel more comfortable—that it is more socially acceptable—to express physical affection toward his or her grandmother, than toward his or her mother).

Despite this vast variation, there are certain principles that apply virtually universally with respect to the expression of affection in children and adolescents. Probably the most damaging thing we can do to our children is to force affectionate expression in a way that does not feel natural to them. Of course, many have read the parenting manuals that emphasize the importance of open expression of warm affectionate feelings in families. In an attempt to be good parents, many will too strongly encourage their children to hug "Aunt Belle" or kiss "Uncle Bud." As we are all too painfully aware, our children/adolescents are often not in the same emotional spaces as we, or in which we would like them to be. Thus, at the exact moment when it would be most politically correct to demonstrate some affection toward a certain relative or family friend, it appears it is the last thing that the young person would prefer to do. So, as a result, the parents cajole (to varying degrees), the child/adolescent eventually gives in, the person on the receiving end of this forced behavior feels embarrassed, and an obviously perfunctory expression of affection transpires.

Clearly, this is not the optimal way to encourage open expression of affection in a child/adolescent. Indeed, this is one case where modeling provides the best and strongest instruction. Simply stated, if you want your child to be openly physically demonstrative, then you should model this type of behavior in your own interpersonal interactions. It is much more likely for a young person to develop a certain pattern of behavior if the people around him engage in that behavior on a regular, consistent basis. Of course, there are certain limitations to this approach. We all know of situations in which the parents behave in a certain manner (e.g., are openly affectionate to each other and those around them), and the child ends up behaving in a diametrically opposite manner (e.g., the child of the aforementioned parents is one of the most emotionally shy individuals in his or her class).

This brings us to another crucial principle: Allow your child to be who he or she is. In many areas, it is very tempting to try to mold our children into some idealized image of who we would like them to be. Then, when our child's actual behavior does not correspond with the idealized image we have formulated in our minds, we become distressed—questioning our parenting abilities, wondering and worrying why we have this bad child. Unfortunately, this is only the beginning of the problems, as such a situation commonly results in our working even harder to force the child to conform to our idealized image. As in most cases of trying to fit a square peg into a round hole, the process is typically quite aversive and uncomfortable, and the results are consistently less than optimal.

For that reason, when confronting the issue of the expression of affectionate feelings (as well as the majority of other issues), parents need to monitor their own responses to minimize tendencies toward attempting to make their child what he or she is not. Parents need to accept that, for example, despite the fact that they are rather reserved in their expression of affectionate feelings, their child may be the type of person who gushes affection all over the place. Similarly, even if parents consistently demonstrate an open expression of affection in their day-to-day lives, their child may well develop into a more emotionally constrained individual who prefers not to be affectionate in public. It best be accepted that our children's behavior does not need to be a mirror image of ours—nor should it be.

A common question, however, is how to determine if the manner in which a child expresses affection is indicative of some problem. Whereas one does not want to ignore an important symptom of a psychological problem, it is similarly unwise to react to a basic aspect of a young person's personality as if it is a symptom that requires professional treatment. When attempting to evaluate such a situation, it is best to adhere to the adage of "never diagnosing an illness based upon one symptom." It is often useful to consider the following in attempting to determine if the manner in which a child/adolescent is expressing affection is cause for concern:

1. Does this manner of expressing affection reflect a major change in the specific child? In other words, is this a child who was previously affectionately quite open, and has now become reserved (or vice versa)?

2. Is the manner in which the child/adolescent is expressing affection consistent with his or her developmental stage? Even if the way in which the particular child expresses affection represents a significant change, remember that a child/adolescent is constantly in the process of change and maturation. Thus, when evaluating the implications of any such change in expression of affection, be sure to do so within the context of developmental maturation.

3. Is the manner in which the child/adolescent expresses affection consistent from person to person? If not, is it consistent with how the child/adolescent conceptualizes his or her relationship with each person? Whereas behavioral consistency is generally a good thing, one would expect that a person's expression of affection may vary somewhat from person to person. However, if it is observed that the young person expresses affection in a rather consistent way, except in the cases of one particular person, a certain type of person, or a certain group of people, it is worthwhile to explore the situation further.

4. Does the young person in question manifest any symptoms consistent with any form of psychological/psychiatric distress that could potentially affect the means of expression of affection? Specifically, are any other symptoms being demonstrated that are consistent with **Anxiety Disorders, Sexual Abuse, Physical Abuse,** and/or depression? Such symptoms in conjunction with a noteworthy change in the manner in which the child/adolescent expresses affectionate feelings also warrant concern and investigation.

Affective Lability

Affective lability is a clinical term used to describe extreme variations and changes in a person's emotional reactions. Contributing to the uniqueness of affective lability is the fact that these changes often occur in the absence of any external events that could be considered as causal. In addition, it is common for the intensity of these changes to appear to be out of proportion to what is actually occurring in the environment. Thus, an individual may be laughing hysterically one minute and, for no observable reason, show signs of volatile anger only a few minutes later. Diagnostically, true affective lability is usually associated with **Schizophrenia,** certain forms of **Organic Pathology,** and **Bipolar Disorders.**

Especially when working with preteens and adolescents, however, it is crucial not to confuse the hormonally and developmentally based mood swings of this age group **(Adolescent Mood Swings)** with clinically significant affective lability.

Age-Appropriate Anxiety

It is important to note that anxiety is a normal, adaptive part of one's psychology—at every age! However, it often appears as if young people manifest more obvious symptoms of anxiety (e.g., fears, terror reactions, etc.) than do adults. As a result, it is rather common for parents to manifest their own anxiety in terms of whether their child's reactions are indeed normal, or require some form of intervention (professional or otherwise). Part of what makes this question so common (and difficult to answer simply) is that research in this field indicates that not only does the frequency of anxiety reactions change as the child goes through different developmental stages, but the focus (i.e., what triggers the anxiety response) and the actual manifestation (i.e., how the young person expresses the anxiety response) also vary as a function of age.

Up through approximately 6 months or so the major source of anxiety and fear seems to focus around sudden, dramatic changes in the baby's environment. For example, unexpected loud noises, unusually bright lights, or intense odors all can evoke a fear response. This is often explained by looking to an evolutionary perspective that relates these dramatic changes in sensory experience to a threat to the baby's physical safety and well-being. At the age of 6 months, fears extend beyond dramatic changes in environment to a focus on animals and heights. In addition, it is around this age that children begin to show a fear of strangers (and similarly, facial masks that distort the appearance of known adults).

Example: Eight-month-old Bobby's father dressed as Santa Claus for Halloween. When he approached Bobby, his son screamed in terror.

As the child enters the first year, the typical focus of anxiety changes to correspond with the child's psychological development. At this point, anxiety and fear are characteristically triggered by separation from parental figures and thoughts of physical injury. Closely related to this latter fear are anxieties around toilet training. In many cases, a reluctance to participate willingly in toilet training procedures is based upon a fear of falling into the toilet bowl, of being flushed away with the urine or bowel movement matter, or otherwise of being physically injured or maimed by objects related to the lavatory.

Example: When her mother was attempting her toilet training, Julie would repeatedly run out of the bathroom when it was time to flush the toilet. During these incidents, Julie would cry, "Not me, Mommy. Not me!"

The more generic fears of bodily injury characteristic of the first year get translated into more specific related fears during the second year. Indeed, as the child turns 2, fears of being eaten (or otherwise harmed) by monsters, imaginary creatures, and villains become more prominent in the child's anxiety schema. It is also at this time that the young child begins to formulate his or her own conceptualization of death and expresses fears of either his or her own death, or fears of abandonment vis à vis the death of parental figures.

Example: Two-and-one-half-year-old Devon has been having nightmares. He wakes up screaming that the monster under the bed is going to eat him. Of course, this monster will eat him only after, first, taking his parents away.

The third and fourth years are characterized by what are often viewed as typical childhood fears. Fears of large animals, being alone, and darkness begin to surface during this time. These fears usually extend into the early school years, but are typically replaced by anxiety around school and embarrassment in social situations by the time the child reaches the early/mid-elementary school years.

Example: Five-year-old Jessica will not go to sleep at night unless her night light is on.

Example: Seven-year-old Danny refuses to go to school on Thursdays because they have computer class. He tells his parents that he cannot go because he "may make a mistake in front of everybody."

In some situations, the fears or anxieties exhibited by a child are not consistent with the developmental level, nor with a realistic appraisal of the danger of the actual situation. In such cases, when the anxiety interferes significantly with the young person's day-to-day functioning, it is appropriate to consider seeking professional intervention. A more detailed explanation in terms of when to seek treatment, the appropriate form of treatment to seek, as well as what to expect when accessing professional help for each form of clinical anxiety is provided in the entries discussing the specific anxiety disorders (see entries for **Generalized Anxiety Disorder, Obsessive-Compulsive Disorder, Phobic Disorders, Separation Anxiety Disorder**).

SUPPLEMENTAL RESOURCES

Serafino, E. P. (1986). *The fears of childhood: A guide to recognizing and reducing fearful states in children.* New York: Human Science Press.

Agnosia

This is a term used to describe a syndrome or symptom in which an individual is unable to either recognize and/or name objects. A variation of this problem, known as *facial agnosia,* refers to the situation in which the individual is unable to recognize faces—that is faces that have been formerly familiar. Agnosia is usually indicative of a type of organically based pathology such as stroke, or one of the various types of dementia (dementia of the Alzheimer's type, vascular dementia, dementia due to multiple etiologies, dementia due to substance abuse, and dementia of unknown etiology). As a matter of fact, in many cases, agnosia is the first symptom of cognitive deterioration to be manifested and noticed by family and friends.

SUPPLEMENTAL RESOURCES

Adams, R. L, Parsons, O. A., Culbertson, J. L., & Nixon, S. J. (Eds.). (1996). *Neuropsychology for clinical practice: Etiology, assessment, and treatment of common neurological disorders.* Washington, DC: American Psychological Association.

Agoraphobia

Agoraphobia is one of the disorders whose symptoms manifest themselves in children and adolescents quite similarly to the manner in which they are manifested in adults. Technically translated as a fear of the marketplace, agoraphobia used to be conceptualized as a fear of open spaces. As knowledge of anxiety disorders accumulated, agoraphobia came to be viewed as a more generic form of anxiety precipitated by being in situations or places from which escape is perceived as difficult. The perception of difficulty of escape is crucial as oftentimes it is not the actual inability to escape from the situation but rather the individual's perception of the consequences of attempting to escape.

The imagined scenario often entails experiencing a panic reaction (usually a panic attack) and being unable to leave the situation due to lack of availability of necessary assistance and/or intense embarrassment. The resulting situation often entails a phobic avoidance of places, situations, and behaviors that are perceived as being outside of a self-defined safety zone (i.e., in which help is immediately available and/or escape can be accomplished without embarrassment). Typical examples of situations that are avoided by agoraphobics include being away from home alone, standing in a crowd, riding on an airplane or other form of public transportation, driving along a highway from which immediate exit is impossible, and traveling on a bridge. The phobic situation varies considerably both within a given individual as well as among different individuals. Such a variation makes sense, however, when one recognizes that it is not the actual situation that is key, but rather the individual's perception that immediate escape or assistance would be problematic.

The issue of whether agoraphobia can occur without the concurrent presence or previous history of **Panic Disorder** remains one of controversy. However, the current edition of the *DSM* distinguishes among three different diagnostic categories, indicating the psychiatric community's support of the independence of panic disorder and agoraphobia: (1) panic disorder without agoraphobia, (2) panic disorder with agoraphobia, and (3) agoraphobia without a history of panic disorder. (Nonetheless, it is noteworthy that the *DSM* reports that virtually 95% of individuals who suffer from agoraphobia also have a current diagnosis or history of panic disorder.) In cases where agoraphobia occurs concurrently with panic disorder, the primary focus of the fears is on the escape from the embarrassment and intense fear associated with the symptoms of the panic attacks. When agoraphobia occurs without the history or presence of panic disorder, the major focus of the fears is similarly on panic symptoms; however, such symptoms do not reach the intensity as during full-blown panic attacks.

The nature of the treatments employed for agoraphobia have ranged a rather wide gamut over the past twenty years or so. In the seventies, the treatment modalities were aimed at the actual avoidance response itself, typically employing some form of exposure therapy or **Systematic Desensitization** to eliminate the fear responses in the specific situation in question. However, it became clear that such a treatment approach would become rather drawn out and impractical in that the situations that required systematic desensitization changed repeatedly for the individual person and, in so doing, would often multiply in number.

In the mid-1980s Diane Chambless introduced the concept of treating not the actual phobic avoidance but rather the fear of fear. This approach led to the now prevalent **Cognitive Behavioral** treatments, which focus directly on the panic symptoms themselves and the thoughts accompanying them. Based upon the premise that one's catastrophic thoughts about the panic symptoms ("I'm going to have a heart attack," "I'm going to be so embarrassed when everybody knows," "Something horrible is going to happen," "These are so bad I just can't stand it," and so on) are at the heart of the disorder, the current treatments work to modify the individual's beliefs and automatic thoughts about the panic symptoms. The cyclical pattern at the foundation of this model of therapy is as follows:

1. Anxiety results in mild panic symptoms.
2. Person cues into these panic symptoms and catastrophizes about their significance.
3. This catastrophizing results in the intensification of anxiety level.
4. Increasing anxiety level further worsens anxiety symptoms.
5. Worsening of anxiety results in more catastrophic thinking (and the pattern continues to cycle as above).

Whereas some clinicians support the use of some of the newer antidepressant medications and/or the antianxiety medications for the treatment of the symptoms of agoraphobia, it must be remembered that there has been only minimal research on these newer medications in terms of their effect on young people, and some of them are not even approved by the FDA for individuals younger than age 12. These factors—coupled with the most recent research supporting the use of cognitive behavioral modalities as being superior to medication-only treatment for agoraphobic symptoms and being equal in efficacy to treatment regimens combining medication and cognitive behavior approaches—seem to support the use of these cognitive behavioral methods as the first line of treatment for this disorder.

Because of its close relationship to panic disorder in terms of the manner in which treatment is approached, the reader is referred to the entry on **Panic Disorder,** specifically such questions as when to seek professional help, questions to ask the clinician, what to expect from the treatment process, and information the clinician will want to know.

SUPPLEMENTAL RESOURCES

Babior, S., & Goldman, C. (1996). *Overcoming panic, anxiety and phobias: New strategies to free yourself from worry and fear.* Duluth, MN: Pfeifer-Hamilton.

Bourne, E. J. (1995). *The phobia and anxiety disorder workbook.* New York: New Harbinger.

Eisen, A. R., Kearney, C. A., & Schaefer, C. E. (Eds.). (1995). *Clinical handbook of anxiety disorders in children and adolescents.* Northvale, NJ: Jason Aronson.

Husain, S. A., & Kashani, J. H. (1992). *Anxiety disorders in children and adolescents.* Washington, DC: American Psychiatric Press.

Kendall, P. C., Chansky, T. E., Kane, M. T., Kim, R. S., Kontlander, E., Ronen, K. R., Sessa, F. M., & Siqueland, L. (1992). *Anxiety disorders in youth: Cognitive behavioral interventions.* Boston: Allyn & Bacon.

White, E. Z. (1995). *An end to panic.* Oakland, CA: New Harbinger.

Akathisia (Akatizia)

Originating from the Greek translation "inability to sit still," Akathisia refers to a physical feeling of restlessness or motor quivering/shaking. At times, akathisia can be so intense that the sufferer is virtually unable to sit still for any period of time. However, it is important to note that sufferers of akathisia may not exhibit any of these traditionally observable motor symptoms. Rather, akathisia can also manifest itself as a high degree of anxiety, angry hostility, and other symptoms that appear to be more psychological than physiological in nature.

Visitors to an inpatient psychiatric ward often observe the patients repeatedly pacing back and forth the length of the ward, in a seemingly aimless pattern. This is rather typical in that akathisia is a common side effect of **Neuroleptic** treatment, which unfortunately may persist long after the drug has been withdrawn. Such symptoms tend to occur within four weeks of beginning the neuroleptic medication (or increasing its dosage). Similarly, akathisia can also be caused by the elimination or reduction of medications prescribed to prevent or treat **Extrapyramidal** symptoms. Indeed, akathisia is considered to be the most common of the extrapyramidal side effects, and, interestingly, the most commonly overlooked.

The American Psychiatric Association is considering a new diagnostic category—neuroleptic induced acute akathisia. Such a diagnosis would be applied if an individual experienced at least one of the following symptoms seemingly as a result of initiating or increasing a dosage of neuroleptic medication, or of reducing medication prescribed to attenuate extrapyramidal side effects:

1. fidgety movements or swinging of the legs
2. rocking from foot to foot while standing
3. pacing to relieve restlessness
4. inability to stand still for at least several minutes (American Psychiatric Association, 1994, p. 746)

SUPPLEMENTAL RESOURCES

Adams, R. L., Parsons, O. A., Culbertson, J. L., & Nixon, S. J. (Eds.). (1996). *Neuropsychology for clinical practice: Etiology, assessment, and treatment of common neurological disorders.* Washington, DC: American Psychological Association.

Akinesia

This is one of the group of antipsychotic side effects classified as **Extrapyramidal Side Effects.** This particular symptom pattern somewhat resembles those observed in cases of Parkinson's disease. Specifically, it involves slowing of motor activity, monotonous speech, an expressionless face (Barlow & Durand, 1995), apathy, rigid posture, decreased or no conversation, and walking with a shorter stride and/or a decreased arm swing (Maxmen, 1996). Akinesia (and the other extrapyramidal side effects) occur in approximately 15% of patients who are taking antipsychotic medication, and they tend to occur more frequently in the high-potency, low-anticholinergic medications (Kaplan & Sadock, 1993) such as **Haldol** and **Stelazine.**

SUPPLEMENTAL RESOURCES

Adams, R. L., Parsons, O. A., Culbertson, J. L., & Nixon, S. J. (Eds.). (1996). *Neuropsychology for clinical practice: Etiology, assessment, and treatment of common neurological disorders.* Washington, DC: American Psychological Association.

Alateen

Soon after **Alcoholics Anonymous** was established in the mid-1930s, there was recognition of a need for a support group, based upon similar principles, for family members of individuals who participate in the Alcoholics Anonymous programs. This self-help group, formulated in the late 1940s, was known as Al-Anon and proceeded along with its own twelve-step format. Since that time, various self-help groups have developed based upon the principles of Alcoholics Anonymous and focusing on various addictive behaviors as well as on various segments of the population. Alateen was one of these groups, designed to provide an Alcoholics Anonymous type of support and fellowship for the teenaged children of alcoholics (and subsequently those with other types of addictive problems).

Alcoholics Anonymous

This is a very popular self-help group designed to help individuals who have an addiction to alcohol, as well as providing services to their spouses and families. Originated in 1935 by two individuals (interestingly enough, both of whom were professionals)—Bill W. and Dr. Bob—this organization has now expanded to include over 20,000 groups holding over 25,000 meetings per week (Nathan, 1993). Based on the premise that alcoholism is a disease that, by definition, precludes the individual from being able to drink in moderation, Alcoholics Anonymous operates on a 7-day-per-week/24-hour-per-day format, with its members having continual access to services and meetings. The self-help philosophy allows members to associate with a peer group, all members of whom are in various stages of sobriety, and to receive input in a nonjudgmental, nonclinical manner.

The nature of each AA group varies greatly—in the composition of its members (age, occupational status, gender); in its meeting format (open meetings, closed meetings, meetings that feature a professional speaker); in its emphasis on religion (and the necessity of recognizing a higher power); as well as in what actually transpires at the meetings. With minor variations on emphasis, the Alcoholics Anonymous groups all are based upon a twelve-step format, with each step to be completed in a prescribed order for the individual to achieve true sobriety. In many ways these 12 steps can be considered to be all encompassing as they are certainly not limited to the person's addictive behavior. For example, taking a moral inventory, admitting one's wrongdoings to the people who were wronged, acknowledging powerlessness over alcohol, and agreeing to turn one's will and life to a higher power are all among these 12 steps. These 12 steps are supplemented by a list of 12 traditions, which further expand upon the philosophy of Alcoholics Anonymous but focus more on the nature of the groups and organization itself, rather than on the individual members.

Interestingly, however, the actual efficacy of Alcoholics Anonymous in its helping individuals combat alcoholism (and other addictive behaviors) is yet to be established. Indeed, the data from the organization itself (see Alcoholics Anonymous, 1990) indicate that 50% of individuals drop out of AA after four months, and 75% stop attending after a 1-year period. This certainly supports the necessity of alternative means of dealing with addictive problems suffered by those individuals for whom the AA format is not optimal.

Of course, those who do continue to follow the AA program on a regular basis are reported to have a greater likelihood of gaining control over their addictive problems. Yet, since individuals attend AA on a strictly anonymous basis, truly systematic research is difficult to complete. The best that can be said is that AA is clearly a beneficial treatment approach for some people in some circumstances. However, a more detailed description of when, for whom, and under what conditions it is the most beneficial has not been established.

It should be noted that the principles of Alcoholics Anonymous have been applied to other addictions besides alcohol, as well as to various psychological/psychiatric problems.

SUPPLEMENTAL RESOURCES

Al-Anon and Alateen. 800-356-9996.

A.A. General Service. (1967). *As Bill sees it: The A.A. way of life—Selected writings of A.A. co-founder.* New York: Alcoholics Anonymous World Services.

Frank, D. (1996). *The annotated AA handbook.* New York: Barricade Books.

Friends in Recovery. (1995). *The twelve steps: A way out.* San Diego, CA: RPI Publishing.

Olitzky, K. M., & Copans, S. A. (1991). *Twelve Jewish steps to recovery: A personal guide to turning from alcoholism and other addictions.* Woodstock, VT: Jewish Lights.

Wassil-Grim, C. (1996). *The twelve step journal.* Woodstock, NY: Overlook Press.

Alcoholism

Alcohol is considered to be the most widely used psychoactive drug worldwide. The *DSM-IV* reports that as many as 90% of adults in the United States have used alcohol in some manner, and 60% of males and 30% of females have had one or more alcohol-related events in their life which could be considered to be "adverse" (American Psychiatric Association, 1994). Indeed, a 1989 report from the National Institute on Drug Abuse reports that alcoholism is the third largest health problem in the United States—exceeded only by heart disease and cancer. With respect to children and adolescents, this same study notes that 50% of individuals between the ages of 12 and 17 have tried alcohol at some time in their lives, with 25% reporting having had at least one drink in the past month. For young adults (ages 18–25), 90% report having tried alcohol, with 65% reporting having had a drink in the past month (National Institute on Drug Abuse, 1989).

The term *alcoholism* is somewhat generic, used to refer to a collection of disorders resulting from the excessive and/or repeated ingestion of alcohol. Clinically, such disorders are divided into four major categories (as per the *DSM-IV*) including alcohol dependence, alcohol abuse (these two classified as alcohol use disorders), alcohol intoxication, and alcohol withdrawal (these latter two classified as alcohol-induced disorders).

Alcohol Use Disorders

Alcohol dependence: This refers to the situation in which the individual continues to use alcohol despite significant problems relating to such use. Specifically, alcohol dependence is characterized by evidence of tolerance (requiring more alcohol to obtain the desired effect) and/or symptoms of withdrawal (development of unpleasant symptoms several hours after the reduction of alcohol intake following significant alcohol ingestion). Because these latter withdrawal symptoms can be so unpleasant, the individual is inclined to continue to drink alcohol to avoid experiencing withdrawal symptoms. It is important to note that there are individuals who have alcohol dependence who never experience withdrawal symptoms.

Alcohol abuse: This is the next level of intensity with respect to excessive use of alcohol. Alcohol abuse is defined primarily by the seriousness of the consequences of the drinking behavior. For example, in cases of alcohol abuse, school/job performance tends to suffer, general life responsibilities are neglected, legal difficulties are common, interpersonal relationships suffer, and the individual continues his or her alcohol consumption despite these occurrences.

Alcohol-Induced Disorders

Alcohol intoxication: This is defined by noticeable behavioral and/or psychological changes during or shortly after ingestion of alcohol. In addition, these changes are often accompanied by slurred speech, incoordination, unsteady gait, attention/memory problems, stupor, or even a coma.

Alcohol withdrawal: This refers to the situation(s) wherein stopping or reduction of heavy, prolonged alcohol usage results in two or more of the following symptoms within several hours to a few days after stopping the drinking: increased pulse rate, intense sweating, increased hand tremor, **Insomnia,** nausea/vomiting, psychomotor agitation, anxiety, grand mal seizures, and/or transient visual, tactile, or auditory hallucinations/illusions. In order for alcohol withdrawal to be diagnosed, the above symptoms need to be severe enough to result in distress and/or impairment in social, occupational, or other important areas of functioning (American Psychiatric Association, 1994).

SUPPLEMENTAL RESOURCES

Alcoholism and Drug Addiction Treatment Center. 800-382-4357.

Black, C. (1995). *My dad loves me…my dad has a disease—A workbook for children of alcoholics.* Denver, CO: Mac Publishing.

Marlatt, G. A., & VandenBos, G. R. (Eds.). (1997). *Addictive behaviors: Readings on etiology, prevention and treatment.* Washington, DC: American Psychological Association.

Meir, S. *If you drink.* (A computer program on 3½" disks). Available through MHS (800-456-3003).

Mothers Against Drunk Driving (MADD). 800-438-6233.

National Clearinghouse for Alcohol and Drug Abuse Information. 800-729-6686.

National Council on Alcoholism and Drug Dependence. 800-NCA-CALL.

Parents' Resource Institute for Drug Education (PRIDE). 404-577-4500.

Paterson, J. H. (1997). *Sweet mystery: A southern memoir of family alcoholism, mental illness, and recovery.* New York: Farrar, Straus & Giroux.

Allowance

The issues of whether to give a child an allowance, and, if so, how much have been questions plaguing parents for several generations. Whereas the actual amount given to a child is best left to the jurisdiction of the particular family (the decision to be based upon the age of the child, the developmental level of the child in terms of how he or she manages money, what the money is to be used for, what the parents will still need to pay for, the general financial situation of the family), the fact remains that there are indeed advantages and disadvantages to the entire allowance process.

When an allowance is given in exchange for a child performing certain chores around the house, many parents feel as if it introduces the child to the concept of being paid for work activities—money "not growing on trees" and not being freely available upon request. However, such a situation often results in a scenario in which a child refuses to do a certain household job or task because he or she is not getting paid for it. Parents will complain that, since the allowance procedure was instituted, their child will not help out unless there is some monetary reward associated with performing the task. This is not at all an uncommon occurrence; however, it should not be used as a justification to eliminate the allowance procedure. Rather, it should be explained to the child that as a member of the family he or she (like everyone else in the family) needs to contribute to the family's optimal functioning.

Since no members of the family (adults included) get paid for everything they do, it is not appropriate for the child to expect that, either. Further, if the child is at a developmental stage such that he or she can understand the concept of "salary," it can be explained that the allowance is for a collection of chores, which can vary from week to week according to the needs of the family. The analogy can then be made how the tasks that adults actually perform in their jobs vary according to the needs of the company, but the salary nonetheless remains constant.

A closely related problem can develop when a child is given an allowance (without any job responsibilities attached to it, or with minimal responsibilities), and then is provided the opportunity to earn extra money for doing supplemental work around the house. Whereas this can be an acceptable practice, it should occur only under the most extreme of circumstances (e.g., a family move, change-of-season cleaning, etc.). If not, it can readily turn into a situation in which the child feels as if he or she is entitled to be paid for any extra tasks performed. This can even develop into the all too common disaster in which a parent is put in a situation of monetary negotiation every time the child is asked to do something! A related term is **Response Cost,** which refers to deducting money from a child's allowance as a consequence of inappropriate behavior.

SUPPLEMENTAL RESOURCES

Bodnar, J. (1997). *Dr. Tightwad's money smart kids.* Washington, DC: Kiplinger Books.
Estes, P. S., & Barocas, I. (1994). *Kids, money and values.* Cincinnati, OH: Better Way Books.
Godfrey, N. S. (1996). *A penny saved.* New York: Simon & Schuster.
Godfrey, N. S. (1998). *Ultimate kids' money book.* New York: Simon & Schuster.
Godfrey, N. S., & Edwards, C. (1994). *Money doesn't grow on trees.* New York: Simon & Schuster.

Alprazolam

This is an antianxiety drug, usually marketed under the trade name of Xanax, belonging to the class of drugs known as benzodiazepenes. Although FDA approved for administering only to children over the age of 18 years, alprazolam has been used for the treatment of various **Anxiety Disorders** in children, specifically **Panic Disorder** and more commonly **Separation Anxiety Disorder,** in dosages ranging from 0.25–5 mg.

SUPPLEMENTAL RESOURCES

Kaplan, H. I., & Sadock, B. J. (1993). *Pocket handbook of psychiatric drug treatment.* Baltimore: Williams & Wilkins.
Maxmen, J. S., & Ward, N. (1996). *Psychotropic drugs—Fast facts.* New York: W. W. Norton.
Rosenberg, D. R., Holttum, J., & Gershon, S. (1994). *Textbook of pharmacotherapy for child and adolescent psychiatric disorders.* New York: Brunner/Mazel.
Werry, J. S., & Aman, M. G. (1993). *Practitioner's guide to psychoactive drugs for children and adolescents.* New York: Plenum.

Amenorrhea

Amenorrhea is the stopping or absence of menstruation in a female who has completed puberty. This condition can be either **Primary** (referring to a situation in which menstruation has never occurred) or **Secondary** (referring to a situation in which menstruation began at puberty but stopped sometime thereafter). Physiologically based causes of amenorrhea include high levels of the hormone prolactin, a deficiency of the hormone estrogen, inadequate secretion of the sex glands, and various organic diseases (problems with ovarian function, uterine disease, etc.). In addition, a woman will shows signs of amenorrhea during pregnancy, when nursing and during menopause. Closely related to the above factors, it is not at all uncommon for an adolescent who has recently begun her menstrual cycle, or who has recently begun a regimen of oral contraceptives, to report missed menstrual periods (sporadic amenorrhea), or, at the very least, irregular menstrual periods.

Also relevant to the current discussion are the more **Psychosocial** causes of amenorrhea, less formally classified as "dietary amenorrhea," "jogger's amenorrhea," and "emotional amenorrhea." In today's current culture, it is disturbingly common to encounter adolescent females with amenorrhea that is more psychologically based. Since regular menstruation is closely related to the percentage of body weight that is fat, any rapid weight gain or loss could potentially result in what is referred to as dietary amenorrhea. Similarly, the sudden onset of strenuous physical exercise (such as, but certainly not limited to, jogging) can also interrupt the menstrual cycle—thus the term "jogger's amenorrhea." These two forms of amenorrhea and their variations are especially pertinent to today's adolescent female and the current cultural emphasis on thinness and physical exercise. Indeed, one of the indications that a female may be suffering from **Anorexia Nervosa** or a related eating disorder is the absence of regular menstrual periods. Along the same lines, females who compulsively exercise in a grueling training regimen (either in the context of an organized sports team, or simply in the pursuit of the "perfect" physique) can also be amenorrheic to varying degrees.

Finally, emotional amenorrhea can be caused by any traumatic event in the female's life, or any event perceived as being significant enough to bring on unusually strong feelings. Such feelings include, but are certainly not limited to, sadness or depression. Rather, feelings capable of causing amenorrhea run the entire gamut from joy to anxiety to anticipation. For example, it is not only marriage, death, and divorce that can have such results, but also such seemingly mundane events as a breakup with a boyfriend, a close friend's moving out of town, or even a final examination. In cases of pure emotional amenorrhea, regular menstruation typically resumes once the immediate cause is addressed.

When to Seek Professional Help

In considering when to seek professional help for amenorrhea, there are a few general rules to follow. First, if there is any possibility of pregnancy, that issue must be investigated as soon as possible. If, for whatever reasons, the individual can rule out pregnancy with absolute certainty, there is a variety of paths from which to choose. Whereas the general medical rule of thumb states that, if pregnancy is not a real possibility, wait until you miss three consecutive periods before seeking medical help, there are certainly caveats to this rule.

By examining various lifestyle issues, try to determine what the potential sources of the missed menstrual periods could be. Specifically, have there been any new medications (prescription or otherwise) introduced, any drastic weight change, or any change in exercise regimen? Should new medications be a possible factor, check with the prescribing physician or pharmacist to see if amenorrhea may be a side effect of the new medication. If it is determined that the amenorrhea may be a function of exercise or weight issues, if other circumstances are consistent, the possibility of an **Eating Disorder** may need to be investigated (see related entries).

Next, move on to consider any potential psychological factors that may be impacting on the regularity of menstrual flow. Look to see if the amenorrhea is actually a sign that something else may be going on psychologically that requires attention. For example, is the person depressed, anxious, worried, or otherwise upset about something else that is transpiring in her life? Should such be the case, the specific issue must be addressed directly to see if the true source of the amenorrhea can be resolved. Of course, if resolution cannot be obtained within a reasonable period of time, professional intervention may be necessary (see related entries).

SUPPLEMENTAL RESOURCES

Casper, R. C. (1998). *Women's health: Hormones, emotions and behavior.* New York: Cambridge University Press.

Jukes, M. (1996). *It's a girl thing.* New York: Knopf.

Madaras, L. (1988). *The what's happening to my body book for girls.* New York: Newmarket.

American Association on Mental Retardation

The American Association on Mental Retardation published the first official classification scheme to describe the different degrees/levels of mental retardation. This occurred in 1921, when the primary intelligence test in use was the Stanford Binet. Thus, the classification system utilized Stanford Binet IQ scores as cutoff criteria for the different levels. Specifically, the term *moron* was used for those individuals with an IQ ranging between 50 and 75, the term *imbecile* for those with an IQ between 25 and 50, and finally the term *idiot* for those individuals with an IQ less than 25.

With respect to actual terminology, it should be noted that this association did not acquire its current name (American Association on Mental Retardation) until 1988. Prior to that time, it was referred to as the American Association on Mental Deficiency (from 1934 until 1988), the American Association for the Study of the Feebleminded (from 1906–1933), and was originally established in 1876 as the Association of Medical Officers of American Institutions for Idiotic and Feebleminded Persons.

Amitriptyline

Amitriptyline is one of the members of the class of **Antidepressant** medications known as the **Tricyclic Antidepressants.** This drug is also known by its trade names of **Elavil** and **Endep.** Unlike some of the other drugs in this class, amitriptyline is not commonly recommended for the treatment of childhood disorders (such as **Enuresis, Obsessive-Compulsive Disorder,** and **Attention Deficit Disorder**) other than depression. Despite the demonstrated efficacy of the tricyclic antidepressants in the treatment of adult depression, such evidence does not exist relevant to young people. Indeed, the currently available studies indicate that amitriptyline (along with the other tricyclics) works no better than a **Placebo** in the treatment of depression in children and adolescents. (Actually, amitriptyline has not yet been approved by the FDA for use in the treatment of depression before the age of adolescence.) Whether these results are a function of problems in research design or actually indicate that this drug class is ineffective for treating this population is yet to be determined.

Despite the results of the research studies, utilizing amitriptyline in the treatment of children and adolescents is a rather common practice. This is somewhat alarming when one considers the potential danger—in that, specifically with respect to amitriptyline, serum levels are not useful for monitoring toxicity (or basic effectiveness, either, for that matter). Further, the **Anticholinergic Side Effects** coupled with the general sedating effect of amitriptyline make it even less desirable as a treatment option for young people.

SUPPLEMENTAL RESOURCES

Breggin, P. (1991). *Toxic psychiatry.* New York: St. Martin's Press.
Kaplan, H. I., & Sadock, B. J. (1993). *Pocket handbook of psychiatric drug treatment.* Baltimore: Williams & Wilkins.
Maxmen, J. S., & Ward, N. (1996). *Psychotropic fast facts.* New York: W. W. Norton.
Rosenberg, D. R., Holttum, J., & Gershon, S. (1994). *Textbook of pharmacotherapy for child and adolescent psychiatric disorders.* New York: Brunner/Mazel.
Werry, J. S., & Aman, M. G. (1993). *Practitioner's guide to psychoactive drugs for children and adolescents.* New York: Norton.

Anaclitic Depression

In the 1940s, research was performed on babies who were born in a penal home for adolescent mothers (Spitz, 1946). Observations of these infants resulted in the characterization of a pattern of symptoms manifested by those children who had lost their mother, father, or other primary attachment figure sometime between the ages of 6 and 8 months. This phenomenon, labeled as anaclitic depression, is characterized by a general apathy or lack of interest in the environment. In addition, these children manifested weight loss, insomnia, increased susceptibility to infection, and slowness in achieving developmental milestones. Emotionally, they became withdrawn from the environment, with their interpersonal interactions characterized by chronically weepy behavior, eventually being replaced by a blank stare. According to this early research (which served as the foundation for studies of childhood/infant depression), the longer the child was separated from his or her primary attachment figure, the worse the symptoms would become (refer also to the entry **Failure to Thrive**).

Anafranil

Anafranil is a **Tricyclic Antidepressant** that is commonly used in the treatment of various psychiatric/psychological disorders of childhood and adolescence. Although anafranil is only considered to be an experimental treatment for depressive disorders in young people, the drug has proven effective in the treatment of **Anorexia Nervosa, Bulimia, Enuresis,** and, even more so, **Obsessive-Compulsive Disorder.** In cases of enuresis, anafranil is recommended only if **Desipramine** and **Imipramine** have been found to be ineffective. Regardless of disorder, child/adolescent dosages of anafranil usually begin at 25 mg per day, not exceeding a maximum of 200 mg per day.

Obsessive-compulsive disorder is the main diagnosis for which anafranil is prescribed. When anafranil is prescribed for obsessive compulsive symptoms in young people, it is often combined with **Prozac.** Whereas such a drug combination can decrease the amount of anafranil required and is known to often increase the benefits of the intervention, this combination may intensify the potential side effects of Prozac.

In all cases in which anafranil is prescribed, it is important that regular monitoring occur, especially with respect to cardiac function. (For a more detailed description of the potential side effects of using antidepressants of this class to treat children and adolescents, the reader is referred to the entry on **Tricyclic Antidepressants.**)

SUPPLEMENTARY RESOURCES

Maxmen, J., & Ward, N. (1996). *Psychotropic drugs: Fast facts.* New York: Norton.
Rosenberg, D. R., Holttum, J., & Gershon, S. (1994). *Textbook of pharmacotherapy for child and adolescent psychiatric disorders.* New York: Brunner/Mazel.
Werry, J. S., & Aman, M. G. (1993). *Practitioner's guide to psychoactive drugs for children and adolescents.* New York: Plenum.

Anatomically Correct Dolls

Anatomically correct dolls tend to appear in two settings: the treatment environment and in everyday play. In the former case, anatomically correct dolls are used in **Play Therapy** and in various forms of psychological assessment (as a prelude to or as a component of psychotherapy). Particularly in cases when physical or sexual abuse is suspected, children are often given anatomically correct dolls to convey to the examiner precisely what transpired. The sensitive nature of abuse, limited verbal ability relevant to sexual issues, as well as the shame that so often accompanies such abuse can result in a situation in which the child/adolescent finds it difficult to verbalize details. Thus, the clinician provides anatomically correct dolls so the child/adolescent can more accurately demonstrate the behaviors that transpired. In addition to assuaging some of the "shame" factor associated with such abuse, the use of anatomically correct dolls can increase the accuracy of what is reported as children/adolescents (especially the very young ones) can either be unable—or find it extremely difficult—to describe abusive situations with the accuracy that is demanded.

The clinical situation, however, is not the only environment in which anatomically correct dolls are found. Indeed, an increasing number of parents are purchasing anatomically correct dolls for their sons and daughters as a means of educating them (in a more indirect fashion, perhaps) about the anatomical differences between the sexes. Especially in cases where a child is not exposed to another (a sibling, for example) of the opposite sex, anatomically correct dolls can neatly illustrate gender differences in a rather nonthreatening manner.

SUPPLEMENTARY RESOURCES

Engel, B. (1995). *Families in recovery—Working to heal the damage of child sexual abuse.* Los Angeles: Lowell House.
Maltz, W. (1992). *The sexual healing journey.* New York: HarperCollins.

Anger and Its Expression

The expression of anger in a family situation is a difficult topic to address, largely because every person has his or her individual norms around the issue. Specifically, our feelings about the expression of anger are formulated largely as a function of our early life experiences. Things become rather complicated as we each bring our own values and expectations into every relationship, with these values and expectations not always consistent with those of the other people in the situation. For example, what may be considered by one person to be a calm, controlled expression of anger may be perceived as another as being withdrawing and devoid of any emotion. On the other hand, what one person may perceive as being an inappropriately loud, almost violent outburst may be viewed by another person as simply expressing one's feelings.

Despite the wide variation between family members as well as between different families, there are certain guidelines with respect to the expression of anger in young people. First, it needs to be accepted that anger is a normal, healthy emotion and, as such, will require expression in some form. Although this sounds rather trite, there are indeed individuals who fail to recognize the expression of angry feelings as a natural part of living. As a result, such individuals tend to (consciously or unconsciously) attempt to prevent, or at the very least discourage, the open expression of angry feelings in their offspring. Therefore, such children grow up with a belief that anger is a bad thing, and its expression should be curtailed at all costs. As is true with people of any age who adhere to such a belief, the psychological (and often physical) costs are significant. Since anger is a natural emotion that needs to be expressed, failing to do so results in pent up, unexpressed feeling—feeling that needs to come out in some form or fashion. Anger that is not expressed as such can be exhibited as physical illness, anxiety, depression, or withdrawal. In addition, in situations where it is perceived that it is unacceptable to express angry feelings, such feelings become displaced onto another individual or situation toward whom or in which the expression of anger feels safer.

Of course, none of the above is meant to imply that children/adolescents should be allowed free reign to express angry feelings in any manner and at any intensity they so choose. Parents should discuss between themselves (based upon their own values and their own means of expressing angry feelings) the family norms for such expression, as well as what will be considered acceptable behavior and what will not. Further, parental figures should be prepared to present various options to their children/adolescents in terms of ways to express angry feelings to allow the young people to be able to choose the manner with which they feel the most comfortable.

It is also important to note that this is one of the many situations in which the old adage "actions speak louder than words" actually applies. Almost regardless of what is actually verbalized, children/adolescents tend to look to the behavior of their parents as a guide to how to best express angry feelings. Whereas, at times, there is a modeling effect in which the young person actually seems to imitate (either directly or indirectly) the behavior of one or both parents, in other situations it appears as if the child/adolescent opts to act in a manner diametrically opposed to the style of the parent. This latter situation typically occurs in families in which parental expression of anger is at one of the extremes of the continuum (i.e., the parent expresses anger very violently or the parent does not seem able to express anger at all).

Things can be especially problematic when one or both parental figures have difficulties themselves with the expression of angry feelings. It is in such situations that it is crucial for the parent in question to recognize his or her limitations in this area, acknowledge such to the child/adolescent, and actively work to change the manner in which angry feelings are expressed.

When to Seek Professional Help

It is important for parents not to rush to pathologize a child/adolescent's means of anger expression simply because the modality differs from his or her own. Similarly, when someone significant (be it another parent or someone else) in a parent's life expresses anger in an abusive or otherwise pathological manner, there is a natural tendency to be overly sensitive to the manner in which the child/adolescent expresses anger, and, at times to be a bit overreactive and quick to view it as pathological. Parents must be able to give the child/adolescent permission to express angry feelings individually, even if the behavior is dramatically different from the particular parent's own preferences.

Of course, there are situations in which a young person's expression of anger does require professional help. Such situations are best recognized when the young person's means of anger expression impedes upon the optimal functioning of the family, or simply negatively affects the young person's own optimal functioning. In these circumstances, the child/adolescent is typically aware (at least on some level) of the detrimental effects of the manner in which he or she expresses angry feelings, but is at a loss as to how to best deal with the situation. At times, one or both parents approaching the young person in a nonthreatening, nonjudgmental manner is sufficient to elicit a discussion, which, in and of itself, could eliminate the need for professional intervention. Indeed, these discussions often reveal the source of the anger (perhaps a single incident or person, the reaction to which is instigating angry reactions in various situations) and allow it to be addressed directly.

For those cases in which the parents and/or the young person feel as if professional help is indicated, there are various options available. At the end of this listing is a brief sampling of books designed to help young people express and deal with their angry feelings. In many cases, exposure to one or more of these resources is sufficient to help the young person remedy the situation on his or her own. Other options include therapy groups designed specifically to address anger management, family therapy sessions, or the more traditional individual psychotherapy formats. For any formalized treatment situation, it recommended that the parents and/or young person be prepared to provide the following information:

- Behavior that led person to therapy, justification, if you will, for feeling that a problem exists
- When the problematic behavior began and what was transpiring in the young person's life at that time
- Any medications (prescription and nonprescription) being taken currently (and any changes in medications)
- Family norms as to how anger (and other feelings) are expressed
- Detailed account of what happens during the problematic behavior
- Reactions of those around young person when problematic behavior is displayed
- Young person's opinion as to whether the behavior is problematic
- What is expected to be accomplished in therapy

Parental figures as well as the child/adolescent (consistent with the developmental stage) should expect to have the following questions answered by the treating professional:

- Is this behavior indicative of some other clinical disorder?
- How normal is the behavior being presented, is treatment indicated?

- Would individual, family, or group therapy be the most appropriate treatment modality?
- What therapeutic techniques will you be using?
- What do you believe to be the cause/source of this problem?
- While the child/adolescent is in treatment, what can we as a family expect with respect to his or her behavior?
- While the child/adolescent is in therapy, how should we as a family react to child/adolescent's expression of anger?
- Will the situation get worse before it gets better?
- Is there anything the family and/or the child/adolescent can do at home to bring improvement at a more rapid rate?
- When is it reasonable to expect to see some improvement?

SUPPLEMENTAL RESOURCES

Abarn, A. (1994). *Everything I do you blame on me.* Secaucus, NJ: Childswork/Childsplay.
Anger management for parents [Video]. (Available from Research Press, Champaign, IL [800-519-2707])
Clark, L. (1998). *SOS—Help for emotions: Managing anxiety, anger and depression.* Bowling Green, KY: Parents Press.
Eastman, M. (1994). *Taming the dragon in your child: Solutions for breaking the cycle of family anger.* New York: John Wiley.
Paul, H. A. (1999). *When kids are mad, not bad: A guide to recognizing and handling your child's anger.* New York: Berkley.
Pincus, D. (1995). *How I learned to control my temper: A storybook and workbook of activities to help children learn self-control.* Secaucus, NJ: Childswork/Childsplay.
Shapiro, L. E. (1994). *The very angry day that Amy didn't have.* Secaucus, NJ: Childswork/Childsplay.
Shore, H. (1995). *Angry monster workbook.* Secaucus, NJ: Childswork/Childsplay.

Anhedonia

Anhedonia is a term used to describe a situation in which an individual seems virtually unable to experience any pleasure. Specifically, activities and pursuits that used to be enjoyable for that individual no longer bring pleasure or enjoyment. For example, hobbies, leisure activities, even certain aspects of one's job or academic commitments that used to be perceived as positive are no longer perceived as such, and may even be perceived as drudgery. Whereas anhedonia is typically considered to be indicative of a depressive condition, such is not always the case.

A temporary, short-lived anhedonia can occur in situations in which the individual is under extreme stress due to life situations. For example, an adolescent whose family has recently moved to a new neighborhood has not been engaging in her usual fashion drawing because she is worried about making friends in her new school. Similarly, there is the 4-year-old boy who seems to no longer be interested in playing with his army men and tanks since his father moved out of the house.

When looking at anhedonia in children and adolescents, it is also important to consider the developmental context. Prior to assuming that the young person is suffering from some type of depressive condition, it is important to consider the possibility that the child/adolescent may simply be beginning to outgrow the particular activity. This maturation process can be distinguished from a depression by examining the nature of the anhedonia in some detail. For example, if the anhedonia seems to extend to several different activities that were previously enjoyable, it is more likely to be due to depression. Similarly, if the waning of the pleasurable experience extends to so many activities that the individual seems to be unable to experience virtually any pleasure whatsoever, it is likely that the anhedonia is indicative of a depressive condition.

Anorexia Nervosa

Anorexia nervosa refers to a self-imposed preoccupation with one's weight—more specifically, being thin. Behaviorally, this translates into a refusal to maintain one's body weight, an intense fear of gaining any weight, as well as a disturbance in the manner in which the individual perceives his or her own body image/weight. As a result, the anorexic individual will commonly refuse to eat, thereby resulting in weight loss of varying degrees of severity. In females, this intense weight loss can result in **Amenorrhea,** whereas in males the weight loss can result in problems with erectile functioning. Young people whose onset of anorexia is prior to puberty may not actually lose weight, but, rather, they may fail to gain the expected amount of weight during periods of active growth. Further, approximately 50% of patients diagnosed with anorexia will exhibit binge and purge behavior at some point during the disorder, during treatment, and/or during recovery.

In addition to the above mentioned psychological aspects of anorexia, there are also physical symptoms that commonly accompany this disorder. For example, anorexic individuals often exhibit an inability to tolerate cold temperatures, constipation, abdominal discomfort (including some bloating), dry skin, lanugo (baby-fine hair on the body), sleep difficulties, diarrhea, and dizziness. A seemingly hyperactive demeanor typifies such individuals, with anorexics often appearing to have an almost **Hypomanic** energy level.

Usually, anorexia nervosa symptoms first appear either during the adolescent puberty weight gain, or following a successful dieting regimen in a previously (slightly) overweight individual. In the first class of situations, the adolescent panics at the changes in his or her body shape and takes dramatic measures in an attempt to control subsequent weight gain. Yet another dynamic that comes into play in these situations is that of control. The young adolescent often perceives body appearance to be assuming changes beyond his or her control. Thus, the anorexic behavior becomes an attempt at regaining control of one's appearance. In the latter class of cases, the dieting is reinforcing in that it indicates to the individual that dieting behavior can result in weight loss. Thus, as a result, the individual is inclined to utilize dieting-like behavior (i.e., anorexic symptoms) as a means of subsequently attempting to control his or her weight.

Estimates of (lifetime) prevalence for anorexia range from 0.1% to 0.7%. Data indicate that somewhere between 90% to 95% of the sufferers are female, although this figure may not be accurate, as young men are able to mask the symptoms of anorexia more easily than are women. Onset of anorexic symptoms can be anywhere from age 8 to the mid thirties, however, there seems to be two peaks of onset at ages 13–14 and at 17–18. In any case, over half of the cases appear before age 20, with approximately 75% having their onset prior to age 25. More specifically, 85% of all anorexics have their onset between the ages of 13 and 20 years of age.

Treatment of anorexia is complicated by the fact that, in the majority of situations, the patient does not perceive any need for professional treatment. Indeed, most individuals with anorexia feel that others are misperceiving the existence of pathology. With the patient's distortion of body image translating into seeing the self as overweight, there is often a resentment of professionals and/or family members who attempt to encourage weight gain. Unfortunately, then, the individual with anorexia often does not engage in treatment until the situation becomes medically dangerous.

The first step in treatment for anorexia is to do everything possible to bring on a gain of weight (at times, in an inpatient facility when necessary). **Individual Psychotherapy** for anorexia focuses on the alteration of the person's eating patterns as well the psychological factors determining this behavior. Actual content of therapy may include **Cognitive Behavior Therapy** to restructure the person's perceptions about body appearance and the necessity of being thin. Typically, this is supplemented by education of the family about the disorder and relevant nutritional issues, behavioral treatment to encourage weight gain, as well as **Family Therapy** to explore the psychological issues that rest at the core of the disorder.

SUPPLEMENTAL RESOURCES

Berg, F. M. (1998). *Afraid to eat: Children and teens in weight crisis.* Hettinger, ND: Healthy Weight Publishing Network.

Buckroyd, J. (1996). *Anorexia and bulimia: Your questions answered.* Boston: Element Books.

Chernin, K. (1985). *The hungry self: Women, eating and identity.* New York: Times Books.

Hall, L., & Ostroff, M. (1999). *Anorexia nervosa: A guide to recovery.* Carlsbad, CA: Gurze Books.

Jantz, G. L. (1995). *Hope, help and healing for eating disorders.* Wheaton, IL: Harold Shaw.

Kano, S. (1989). *Making peace with food.* New York: Harper Row.

Krasnow, M. (1996). *My life as a male anorexic.* Binghamton, NY: Haworth Press.

Normandi, C. E., & Roark, L. (1998). *It's not about food.* New York: Grosset-Putnam.

Palmer, R. L. (1989). *Anorexia nervosa: A guide for sufferers and their families.* New York: Penguin.

Pierre, P. C. (1997). *The secret language of eating disorders.* New York: Random House.

Pipher, M. (1997). *Hunger pains: The modern woman's tragic quest for thinness.* New York: Ballantine.

Ray, S. (1981). *The only diet there is.* Berkeley: Celestial Press.

Rosen, J. (1997). *Eve's apple.* New York: Random House.

Sacks, I. M., & Zimmer, M. A. (1987). *Dying to be thin.* New York: Warner Books.

Siegel, M., Brisman, J., & Weinstel, M. (1997). *Surviving an eating disorder—Strategies for families and friends.* New York: Harper Perennial.

Anticholinergic Side Effects

Anticholinergic side effects are commonly associated with the use of certain **Antipsychotic Medications.** Typical side effects in this class include dry mouth, nasal congestion, dry eyes, constipation, and problems with vision (blurred vision, problems with intense light, and glaucoma). There is also a subclass of anticholinergic side effects known as *central anticholinergic effects,* which are considerably more severe in their manifestation. Included in this subcategory are agitation, seizures, fever, **Hallucinations,** and general disorientation.

The antipsychotics vary considerably with respect to likelihood of causing an anticholinergic side effect. For example, those antipsychotics with a high probability of evoking these side effects include **Clozaril, Thorazine,** and serentil, while those drugs that are less prone to inducing anticholinergic side effects include **Haldol, Navane,** and **Prolixin.**

Antidepressants

Generally speaking, the antidepressant medications currently available can be divided into three major classes: **Tricyclic Antidepressants, Selective Serotonin Reuptake Inhibitors (SSRIs),** and **Monoamine Oxidase Inhibitors (MAOIs).** Although antidepressant medications from each of these three groups are used to treat various psychological/psychiatric problems in children and adolescents, the tricyclic antidepressants are the only antidepressants that have been actually approved in children as young as 12 years of age.

When considering appropriate dosages in prescribing antidepressant medications for young people, the physician must keep in mind that these medications are processed by children's bodies differently than they would be in adults. First, since children have a lower fat-to-muscle ratio, there is a greater risk of *toxicity* as a result of there being too much of the drug circulating in the system. Further complicating the issue is the fact that, since young people have a proportionately larger liver, the drugs are metabolized more quickly. Thus, in order for the dosage to be effective, a greater proportion of drug must be in the system (in proportion to body weight) than would be required in adults.

Although in the majority of situations when they are used in the treatment of children and adolescents, antidepressant medication is used as an adjunct to psychological treatment, the various antidepressants are used to treat a wide variety of disorders in young people. Included among these disorders are depressive disorders, **Enuresis, Attention Deficit Disorder,** tic disorders, **School Phobia, Obsessive-Compulsive Disorder,** as well as various sleep problems.

SUPPLEMENTAL RESOURCES

Breggin, P. (1991). *Toxic psychiatry.* New York: St Martin's Press.
Campbell, M., Green, W. H., & Deutsch, S. I. (1985). *Child and adolescent psychopharmacology.* Beverly Hills, CA: Sage.

Kaplan, H. I., & Sadock, B. J. (1993). *Pocket handbook of psychiatric drug treatment*. Baltimore: Williams & Wilkins.

Maxmen, J. S., & Ward, N. (1996). *Psychotropic drugs: Fast facts*. New York: W. W. Norton.

Norden, M. J. (1996). *Beyond Prozac*. New York: HarperCollins.

Rosenberg, D. R., Holttum, J., & Gershon, S. (1994). *Textbook of pharmacotherapy for child and adolescent psychiatric disorders*. New York: Brunner/Mazel.

Werry, J. S., & Aman, M. G. (1993). *Practitioner's guide to psychoactive drugs for children and adolescents*. New York: Plenum.

Antipsychotics

This class of medications is also referred to as the **Major Tranquilizers** and as the **Neuroleptics.** Although they are used primarily in the treatment of the symptoms of psychotic disorders, their application has come to extend beyond the treatment of the psychotic disorders, especially in children. Antipsychotics are generally divided into two classes: (1) the high-potency drugs, which typically required a lower dosage (such as **Navane, Haldol,** and **Stelazine**), and (2) the low-potency drugs, which typically require a higher dosage and tend to be more highly sedating (such as **Mellaril** and **Thorazine**). There are also two newly developed antipsychotic drugs (**Clozaril** and **Risperidone**), which are not classified into either of the two original categories and are often referred to as the *atypical antipsychotics.*

In addition to being prescribed to treat the symptoms of the various schizophrenic disorders, antipsychotic drugs have been approved for and are also used in the treatment of the following child/adolescent disorders: **Conduct Disorder, Pervasive Developmental Disorders,** and **Tourette's Syndrome.** In most of these cases, the antipsychotic medications are used to address some form of behavioral acting out as opposed to being utilized as a potential cure for the disorder itself.

SUPPLEMENTAL RESOURCES

Degen, K. (1996). *Return from madness: Psychotherapy with people taking the new antipsychotic medications and emerging from severe, lifelong, and disabling schizophrenia*. Northvale, NJ: Jason Aronson.

Kaplan, H. I., & Sadock, B. J. (1993). *Pocket handbook of psychiatric drug treatment*. Baltimore: Williams & Wilkins.

Maxmen, J. S., & Ward, N. (1996). *Psychtropic drugs: Fast facts*. New York: W. W. Norton.

Rosenberg, D. R., Holttum, J., & Gershon, S. (1994). *Textbook of pharmacotherapy for child and adolescent psychiatric disorders*. New York: Brunner/Mazel.

Weiden, P. J., Scheifler, P. L., Diamond, R. J., & Ross, R. (1998). *Switching antipsychotic medications: A guide for consumers and families*. Arlington, VA: National Alliance for the Mentally Ill.

Antisocial Personality Disorder

This is one of the eleven **Personality Disorder** diagnoses described in the *DSM-IV.* Although it is technically an adult diagnosis (in that the diagnosis cannot be applied to individuals younger than age 18), it is closely related to behaviors exhibited earlier in life in that one of the requirements for this disorder to be diagnosed is the presence of **Conduct Disorder** during the childhood years (specifically prior to age 15).

Antisocial personality disorder is characterized by a pattern of disregard for the feelings of others as well as for established rules of society. The *DSM-IV* (American Psychiatric Association, 1994) requires at least three of the following symptoms to be present for this diagnosis to be made:

1. failure to conform to social norms with respect to lawful behaviors as indicated by repeatedly performing acts that are grounds for arrest
2. deceitfulness, as indicated by repeated lying, use of aliases or conning others for personal profit or pleasure
3. impulsivity and aggressiveness, as indicated by repeated physical fights or assaults
4. irritability and aggressiveness, as indicated by repeated physical fights or assaults
5. reckless disregard for safety of self or others
6. consistent irresponsibility, as indicated by repeated failure to sustain consistent work behavior or honor financial obligations
7. lack of remorse, as indicated by being indifferent to or rationalizing having hurt, mistreated, or stolen from another.... (pp. 649–650)

It is especially interesting that, despite the behaviors described above, many individuals with antisocial personality disorder can be charming and pleasant to be around. A partial explanation for this apparent inconsistency is their lack of anxiety and/or guilt stemming from the consequences of their actions. Indeed, some even describe individuals with antisocial personality disorder as appearing to lack a conscience and/or sense of right and wrong.

Issues of substance usage/abuse often complicate the diagnostic process in cases where antisocial behavior is observed. Since the process of substance abuse often seems to necessitate various types of antisocial behavior, it is inappropriate to diagnose an individual with antisocial personality disorder when the behaviors are **Secondary** to the substance abuse problem. In other words, if the individual's antisocial behavior is a consequence or result of the substance abuse (e.g., lying to mask drug usage, stealing money from others to obtain funds to purchase drugs, etc.), a diagnosis of antisocial personality disorder is inappropriate. However, there are indeed cases in which both the substance abuse as well as the antisocial behavior have been occurring since childhood. In such cases, both diagnoses are appropriate and relevant.

Again, whereas antisocial personality disorder is indeed an adult diagnosis, it cannot be diagnosed unless the individual has manifested antisocial personality disorder symptoms during childhood (i.e., prior to age 15 years), and unless these same symptoms have continued on until adulthood. Although statistical data indicate that this disorder is more common in males than in females (with a reported incidence of 3% in men and 1% in women), this could very well be a function of the diagnostic criterion in **Conduct Disorder** requiring aggressive behavior to be present (a characteristic more common in boys than in girls).

SUPPLEMENTAL RESOURCES

Black, D. W., & Larson, C. L. (1999). *Bad boys, bad men: Confronting antisocial personality disorder.* New York: Oxford University Press.

Magid, K., & McKelvey, C. A. (1989). *High risk children without a conscience.* New York: Bantam.

Masterson, J. F. (1988). *The search for the real self: Unmasking the personality disorders of our age.* New York: Free Press.

Anxiety Disorders

During the early years of psychiatry and psychology, all types of mental disorders were considered to be caused by (or, at the very least, severely influenced by) anxiety. As a matter of fact, until relatively recently, diagnosticians and clinicians distinguished between those disorders that interfered with a person's perception of reality (classifying these under the rubric of **Psychotic Disorders**) and other disorders that were believed to be due to problems with the management or intensity of anxiety (classifying these under the rubric of *neurotic disorders*). Indeed, the original *DSM (Diagnostic and Statistical Manual)* published in 1952 grouped all of the anxiety disorders under the heading "psychoneurotic disorders," further classifying them into four subgroupings: (1) anxiety reactions, (2) phobic reactions, (3) obsessive compulsive reactions, and (4) psychoneurotic and other reactions. Interestingly, formal diagnoses for anxiety disorders experienced by young people were not established formally until 1980, as (1) **Separation Anxiety Disorder,** (2) **Avoidant Disorder of Childhood and Adolescence,** and (3) **Overanxious Disorder.**

Currently, the only anxiety disorder diagnostic category remaining that is exclusive to children and adolescents is that of separation anxiety disorder. Of course, this is not to imply that young people do not suffer from any of the other anxiety disorders! Rather, instead of providing separate diagnostic categories, the most popular diagnostic system in current use in the United States conceptualizes children and adolescents as experiencing the same anxiety disorders as do adults. However, the actual symptoms observed are different as a function of developmental level. Thus, as with adults, the anxiety disorders experienced by young people include **Phobic Disorders, Panic Disorder, Generalized Anxiety Disorder,** and **Obsessive-Compulsive Disorder.**

SUPPLEMENTAL RESOURCES

Bourne, E. J. (1995). *The phobia and anxiety disorder workbook.* New York: New Harbinger.

Greist, J., Jefferson, J., & Marks, I. (1986). *Anxiety and its treatment.* Washington, DC: American Psychiatric Press.

Knowles, J. J. (1994). *What of the night: A journey through depression and anxiety.* Fort Erie, Ontario: Magpie.

Anxiety Disorders Scale for Children

This is an assessment instrument designed to measure the presence and severity of anxiety symptoms in children and adolescents. Often referred to as the ADIS, it contains various questions dealing with the symptoms characteristic of the different anxiety disorders. The majority of the questions are designed to be answered in a yes/no format. The instrument itself consists of two parts—one for the parental figure to complete (ADIS-P) and the second for the child or adolescent to complete (ADIS-C).

Anxiolytics

This term refers to a category of drugs used to treat an individual's anxiety or to produce sedation. Interestingly, however, despite the term anxiolytic (meaning antianxiety), when drugs are used in the treatment of **Anxiety Disorders** of young people, it is typically drugs of the **Antidepressant** group as opposed to anxiolytics! Indeed, anxiolytics (benzodiazepines, antihistamines, and buspirone) are seldom actually used as treatments for child/adolescent anxiety.

SUPPLEMENTAL RESOURCES

Kaplan, H. I., & Sadock, B. J. (1993). *Pocket handbook of psychiatric drug treatment.* Baltimore: Williams & Wilkins.

Maxmen, J. S., & Ward, N. (1996). *Psychotropic drugs: Fast facts.* New York: W. W. Norton.

Rosenberg, D. R., Holttum, J., & Gershon, S. (1994). *Textbook of pharmacotherapy for child and adolescent psychiatric disorders.* New York: Brunner/Mazel.

Werry, J. S., & Aman, M. G. (1993). *Practitioner's guide to psychoactive drugs for children and adolescents.* New York: Plenum.

Aphasia

Aphasia (also referred to as *dysphasia)* refers to any loss of the ability to produce or understand language. This term is used when the language loss is physiological in basis, as opposed to those cases in which the individual chooses not to talk in certain or all situations (i.e., *elective mutism).* Potential physiological causes of aphasia are many in number, including dementia, brain tumors, and trauma. However, when aphasia presents itself as an isolated symptom, it is usually a function of a stroke or some type of brain injury.

There are eight basic types of aphasia, differentiated by the type and extent of language impairment as well as the portion of the brain that is injured:

Global aphasia: Complete aphasia in which fluency, writing, naming, repetition, reading comprehension, reading aloud, and general comprehension are all impaired; the most severe type of aphasic condition.

Broca's aphasia: Also referred to as *motor aphasia, expressive aphasia,* and *nonfluent aphasia;* person is able to comprehend both spoken and written language; however, impairment exists in all aspects of speech and writing.

Wernicke's aphasia: Also referred to as *sensory aphasia, central aphasia,* and *receptive aphasia;* individual's speech is fluent but disordered in both writing and verbalization; individual is unaware of problems in his or her verbalization; comprehension is also impaired.

Anomic aphasia: The only impairment in this type of aphasia is in the areas of naming objects—both verbally and in writing.

Conduction aphasia: So named because of the nature of the brain lesion (i.e., lesion in the area connecting Broca's area with Wernicke's area); all aspects of comprehension are normal, but impairments exist in repetition and reading aloud; similarly, there are problems in speech.

Transcortical motor aphasia: Similar to Broca's aphasia except that in transcortical motor aphasia repetition abilities are not impaired; ability to read aloud is impaired, as are writing abilities.

Transcortical sensory aphasia: Similar to Wernicke's aphasia without impairment in the ability to repeat; reading and writing abilities are impaired.

Mixed transcortical aphasia: Similar to global aphasia, however in mixed transcortical aphasia the ability to repeat is unimpaired.

Aphasia is diagnosed and assessed by a variety of **Neuropsychological** tests and batteries. These assessment instruments present tasks that require the use of the various language abilities. Thus, the clinician is able to evaluate which aspects of language are actually impaired, and to what degree.

SUPPLEMENTAL RESOURCES

Adams, R. L., Parsons, O. A., Culbertson, J. L., & Nixon, S. J. (Eds.). (1996). *Neuropsychology for clinical practice.* Washington, DC: American Psychological Association.

Apnea

Technically, apnea (or more specifically, sleep apnea) is defined as the stopping of a person's breathing (for at least ten seconds) while he or she is asleep. In order for sleep apnea to be diagnosed, both nasal (nose) and oral (mouth) airflow needs to stop for longer than ten seconds at a time, and for more than thirty times during a 7-hour period of sleep. When an incident of apnea occurs, there is a decrease in the amount of oxygen in the blood, with a similar increase in the amount of carbon dioxide.

Whereas sleep apnea most commonly affects middle-aged males, it can and does occur at any age. Infant sleep apnea (in babies 37 weeks or older) and apnea of prematurity (in babies younger than 37 weeks) can be potentially life threatening as they involve various central or obstructive apneas that occur while the baby is asleep. When children and adolescents suffer from sleep apnea, there are often secondary psychological symptoms associated with the lack of sleep and the apnea physiological process. Included among commonly observed secondary symptoms are decline in school performance, periodic sleeping spells, hyperactivity and **Enuresis** (especially at night).

The *DSM-IV* (American Psychiatric Association, 1994) describes diagnostic criteria for Breathing Related Sleep Disorder as "sleep disruption, leading to excessive sleepiness or insomnia, that is judged to be due to a sleep-related breathing condition (e.g., obstructive or central sleep apnea syndrome or central alveolar hypoventilation syndrome)." Whereas obstructive sleep apnea is typified by incidents of upper airway obstruction, central sleep apnea (also referred to as nonobstructive sleep apnea) is more characteristically typified by a decrease or actual stopping of ventilation during sleep.

Arguing between Parents

A certain amount of disagreement is inevitable whenever two or more individuals live in close proximity for any period of time. Indeed, it is unreasonable to expect that the situation should be any different when these two individuals are man and wife, or when these two individuals become parents. Actually, there are many who would say that the introduction of offspring into the scenario actually exponentially increases the opportunities for disagreement and arguments. However, in no way is arguing between parents, in and of itself, a negative occurrence. Actually, if it is done right, it is yet another way that parents can model a human interaction in a manner that is helpful to their child or adolescent. Since disagreements are a natural part of the human condition, as noted above, it is important that children mature in such an environment that they learn to deal with such occurrences appropriately.

Thus, it is not *whether* children/adolescents view arguing between their parents, but, rather, *what* they view when they experience this occurrence that is of significance. If the parents are able to discuss their disagreement in a nonabusive, nonthreatening manner, even if anger is a part of the scenario, they are able to model a very important component of day-to-day life for their offspring. Without saying anything to them directly, this behavior teaches young people that individuals can disagree, argue, and even become angry with each other, but the relationship can still remain loving and intact. Within reason, then, parents who attempt to hide arguments from their children, and therefore convey the impression that the parents "never argue," are indeed doing their children a disservice by failing to provide them with a demonstration of crucial interpersonal interaction.

On the other hand, there are situations in which arguments between parents develop into hateful, ugly scenes. Some are complete with name-calling, physical violence, emotionally abusive language, and other dysfunctional behaviors. In cases such as these, children become anxious and fearful and view these scenarios as possible precursors of the destruction of their world as they know it (i.e., parental separation or divorce). To make matters worse, such situations convey to the child that disagreement is synonymous with scary behaviors and, as such, needs to be avoided and feared at all costs. Indeed, this type of behavior also teaches children important lessons about how to argue—lessons that are probably better left unlearned. Yet, it is important to emphasize, again, that it is not the actual arguing that is detrimental to the child in these cases, but rather the unhealthy manner in which the parents express their disagreement. Thus, the solution here is not to protect the children from hearing the parents argue, but rather to help the parents learn to argue in a more functional, less destructive manner.

Two other issues need to be addressed regarding this topic. First, in the majority of cases, regardless of the quality of the interaction style between the parents, it is better for the child not to be witness to a disagreement between the parents that focuses on an issue directly concerning the child himself or herself. Whereas it is perfectly appropriate to inform the child that the parents have differing opinions on a given subject and need to discuss the issue in private, it is important for the child not to be informed as to which parent takes what position, nor the actual content of the discussion. Rather, the child should be approached after the parents have discussed the issue and presented with a unified decision. Second, at times, upon hearing their parents argue, children express concerns that the parents are going to divorce, separate, or hurt each other. Again, this is an ideal opportunity to explain to the children that it is most normal for individuals to argue, and, that such arguments and disagreements do not signify the end of a relationship nor a lack of love between the two people involved.

SUPPLEMENTAL RESOURCES

Carlson, R. (1998). *Don't sweat the small stuff with your family.* New York: Hyperion.
Pipher, M. (1996). *The shelter of each other—Rebuilding our families.* New York: Ballantine Books.

Arguing between Siblings

Arguing between siblings, as is arguing between or among any members of the family, is natural, healthy, and inevitable. However, there is an idealized conceptualization of the image of family held by most parents that prevents them from being able to accept and allow dissention among their offspring. To make matters worse, parental reaction to their children's spats often inadvertently reinforces the arguing behavior. Desperate pleas from parents such as "Why can't you two get along?" and threats from parents conveying "I'd better not hear anymore arguing between you guys" along with lectures as to how people in the same family should treat each other often seem to fall upon deaf ears as the arguing, playful (and sometimes not so playful) physical and verbal aggression, teasing, and taunting seem to continue without end.

One major dynamic behind arguing among siblings centers around rivalry—rivalry for parental attention, rivalry for earning the title of "the best child," rivalry for earning the title of "the worst child," rivalry for a chosen toy, rivalry for a certain seat in the family car or at the family table, rivalry for…the list goes on endlessly. Whereas some would conceptualize the ideal situation as children not engaging in a competitive relationship with their siblings, a certain amount of such rivalry is a necessary learning experience of growing up. Such feelings help the child learn about issues of sharing, respecting, understanding and acknowledging the feelings of others, compromise, and learning to deal with disappointment. Toward that end, parents should refrain from both intervening at the first indication of arguing and immediately attempting to solve the problem at hand.

Of course, there are indeed sibling argument situations in which the parents do need to intervene. As in most such cases, there is wide variation among families, and oftentimes within families as to when this particular time is. Decisions as to when parents need to enter the scene are based upon parental values, what is considered tolerable behavior, and what is considered acceptable behavior. Whatever position a parent chooses to take, however, it is crucial to recognize that children tend to view parental intervention as reinforcing. As a result, they may escalate the situation's intensity to such a degree until parental involvement is forced to occur. As a prime example of this phenomenon, note the frequency with which some variation of the following situation occurs.

> The brothers and sisters have been alone with the babysitter all day while the parents are at work. During this time, there has been virtually no arguing or bickering between the children, and the overall behavior has been without problem. However, within 5 minutes of Mom's walking in the door, intense arguing among the children begins…intense enough to demand the mother's intervention.

Whenever a parent needs to intervene, however, a major part of the parental message should be that it is not the arguing itself that is problematic (emphasizing the normality of disagreement), but rather the methods of expressing disagreement that are being used.

Despite the more covert dynamics, most cases of sibling rivalry stem from a more generic attempt to achieve perceived importance. (After all, would Mom and/or Dad intervene if the incident were not truly important in the grand scheme of things?) Again, the exact nature of the need for importance may vary, however the underlying dynamic remains consistent. Thus, the natural question is what can parents do, as a preventive measure so to speak, to minimize the frequency and intensity of sibling arguing?

> *Allow each child to feel special and unique in his or her own right:* Much competition among siblings can be eliminated when each child has a sense of playing a significant and important role in the family system, as well in his or her own world. Thus, when parents make a definitive effort to reinforce each child for his or her talents, strengths, and abilities, by definition, the child's sense of self is strengthened. It is quite important, then, that parents take advantage of every attempt to *sincerely* offer a compliment to a child/adolescent, especially when the source of that compliment is unique to that particular young person.

> *Recognize each child as an individual as well as a family member:* Despite the time limitations of today's world, parents should try to spend some individual time with each child. Oftentimes, there are special activities that can be enjoyed between parent and child that are unique to the relationship between the parent and the individual child.

> *Reinforce children for appropriate interactions with siblings:* When parents observe children playing together (or otherwise interacting) for any period of time, it is useful for parents to approach the siblings and comment upon how nice they are playing together, or to simply go over to the group and briefly converse. This serves multiple purposes—not the least of which is providing the children with parental attention when a desired interaction is occurring (as opposed to when problems are occurring).

SUPPLEMENTAL RESOURCES

Bullard, J. (1996). *Teaching tolerance.* New York: Doubleday.
Canter, L. (1993). *Surviving sibling rivalry.* Santa Monica, CA: Lee Canter and Associates.
Faber, A., & Mazlish, E. (1987). *Siblings without rivalry.* New York: Avon Books.
Goldenthal, P. (1999). *Sibling rivalry.* New York: Henry Holt.

Asperger's Disorder (Syndrome)

One of the **Pervasive Developmental Disorders,** Asperger's disorder (also referred to as Asperger's syndrome) was first formally described in the mid-1940s. For quite some time (and even now, to some extent), there has been controversy as to whether Asperger's disorder is indeed a distinct diagnostic entity, or, if in reality, it is simply a less severe form of **Autistic Disorder.** Initially, this disorder was referred to as *autistic psychopathy* prior to it having its current name—named after the Austrian physician Hans Asperger (1844–1954). Estimates of frequency range from 0.6 to 26 per 10,000 children with a definite trend showing considerably more male Asperger sufferers than female.

Unlike autism, in Asperger's disorder there is no delay in the development of language or cognitive skills. Specifically, most Asperger's sufferers are able to use individual words by two years of age, and are able to use full phrases by three years of age. Further, somewhat dissimilar to autistic children, children with Asperger's disorder actually appear to enjoy the company of others. However, the peer relationships are not at an appropriate developmental level, and there is a lack of social and/or emotional reciprocity. Similar to autistic children, however, those with Asperger's manifest ritualistic, repetitive behavior patterns. These behaviors can involve meaningless routines or rituals, a preoccupation with one or more interests, a preoccupation with parts of objects, and/or an apparent inflexibility with respect to daily routines. Often, Asperger's children are perceived as being clumsy or awkward in their motor behaviors, at times slow in achieving developmental motor milestones.

Treatment

Treatment for Asperger's disorder will usually involve three components: (1) drug interventions, (2) psychotherapy, and (3) work on social and motor skills. The drug therapy is variable in its type—usually using whatever medications are employed to address the specific symptom(s) in question. Thus, if some compulsive ritual is being targeted, a drug usually used for **Obsessive-Compulsive Disorder** would be employed. Similarly, if general anxiety is being targeted, the medication would be chosen accordingly. The psychotherapy component usually entails both individual work with the child as well as some parent/family interventions. These latter approaches are designed to provide the family members with information about the disorder itself, as well as to provide coping strategies to deal optimally with the Asperger's child. Finally, those treatment approaches aimed at developing and maximizing social and motor skills are provided both at the individual patient level as well as at the school level.

SUPPLEMENTAL RESOURCES

Attwood, T. (1998). *Asperger's syndrome: A guide for parents and professionals.* Philadelphia: Jessica Kingley.
Freeman, S., & Drake, L. (1996). *Teach me language.* Austin, TX: ProEd.
Myles, B. S., & Simpson, R. L. (1998). *Asperger syndrome: A guide for educators and parents.* Austin, TX: ProEd.
Simons, R. (1987). *After the tears: Parents talk about raising a child with a disability.* San Diego, CA: Harcourt, Brace.

Attachment Theory

This is a theory of interpersonal relationships that has been expanded to explain psychological development as well as the development of psychological/psychiatric symptoms. It focuses primarily on the relationship between the child and his or her primary caretaker, from birth onward. Proposed initially in the 1950s by psychoanalyst **John Bowlby,** the basic premise of attachment theory is that, from birth, infants naturally engage in various behaviors in an attempt to maximize proximity to the mother figure.

The theory lists four developmental phases through which the proximity seeking behavior progresses. The first phase occurs from birth through 3 months, during which time the infant manifests an undiscriminating social responsiveness. At this time, the infant's reactions are not at all dependent upon to whom they are actually reacting. The second phase (from 3 through 7 months of age) is characterized by the beginning of discriminating social responsiveness, at which point the baby begins to respond differently to different people. Stage three (lasting from 7 months through 3 years of age) is marked by the child's beginning to take initiative in seeking proximity to and contact with the primary caregiver. The fourth and final phase (beginning at age 3 years) is marked by the development of the goal-directed partnership behavior.

This theory goes on to specifically delineate several types of attachment behaviors such as differential crying (crying in certain situations but not others), differential vocalization (vocalizing in certain situations but not others), differential smiling (smiling in certain situations but not others), greeting responses, and reactions to the maternal figure's leaving the immediate environment. The actual manner in which the infant performs each of these behaviors varies according to his or her perception as to what would increase the chances of closeness to the maternal figure. The details of these behaviors are refined and modified by the baby according to the reactions of the caretaker: In other words, those behaviors that are reinforced by increased proximity to the caretaker continue to be performed, while those behaviors that result in decreased proximity to the caretaker tend not to continue to occur, or to occur less frequently.

A crucial component of attachment theory is the premise that the behaviors of the caretaker and those of the infant are reciprocal in nature, with the behaviors of one having an impact on the behaviors of the other. The theory goes on to say that the quality of this relationship between caretaker and child actually determines the young person's subsequent psychological adjustment, or lack thereof. In sum, it is a form of inner distress causing the infant/child anxiety. It is this anxiety that initially directs much of the infant's behavior, and it is the care giver's response to this anxiety that forms the child's subsequent expectations of others in later life.

SUPPLEMENTAL RESOURCES

Bowlby, J. (1973). *Separation: Anxiety and anger.* New York: Basic Books.

Attention Deficit Disorder

Few childhood diagnoses have generated as much controversy as **Attention Deficit Hyperactivity Disorder** (ADHD)—the most commonly diagnosed condition in child psychiatry clinics. The actual cause of ADHD, who should be diagnosed with ADHD, how ADHD is best treated, and whether ADHD is indeed a real disorder all are current foci of controversy in the ADHD field. Reams of writings exist addressing these issues—writings ranging from the most scholarly to those written by concerned parents and other lay people. There is certainly no shortage of information about ADHD, aimed at various different audiences.

A psychiatric textbook (Weiss, 1991) summarizes the primary symptoms of this disorder as characterized by a core of seven symptoms. As will be discussed below, although the symptoms do indeed vary according to the age and/or developmental level of the child, in many ways, the following list of symptoms does indeed present a valid conceptualization of the disorder:

1. Inappropriate or excessive activity, unrelated to the task at hand, which generally has an intrusive or annoying quality
2. Poor sustained attention
3. Difficulties in inhibiting impulses in social behavior and on cognitive tasks
4. Difficulties getting along with others
5. Other, coexisting externalizing behavior disorders (i.e., **Oppositional Defiant Disorder** or **Conduct Disorder**) and frequently concommitant specific *learning disabilities*
6. School underachievement
7. Poor self-esteem secondary to the above

Similarly, *Pay Attention: Answers to Common Questions about the Diagnosis and Treatment of Attention Deficit Disorder* (Liden, Zalenski, & Newman, 1989)—a manual designed for parents of ADHD children and adolescents—also presents symptom checklists designed to illustrate the different manner in which ADHD presents itself in different age groups.

Toddlers (1–3 years): excessive moving about that appears to be unfocused; proneness to have accidents; ingestion of nonedible household items; difficulty responding appropriately to limits; seeming to repeatedly "get into things"

Preschool age (3–6 years): inability or refusal to take turns during play activities; failure or inability to share during play; repeatedly switching from one play activity to another; inability to sit at the table for the entire meal (until all family members have finished eating); impulsive aggressive behavior toward peers (such as hitting, pushing, biting); seeming not to hear; failure to remain still for a story, puzzle, or other sedentary activity; inability to maintain concentration in academic activities

School age (6–12 years): failure to complete activities; interruption of the conversations of others; inability to take turns; frequent digression from topic of conversation; failure to make eye contact during conversation; inability to complete basic chores without constant supervision; subadequate appearance; seeming to walk into doors and furniture; being accident prone; physical aggression with peers; having friends who are much younger or much older; seeming failure to respond to discipline

Specific school problems: rushing through schoolwork, often not completing it and/or without checking it; disorganization; talking out of turn in class; forgetting and losing things—especially assignments; losing place during reading

Adolescence: substance usage/abuse (often extending beyond the typical experimentation characteristic of this age group); legal problems; temper outbursts; inadequate responsibility level; inability to remain on a given topic when conversing; interruption of others when they are conversing; poor organizational and planning skills; inadequate attention to personal hygiene; poor social skills; impairment in comprehension of higher-level reading materials

Diagnostically, the *DSM-IV* (American Psychiatric Association, 1994) divides the symptom categories of attention deficit hyperactivity disorder into three major categories: (1) inattention, (2) hyperactivity, and (3) impulsivity. In order for such a diagnosis to be applied, it is required that six or more symptoms of inattention have persisted for at least 6 months, or that six or more symptoms of hyperactivity/impulsivity have persisted for at least 6 months. For both cases, it is also required that the symptoms be severe enough that they result in a situation that is "maladaptive and inconsistent with developmental level" for the diagnosis to be applied. Further, the impairment needs to be present prior to the age of 7 years, in two or more settings and, to result in difficulties in social, academic, as well as occupational functioning.

A description of the specific symptoms incorporated into each of the three *DSM-IV* symptom categories mentioned above are as follows:

Inattention
1. Makes mistakes in schoolwork (or other activities) that can be described as "careless"; does not pay appropriately close attention to details.
2. Has frequent problems with maintaining attention for any period of time.
3. Does not seem to be listening when spoken to directly.
4. Does not follow through on instructions, and generally fails to complete tasks.
5. Has problems with organizing tasks.
6. Avoids, dislikes, or is reluctant to engage in activities that demand sustained attention or concentration.
7. Is easily distracted.
8. Is perceived as "forgetful."

Hyperactivity
1. Fidgets with hands or feet, squirms in seat.
2. Leaves seat in situations in which it would be expected to remain in seat.
3. Runs about or climbs inappropriately; has feelings of restlessness.

4. Has difficulty playing or engaging in leisure activities quietly.
5. Is frequently moving—acting as if driven by a motor.
6. Engages in excessive talking.

Impulsivity
1. Blurts out answer even before question is completed.
2. Has problems waiting to take turn.
3. Interrupts or intrudes upon the activities of others. (pp. 83–84)

When considering a diagnosis of attention deficit disorder, it is important to remember that several other diagnoses have similar symptoms as part of their clinical presentation. Further, it is not at all uncommon for attention deficit disorder to exist together with other psychopathologies. Among the psychopathologies whose symptoms are most commonly confused with those of attention deficit disorder and those that tend to be observed in conjunction with ADHD are the following:

Disorder	*Differential Diagnosis*
Adjustment Disorders	Symptoms of adjustment disorders are typically shorter in duration. The age of onset is later in adjustment disorders, and symptoms tend to occur following a specific incident.
Conduct/Oppositional Defiant Disorders	Behavioral symptoms are more severe than are attentional symptoms in the conduct/oppositional defiant disorders.
Learning Disabilities	In learning disabilities cases, attention deficit symptoms are due to the child's boredom/frustration as a function of his or her cognitive difficulties.
Psychotic Disorders	Attention deficit disorders do not have the accompanying delusional and/or hallucination symptoms.
Mania	Children with manic disorder tend to show an increase in self-esteem; those with attention deficit show a decrease in self-esteem; in addition, children with mania tend to manifest more emotion overall—especially that which is euphoric or irritable in nature; age of onset in attention deficit disorder is earlier than that in mania.

Finally, it is imperative that parents, school personnel, and clinicians as well be familiar with the developmentally appropriate behavior for children in various age groups. It has often been said that attention deficit disorder is the most "overused" diagnostic category in child clinical practice. One reason for this perception is the rather pervasive belief that lay people and professionals alike tend to pathologize overactivity without regard to age appropriateness. (Estimates of prevalence of attention deficit disorder in the general population range from 3%

for girls to somewhere between 9% and 10% for boys. However, when the sample population is restricted to child psychiatric outpatients, the overall figure hovers closer to 40–70%!)

The theories with respect to the **Etiology** of attention deficit hyperactivity disorder are wide in their range, predominantly because there is currently no closure in terms of determination of the specific cause(s). Controversy regarding the causes of ADHD is far from over, with postulated causes ranging from the biological, to the **Psychosocial,** to some combination of the two. Indeed, the current state of the field in terms of theories regarding the cause of attention deficit hyperactivity disorder is certainly in its developmental stages as opposed to being any more finalized.

One group of theories about the etiology of ADHD dates back to the early 1900s. Viewing the disorder as a form of minimal brain dysfunction, early theorists conceptualized it as stemming from some type of brain injury. When subsequent research showed that the majority of children suffering from ADHD did not have any form of brain pathology, the focus moved on to other neurological factors. Thus, the more current explanations look to neurological imbalances, retardation in the maturation of the brain and spinal cord, and general dysfunction in the prefrontal lobes of the brain of the limbic system as possible etiological explanations. Yet another group of biologically oriented theories hypothesize attention deficit hyperactivity disorder to be related to the **Neurotransmitter** dopamine and problems with its metabolism.

Other researchers have put forward developmentally oriented theories of the etiology of ADHD. The nature of ADHD symptomatology has led some to suggest that the disorder is due primarily to a developmental delay. Still others have investigated the influences of toxic chemicals in the child's environment in the development of ADHD. The most popular example of this type of theory is that proposed in the mid 1970s claiming that the additives and chemicals in certain food substances were sufficient to initiate attention disorder symptoms. Yet another theory regards lead as a primary cause of ADHD symptoms. Ingestion of lead can cause swelling of the brain, in turn, impairing brain function. Indeed, many studies have demonstrated a correlation between ADHD symptoms and higher blood lead levels. However, such data merely indicate that these conditions often coexist; no causal relationship has yet been demonstrated. Finally, among the biological theories are those that look to genetics. Citing the increased incidence of ADHD in the parents as well as the biological relatives of children with attention deficit disorders, as well as the twin studies showing increased incidence, such theories use this as evidence of a hereditary component.

Other theories of the etiology of attention deficit hyperactivity disorder are more psychologically based. Many of these focus on the interaction between the parents and hyperactive child. As one would expect intuitively, parents of ADHD children/adolescents manifest increased stress, increased marital discord, and overall psychopathology. However, whether the ADHD is a result or a cause of such a trend, or if there is indeed any causal relationship whatsoever between the presence of ADHD in offspring and parental pathology, still remains to be determined.

Treatment

The traditional modalities of treating children with ADHD involve a combination of psychopharmacological and behavioral methods. As far back as the 1960s and 1970s, several studies reported the effectiveness of stimulant medication in treating this disorder. As a matter of fact, some studies claimed as high as a 70% success rate. At about this same time, **Behavior Therapy** was also gaining popularity, and it seemed to be a "natural" treatment for ADHD. Today, some thirty years later, in the midst of considerable controversy, nonetheless some combination of stimulant medication and behavior therapy remains the primary mode of treatment for attention deficit disorders.

Psychopharmacological Approaches.   Attention deficit hyperactivity disorder is one of the few psychopathologies of childhood and adolescence for which medication is not viewed as a last resort with respect to treatment. Indeed, approximately three fourths of all ADHD children respond positively to a treatment regimen of either **Stimulants** or **Antidepressants.**

Perhaps the most commonly used of the stimulants prescribed for the treatment of ADHD is **Methylphenidate (Ritalin).** Despite its official classification as a stimulant, Ritalin induces positive behavioral changes in the ADHD individual, including improved focusing ability, increased alertness, a decrease in impulsive behavior, and an improved attention span. Some studies have also reported improvement in academic performance as well as in peer relationships. Although the majority of ADHD sufferers do respond positively to Ritalin, the degree of improvement is variable. (When a child does not improve with Ritalin, often another medication is tried.)

Beneficial effects of a dose of Ritalin can be observed within twenty minutes. Maximum concentration in the blood is reached some 60 to 150 minutes after administration, so Ritalin is typically administered just before the child goes to school and, again, sometime during the lunch break. It is important to be aware that Ritalin use can result in a *rebound effect.* Children who take their medication early in the day may exhibit an exacerbation of their symptoms in the late afternoon or early evening. Such a problem occurs as the serum level of Ritalin drops and can be potentially alleviated by altering the dosage scheduling. Further, Ritalin is now also available in time-release capsules that can prolong the medication's effectiveness for anywhere between 8 and 10 hours. Although Ritalin is not indicated for children under the age of 6, it is without question the most commonly prescribed drug for the treatment of attention deficit hyperactivity disorder. The initial dosage is usually 5 mg once or twice daily with the possible dosage increased to a potential maximum of 60 mg per day.

When Ritalin or other stimulants result in untoward side effects (e.g., tics, seizures) or when the rebound effect is intense, antidepressant medications can be prescribed for treatment of attention deficit hyperactivity disorder. **Tricyclic Antidepressants,** especially **Imipramine,** are among the most commonly used. Although imipramine does not have FDA approval for the treatment of ADHD, it is generally considered to be the drug of first choice if stimulant medication is not successful. Other alternatives or supplements to the stimulants include beta blockers such as inderal or nadolol.

Despite the impressive benefits of psychopharmacological intervention in the treatment of ADHD, drug treatment does indeed have its limitations. A 1992 article (Pelham & Hinshaw, 1992) lists three negative effects of psychopharmacological intervention, specifically the use of psychostimulants: (1) This type of intervention does not work for all individuals, and even in those for whom psychostimulant intervention is considered effective, there are clear limitations to the results expected in terms of interpersonal and academic functioning. (2) The beneficial effects of the medication are observed only during those times when the drug is at a certain level in the individual's system. Thus, there is a limited period during which the patient can benefit from the medication without administration of subsequent doses. (3) The empirical studies that are currently available do not support long-term improvement.

Psychological Approaches.   The aforementioned limitations of drug treatment for ADHD have resulted in the situation in which most clinicians prefer some combination of pharmacological and behavioral approaches. Toward this end, the variety of psychological (i.e., nondrug) treatments for this disorder has expanded over the past several years. The most popular nonpharmacological treatments for ADHD include several types of behavior therapy, **Cognitive Behavior Therapy, Parent Training, Family Therapy,** social skills training, and dynamically oriented individual psychotherapy (probably the least effective of these methods).

Traditional behavioral therapy uses **Contingency Management** involving the child's parents and teachers. The child is reinforced and/or punished for certain behaviors in accordance with a mutually agreed upon plan. Although research has yielded conflicting data on the overall efficacy of such an approach, the general consensus is that it leads to considerable improvement with respect to global level of functioning. However, one criticism of the more traditional behavior therapy approach utilizing contingency management procedures is that the responsibility for the behavioral intervention is somewhat removed from the child. In other words, it is the therapist, parent, teacher, or other adult in an authority position who is responsible for implementing the treatment strategies, and therefore the results of the strategies are not attributed to the child. In response to this criticism, cognitive behavioral strategies that use techniques such as self-talk, self-guidance, cognitive self-monitoring, and training in problem-solving skills allow the child/adolescent more responsibility for the implementation of the treatment modality.

Parent training programs include instruction modules designed to train the parents/teachers so that they can act as cotherapists in the children's treatment. The adults are instructed in the basic principles of behavior therapy so that they can help in achieving the desired results with their children. Preventive strategies teach the adults to intervene even before any symptoms of ADHD manifest themselves. With preventive strategies, the parents are shown how to make modifications in the home environment as well in their own approach to the child. In contrast, the reactive strategies, which are used after undesirable behavior is shown, involve modifications to the environment and responses directed specifically toward the child. Usually viewed as punitive to some degree, examples of reactive strategies include **Differential Reinforcement of Other Behavior (DRO)**, time out, **Overcorrection,** and ignoring.

With recent literature and research on ADHD focusing on the interpersonal difficulties encountered by children and adolescents with ADHD, various forms of social skills training are being integrated with increasing frequency into the treatment protocols for ADHD people. Social skills approaches attempt to facilitate accurate self-perceptions in ADHD sufferers via self-monitoring and practice (role playing, modeling) in various social situations. Typically, social skills training is not used as a single modality, but rather as an important adjunct.

SUPPLEMENTAL RESOURCES

Armstrong, T. (1997). *The myth of the ADD child.* New York: Penguin.

Barkley, R. A. (1995). *Taking charge of ADHD: The complete, authoritative guide for parents.* New York: Guilford.

Brakes: The Interactive Newsletter for Kids with ADD. (Can be ordered by calling 212-924-3344).

Children and Adults with Attention Deficit Disorder (CHADD). 954-587-3700.

Debroitner, R. K., & Hart, E. (1997). *Moving beyond ADD/ADHD: An effective holistic mind body approach.* Chicago: Contemporary Books.

Dendy, C. A. Z. (1995). *Teenagers with ADD: A parent's guide.* Bethesda, MD: Woodbine Press.

Dornbush, M. P., & Pruitt, S. K. (1998). *Teaching the tiger: A handbook for individuals involved in the education of students with Attention Deficit Disorders, Tourette syndrome or OCD.* Duarte, CA: Hope Press.

Flick, G. L. (1996). *Power parenting for children with attention deficit disorder.* West Nyack, NY: Simon & Schuster.

Frank, K. T., & Smith, S. J. (1994). *Getting a grip on ADD—A kid's guide to understanding and coping with attention disorders.* Minneapolis, MN: Education Media.

Friedman, R. J., & Doyal, G. T. (1992). *Management of children and adolescents with attention deficit–hyperactivity disorder.* Austin, TX: ProEd.

Galvin, M. R. (1996). *Otto learns about his medicine.* New York: Magination Press.

Garber, S. W., Garger, M. D., & Spizman, R. F. (1996). *Beyond Ritalin.* New York: HarperCollins.

Goldstein, S., & Goldstein, M. (1990). *Managing attention disorders in children: A guide for practitioners.* New York: John Wiley and Sons.

Gordon, S. B., & Asher, M. J. (1994). *Meeting the ADD challenge: A practical guide for teachers.* Champaign, IL: Research Press.

Greenberg, G. S., & Horn, W. F. (1996). *Attention deficit hyperactivity disorder: questions and answers for parents.* Champaign, IL: Research Press.

Hallowell, E. M., & Ratey, J. J. (1994). *Driven to distraction.* New York: Simon & Schuster.

Hallowell, E. M., & Ratey, J. J. (1995). *Answers to distraction.* New York: Simon & Schuster.

Hughes, S. (1995). *Ryan—A mother's story of her hyperactive/Tourette syndrome child.* Duarte, CA: Hope Press.

Janover, C. (1997). *Zipper—The kid with ADHD.* Bethesda, MD: Woodbine House.

Johnston, H. (1990). *Stimulants and hyperactive children: A guide.* Lithium Information Center, University of Wisconsin, Department of Psychiatry.

Jordan, D. R. (1998). *Attention deficit disorder: ADHD and ADD syndromes.* Austin, TX: ProEd.

Kajender, R. (1995). *Living with ADHD.* Minneapolis, MN: Institute for Research and Education.

Kelley, K., & Ramuntos, P. (1997). *The ADDed dimension.* New York: Simon & Schuster.

Moss, D. M. (1989). *Shelley the hyperactive turtle.* Bethesda, MD: Woodbine House.

Nadeau, K. G. (1994). *Survival guide for college students with ADD or LD.* New York: Magination Press.

Nadeau, K. G. (1997). *ADD in the workplace.* New York: Brunner/Mazel.

National Attention Deficit Disorder Association. 800-487-2282.

Neuville, M. B. (1995). *Living with attention-deficit/hyperactivity disorder: Sometimes I get all scribbly.* Austin, TX: ProEd.

Nussbaum, N. & Bigler, E. (1990). *Identification and treatment of Attention Deficit Disorder.* Austin, TX: ProEd.

Parker, H. C. (1994). *The ADD hyperactivity handbook for parents, teachers, and kids.* Plantation, FL: Special Press.

Quinn, P. O., & Stern, J. M. (1991). *Putting on the brakes.* New York: Magination Press.

Quinn, P. O., & Stern, J. M. (1993). *Putting on the brakes activity book.* New York: Magination Press.

Rief, S. F. (1993). *How to reach and teach ADD/ADHD children.* West Nyack, NY: Simon & Schuster.

Teeter, P. A. (1998). *Attention-deficit/hyperactivity disorder: Treatment in developmental context.* New York: Guilford Press.

Weiss, G., & Hechtman, L. T. (1993). *Hyperactive children grown up (2nd ed.).* New York: Guilford Press.

Weiss, L. (1997). *ADD and creativity.* Dallas, TX: Taylor.

Wells, K. (1996). *Parent management training for attention-deficit/hyperactivity disorder* [Three audio-tapes and a handbook]. Available through MHS (800-456-3003).

Wright, J. (1997). *Do we really need Ritalin?* New York: Avon Books.

Auditory Hallucinations

Of all the hallucinatory experiences, research and clinical data indicate that auditory hallucinations are the most commonly experienced form. Although typically associated with some type of schizophrenic or other psychotic conditions (observed in 60–90% of schizophrenic patients and 80% of all children and adolescents diagnosed with schizophrenia), auditory hallucinations are not limited to those with psychotic diagnoses. Organic problems, deafness, depression, and affective disorders are all diagnostic categories in which auditory hallucinations can play a major role in the symptom profile. Generally speaking, the actual content of auditory hallucinations becomes more complicated and involved as one moves along the psychotic spectrum. For example, auditory hallucinations associated with organic diagnoses tend to be primarily nonverbal, unstructured sounds (such as buzzing, blowing of the wind, etc.), whereas those auditory hallucinations associated with the psychotic disorders are more involved and tend to involve a greater degree of verbalization. With respect to those auditory hallucinations in the latter category, there are basically four types (classified according to their content): (1) command hallucinations, (2) arguing voices, (3) running commentary, and (4) thought verbalization.

Command hallucinations consist of one or more voices actually instructing the patient as to how he or she should behave. These command hallucinations run the gamut in content from the simple and trivial (i.e., telling the patient what to have for dinner or what outfit to wear to a meeting) to those involving suicidal or homicidal ideation. Command hallucinations of the latter type are frequently used in legal situations to add credence to an individual's plea for an insanity defense (i.e., reporting to the court that a crime was committed because one or more voices instructed the individual to behave as such).

> *Example:* Seventeen-year-old Danny drove his car off a bridge because voices inside his head told him that he was evil, and this was the only way to purge the devil from his soul.

> *Example:* The father of 10-year-old Natasha woke up in the middle of the night to find his daughter standing over him with a knife. She explained that two women in her head told her that she had to stab her father three times in the right forearm; otherwise, he would die within the next 24 hours.

> *Example:* Seven-year-old Mark was found by his parents pouring the entire container of flaked fish food into the family aquarium. The child later told his family that the fish gods in his head told him that he must do this to prevent the fish from dying of starvation.

The second type of auditory hallucinations involves two or more voices arguing, oftentimes with the topic of argument being the patient. In this form of auditory hallucination, the patient is somewhat of a passive observer/listener to the two or more voices, at times feeling as if he or she would like to participate in the argument, or, more often than not, to terminate the discussion. What sufferers of this form of hallucination report to be the most bothersome is the annoyance of hearing the repeated arguing, but not being able to do anything to intervene to stop it.

> *Example:* Twelve-year-old Richard reports hearing two voices arguing in his head, debating as to whether or not he will be allowed to live past the age of 21.

> *Example:* Fifteen-year-old Jillian tells her psychiatrist that she is bothered at night by voices arguing as to whether or not she should have sexual intercourse with her boyfriend.

Running commentary is the third major type of auditory hallucination. In this type the sufferer hears one or more voices commenting on his or her thoughts and/or activities. The precise character of the commentary can vary from being judgmental and critical to being virtually neutral and noncommittal. In any case, the individual usually reports being frustrated with hearing the almost constant commentary on his or her behavior, and being unable to stop or in any way affect it.

> *Example:* Fifteen-year-old John complains of having "CNN in my head." He speaks of hearing three male voices describe his every move, and, more often than not, make disparaging comments about what he is doing.

Example: Ten-year-old Amanda tells her parents that she makes decisions as to whether or not she should do something based upon two voices in her head, who inform her as to the merit of each choice.

The fourth and final type of auditory hallucination is known as thought verbalization. Somewhat similar to the running commentary type described above, thought verbalization involves the individual's thoughts being spoken as they are being articulated. Worded another way, whereas in running commentary the voices are commenting on the individual's behavior (in the voice of a third person), in thought verbalization the voices are actually speaking the person's thoughts in the individual's own words.

Example: Twelve-year-old Aaron complains that his thoughts are being spoken aloud in his head, almost before he is aware that he is even thinking them. Aaron finds this most distressing and scary in that he wonders how anyone else knows what he is thinking; he is also concerned that others will hear these voices as well, knowing all of his thoughts.

Whereas the presence of auditory hallucinations should in no way be minimized in terms of its clinical significance, it is crucial that the symptom be conceptualized within the appropriate developmental context. For example, imaginary friends are certainly a common developmental phase of childhood, and it is not at all unusual for these friends to speak to the child. Certainly, reports of such behavior are not to be taken as evidence that the child suffers from some schizophrenic or other psychiatric disorder. Yet, how is a concerned adult to distinguish between the imaginary friends of childhood (which, to some extent, are to be expected) and true auditory hallucinations, which are likely to be indicative of some serious psychiatric disorder? The following criteria should be helpful to parents in determining the implications of the child/adolescent's behavior:

Developmental stage: Imaginary friends and their associated behaviors tend to disappear by the time the child reaches 9 or 10 years of age. Thus, a 14-year-old sharing the comments of an unseen individual would have potentially more serious implications than if a 5-year-old shared the same information.

Functional level: One of the major diagnostic criteria for schizophrenia is a deterioration from a previous/earlier level of functioning. If a young child is continuing to achieve all of the developmental milestones in a timely fashion, and does not indicate any signs of deterioration or regression, it is likely that the source of the auditory voices is something other than a schizophrenic process.

Context: If a young person's behavior changes rather dramatically, it is useful to evaluate the surrounding life circumstances. For example, the experiencing of a traumatic event or other form of intense anxiety can be sufficient to evoke rather bizarre behavior patterns and unusual symptoms (refer to entry **Acute Stress Disorder; Post-Traumatic Stress Disorder**).

Other symptoms: Very few psychological or psychiatric disorders manifest themselves with only one isolated symptom. Schizophrenic disorders being no exception, if a young person begins showing symptoms resembling auditory hallucinations, it is important to see if other psychiatric symptoms are also being manifested. If it appears as if the so-called auditory hallucinations seem to exist in isolation, it is considerably less likely that they are true auditory hallucinations!

When to Seek Professional Help

If a parent remains unsure and decides to seek professional help, it is important that he or she be able to provide the clinician with as much detail regarding the symptoms observed as possible. The frequency, content, as well as the history of the possible auditory hallucinations should be available. Further, the parent should also be prepared to provide the clinician with a medication history, history of recent illness, as well as the details regarding any event that has occurred in the child/adolescent's life that could potentially have had a psychological impact. A more complete description of treatment approaches can be found in the relevant entries on **Schizophrenia, Post-Traumatic Stress Disorder,** and **Imaginary Friends.**

Autistic Disorder

Autistic disorder is one of the four disorders included among the **Pervasive Developmental Disorders.** It was first formally acknowledged as a diagnostic entity with the writing of Leo Kanner in the 1940s. At that time, it was referred to as *infantile autism,* with the sufferers believed to be experiencing the early stages of **Schizophrenia.** Since then, the conceptualization of this disorder has gone through many modifications and changes, until a 1978 publication by the Professional Advisory Board of the National Society for Children and Adults with Autism presented four basic diagnostic characteristics of the disorder: (1) impairment in development, with respect to both sequence and rate; (2) impairment in ability to respond to sensory stimulation; (3) problems with nonverbal communication, speech, language, and cognition, and (4) difficulties in relating interpersonally as well as in relating to events and objects. The criteria proposed in this document served to lay the foundation for the current conceptualization of autistic disorder.

As indicated above, the autistic child's impaired ability to engage in expected social interaction is one of the central symptoms of this disorder. The social interaction patterns of these children are typically perceived as an overall lack of responsiveness to others in the environment. It is almost as if the autistic child is not aware of or simply does not care about the presence of other beings. Indeed, not only is physical affection not sought out by autistic children, it is often reacted to as if it is actually aversive. In most cases, the autistic child will react the same to perfect strangers as he or she would react to parental figures or familiar family members. Often content to be left alone for extended periods of time, the child exhibits an apparent lack of sensitivity to the feelings and emotional needs of others. This trend can even be extended to the point at which it appears as if the autistic child has closer relationships with, or prefers to interact with, inanimate objects as opposed to people.

One of the symptoms that distinguish sufferers of autism from those of the other pervasive developmental disorders is the exhibiting of what are often referred to as "bizarre behaviors." These can include repetitive behaviors often performed to the exclusion of involvement in other more normal activities. Examples of these repetitive behaviors include but are not limited to spinning, rocking, and finger flicking. In addition, autistic children will appear to be completely preoccupied with a single event, object, or activity—again to the seeming exclusion to anything else that is transpiring. Interestingly, despite this rather singular preoccupation, autistic children appear to be extremely sensitive to changes in their environment—even trivial ones.

Symptoms of autism extend to the cognitive realm as well. With respect to speech, most young people with autistic disorder do not speak at all. As infants, autistics express their needs by crying and screaming. As they get older, young children communicate by pulling the adult's hand, using similar gestures even into middle/late childhood. Approximately half of all autistic sufferers remain mute for their entire lives. When speech does indeed develop, it is more a robotlike babble and is typically described as being primarily self-stimulatory in function.

Intellectually, 70–80% of autistic children and adolescents have an IQ in the mentally retarded range (i.e., below 70). It is interesting, however, that autistic children do not respond to intelligence testing the same way as do mentally retarded children. Although there is a preponderance of low IQ scores, examples of *idiot savant* behavior as well as unusually high scores on visual/spatial tasks and short-term memory tasks both support the notion that the cognitive impairment in autistic disorder is qualitatively different from what one would find in mental retardation.

Three assessment instruments are most commonly used in clinical practice to diagnose autistic disorder: the Diagnostic Checklist for Behavior-Disturbed Children (Form E-2); The Behavioral Observation System (BOS); and the Childhood Autism Rating Scale (CARS). In addition to these three instruments, there is also a Parent Interview for Autism (PIA)—a structured interview for parents to assess the presence and intensity of autistic symptoms.

Precisely what factors are involved in causing autistic disorder are yet to be firmly established. Although many of the early theories emphasized disturbed relationships between parent and child as the primary cause of autism, subsequent studies provided minimal or no support for such a correlation. At the present time, the majority of theories of the causes of autistic disorder focus on more biologically oriented factors. These theories are based on the fact that certain biological abnormalities appear to exist more frequently (or to more severe degree) in autistic children than they do in nonautistic children. Dawson and Castile (1992) summarize the primary categories of biological factors proposed to contribute to the development of autism as follows: neurological findings (such as prenatal factors, seizures); **Neuropsychological** factors (such as frontal lobe dysfunction, cerebellar dysfunction); genetic factors; and biochemical factors.

Treatment

If one wished to be completely accurate, it would be appropriate to say that indeed there is no treatment, per se, for autistic disorder. In reality, the treatment approaches for autism are designed to address the symptoms rather than actually alter the intensity or nature of the clinical course. These treatments are both psychological (therapy treatment) and biological (drug treatment) in nature; the goals of the former are more educational and behavioral in nature whereas the goal of the latter is to lessen the severity of the symptoms.

The drug therapies used for autism aim at controlling especially severe symptoms. Whereas there are no drugs designated as being "for autism," there are drug interventions that are commonly used with autistic patients. For example, **Neuroleptics** are prescribed to control self-injurious behavior, while opiate antagonists are prescribed to address symptoms of withdrawal. Other drugs commonly prescribed include vitamin B and fenfluramine (more commonly prescribed twenty years ago as, when was believed to be effective in controlling a variety of autistic symptoms).

Despite the use of drug therapy in managing autistic symptoms, the majority of treatments for autistic disorder are based upon some combination of **Behavior Therapy** and education. The more behaviorally oriented approaches have been used to target communication skills, appropriate emotional expression, and the reduction of self-injurious activities. Based on the principles of **Reinforcement,** the therapy aims at helping the child develop more socially adaptive/acceptable habits to replace those that are clearly symptomatic and/or harmful. In many situations, these therapies work by utilizing the parents and others in the child's immediate environment as cotherapists, wherein the other family members observe the therapeutic interactions between child and therapist, and are then taught how to carry on a similar protocol outside of the actual session. One such key model, the TEAACH program, was developed approximately ten years ago (Marcus & Schopler, 1991) and is based upon the premise that parents and therapists be viewed as collaborators in the child's treatment. Thus, this particular program includes not only traditional therapy sessions, but a home teaching process as well as emotional support for the parents. As in many of the newer treatment approaches, the clinician encompasses the psychological and emotional needs of the entire family in the treatment process.

SUPPLEMENTAL RESOURCES

Autism Research Institute. 619-469-6618.

Faith, U. (1989). *Autism: Explaining the enigma.* Cambridge, MA: Blackwell.

Fullerton, A., Stratton, J., Coyne, P., & Gray, C. (1996). *Higher functioning adolescents and young adults with autism.* Austin, TX: ProEd.

Harris, S. L., & Handleman J. S. (Eds.). (1994). *Preschool education programs for children with autism.* Austin, TX: ProEd.

Hart, C. A. (1993). *A parent's guide to autism.* New York: Pocket Books.

Maurice, C. (Ed.). (1996). *Behavioral intervention for young children with autism: A manual for parents and professionals.* Austin, TX: ProEd.

Perk, C. C. (1982). *The siege: The first eight years of an autistic child.* Boston: Little Brown.

Powers, M. D. (1989). *Children of autism.* Kensington, MD: Woodbine House.

Siegel, B. (1996). *The world of the autistic child.* New York: Oxford Press.

Simons, J., & Oishi, S. (1987). *The hidden child.* Kensington, MD: Woodbine House.

Simpson, R. L., & Reagan, M. (1986). *Management of autistic behavior.* Austin, TX: ProEd.

Simpson, R. L., & Zionts, P. (1992). *Autism: Information and resources for parents, families and professionals.* Austin, TX: ProEd.

Aventyl

This is the trade name of the tricyclic antidepressant generically referred to as **Nortriptyline.** Refer to that entry for a description.

Avoidant Disorder of Childhood and Adolescence

This is a diagnosis that is no longer being used in the current edition of the *Diagnostic and Statistical Manual (DSM-IV).* In the two previous editions of the diagnostic manual, there was a separate section listing diagnostic criteria for various anxiety disorders specific to children and adolescents. Avoidant disorder of childhood and adolescence was one of these disorders; however, its symptoms are now incorporated under the current diagnoses of **Phobic Disorders, Panic Disorder** with **Agoraphobia,** and/or **Generalized Anxiety Disorder.**

Avoidant Personality Disorder

Avoidant personality disorder is one of the Axis II **Personality Disorders.** This specific diagnosis is characterized by the individual's (1) feeling generally inadequate in social situations and (2) being extremely sensitive to perceived negative evaluation; these two tendencies result in the person's becoming inhibited in any situation in which other people are present or involved. Although it is similar to **Social Phobia,** avoidant personality disorder can be distinguished from social phobia in that in social phobia the anxiety is limited to issues of "performing" in social situations, whereas in avoidant personality disorder the symptoms are evoked by a wider range of situations—that is, by simply engaging interpersonally.

The *DSM-IV* (American Psychiatric Association, 1994) requires at least four of the following symptoms to be present for this personality disorder to be diagnosed:

Avoidance of occupational activities that involve interpersonal interactions: In some cases, the individual may very well be gainfully employed but make excuses to avoid participating in work situations perceived as potentially threatening (i.e., in terms of possibly involving disapproval or criticism). What is crucial here is that the real possibility of these threatening experiences occurring is not necessarily the relevant issue. Rather, it is the person's perception of such. In other cases, the individual with avoidant personality disorder will actually avoid beginning work assignments or terminate involvement in those that are perceived as interpersonally threatening.

Unwillingness to become involved with others without "guarantee" of being liked: Because perceived rejection and/or criticism is so threatening to individuals with avoidant personality disorder, they seek reassurance of a positive outcome in interpersonal interactions (i.e., defined as being free from criticism and rejection) prior to initiating any contacts.

Restraint in interpersonal reactions as a protection against being rejected: Because of the fear of possibly being criticized, ridiculed, or otherwise rejected, an individual with avoidant personality disorder will set up emotional/psychological boundaries in interpersonal relationships so as not to reveal aspects of himself or herself that could potentially be a source of potential negative feedback.

Preoccupation with being criticized or rejected in social situations: Individuals with avoidant personality disorder are worrying almost constantly about having a less than positive experience in their social situations.

Inhibition in new social situations due to inadequacy issues: People with avoidant personality disorder have a tendency to withdraw in new or unfamiliar social situations because of a fear of "not being able to handle it" or feelings of general social inadequacy.

A self view of being interpersonally inferior in comparison to others: Those with avoidant personality disorder see themselves as being incompetent in social situations, especially when their social skills are compared to those of others. As a result, they anticipate being criticized, rejected, or otherwise reacted to in a negative manner.

Reluctance to take interpersonal risks: Individuals with avoidant personality disorder are extremely cautious in their interpersonal relationships out of fear that, if they cease to be so, they will behave in such a manner to evoke criticism, and/or rejection from others.

Although the diagnosis of avoidant personality disorder is not one exclusive to childhood or adolescence (actually, it is in the adult section of the *DSM-IV*), clinical and research data indicate that this disorder typically has its origins in late adolescence/early adulthood. Occurring with relatively equal frequency in males and females, it is estimated to be present in approximately 0.5–1.0% of the general population. Although treatment for avoidant personality virtually always involves some type of psychotherapeutic intervention, in some cases, psychopharmacological intervention is used in an attempt to control the anxiety associated with social interactions.

SUPPLEMENTAL RESOURCES

Masterson, J. F. (1988). *The search for the real self—Unmasking the personality disorders of our age.* New York: Free Press.
Millon, T., & Everly, G. S. (1985). *Personality and its disorders.* New York: John Wiley.

B Baseline–Burping

Baseline

This is a term referring to the level or quality of an individual's behavior under "normal," nonpathological circumstances. It is often used as a standard against which the person's current behavior is compared to determine if indeed there is a problem, or if clinical pathology exists. Since much of psychological behavior is highly unique to the individual in question, it is often necessary to have an established criterion of "normalcy" to evaluate a currently observed behavior. Assessing the extent to which the current behavior deviates from what is typically observed provides useful data in determining whether clinical pathology indeed exists, and, if so, at what level of severity.

> *Example:* Nine-year-old Aaron has been a model student ever since kindergarten. However, over the past two months, there have been three letters sent home to Aaron's parents complaining of the child's disruptive behavior. When attempting to evaluate the significance of this, it is crucial to keep in mind Aaron's baseline behavior of being a model student, and the potential implications of this deviation from the status quo. In contrast, however, if Aaron were a child whose behavior was typically erratic, the same three letters sent home over a 2-month period would not have the same clinical implications.

> *Example:* Sixteen-year-old Latricia has been showing some rather unusual emotional behavior lately. Always a girl who would keep her emotions very much in control, she now is crying several times per week. What is especially noteworthy is that, most of the time, there is no recognizable trigger for these tearful outbursts. Again, this is an example of a situation in which the adolescent's behavior deviates significantly from her baseline, and therefore requires some concern and/or further exploration.

Bedtime Problems

Difficulties around bedtime are relative common in households and seem to be prevalent among a wide range of ages—from the very young to school age. Typical problems around bedtime focus on the child's not wanting to go to bed at a prescribed time, as well as the variety of problems that stem from that resistance. Parents complain about the child's uttering multiple requests around bedtime (snacks, needing to use the lavatory, asking for a drink of water, etc.), suddenly remembering uncompleted tasks or chores, and asking parents all sorts of seemingly irrelevant questions, recognizing that these are all attempts on the part of the child to postpone going to bed.

Most of the time when such problems arise they are due to some disruption in the usual family routine, or even the actual absence of such a routine. In the large majority of cases, a bedtime routine to which one adheres relatively consistently tends to eliminate many of the common bedtime problems. If the family has not established such a routine, the development of bedtime problems often serves as the motivating factor to do so. Although flexibility is a prime feature of good parenting, routines around bedtime should include the following:

- Regular bedtime for school nights as well as a separate one for week ends and nonschool nights.
- An established time to begin "bedtime prep" so that the necessary behaviors are completed prior to the actual bedtime; if a child tends to prolong these preliminary behaviors, the "bedtime prep" time needs to be made earlier.
- Establishment of certain **Bedtime Rituals** that are adhered to relatively regularly; as described in more detail in that entry, these provide a certain amount of structure around bedtime that can be reassuring to the child and serve positive functions for the adults.

If the parents have a situation wherein there has never been an established bedtime routine, or if the parents allowed this to slide and are now reinstituting it, it is predictable that the child's bedtime problems will worsen for a brief period as the routine is being (re)instituted. Whenever more structure is imposed upon a disrupted situation, it is a general tendency that the target behaviors worsen prior to improving. This is partially because the child's routine (or lack thereof) is being altered, and there is a natural tendency to want to return the situation to the status quo. However, after children have completed their "testing period," and recognize that this newly instituted regimen is here to stay, their behavior will respond positively to it.

In rare cases, bedtime problems are **Secondary** to some underlying psychopathology such as a **Phobia** of the dark or some other **Anxiety Disorder.** Whereas the aforementioned techniques can be helpful in such cases, the underlying issues must be addressed in order for the bedtime problems to be thoroughly resolved.

SUPPLEMENTAL RESOURCES

Coren, S. (1996). *Sleep thieves.* New York: Free Press.
Eberlein, T. (1996). *Sleep—How to teach your child to sleep like a baby.* New York: Pocket Books.
Farber, R. (1985). *Solve your child's sleep problems.* New York: Simon & Schuster.

Bedtime Rituals

Ritualistic behaviors around bedtime are very common in children of various ages. Indeed, one need only look at the behaviors in which adults engage prior to bedtime to recognize that bedtime rituals are by no means restricted to children, to individuals with some form of psychological disorder, or to a small minority of the population. As with the large majority of ritualistic behaviors, rituals around bedtime are designed to mitigate against anxiety by providing the certain amount of comfort that goes along with predictability. One need only look to general trends in human behavior to recognize the almost universal tendency to engage in ritualistic and/or superstitious behavior when one's sense of security is threatened.

For young children, going to bed can be associated with several negative emotions. Be it a fear of the dark, a feeling of abandonment, the experience of nightmares, or the existential fear of not waking up, bedtime is typically associated with a myriad of threatening images. Since going to bed in and of itself is a necessary part of life, parents will develop various techniques to make the bedtime hour less stressful for their child, and, therefore less stressful for them. In so doing, rituals get established (sometimes intentionally and sometimes inadvertently) that tend to perpetuate into later childhood, adolescence, and even the adult years.

Example: When Mr. Patterson was a young boy, he resisted going to bed because he was afraid of the dark. To help calm his fears, his parents would allow him to sleep with a night light plugged into a wall socket in his bedroom. Now an adult in his mid-thirties, Mr. Patterson is unable to sleep in a completely dark room, requiring (at least) a small night light in order to fall asleep.

Example: As a young child, Miranda would always get a treat prior to going to bed. This treat could consist of anything from cookies and milk, to ice cream, to a dish of fresh fruit. Miranda is now in graduate school and continues to prepare herself a snack virtually every night prior to going to bed.

When not carried to a compulsive extreme, bedtime rituals can provide the child with the security needed to make going to bed less anxiety provoking. As all parents know, children generally derive comfort from predictability and routine. Thus, it only makes sense that, in situations (such as bedtime) that evoke more anxiety than most, rituals have a valuable role to play. As alluded to above, in some families it is the parents who formulate these rituals; in other families it is the child; in most cases, it is some combination of the above.

Because rituals that may begin as simple bedtime stress busters can easily develop into more rigidly embedded routines, parents are advised to pay some attention to the behaviors they initiate associated with bedtime. Behaviors that would be impractical to carry out under less traditional circumstances are best avoided. For example, limiting the bedtime snack to a certain type of gourmet food (which may not be easily accessible in another home) or the child's needing to be surrounded with several stuffed animals (which would not be practical in a trip or camp situation) are types of bedtime rituals that could eventually prove to be more detrimental than helpful. Examples such as these give bedtime rituals a "bad name" and lead parents to be reluctantly anxious around employing bedtime routines with their children.

Although it sounds contradictory, the key to preventing pathology from developing as a result of a bedtime ritual (or from any ritual for that matter) is to maintain flexibility. Parents need to take responsibility for allowing their children the desired bedtime rituals, as they gently introduce variations in the routine. Dramatic alterations in practice around bedtime are certainly not indicated, as such behavior would eliminate the benefits of having the rituals in the first place. However, periodically introducing minor changes to the routine (always with reassurance—e.g., "we can do it this way sometimes too") prevents the child from becoming too rigidly fixated in a given way of doing things. Such a matter-of-fact introduction of variation in routine also communicates to the child that change need not be threatening, nor need it result in anxiety-provoking consequences.

Behavior Assessment System for Children (BASC)

First released in 1992, this is a generic assessment instrument designed to screen for various aspects of psychopathology in children and adolescents. There are eight variations of this instrument—designed for children of different ages (ages 4–5, ages 6–11, ages 12–18) and for different people to complete (a form to be completed by parents, teachers, and, for the older two age groups, by the child/adolescent himself or herself). The forms to be completed by parents and school personnel are composed of several statements to which the adult is instructed to respond along a four-point scale (never, sometimes, often, always), indicating how frequently the child/adolescent in question engages in the specific behavior. Those forms designed as self-report measures are constructed in a true/false format asking the child/adolescent whether each particular statement applies to him or her (true) or not (false).

This assessment results in standardized scores indicating the validity of the profile, as well as the degree to which the child/adolescent is experiencing difficulty in various diagnostic areas. These clinical scales are divided into the two major categories of externalizing and internalizing disorders. Included among the externalizing diagnoses are those related to hyperactivity/**Attention Deficit Disorders,** aggression and general **Conduct Disorders.** In contrast, included among the internalizing diagnoses are those classified as depressive disorders, **Anxiety Disorders** and those that would be considered **Psychotic Disorders.** Computerized scoring for this instrument also provides suggestions as to possible diagnoses to be considered.

Behavior Therapy

Behavior therapy refers to a variety of different therapeutic approaches, all of which are based upon the premise that behavior (whether healthy or maladaptive) is learned. As such, all behavior (whether healthy or maladaptive) can be modified (or unlearned, if necessary) in a similar manner. In addition, adherents of behavior therapy place a strong emphasis on measurable, objective, reliable, and replicable results. Although the introduction of behavior therapy is relatively new to the field of child/adolescent psychology and psychiatry, a survey taken in the mid 1980s (O'Leary, 1984) reports that somewhere around 50% of all psychologists considered themselves to be behaviorists. Behavior therapies vary in form, with the four major types classified as: (1) those based upon the classical conditioning (or respondent) models, (2) those based upon the operant conditioning models, (3) those based upon the social learning models, and (4) those based upon the cognitive behavioral models. Each of these will be described in more detail in their individual entries.

The oldest form of behavior theory, using approaches based on classical conditioning, dates back to the work of the nineteenth-century Russian researcher Ivan Pavlov. Studying the digestive process in dogs, Pavlov's work demonstrated that, after repeated pairing of a neutral stimulus with a stimulus that reliably evokes a certain response, eventually the neutral stimulus will evoke a similar if not identical response. A more specific example of Pavlov's actual work may prove helpful in illustrating this principle:

> Pavlov noticed that his dogs would salivate prior to eating when presented with their food. He then repeatedly paired a buzzer with the presentation of the dogs' food. Eventually, Pavlov found that the dogs would exhibit the salivation response to the buzzer alone, even when it was sounded without presentation of the food at the same time.

Whereas this is certainly an interesting phenomenon, its application to the treatment of children and adolescents may not be especially clear. Although classical conditioning approaches are probably the least commonly used, when they are used today, it is typically for the treatment of anxiety or fear reactions. Such treatment approaches usually involve the pairing of exposure to the anxiety-provoking object or situation with a behavior that is inherently incompatible with anxiety (such as relaxation, food, a positive mental image). Examples of such treatment modalities would include **Systematic Densitization** and **Implosive Therapy**. Again, when these modalities are used, it is usually in the treatment of anxiety responses. (However, more current research has indicated that **Cognitive Behavior Therapy** tends to be the treatment of choice in the majority of such cases.)

Operant conditioning therapies are certainly the most popular of the behavior therapies used today in the treatment of child/adolescent disorders. These therapies are based upon a single principle: that certain behaviors are learned (and continue to be performed) because they result in positive or reinforcing consequences for the individual performing them. Thus, those behaviors considered desirable can be maintained by following them with positive consequences, whereas those behaviors that are aversive or less desirable can be eliminated by following them with unpleasant consequences. Examples of such measures include **Differential Reinforcement of Other Behavior, Contingency Management, Response Cost,** and **Overcorrection.** Utilizing such procedures involves having the parent and/or teacher act as a therapist so that he or she can maintain the operant connection made during the actual therapy session. Common everyday instances of such an approach can be seen in the following situations:

■ Sticker charts posted in a prominent place in the home that allow for the child to place a sticker on the chart for every time a positive behavior is performed; a given quantity of stickers can be redeemed for a special treat or outing.

■ Having a coin bank in the kitchen into which every family member must deposit fifty cents each time a swear word is uttered; contents of the coin bank are donated to a favorite family charity every 3 months.

The *social learning* approaches present somewhat of a combination of the classical conditioning and the operant conditioning models. Designed to primarily address interaction skills, social learning is somewhat educational in character as it can involve role playing, actual teaching, modeling, or even instruction in problem solving.

One of the newest types of behavior therapy, **Cognitive Behavior Therapy** works by focusing on the person's thought process as a means of impacting upon his or her behavior. It is based upon three major postulates (Zarb, 1992): (1) cognitions or thoughts are the primary mediators of behavior, (2) a predictable relationship exists between cognitions or thoughts and the person's emotional experience, and (3) maladaptive ways of thinking are directly connected with the development of certain psychological/psychiatric problems. Thus, the basic procedure of cognitive behavior therapy involves identifying the target symptom(s), identifying the thoughts or cognitions that characteristically accompany (or precede) these symptoms, and then working with the child/adolescent to change the thought process appropriately. (For a more detailed description, please refer to entry cognitive behavior therapy.)

SUPPLEMENTAL RESOURCES

Azdin, N. H., & Besalel, V. A. (1980). *How to use overcorrection.* Austin, TX: ProEd.

Azdin, N. H., & Besalel, V. A. (1980). *How to use positive practice.* Austin, TX: ProEd.

Baer, D. M. (1980). *How to plan for generalization.* Austin, TX: ProEd.

Dawson, K. E., & Kazdin, A. E. (1980). *How to use self control.* Austin, TX: ProEd.

Hall, R. V., & Hall, M. C. (1980). *How to negotiate a behavioral contract.* Austin, TX: ProEd.

Hall, R. V., & Hall, M. C. (1980). *How to select reinforcers.* Austin, TX: ProEd.

Hall, R. V., & Hall, M. C. (1980). *How to use planned ignoring (extinction).* Austin, TX: ProEd.

Hall, R. V., & Hall, M. C. (1980). *How to use systematic attention and approval (social reinforcement).* Austin, TX: ProEd.

Hall, R. V., & Hall, M. C. (1980). *How to use time out.* Austin, TX: ProEd.

Kazdin, A., & Dawson, K. E. (1980). *How to maintain behavior.* Austin, TX: ProEd.

Panyan, M. (1980). *How to use shaping.* Austin, TX: ProEd.

Striefel, S. (1980). *How to teach through modeling and imitation.* Austin, TX: ProEd.

Turner, S. M., Calhoun, K. S., & Adams, H. E. (Eds.). (1992). *Handbook of clinical behavior therapy,* 2nd ed. New York: John Wiley and Sons.

VanHouten, R. (1980). *How to motivate others through feedback.* Austin, TX: ProEd.

Who did what to whom: Recognizing four behavioral principles in action [Video]. (1982). (Available from Research Press, Champaign, IL [800-519-2707])

Biofeedback

Biofeedback is a specialized technique usually used to supplement other forms of psychological or psychiatric intervention. It works by providing the patient (and clinician) with information about the functioning of specific body processes. The basic premise behind biofeedback is that certain biological/physiological functions of the body correlate with various emotional processes. For example, when we are anxious, the heart tends to beat more quickly. Another example centers around individuals who suffer migraine headaches: Research has documented a correlation between migraine headaches and a low hand temperature. Biofeedback works by first illustrating the relationship to the individual between the body process and the emotional reaction. The next step entails instructing the individual as to how to control the specific physiological process, and, therefore, attain increased control over the specific emotional dimension.

In the majority of cases, the practice of biofeedback requires the use of elaborate instruments (usually to measure the physiological processes in question). Thus, initial biofeedback sessions typically take place in the office of the practitioner so that the patient can learn to recognize and take advantage of various body cues associated with the physiological process being worked on. Then, with practice, the patient is able to work with these body cues without the actual feedback of the machine, and is thereby able to work with the body processes (and explore their relationship with emotion) on his or her own. Included among the psychological areas to which biofeedback treatment has been applied are sexual dysfunction, chronic/acute pain, anxiety, excessive defense mechanisms, migraine headaches, Raynaud's disease (chronically cold hands), and phobias.

Bipolar I Disorder

This is one of the major classifications of bipolar disorders, all of which involve the presence of **Manic** or **Hypomanic** symptoms. A diagnosis of bipolar I disorder is given when there is at least one incident of a manic or mixed episode. This diagnosis is given whether or not there has also been an occurrence of a depressive episode in the patient. For example, in cases in which there has been only one manic episode, but there have been no major depressive episodes, the appropriate diagnosis would be *bipolar I disorder, single manic episode.* For those cases in which the most recent (or current) episode is a manic episode, and there has been a history of at least one other type of mood pathology, the appropriate diagnosis would be *bipolar I disorder, most recent episode manic.* Similarly, for those cases in which the most recent (or current) episode is a mixed episode, and there has been a history of at least one other type of mood pathology, the appropriate diagnosis would be *bipolar I disorder, most recent episode mixed.* In those cases where the most recent (or current) episode is that of major depression, and there has been a history of at least one other type of mood pathology, the appropriate diagnosis would be *bipolar I disorder, most recent episode mixed.* Finally, for those cases in which the most recent (or current) episode meets all of the criteria for either a manic, mixed, or depressed episode but simply has not lasted long enough, the appropriate diagnosis would be *bipolar I disorder, unspecified.*

SUPPLEMENTAL RESOURCES

Berger, D., & Berger, L. (1991). *We heard the angels of madness: A family guide to coping with manic depression.* New York: Quill.

Jefferson, J., & Bohn, M. (1990). *Lithium and manic depression: A guide.* Lithium Information Center, University of Wisconsin, Department of Psychiatry.

Jefferson, J., & Greist, J. (1990). *Valproate and manic depression: A guide.* Lithium Information Center, University of Wisconsin, Department of Psychiatry.

Medenwald, J. (1990). *Carbamaxepine and manic depression: A guide.* Lithium Information Center, University of Wisconsin, Department of Psychiatry.

Bipolar II Disorder

This diagnosis of bipolar II disorder is given when the individual suffers alternating major depressive episodes and **Hypomanic** episodes. In other words, individuals who suffer manic episodes are not to be diagnosed with bipolar II disorder and would be classified as having some form of bipolar I disorder as described in that entry. Further, in order to be diagnosed with bipolar II disorder, there must never have been any history of any full-blown manic episodes or mixed episodes. Rather, the diagnosis of bipolar II disorder implies that the individual has suffered at least one hypomanic episode as well as one major depressive episode during the course of the disorder.

SUPPLEMENTAL RESOURCES

Berger, D., & Berger, L. (1991). *We heard the angels of madness: A family guide to coping with manic depression.* New York: Quill.

Jefferson, J., & Bohn, M. (1990). *Lithium and manic depression: A guide.* Lithium Information Center, University of Wisconsin, Department of Psychiatry.

Jefferson, J., & Greist, J. (1990). *Valproate and manic depression: A guide.* Lithium Information Center, University of Wisconsin, Department of Psychiatry.

Medenwald, J. (1990). *Carbamaxepine and manic depression: A guide.* Lithium Information Center, University of Wisconsin, Department of Psychiatry.

Birth of a Sibling

Just as the birth of a new child requires major adjustments on the part of the parents, it requires similar adjustment on the part of the other children in the household. It is in some ways a more significant occurrence for the siblings in that the parents (as adults) have more highly developed coping skills to deal with such major life changes. In addition, it is the likely case in most situations that the adults played a greater role in the determination of the decision to have another child than did the children in the home. Thus, the children have a major change in their lifestyle flung upon them without their feeling that they have any control over the occurrence. Superimposed upon all of that frustration is the aforementioned fact that their developmental stage may preclude their having the optimally adaptive coping skills for dealing with this disruption in their lives.

Whereas the birth of a new baby (or the addition of an older adopted child) confronts the parents with issues around time management, financial resources, health, and purchasing of necessary supplies, the introduction of a new sibling into the family confronts the children in the home with a set of concerns all of their own. Whereas the specific nature of the concerns associated with the arrival of new sibling varies according to the developmental level of the children, there are certain basic themes that tend to be rather uniform. Included among these concerns are the following:

> *Physical abandonment by parents:* With the mother's needing to go to the hospital to have the baby (or in cases of adoption, both parents needing to attend several meetings and otherwise be away from the home), children have worries as to whether the mother (and/or father) will actually disappear forever, leaving nobody to care for them.
>
> > *Solution-oriented approach:* Assure the child that he or she will not be left by the parents, and no matter how many new children come into the family, the parents will always be there to assure that the child will be taken care of.
>
> *Emotional abandonment by parents:* Children's fears can even go so far as to wonder "Will Mommy still be my Mommy" when the new sibling arrives. Such concerns can be taken literally, or they can be internalized more metaphorically, wherein the child is unsure if the parents will still provide the emotional comfort and security as in the past. In such situations, it is common for the child to artificially create emotionally demanding situations as a means of "testing" the parents to see if they are still able to meet his or her emotional needs.
>
> > *Solution-oriented approach:* During the first few days of the new baby's arrival, go out of the way to spend time with the older child and be particularly attentive to his or her emotional needs, anticipating problems before they are created.

Insecurity about their place in the family: With the arrival of a new child or baby, everybody's position and role in the family unit is by definition altered. For the children, it becomes an issue of feeling displaced (for example, as the youngest, only boy, only girl, etc.) and then feeling a need to establish and define a new role. The attention naturally lavished on the new arrival only contributes to the older child's sense of insecurity and concern that he or she is being displaced, and, possibly even worse, no longer significant.

> *Solution-oriented approach:* Attempt to spend time with the older child (alone) without the presence of the new arrival. During this time, repeatedly reinforce to the child that he or she is special, and, as such, will always have a special relationship with the parent. In addition, in day-to-day activities, work to maintain as much consistency as possible in terms of the child's previous role in the family system (e.g., chores, errands, etc.).

What about me? A rather generic concern of being ignored, deprived, unloved, and unwanted pervades the child's sense of being. It is only natural that the new arrival is blamed for this unpleasant situation, and the child typically has some significant anger around this. In his or her attempt to continue to be noticed, the child may engage in behavioral extremes—sometimes positive, sometimes negative.

> *Solution-oriented approach:* Be proactive in anticipating potential problems by speaking with the child (at a level consistent with his or her development) about what he or she may be feeling. In these talks (and, more importantly, in the behaviors of the adult) work to assuage the child's fears and demonstrate his or her continued significance in the family unit.

Whereas the above issues are rather pervasive when a new child enters the family, and, as such, are difficult to eliminate entirely, an awareness of these dynamics can help the parent interact with the child in such a way to eliminate any major psychological stress on the part of parent as well as child. Recognizing these emotional needs in the child—and identifying some less than optimal behaviors that result—allows the parent to address the true problem (i.e., the child's feelings) rather than focusing exclusively on the aversive symptoms. While it is not recommended that the child's inappropriate behavior be excused or allowed to continue, the parents can make better inroads at modifying this behavior when the source of it is understood and addressed at that level.

SUPPLEMENTAL RESOURCES

Canter, L. (1993). *Surviving sibling rivalry.* Santa Monica, CA: Lee Canter.
Cole, J. (1985). *The new baby at your house.* New York: William Morrows.

Corey, D. (1995). *Will there be a lap for me?* Morton Grove, IL: Albert Whitman.

Faber, A., & Mazlish, E. (1998). *Siblings without rivalry.* New York: Avon Books.

MacGregor, C. (1996). *Why do we need another baby?* New York: Carol Publishing Group.

Bisexuality

Bisexuality is a term that refers to an individual's sexual orientation—that is, the gender of people to whom the person is attracted. Technically speaking, bisexual individuals are defined as being attracted to people of both sexes and able to form sexual relationships with people of both sexes. Such a definition is less straightforward than it sounds, however, as studies indicate that many people who are sexually aroused by both genders indeed limit their actual sexual activity to one gender or another. In fact, as far back as the classic studies by Kinsey in the 1940s, data report that one third of all males acknowledged having at least one sexual relationship with a member of both sexes, whereas an additional 13% of the sample acknowledged having erotic feelings toward members of both sexes, however were only behaviorally sexual with one. When we take into account the distortion in these statistics as a function of what respondents were willing to admit, coupled with the fact that the data were gathered some sixty years ago, one can only assume that the true figures for incidence of bisexual feelings as well as for bisexual activity are considerably higher.

In the majority of cases, individuals who describe themselves as bisexual have a preference for one gender over the other as a sexual partner. Nonetheless, some bisexuals alternate their choice of gender of sexual partners, sometimes merely as a function of availability and circumstances at any given point in time. There is also a subgroup of bisexual individuals, described by Masters and Johnson as *ambisexual.* These are men and women who describe themselves as bisexual but have absolutely no preference with respect to the gender of their sexual partners, have a history of frequent sexual interaction with both males and females, and have never become involved in a committed sexual relationship.

SUPPLEMENTAL RESOURCES

Masters, W. H., Johnson, V. E., & Kolodny, R. C. (1986). *Sex and human loving.* Boston: Little, Brown.

Biting

Two general types of biting behavior are observed in children. The first involves mouthing, sucking and possibly chewing on objects (or people for that matter) during the teething period. This type of behavior is exploratory and also provides the child with oral stimulation to ease some of the discomfort of the teething process. The second type of biting behavior is aggressive in nature and is utilized by the child as a way to express anger and/or frustration, as well as an attempt by the child to obtain control over the situation. Naturally, the more dramatic the response by the person who has been bitten (and by the parental figure if he or she is not the one who has bitten) the more reinforcing the biting experience is for the child.

Under no circumstances is biting (as is true for any other unacceptable behavior or aggression) to be tolerated. However, it should be addressed as is any other such behavior that involves inappropriate expression of anger via inflicting pain on another person. Whereas some parents advocate biting the child so he or she can see how it feels, such an approach is not recommended as it models the precise behavior you are trying to eliminate. Rather, parents should decide on an approach similar to what would be applied in a **Tantrum Behavior** situation. The following guidelines should be helpful in determining a useful approach:

- Parents should react in a calm, matter-of-fact matter.
- Punishment should occur as quickly as possible after the biting event.
- For very young children, a firm "no biting" with a disapproving look may suffice, whereas for older children a more severe punishment may be necessary.
- When determining the consequences of biting, it should be kept in mind that aggressive behavior should not be punished with aggressive behavior because of the maladaptive modeling component.

Especially with older children, it is important to determine the reason behind the biting. While it is crucial to address the biting behavior itself, it is often necessary to look into the reasons why it is occurring. In no way is this meant to excuse the biting behavior, but rather to explain it so that the source of the problem can be eliminated, as well as the actual problematic behavior. This way, elimination of the biting behavior will not result in symptom substitution (where the child develops another negative behavior to replace the biting). Possible reasons for a child to engage in biting behavior include the following:

- inability to express anger
- feelings of great frustration with a situation
- feelings of powerlessness
- need to get attention from adult figures
- inability to express aggressive impulses in any other way
- reinforcing qualities of reactions of those around him or her to biting

SUPPLEMENTAL RESOURCES

Beranstein, S. (1987). *The Beranstein bears and the bad habit.* Westminister, MD: Random House.
Minarik, E. H. (1987). *No fighting—No biting.* New York: Harper.

Blanket Carrying

When a young child carries a blanket, it is usually as an element of security, as he or she associates the blanket with the safe feelings of being in bed, as well as with the safety of parental connection. Similarly, when an older child carries a blanket it is for similar reasons. However, what is perceived by others as being cute and acceptable in young children can be viewed as marginally tolerable in older children. Thus, the disapproval of the adults in the environment, coupled with the taunts of peers, often results in a child needing to wean himself or herself from carrying a blanket before feeling ready.

Once the child has accepted the need to relinquish the blanket, there are several techniques that can mitigate against the associated anxiety. First and foremost, the weaning away from the blanket should be a gradual process, the steps and timing of which to be scheduled in advance together with the child. A possible schedule for this could incorporate the following steps:

- Sit down with the child and establish a tentative target date to be completely blanket free; then establish a timeline with various behavioral steps approximating the goal.
- Included among the possible steps along the hierarchy would be
  - decreasing the amount of time per day that the blanket is carried.
  - limiting the carrying of the blanket to within the house only.
  - limiting the carrying of the blanket to within the bedroom only.
  - limiting the carrying of the blanket to bedtime only.
  - Throughout all of the above steps, if necessary, consider acquisition of another transitional object to carry instead of the blanket; this new object should be smaller and therefore less obvious and more easily hidden.

During this process there may be some backward movements, as progress will not always be consistent. It is important that these setbacks are presented to the child as merely temporary, and are not interpreted as failures. After discussing why a specific step was not successful, without placing too much emphasis on this, the parent should matter of factly encourage further movement along the hierarchy.

Blunted Affect

This is a phrase used to describe the intensity or degree with which an individual expresses his or her emotions. Phrased another way, blunted affect is a means of describing the amount of energy or force a person exerts in conveying a feeling state. When a person's affect is described as blunted, we are talking about a situation in which the person exhibits a decreased or low intensity. If one looks at the expression of emotion along a continuous scale, blunted affect can be considered more animated than **Flat Affect,** but, considerably less animated than would be normally expressed affect.

As with the case of flat affect, blunted affect is often characteristic of various psychological/psychiatric diagnoses. **Schizophrenia,** dementia, **Obsessive-Compulsive Disorder,** as well as depression all can have blunted affect as a visible symptom. However, certain developmental and individualized concerns must be taken into account when evaluating the implication of blunted affect in the young people. First of all, it must be recognized that what may be correctly classified as blunted affect in one person may actually be perfectly normal expression of affect in another. Thus, it is important to have a good sense of the **Baseline** level of emotional expression for a given individual prior to diagnosing blunted affect. Second, there is considerable cultural variation in the intensity of emotional expression, and oftentimes this variation is further complicated by gender differences. Finally, despite the reputation of adolescents as being hyperemotional and melodramatic, it is not at all uncommon for adolescents to attempt to present a calm, cool demeanor with respect to emotional expression—to seem as if nothing phases them one way or the other.

Whereas no parent or teacher would want to ignore significant symptoms that may be indicative of serious pathology, in certain situations it is equally important not to attribute too much meaning to blunted affect. As stated, it is crucial to be very familiar with the manner in which the child/adolescent in question typically expresses affect (and behaves in general). Using that knowledge of baseline behavior, the next step is to evaluate whether or not the current behavior represents a clinically significant change. If such a change is documented, it needs to be looked at within the entire context of the child/adolescent's behavioral profile. Recognizing that the development of blunted affect does not exist in isolation, then determining if it is a part of a larger symptomatic profile or rather one of other more natural developmental stages, aids the concerned adult in deciding whether professional help needs to be sought.

Body Dysmorphic Disorder

This is a diagnosis applied to individuals who are virtually preoccupied with one (or more) parts of their body or aspects of their anatomy. Usually beginning during adolescence, the preoccupation has a negative valence to it, with the person suffering from body dysmorphic disorder being so focused on the particular aspect of his or her appearance that there is significant impairment in day-to-day functioning. In some cases, there is an element of truth relevant to the preoccupation (e.g., an individual who has a moderately large nose is so preoccupied with how her nose appears to others that she is spending hours per day looking in the mirror, rehearsing different poses that deemphasize the size of her nose), whereas in other cases, the object of preoccupation in body dysmorphic disorder has virtually no basis in reality (e.g., an individual with average-sized feet is convinced that his feet are enormous and consistently wears pants that are too long in an attempt to cover them).

The key feature of body dysmorphic disorder is the intense distress resulting from the preoccupation with the specific physical feature as well as the disruption in lifestyle associated with it. As indicated above, this preoccupation tends to be negative in character, with the sufferer perceiving the specific aspect of his or her anatomy as being grossly aversive and significantly impacting upon the quality of his or her appearance. Tending to accompany this preoccupation and distress are certain behaviors that impair interpersonal, occupational, and/or academic functioning.

Whereas facial imperfections/flaws are the most common focus of individuals with body dysmorphic disorder, symptoms are by no means restricted to the facial area. Indeed, feet, genitalia, hair, and virtually any aspect of appearance can be targets of a body dysmorphic disorder sufferer's distress. In an attempt to rectify the perceived flaw, the individual with body dysmorphic disorder will often seek medical assistance (usually in the form of surgical intervention). Interestingly, even in those cases in which medical intervention can be employed, subsequent medical treatment will often be sought (the reasoning being that the initial intervention made an improvement, but there is more work to be done), or, the individual's focus will switch to yet another physical feature.

> *Example:* Seventeen-year-old Mariella had severe acne when she was in her early teens. She views the two or three minor scars on her face as being "deep pits" that demand everybody's attention the minute they see her. In an attempt to minimize the extent to which these scars are visible, Mariella takes considerable time each morning applying concealer makeup. Difficulties arise, however, in that Mariella requests lavatory passes several times during each class period in order to go the ladies room and carefully check to ensure that the makeup has remained on properly so that no acne scars show.

> *Example:* Fifteen-year-old Jon has an extremely difficult time on school days when he has gym. Although he does not mind participating in the physical activity, Jon will not undress in front of his classmates because of his belief that his penis is smaller than everybody else's. For that reason, on gym days, Jon wears loosely fitting clothing and puts his gym shorts on underneath his pants so that he does not have to change in front of anybody.

Body dysmorphic disorder has much similarity to and is often confused with **Obsessive-Compulsive Disorder, Anorexia Nervosa,** and psychotic disorders. Indeed, because of the similarities to these disorders (among others), the *DSM* specifically indicates that body dysmorphic disorder is only to be diagnosed if "The preoccupation is not better accounted for by another mental disorder (e.g., dissatisfaction with body shape and size in anorexia nervosa...)". Specifically, body dysmorphic disorder differs from obsessive compulsive disorder in that, despite the sufferer's preoccupation with one or more aspects of his or her appearance, the preoccupation does not have the intrusive, uncontrollable obsessive qualities as in OCD. Further, in OCD, there is typically some awareness that the thought process is less than natural, and due primarily to anxiety. However, in body dysmorphic disorder, the ability to step back and objectively recognize the absurdity of the thought process is typically absent. The distortion of body image associated with anorexia nervosa is, in some ways, a specialized type of body dysmorphic disorder. However, because of the other associated symptoms, this distortion is conceptualized as one of a cluster of symptoms comprising those of this separate disorder. Finally, in psychotic disorders in which there is delusional ideation, the content of the delusions is typically not limited to distortion of body image and encompasses other content areas.

When to Seek Professional Help

At times it may be difficult, particularly with an adolescent, to determine if professional intervention is necessary in cases where symptoms of body dysmorphic disorder are being exhibited. Quite frequently, as part of their becoming more comfortable with a more adultlike body, adolescents manifest an almost obsessive preoccupation with their physical appearance. Part of this pattern can include a focus on one or more aspects of appearance, often to a degree at which others around them find it rather obnoxious! This narcissistic component of adolescent development, albeit a bit annoying, does not in and of itself warrant professional intervention. The teen who spends exaggerated amounts of time preening in the mirror, or verbally bemoans the appearance of one aspect of his or her anatomy, is certainly not in need of clinical treatment for body dysmorphic disorder.

However, when the situation is such that the preoccupation with one or more aspects of appearance is so intense that it affects day-to-day functioning in a significant manner, treatment for body dysmorphic disorder should be considered. The following questions should be useful as guides in determining whether the symptoms being exhibited are merely a part of adolescent development, or are to be more accurately approached as a possible case of body dysmorphic disorder requiring treatment:

> *Is the preoccupation with appearance in general, or simply with one or two aspects of appearance?* Nonclinical adolescent narcissism tends to extend beyond a focus on one or two body parts, and is more general in its focus.

> *When did the symptoms begin and what has been the general course of development?* Whereas body dysmorphic disorder tends to have its onset during adolescence, there is often a gradual progression of symptoms in terms of intensity and visibility, at times beginning during an earlier period in life. If onset is more sudden (acute) in nature, it is worth exploring to see if there was some triggering event that precipitated this concern with body image.

> *Are there any other psychological/psychiatric symptoms that have been noticed either prior to or as a result of the preoccupation with the specific body part?* The symptoms of body dysmorphic disorder can result in clinical manifestations of depression and/or anxiety secondary to concerns regarding the preoccupation itself. On the other hand, other psychiatric/psychological disorders can have symptoms of body dysmorphic disorder as secondary symptoms. Thus, if clinical symptoms of anxiety or depression, for example, are evident in addition to those of body dysmorphic disorder, it is recommended that professional consultation be sought.

What to Expect from Treatment

Many different approaches have been tried in the treatment of body dysmorphic disorder, with varying degrees of reported effectiveness. Whereas there is no body dysmorphic disorder drug, per se, several different **Antidepressant** medications have been tried. The success of some of the **Tricyclic Antidepressants** in some cases has led people to conclude that body dysmorphic disorder is some form of depressive disorder. Of course, another explanation for the sporadic success of these agents would be that the individuals who manifest improvement actually were indeed suffering from some form of depressive disorder to which the body dysmorphic symptoms were actually **Secondary.** More recently, the antidepressants of the **Selective Serotonin Reuptake Inhibitors (SSRI)** have also been utilized in the treatment of body dysmorphic disorder. Specifically, those drugs which have been known to be useful in cases of obsessive-compulsive disorder (e.g., **Prozac, Anafranil, Luvox**) have been used to treat body dysmorphic disorder with varying degrees of success.

In cases of young people with body dysmorphic disorder, psychotherapeutic approaches tend to be the treatments to try first. Indeed, this writer has had particular success utilizing **Cognitive Behavioral** methods to treat this condition, especially in situations in which there are not other major psychiatric/psychological disorders complicating the diagnostic picture. This approach provides the sufferer with the opportunity to reevaluate his or her thought patterns and experiment with alternative ways of conceptualizing self-image, especially relevant to the part(s) of the body being focused upon. Other psychotherapeutic approaches can also be used, typically depending upon the **Theoretical Orientation** of the clinician.

Since there is not a vast amount of research or clinical literature regarding the psychotherapeutic treatment (or any type for that matter) of body dysmorphic disorder, there is no single treatment modality that is universally accepted as being superior to the others. Similarly, body dysmorphic disorder is not among the most commonly presented disorders. Thus, when seeking professional treatment, it is crucial that the following questions be asked of the clinician prior to engaging in a treatment relationship:

- What is your experience in treating body dysmorphic disorder?
- What is your experience treating body dysmorphic disorder in this age group?
- How do you conceptualize the disorder (as being a form of depression, a type of obsessive compulsive disorder, etc.)?
- Do you typically treat this disorder with or without medication?
- What is your treatment orientation and what modality do you use in body dysmorphic disorder?

Keep in mind that there are no right or wrong answers to these questions, but that the important thing is that the answers are consistent with the values and mindset of the family and patient.

SUPPLEMENTAL RESOURCES

Thompson, J. K., Heinberg, L. J., Altabe, M., & Dunn, S. T. (1999). *Exacting beauty: Theory, assessment and treatment of body image disturbance.* Washington, DC: American Psychological Association.

Body Noises

At some point during the late preschool or early elementary school period, children commonly become fascinated with various body noises. Whether it is burping, flatulence, or the various noises they can make with different body parts, such noises become the basis for hysterical laughter, more subtle giggling, and, in many cases, intense frustration on the part of the adults in the immediate environment. Indeed, sometimes it is this expression of anger, disgust, and/or frustration by those in the immediate environment that actually proves to be more reinforcing to the child than the actual utterance of the noises themselves.

What is the source of this almost obsessional preoccupation with body noises? First, this has to do with the fascination with that which is prohibited, dirty, or—in the children's language—gross. Since this is a developmental period in which children are bombarded with new sets of rules at preschool/school and are expected to act in a more mature, less babyish manner, there is an inherent tendency to rebel against all of these newly imposed prohibitions. This focus on body noises in terms of expressing them, laughing at them, and most of all shocking others by this behavior allows the child to experience a combination of regression and rebellion at the same time. A second component behind this behavior rests in the fact that the children are still struggling somewhat to maintain control over such body processes. When accidents happen, it is less embarrassing for the child to act as if it was intentional and laugh along with his or her peers at the behavior than it would be to utter a more mature "excuse me" and acknowledge that the utterance was beyond his or her control. As alluded to above, the laughter along with peers is reinforcing, as it provides the child a feeling of belonging. Thus, as with other behaviors found to be reinforcing, the child will continue the pattern.

How Is the Adult to React?

Reacting to body noises poses for adults a rather difficult situation. Whereas the adult naturally wants to convey a sense of disapproval of the seemingly haphazard utterance of the various body noises, the manner in which this disapproval is conveyed is crucial. Such is the case because, to some extent, as alluded to above, it is the adult's expression of shock and disgust that is one of the most reinforcing components of engaging in the behavior in the first place! Thus, the adult is in the tricky position of needing to indicate that the behavior is unacceptable without unintentionally reinforcing it by doing so.

In most situations dealing with body noises, the less dramatic the adult's reaction, the better. In order to eliminate the behavior, it is optimal to set up a behavioral schedule with identified consequences—consequences that are enforced with a minimum of drama on the part of the adults enforcing them. Whatever behavioral program is established, it is best done together with the child at a time when both parent and child are calm and rational. It should be explained to the child that his or her behavior around body noises is unacceptable and needs to stop. The parent needs to be specific as to what type of behavior will not be tolerated. Should it not cease, there will be certain consequences that will be enforced every time the child behaves inappropriately with respect to body noises. Choice of a particular consequence should be made based upon a consideration of what would make an impact on the child, as well as what would be practical for the adult to administer on a consistent basis. Whichever consequences are utilized (depending upon what is perceived as being more effective with a particular child), it is essential that they be announced to the child in advance of the infraction (maybe even written down), are followed through with consistency, and, finally, are delivered with a minimum of emotion on the part of the adult. Examples of possible such consequences are listed below:

Fine: The child is required to give up a certain amount of money every time he or she acts inappropriately with respect to body noises. (This can be deposited in a family bank, whose contents will eventually be donated to a charitable cause of the family's choosing.) Alternatively, the money can be deducted from the child's weekly allowance.

Bedtime: A certain amount of time is deducted from the child's bedtime hour every time he or she engages in the target behavior. Thus, if the agreed upon time interval is 10 minutes, every time the child acts inappropriately with respect to body noises bedtime is made earlier by 10 minutes.

Removing privileges: The child is not allowed to engage in a desirable activity (television, video game, telephone, playing with friends, etc.) for a prescribed period for every time he or she violates the rule. For example, a child may be have to come in from playing outside 10 minutes early for each infraction, a child may be denied privileges to watch a given television program for a single infraction, and so forth.

Time out: A child is required to be placed in a nonreinforcing time out situation for a given period with each violation of the rule.

SUPPLEMENTAL RESOURCES

Cho, S. (1994). *The gas we pass: The story of farts.* Secaucus, NJ: Childswork/Childsplay.
Gomi, T. (1993). *Everyone poops.* Brooklyn, NY: Kane Miller.

Borderline Personality Disorder

Borderline personality disorder is one of the **Personality Disorders** diagnoses. Although this is a diagnosis formulated for adults, the clinical literature has contained descriptions of borderline children and adolescents as far back as the early 1900s. However, these earliest descriptions of borderline disorder in young people did not actually use the term *borderline,* but rather looked at these conditions as a mild form of schizophrenic disorder. As more clinical and research data were accumulated on schizophrenic disorders, it became obvious that these children and adolescents represented a different diagnostic category than did those who now carry a borderline diagnosis.

Part of the lack of clarity around diagnosing this condition centers around the fact that the clinical presentation of borderline disorders is indeed variable. Partly because the diagnostic criteria are somewhat ambiguous and partly because of the disorder's questionable association with the corresponding diagnosis for adults, the descriptions of borderline personality disorder for children are certainly not uniform. In any case, this disorder in children and adolescents is best conceptualized as a severe impairment in the young person's sense of who he or she is as a person. The borderline child or adolescent has never developed a sense of identity and therefore requires the input of others to determine and maintain one. This dependence tends to be focused on one or a few significant others in the young person's immediate environment. When the borderline individual believes that these others are failing to provide sufficient input with respect to his or her psychological needs, the sense of well-being is severely threatened. This can occur to such a degree that a young person with this disorder may even feel that his or her existence is actually in danger.

This intense anxiety precipitated by the lack of interpersonal feedback the child or adolescent requires results in the symptom pattern characteristic of the borderline individual. The actual manifestation of borderline symptoms is variable, with the same patient reacting differently at different times. However, clinical and empirical studies support the adult diagnostic criteria for borderline personality disorder as being relevant to this syndrome in young people. In sum, borderline personality disorder is characterized by a pattern of instability in interpersonal relationships, self-image, and impulse control. It tends to begin in early adulthood and requires at least five of the following symptoms for a diagnosis to be applied:

Avoidance of abandonment at all costs: Individuals with borderline personality disorder will do anything in their power to avoid real or perceived abandonment, or even the threat of abandonment by significant individuals in their lives.

Lack of stability in relationships: The relationships of people with borderline personality disorder are characterized by frequent ups and downs wherein the people with whom they are involved are at times idolized, and at other times virtually demonized.

Identity disturbance: People with borderline personality disorder have an unstable, shaky image of themselves.

Impulsivity: Impulsive behavior is observed in at least two areas of the borderline personality disorder person's life (e.g., interpersonal relationships, substance abuse, shopping, etc.). This impulsive behavior is severe enough that it is potentially damaging to the person's life.

Self-injurious behavior: Individuals with borderline personality disorder have repeated incidents of suicidal behavior, threats of hurting oneself, and/or self-mutilating behavior.

Instability of mood: Borderline personality disorder is often characterized by intense expression of moods that tend to last only a brief period of time.

Chronic feelings of emptiness: Individuals with borderline personality disorder, despite their intense emotional reactions, will often report feeling emotionally numb and empty inside. This occurs most commonly when the individual's significant person is absent.

Problems controlling expression of anger: For people with borderline personality disorder, the expression of anger is usually out of proportion in intensity with respect to the context of the situation. Thus, it is common to see frequent temper outbursts, to have a sense of the person being always angry, and, in more severe cases, to witness physical outbursts.

Occasional psychotic symptoms: When life becomes especially stressful for an individual with borderline personality disorder, the person may exhibit symptoms characteristic of a psychotic disorder. Specifically, paranoid thinking and/or **Dissociative** symptoms may be observed. (American Psychiatric Association, 1994)

(It is interesting to note that borderline personality disorder appears to be more prevalent in cases in which there was alcohol/substance abuse in the family of origin, a history of sexual or physical abuse, and/or where there are also problems with some form of eating disorder.)

Professional Treatment

If a parent observes his or her child or adolescent exhibiting a significant number of the named symptoms, it is recommended that a professional evaluation be sought. However, it is important to recognize that many of the symptoms are, in many ways, simply common to the developmental stage of preadolescence and adolescence (refer to entry on **Adolescent Mood Swings**). Nonetheless, if such symptoms are observed for a prolonged period of time, and they are perceived to be significant enough to interfere with the child/adolescent's optimal day-to-day functioning, a professional consultation is advised.

Treatment for borderline personality disorder is both symptom focused as well as more global. When the symptoms are especially severe, they are addressed after an exploration of the psychological sources/explanations of these behaviors. All approaches to the treatment of this disorder, however, have the following primary objectives:

Reduction of impulsive behaviors: Since the impulsive behaviors of individuals with borderline personality disorder tend to be self-destructive in nature (e.g., in the areas of sexual behavior, substance abuse, self-mutilating behaviors, temper outbursts), one universal goal in therapy is the management and eventual elimination of the impulsive behaviors.

Improvement of reality testing: In those cases where the borderline symptomatology has reached the point at which the individual is experiencing psychotic symptoms, a major (and perhaps initial) goal of treatment is the elimination of these symptoms and development of a more accurate perception of reality.

Reduction of cognitive distortions: Using cognitive behavior methods, the therapist works with the borderline patient to illustrate and then correct faulty thought processes. For the most part, it is this maladaptive, distorted way of thinking that actually results in the symptomatic behavior that must be addressed.

Reduction of interpersonal conflicts: Much of the therapy done with individuals with borderline personality disorder is designed to improve their relationships with people, especially those closest to them. This is done not only through work in interpersonal interactions but also through the teaching of more specific skills such as anger management, delay of gratification, and increasing of frustration tolerance.

In some cases, the treatment of child/adolescent borderline personality disorder incorporates drug treatment as well as psychotherapeutic interventions. Then, the range of drugs used covers virtually the entire range of possible medications. This is true because in young people with borderline disorders, drug treatment is used mostly to address symptomatology that is either too severe for, or simply not amenable to, psychological interventions. Medications, then, are prescribed to address mood symptoms (e.g., **Antidepressants, Lithium**), **Attention Deficit Disorder** (e.g., **Ritalin, Imipramine**), seizure disorders (e.g., **Tegretol**), and **Conduct Disorders** (e.g., **Lithium, Haldol**).

SUPPLEMENTAL RESOURCES

Conterio, K., & Lader, W. (1998). *Bodily harm.* New York: Hyperion.
Kreisman, J. C. (1991). *I hate you—don't leave me.* New York: Avon Books.
Masterson, J. F. (1988). *The search for the real self: Unmasking the personality disorders of our age.* New York: Free Press.
Millon, T. & Everly, G. S. (1985). *Personality and its disorders: A biosocial learning approach.* New York: John Wiley.

Bowlby, John

John Bowlby was a psychoanalyst who published in the 1950s. His name is most closely associated with the development of **Attachment Theory** (see separate entry).

Bradykinesia

Bradykinesia is a rather generic term referring to a general slowing in motor movements. It can be brought on by either psychological (functional) or physiological factors. In the former case, bradykinesia is most commonly seen in cases of depression or as one of the **Negative Symptoms** of schizophrenia. When the **Etiology** of bradykinesia is primarily physiological, it tends to be one of the side effects of the initiation or increase in dosage of a **Neuroleptic** medication.

Brief Psychiatric Rating Scale for Children

This is an assessment instrument that is designed to be completed by the clinician. Originated in 1979 and modeled after the adult version (Brief Psychiatric Rating Scale—BPRS), this is a rating scale composed of a list of items, each of which is to be rated along a seven-point scale. It is more of a generic rating of psychopathology (as opposed to focusing on one specific form of disorder) and provides ratings with respect to depression, anxiety, behavior problems, organicity, withdrawal, cognitive distortion, and psychomotor agitation.

Briquet's Syndrome

This is an obsolete term that was used to refer to *somatization disorder*. For a detailed description of the syndrome, please refer to entry **Somatoform Disorders.**

Bruxism

Bruxism is classified as a *stereotypic movement disorder,* specifically one that is commonly observed in young children and adolescents. The behavior of bruxism itself involves the grinding of the teeth together. Thus, this behavior is not seen in young infants until after the actual eruption of the first teeth. It is especially prevalent during sleep and is reported to occur in over half of normal infants.

Bulimia Nervosa

Bulimia nervosa is characterized by two major symptom patterns: episodes of uncontrolled eating (referred to as *binging*) and some attempt (referred to as *purging*) by the bulimic individual to prevent any weight gain as a result of the binging be-havior. The behavioral attempts to eliminate any weight gain vary significantly from person to person as well as within a single person. Specifically, such behav-iors include self-induced vomiting and/or the use of laxatives or diuretics. The actual foods ingested during the binges are typically high in calories, sweet, and smooth in texture. For some bulimic individuals, a depressive period (referred to as *postbinge anguish)* often follows the binge/purge cycle.

As with individuals diagnosed with **Anorexia,** bulimics are usually ex-tremely preoccupied with their own body weight. There is some controversy, however, as to whether this is true for all bulimics and whether individuals who otherwise fit the criteria for bulimia but do not manifest this intense preoccupa-tion should be diagnosed as bulimic. In an case, bulimia and anorexia may occur separately, concurrently, or even sequentially in the same patient.

With respect to personality, the self-esteem of bulimics tends to be low. These individuals usually work below their capacity, and they are overly concerned about how others perceive them. The binge/purge cycle, usually engaged in pri-vately, results in secrecy, sneakiness, and socially isolating behaviors. In addition, interpersonal relationships are further compromised because a significant portion of the bulimic's time and money is spent obtaining foods for the binges. These fac-tors, as well, can precipitate feelings of guilt and shame thereby further intensify-ing the individual's feelings of low self-esteem and guilt.

Dissimilar to the typical patient with anorexia, the bulimic individual is not unusually thin. Again, unlike the nonbulimic person with anorexia, bulimic people are likely to be sexually active and to acknowledge obtaining pleasure from eating. The clinical course of bulimia is usually a chronic one, with repeated relapses throughout the person's life. Similar to anorexia, however, bulimia is as-sociated with several medical, psychological, and psychiatric conditions.

The *DSM-IV* (American Psychiatric Association, 1994) requires that the fol-lowing criteria be met in order for a diagnosis of bulimia nervosa to be applied:

Recurrent binges characterized by

> *Eating large amounts:* The bulimic individual will eat a quantity of food in a two-hour period that exceeds what most people would eat in that period of time and under those circumstances.

> *Lack of control:* During the binging episode, the bulimic individ-ual experiences a feeling of being unable to stop eating and/or being unable to control the quantity of food being ingested.

Repeated purging behavior: The bulimic individual engages in repeated behaviors designed to prevent weight gain as a result of the binging. Such behaviors include self-induced vomiting, misuse of laxatives, di-uretics, enemas or other medications, fasting, or excessive exercise.

Regular binging and purging: The binging and purging behaviors both occur at least twice a week for a period of 3 months.

Self-evaluation issues: Person negatively evaluates self based upon perceived body shape and weight.

Estimates of the frequency of bulimia range from 1% to 4% for adolescent females in the United States, with an estimate of 1.9% for the general population. Of course, such estimates are probably inaccurately low because of the shame and secretive behaviors typical of bulimics. Peak age of onset for bulimia is late adolescence or even early adulthood—considerably later than the peak onset ages for anorexia.

Issues of Professional Treatment

As is true with the treatment of anorexia, the first and primary goal in the treatment of bulimia is the restoration of physical health (when necessary) and the minimization of the chances of subsequent or increased medical illness. Psychotherapy will usually focus on the cessation of the binge/purge cycles as well as the problems arising because of the actual bulimic behaviors. A vast range of treatment approaches are utilized—all having been reported to be effective to varying degrees depending, of course, on the specific clinical needs of the patients.

Most clinicians treating bulimia support a multidisciplinary approach, employing the expertise of professionals in the fields of medicine, nutrition, psychiatry, addictive disorders, and psychology. The actual techniques and modalities are similar in scope and content to those utilized with patients diagnosed with anorexia. The one exception here is the more frequent use of drug interventions in bulimic patients. Although drug therapy for this disorder is currently an issue of controversy, **Antidepressant** medications, antianxiety drugs, **Antipsychotics,** and **Lithium** have all been used with various degrees of success in the treatment of bulimia.

SUPPLEMENTAL READINGS

Buckroyd, J. (1996). *Anorexia and bulimia: Your questions answered.* Boston: Element Books.
Fairborn, C. (1995). *Overcoming binge eating.* New York: Guilford Press.
Jantz, G. L. (1995). *Hope, help and healing for eating disorders.* Wheaton, IL: Harold Shaw.
Kano, S. (1989). *Making peace with food.* New York: Harper and Row.
Pierre, P. C. (1997). *The secret language of eating disorders.* New York: Random House.
Pipher, M. (1997). *Hunger pains—The modern woman's tragic quest for thinness.* New York: Ballantine.
Sherman, R. T., & Thompson, R. A. (1990). *Bulimia: A guide for family and friends.* San Francisco: Jossey-Bass.
Siegel, M., Brisman, J., & Weinstel, M. (1997). *Surviving an eating disorder—Strategies for families and friends.* New York: Harper Perennial.
White, M. B., & White, W. C. (1991). *Bulimarexia.* New York: W. W. Norton.

Bullies

In spite of the annoyance it causes for young people, parents, and teachers alike, bullying behavior is far from uncommon among children and young adolescents.

This process of bullying is allowed to occur because it is fostered by a cycle of insecurity involving the bully and the one who is bullied. A bully behaves in the way he or she does because of insecurity, lack of confidence, and poor self-esteem. Not feeling adequate with respect to his or her sense of self and overall abilities as a person, the bully attempts to demonstrate personal adequacy to others (as well as to himself or herself) by bossing around, making fun of, and/or otherwise terrorizing others in the peer group. In so doing, the bully attempts to gain status within the peer group. ("If I can put someone else down, dominate another, etc., that must mean I have a certain amount of power.") Thus, the actual process of bullying is reinforcing for the bully in that it meets his or her needs to feel as if he or she plays an important, significant leadership role in the peer group.

However, there are two additional components of insecurity that allow the entire bullying process to continue. First, often as a corollary of the developmental stage, the peer group itself is looking for a leader, and, in some cases, that means the group bully. The bully assuming a leadership role (even though he or she is probably less appropriate for this role than most of the others in the peer group!) provides an element of security and reassurance to the rest of the group. In addition to giving the group members someone to assign the responsibilities of a leadership role, by supporting the bullying, the others in the group can feel reassured that they are members of the "in" group or clique. Further, by actively or passively supporting the bully, those in the peer group can feel more confident that they will not be the target of the bullying!

The final component of insecurity that completes the bullying cycle rests in the individual(s) being bullied. Individuals who allow themselves to be the victim of bullies tend to suffer a considerable amount of insecurity themselves. With the bully taking advantage of the person's self-conscious nature, he or she builds upon it. Actually, being the recipient of repeated bullying is a prime cause of developing insecurities—at times, in areas where they did not exist previously. All it takes is being teased about one's clothing, some aspect of one's appearance, a parent or other family member, the house one lives in, or any other such detail to change the object of the teasing into a source of anxiety and shame for the person being bullied.

Thus, a virtually perpetual cycle of insecurity is in full force wherein the insecurity in the bully leads him or her to bully others, whose own insecurities are actually fostered by the bullying process. Further, it is not at all uncommon for a child (or adult, for that matter) who is a victim of bullying by someone in his or her peer group to attempt to apply similar bullying tactics to another in an attempt to reestablish their own personal sense of self worth. As an adult involved with a child involved in bullying, there are various techniques to employ to address the situation:

> *When the child is the bully:* When the child with whom you are dealing is the aggressor in a bullying situation, the first thing to be done is to attempt to determine where the child learned this behavior. It is considerably more difficult to modify a child's bullying behavior when he or she is consistently exposed to bullying behavior by role models in the

home. Once this issue is addressed, answers to the following questions can be a major step in helping to stop the bullying behavior:

- When did the bullying behavior first start?
- What is the nature of the bullying behavior?
- Is more than one child a target of the bullying, or is it predominantly one child?
- What particular characteristic does the bully focus upon when mocking or attacking his or her target?
- How do others in the peer group react to the bully's behavior?
- Does the child/adolescent engage in the bullying behavior on his or her own, or are these accomplices?

In such situations where you are the adult who has the primary relationship with the child who is engaging in the bullying behavior, it is incumbent upon you to convey to the child that such behavior is by all means inappropriate and needs to cease. The developmental stage of the child, your particular parenting style, as well as the actual personality/psychological makeup of the child should determine the extent to which you as the adult engage the child in a discussion of the phenomenon. In any case, the bullying behavior best be handled as would any other unacceptable behavior (i.e., with negative consequences for it continuing). Since, in many cases, the child doing the bullying may not be the most accurate source as to the status of behavior, the child should be informed that the parent will be checking with external sources as to whether the behavior has ceased.

Professional Help need be sought only when it appears as if there are strong psychological factors that are preventing improvement in the behavior. Keeping in mind that, in most cases, parents are the primary (and often the most influential and effective) therapists, the situation best be addressed within the family (as described above) prior to consulting a professional. If a professional does indeed need to be consulted, it is recommended that parents be prepared to provide the treating clinician with data consisting of answers to the questions posed above.

When the child is the one being bullied: When the child with whom you are dealing is being bullied, consider the answers to the following questions:

- Is this bullying behavior a recent occurrence, or has the child historically been a victim of bullying behavior?
- What is (are) the target(s) of the bully's attacks? To what extent has the child begun to internalize the messages of the bully?
- Is the child the only one being targeted by this bully, or are there other victims?
- What is the nature of the bully's attacks?
- What is the previous relationship between the child and the person doing the bullying?

- What is the child's reactions to the bully's behavior?
- What are the reactions of others in the peer group to the bully's behavior?
- Has the child made any attempts on his or her own to address the situation? If so, what were they and how were they received? If not, why not?

When you are the parent of a child who is the victim of a bully's attack, the degree to which you intervene can be a tricky decision. Whereas you certainly want to convey your support to the child, it is similarly important that you similarly convey to him or her your confidence in his or her ability to handle the situation. Finally, issues of peer reactions also need to be considered when an adult decides to intervene on behalf of a child who is being bullied. There are times when peer knowledge of the direct intervention of an adult can make matters worse rather than better.

Toward that end, it is important to first evaluate the level and extent of the bullying behavior, then, based on these findings, to discuss with the child the various options for dealing with the problem. Discuss how the child has attempted to deal with this on his or her own, and to what extent his or her efforts have been successful. Make it clear to the child that you respect his or her judgment and ask him or her directly as to how he or she feels the situation should be handled. Without denigrating these suggestions, explore their pros and cons as well as the advantages and disadvantages of other approaches. When agreeing upon a solution, whenever possible, try to choose the one that maximizes the role of the child and minimizes your direct involvement. This will not only increase the child's sense of empowerment and confidence, but will also reduce the chances of peers increasing bullying behavior based upon the fact that the child "ran home to mommy, daddy," and so forth.

SUPPLEMENTAL RESOURCES

Doyle, T. W. (1996). *Why is everybody always picking on me?: A guide to handling bullies.* Secaucus, NJ: Childswork/Childsplay.
Nass, M. S. (1994). *No more bullies.* Secaucus, NJ: Childswork/Childsplay.
Petty, K., & Firmin, C. (1991). *Being bullied.* Hauppauge, NY: Barrons.
Rigby, K. (1998). *Bullying in schools and what to do about it.* New York: Pembroke.
Romain, T. (1997). *Bullies are a pain in the brain.* Secaucus, NJ: Childswork/Childsplay.
Shapiro, L. E. (1995). *Sometimes I like to fight, but I don't do it much anymore: A self esteem book for children with difficulty in controlling their anger.* Secaucus, NJ: Childswork/Childsplay.

Burping

Please refer to entry on **Body Noises.**

C

Catatonia–Cylert

Catatonia

Catatonia is a general term used to refer to motor symptoms that are associated with psychiatric/psychological disorders. In order for catatonia to be diagnosed, the observed symptoms must be a function of a psychological/psychiatric disorder (as opposed to an organic disorder), and the symptoms need to be expressed via motor activity (as opposed to cognitive functioning). In their *Concise Textbook of Clinical Psychiatry*, Kaplan and Sadock (1996) list the following variations of catatonic behavior:

Catalepsy: Term used for an individual who is virtually immobile despite efforts to move him/her.

Catatonic excitement: An almost hypomanic/manic state in which the individual is engaged in virtually continuous movement and agitation, seemingly without purpose and seemingly unaffected by what is transpiring in the environment.

Catatonic stupor: A significant reduction in motor activity—at some times to the point of no movement whatsoever—again, as with catatonic excitement, seemingly unaffected by what is transpiring in the environment.

Catatonic rigidity: Rigid, virtually immobile posture (assumed voluntarily) that resists all attempts at movement by others.

Catatonic posturing: A bizarre, awkward, or otherwise unusual posture is maintained (assumed voluntarily) by the individual, with such posture being resistant to attempts at movement or change.

Waxy flexibility: Position of the individual can be molded and moved at will by another, seemingly without any resistance or effort on the part of the person; also referred to as *cerea flexibilitas*.

Catatonic Schizophrenia

This is a form of schizophrenia that is seen less commonly now with the newer **Antipsychotic** medications. As one would assume by the name, this type of schizophrenia is characterized by symptoms that affect the individual's motor movements. The symptoms observed can vary in the type of **Catatonia** in that the possibilities encompass the full range from complete immobility to excessive motor activity (i.e., catatonic excitement).

According to the *DSM-IV* (American Psychiatric Association, 1994), a patient suffering from schizophrenia must meet at least two of the diagnostic criteria in order to have a diagnosis of catatonic schizophrenia:

Immobility: With respect to the motor movements, which can be expressed in terms of waxy flexibility, catalepsy (as described above), or total stupor.

Excessive motor activity: Which appears to be purposeless and unaffected by environmental factors; also referred to as catatonic excitement.

Extreme negativism: As demonstrated via a lack of motivation, resistance to directions (especially directions regarding movement), and/or a maintaining of a rigid posture (i.e., catatonic posturing).

Peculiarities of voluntary movements

Echolalia or **echopraxia**

(It is noteworthy that individuals with catatonic schizophrenia may also alternate between exhibiting symptoms of lack of movement and those of catatonic excitement.)

Treatment of catatonic schizophrenia often entails immediate attention to ensure that the patient does not injure himself, herself, or others as a result of the bizarre movements, as well as to ensure that the individual is not in any danger from complications associated with malnutrition and/or exhaustion. Aside from this, **Antipsychotic** medications used to treat other forms of schizophrenia are typically employed as the major treatment intervention.

Child Assessment Schedule

This is a semistructured interview assessment designed to evaluate children with respect to various forms of psychological/psychiatric problems. The clinician doing the assessment is provided with a list of questions addressing twelve different content areas, the responses to which are tallied. Cutoff scores are provided to be used as criteria to determine whether the child is exhibiting symptoms severe enough to warrant a clinical diagnosis.

Child Behavior Checklist

This is an instrument designed to identify the existence of psychological problems in individuals ranging in age from 4 to 16 years. Designed in the early 1980s

(Achenbach & Edelbrock, 1982), there are separate versions to be completed by parents and teachers. Each version requires approximately 30 minutes to complete and is composed of 112 statements. The respondent is asked to rate each of the statements along separate scales so that behaviors related to depression, school, adaptive functioning, and general behavior can be assessed.

Childhood Anxiety Sensitivity Index

This is a self-report instrument designed to assess the presence of anxiety disorder symptoms in children and adolescents. Based upon the model of anxiety disorders that focuses upon the importance of the individual's interpretation of the anxiety symptoms (as opposed to the actual presence of the anxiety symptoms themselves), this measure asks the respondent to indicate how he or she views or interprets the presence of various anxiety symptoms. Thus, rather than collecting information relevant to the frequency or intensity of the anxiety symptoms, this measure assesses the meaning the child/adolescent attributes to these symptoms—the basic premise being the more negatively the individual views the presence of anxiety symptoms, the more likely it is that a true anxiety disorder exists.

Childhood Depression

For a surprisingly long time, the existence of depression in young people was not acknowledged by the professional community. Actually, it was not even 30 years ago (in the mid 1970s) that the National Institute of Mental Health first recognized depression as a valid diagnosis for children and adolescents. Now, there is universal consensus among the lay and professional communities that depression indeed exists as a clinical problem for young people, with current estimates putting the number of depressed children and adolescents somewhere between one and three million. The feelings experienced by depressed children and adolescents closely resemble those experienced by depressed adults, with the actual symptoms varying as a function of the age of the child and his or her developmental level.

Infants

Depression in infants was talked about in the clinical literature as far back as 1946. Then referred to as **Anaclitic Depression** or *emotional deprivation,* depressive symptoms in babies as young as 6 months were described. This syndrome, believed to be due to lack of adequate mothering, was characterized by an increased susceptibility to infection, weight loss, insomnia, difficulties in interacting with people, slowness or failure to achieve developmental milestones, and withdrawn behavior eventually deteriorating to an almost constant blank stare.

More recent studies on infant depression describe a cluster of symptoms referred to as **Failure to Thrive.** Such babies, usually suffering from neglect, show problems in social as well as physical development. When such a situation tends to be more short term, it is referred to as *sensory motor depression*. These young babies are characterized by constantly having a sad facial expression as well as an irritable tone to their cry. In addition, there are the sleep problems, frequent physical ailments, weight loss, and social withdrawal as described above. Oftentimes, this is also accompanied by a delay in language and cognitive development as well as limited curiosity. Such symptoms are typically first observed by the primary caretaker.

Young Children

Depression in young children (ages 1 to 3 years) is usually characterized by either a delay or a failure to achieve the normal developmental milestones typically expected of children of this age. Worded another way, the child may appear "slow" in acquiring the physical and cognitive skills expected from children of this given age. This is often referred to as **Developmental Arrest** (the typical developmental accomplishments appear to almost "stop" in mid sequence) or *developmental regression* (the child can seem to be going "backwards" in terms of his or her abilities). Behaviorally, this can be observed as problems with language, various sleep disturbances, problems with gross motor skills, difficulties with toilet training, and/or an increase in self-stimulating behaviors (touching self, biting self, rocking, masturbating, thumb sucking, etc.), often as a substitute for age-appropriate activities.

In addition, depressed children ages 1 to 3 often show exaggerated behavioral problems in terms of negativism and oppositional behavior. Whereas the so-called **Terrible Twos** are often considered to be a prime time for such problem behaviors, depressed children of this age group show these behaviors to a more advanced degree. Thus, besides the usual "no" and seeming refusal to cooperate with any request, depressed children of this age group will also show a distrustful attitude toward any parental or authority figure.

Preschoolers

When a child reaches preschool age, symptoms of depression begin to more closely resemble those considered characteristic of older individuals. As with the younger children, 3- to 5-year-olds do show the disturbed eating and sleeping patterns as well as some decline/delay in cognitive functioning. However, more stereotypical indications of depression also become evident, such as actual expression of sadness and an inability to experience pleasure regardless of the activity (technically referred to as **Anhedonia**). In addition, depressed children of this age group are often preoccupied with negative or punitive themes (for example, "I am bad," "This will never work," "I am stupid," or "Nobody likes me") that can, at times, escalate into expression of suicidal ideas. Involvement with peers is often reported as markedly decreasing, with an overall lack of interest in newly learned motor skills.

School-Aged Children

Depressive symptoms of school-aged children are easier to recognize, primarily because children of this age group tend to be more verbal in expression of their feelings. Speaking with depressed 6- to 12-year-old children will often elicit direct verbalization of feelings of sadness and/or an inability to have fun/enjoy anything. These complaints often extend to problems getting along with peers and/or parents and teachers. In-depth discussions with these children can also reveal a deterioration in school work, morbid fantasies (often of self-harm), nervousness, self-criticism, and generalized anger. At times, when the depression is sufficiently severe, the child will share feelings of intent and/or plans to end his or her own life.

Causes

Many different factors have been put forth to explain the causes of depression in young people. Whereas it is common to classify these theories into those that are biologically based and those that look more to **Psychosocial** factors to explain the disorder, there is some degree of overlap between the two theoretical categories.

Biological theories tend to focus on issues of genetics and heredity or on some form of chemical imbalance. Although the data remain far from conclusive, those that focus on the genetic component cite studies that report a higher frequency of depressed individuals among family members of depressed people. Chemical imbalance theories look specifically to various **Neurotransmitters** (such as serotonin, dopamine, norepinephrine) and their different levels in the person's system to explain the presence or absence of depressive symptoms. Such theories are closely tied in with the rationale behind the usage of the various antidepressant medications, some of which work via altering the amount of these various neurotransmitters.

Those theories that explain depression as being caused by nonbiological factors are many. Life occurrences (often conceptualized as stress) that have been considered possible causal factors in the developmental of depression tend to be those that entail some form of loss of, or separation from, a significant person or object. This can assume the form of death, divorce, forced separation, perceived rejection, or other loss of some strong attachment relationship. Finally, the **Cognitive Behavioral** approach to explaining depression focuses on the depressed person's interpretation of his or her world. More specifically, this theory emphasizes the depressed individual's maladaptive way of interpreting environmental events, these interpretations typically involving negative perceptions of the self, world, and the future.

Professional Help

Although it is crucial to respect a parent's understanding of his or her child's emotional state, it is not always an easy decision as to whether to seek professional help for a child's depressive symptoms. Like so many other psychological/psychiatric diagnoses, it is seldom easy to acknowledge that one's child is so bad that he or she requires professional intervention. Adding to the complexities of the struggle are the issues specific to the depressive condition—the fear that failing to seek help at the appropriate time may have disastrous consequences. In any case, however, it is best to attempt to keep things in the proper perspective—not overcatastrophizing at the first sign that may possibly be viewed as a symptom of depression!

The optimal approach is to evaluate the degree to which the symptoms of a concern are negatively affecting the child/adolescent's quality of life. More specifically, how are the depressive symptoms affecting school work, social interactions with friends, family relationships, and the like? Also, what are the specific symptoms exhibited by the young person? For example, a previously socially active child expressing a desire to be left alone this weekend clearly does not send as dramatic a message as a child talking about wanting to die. The timing of the depressive symptoms also needs to be taken into account. Have these symptoms been around for several weeks or months, or did they seem to surface rather suddenly? If it is the latter, is there some event or occurrence that could be prompting these symptoms? Should such be the case, once the initial impact of the event has passed, does the young person still manifest the depressive symptoms? In sum, if in the opinion of the parents and/or the child, the symptoms seem uncomfortably serious, uncharacteristic, or to be lasting for an uncomfortably long time (not responding sufficiently to common interventions), it is recommended that professional help be considered.

When dealing with infants and young children, it is best to first consult the pediatrician in order to rule out any physiological (medical) basis for the observed symptoms. It is not at all uncommon for young people (and older people, too, for that matter!) to translate physical discomfort into behavior appearing to be more emotional than medical. When presenting the case to the pediatrician, try to be as specific as possible regarding what you have observed in terms of the details of the behavior, when you first noticed it, any changes you have noticed, and if the child has ever shown similar behavior in the past.

If physiological (medical) causes for the child's behavior can be eliminated, it's safe to assume that the depressive symptoms being observed are probably psychological in nature. After scheduling an appointment with a professional with whom you believe you and your child/adolescent would feel comfortable (refer to entries **Professional Help, Locating; Therapist: What To Expect at the First Visit; Therapist: Preparing the Child for the First Visit**), you and your family should feel assured, as depression is known to be the most "treatable" psychiatric diagnosis.

The initial one or two sessions with the therapist will consist of various assessment procedures to determine if indeed the child is depressed and, if so, to what extent. This process is carried out via **Clinical Interviews** with the young person and accompanying family members, and is often supplemented by more formal assessment instruments of more structured interview procedures. Some of these assessment instruments are designed specifically to assess the degree of depression in young people (e.g., **Interview Schedule for Children,** *Bellevue index of depression,* **Children's Depression Inventory, Depression Self-Rating Scale**), whereas others are more general and assess depression as well as other possible disorders (e.g., **Child Behavior Checklist, Brief Psychiatric Rating Scale for Children**).

Also often evaluated (although a bit more indirectly) during these initial sessions are factors that would help the therapist determine the best form of therapeutic intervention. In other words, what type of format (e.g., **Individual Psychotherapy, Group Therapy, Family Therapy**) and to what particular form of therapeutic intervention (e.g., **Cognitive Behavior Therapy, Play Therapy,** etc.)

would the child/adolescent respond most positively? (Refer also to the entry **Therapeutic Modalities.**)

There are three general paths that treatment for depression can take: psychotherapy alone; medication alone; or some combination of psychotherapy and medication. Since the majority of antidepressants have not been approved for young children, nor have they been researched extensively with young people, in most cases the first approach tried is psychotherapy without medication. Although cognitive behavior therapy is considered the treatment of choice for adults, it is most important that the therapeutic modality is consistent with the child/adolescent's developmental level and preferences. Thus, for example, while cognitive behavioral therapy may be the intervention of choice for a 13-year-old depressed girl who enjoys reasoning out her problems, it certainly would be inappropriate for a 3-year-old little boy who was depressed because of a recent parental divorce. Therefore, although the actual form the therapy may take can range anywhere from play therapy, art therapy, **Psychodynamic Psychotherapy,** to some form of systems oriented family therapy, what is crucial is that it corresponds well to the young person's developmental level, communicative style, and overall preference.

If it is decided that some type of medication is going to be tried, a psychiatrist or other medical doctor will need to be involved. (Note that is strongly recommended that the medication be used in conjunction with psychotherapy, not instead of it.) It is further crucial that it be explained to the child that the medication is being tried not because the psychotherapy didn't work or because "this case is more serious than we thought." Rather, it should be explained to the child/adolescent, at a level that he or she can comprehend, that different cases respond differently to different types of help (refer to entry **Psychiatric Medication, Children on**). The relative advantages and disadvantages as well as what can be expected in terms of improvement and side effects are explained in detail in the related entry on **Antidepressants.**

SUPPLEMENTAL RESOURCES

Cytryn, L., & McKnew, D. (1998). *Growing up sad*. New York: W. W. Norton.

Dubuque, N., & Dubuque, S. E. (1996). *Kid power tactics for dealing with depression*. Secaucus, NJ: Childsplay/Childswork.

Dubuque, S. E. (1996). *A parent's survival guide to childhood depression*. Secaucus, NJ: Childsplay/Childswork.

Dudley, C. D. (1997). *Treating depressed children: A therapeutic manual of cognitive behavioral treatments*. Oakland, CA: New Harbinger.

Fassler, D. G., & Dumas, L. S. (1998). *Help me, I'm sad*. New York: Penguin.

Gordon, S. (1985). *When living hurts*. New York: Union of American Hebrew Congregations.

Knowles, J. J. (1994). *What of the night: A journey through depression and anxiety*. Fort Erie, Ontario: Magpie Press.

Mandler, A. N. (1990). *Smiling at yourself: Educating young people about stress and self esteem*. Santa Cruz, CA: Network.

Miller, J. A. (1998). *The childhood depression sourcebook*. Lincolnwood, IL: Lowell House.

Childhood Depression Inventory

Published in 1985, the Childhood Depression Inventory (CDI) is one of the most widely used assessment instruments to evaluate clinical depression in children and adolescents. It is composed of 27 items, each of which is to be rated on a three-point scale. Extensively researched, the scale is designed to tap into the various components of the depressive condition such as behavioral (how/if the depression is affecting the child/adolescent's activities and observable behavior), motivational (how/if the depression is affecting the child/adolescent's initiative and willingness to engage in typical day-to-day activities), affective (how/if the depression impacts on the child/adolescent's observable mood) and cognitive (how/if the depression affects the child/adolescent's thought patterns and way of perceiving the world).

Childhood Disintegrative Disorder

This is a diagnostic category that was not officially recognized until the most recent revision of the **Diagnostic and Statistical Manual (DSM).** However, the clinical literature has described the disorder as far back as 60 years ago. Childhood disintegrative disorder belongs to the class of disorders known as the **Pervasive Developmental Disorders** and is remarkable in that the sufferers of this disorder manifest virtually no symptoms up through the age of 2, 3, or even 4 years. Then, much to the horror of the parents, these children manifest clinically significant signs of deterioration without any warning or **Prodromal** signs.

This deterioration is evidenced in the psychological, cognitive, and physical arenas. In addition, these children begin to show changes in their personality. Specifically, there is a noticeable increase in angry acting out, anxiety, and general **Conduct Disorder** types of behaviors. Cognitively, these children are known to lose virtually all language as well as social skills within a period of several months. In addition, these children often require assistance with the most basic tasks including feeding and bathroom behavior (partially due to a deterioration in motor skills). It is important to note that, in some children, the deterioration in functioning is not completely uniform. In these cases, there are some areas of functioning that remain intact, whereas others deteriorate as described. This period of deterioration in functioning lasts anywhere from 6 to 8 months. Following this stage, there is a stabilizing of functional level, during which time there is no further deterioration, and, in some cases, there is some minor restoration of functioning.

In addition to the aforementioned areas of deterioration, a diagnosis of childhood disintegrative disorder also implies at least one of the following: problems in social interactions (manifested as impairment in nonverbal behaviors, difficulties with peer interactions and with social interactions in general); problems with communicative skills (manifested via poor conversational skills, inadequate spoken language, inability to engage in age-appropriate make-believe play, repetitive use of language); or restricted and repetitive behavior patterns, interests, and activities (American Psychiatric Association, 1994).

Whereas the etiology of childhood disintegrative disorder remains a mystery, it has been noted that the disorder seems to be associated with various neurological conditions. However, the data regarding any actual causal association remain (at the very best) extremely tentative.

Treatment

Unfortunately, at this point there is no established "treatment" per se of childhood disintegrative disorder. As is true with many of the pervasive developmental disorders, professional intervention for childhood disintegrative disorder is limited to symptom management and support/educational programs for the family members. Such interventions take the form of special education classes for the child, pharmacological interventions (again, primarily for the purpose of symptom management), and those interventions aimed at parents and other family members. This third class of treatment modalities includes parent education, self-help/support groups, and supportive psychotherapy.

SUPPLEMENTAL RESOURCES

Hamaguachi, P. M. (1995). *Childhood speech, language and listening problems—What every parent should know*. New York: Wiley.

Meyer, D., & Vandasy, P. (1996). *Living with a brother or sister with special needs—A book for siblings*. Seattle: University of Washington Press.

Simons, R. (1987). *After the tears: Parents talk about raising a child with a disability*. San Diego, CA: Harcourt, Brace.

Children's Manifest Anxiety Scale

This is the first measure specifically designed to assess anxiety symptoms in young people. The first version of this measure (the CMAS) was published in the 1950s and consisted of 42 true/false and yes/no items designed to detect anxiety symptoms. In 1984, this instrument was revised and renamed "What I Think and Feel" (but is often referred to as the CMAS-R). The new instrument was written at a third-grade level and is comprised of 37 items (27 of which are taken from the original instrument). These items are designed to assess the presence of physiological symptoms of anxiety, oversensitivity, and worry, as well as cognitive symptoms of anxiety.

Chlorpromazine

This is the generic name of the antipsychotic (neuroleptic) marketed as **Thorazine.** Please refer to that entry for more detailed information.

Clinical Interview

Although not technically a formal test or measurement instrument, the clinical interview is regarded by most clinicians as one of the most useful assessment tools. A clinical interview can assume many different forms depending upon the degree of structure involved and the individuals who are interviewed. Some form of clinical interview typically occurs during the first session(s) with any therapist, since the data gleaned in the clinical interview are used to formulate the treatment regimen. Although clinical interviews vary as a function of the clinician's **Theoretical Orientation,** the purpose and goals of the interview, and the person or people being interviewed, there are certain components that are common to most psychological/ psychiatric clinical interviews with children and adolescents. Thus, when bringing a young person to an initial psychotherapy session, one can expect the following information to be sought:

Developmental History

Prenatal factors: Was there anything unusual about the pregnancy?

Developmental milestones: Were they reached at expected times?

Childhood illnesses: What were they and when did they occur?

Environmental Issues

Home environment

Family structure: Who lives in the home? Have there been any separations or divorces? Have any significant figures in the child's life died?

Substance abuse: Are there any alcohol or substance abuse problems with any person in the child's family?

Psychosocial stressors: What are the significant stressors (past and present)?

School performance and behavior

Academic performance: How is the child doing in school? Have there been any changes for the better or for the worse?

Achievement as compared with ability: Does the child attain grades consistent with his or her cognitive abilities?

School behavior and conduct: How does the child behave in school? Does this represent any significant change?

Interpersonal Behavior

Parents

Nature of marital relationship: Are there any changes or tensions in the parents' marriage that may be impacting on the child?

Psychosocial stressor affecting parents: Which stressors in the lives of the parents may be affecting the child?

Psychological status of parents: Are the parents experiencing any psychological/psychiatric symptoms that are affecting the child?

Siblings and other family members

Birth order issues: Is there a new child in the family? Does the child have psychological issues with respect to his or her place in the family relevant to siblings?

Sibling relationships: How is the child getting along with his brothers and sister? How are his or her brothers or sisters getting along with each other?

Psychological status of siblings: Do any of the child's brothers or sisters have any psychological/psychiatric issues that may be affecting the child?

Peers

Quality and quantity of peer relationships: How does the child get along with his or her peers? Does he or she have many friends with whom he or she socializes? Have there been any significant changes in his or her peer relationships?

Clinical Psychologist

A clinical psychologist is usually a professional psychologist who has attained some form of doctorate degree (either a Ph.D. or a Psy.D.) in psychology and specializes in the treatment of psychopathology (i.e., psychiatric/psychological disorders). Clinical psychologists can be found in a wide variety of settings ranging from academic (usually teaching and/or doing research in a university), to business, to hospital, to mental health center, to private practice. Whereas many clinical psychologists are employed in practical settings in which they actually treat individuals with psychiatric/psychological disorders, others are engaged in consultative or research positions. Most clinical psychologists are licensed (either nationally and/or by their state) and have one or more areas of specialization.

Clomipramine

Clomipramine is the generic name for the **Antidepressant** medication most commonly marketed as **Anafranil.** Please refer to those entries for a description.

Clozapine

Clozapine is the trade name for the atypical **Antipsychotic** drug **Clozaril.** Please refer to the entry on clozaril for a more detailed explanation.

Clozaril

Clozaril is one of the newer **Antipsychotic** or **Neuroleptic** medications, classified as an *atypical antipsychotic* because of its chemical structure. It is recommended for schizophrenic sufferers who have shown little or no improvement with the more traditional antipsychotics, who tend to exhibit **Extrapyramidal Side Effects** with even minimal dosages of more conventional antipsychotic drugs and/or who are experiencing relatively severe cases of **Tardive Dyskinesia.** Because of the potential for some 1–2% of the patients on clozaril to develop potentially lethal problems, with their white blood count dropping dramatically (specifically *leukocytopenia* and *agranulocytosis*), all patients who are taking clozaril are required to have weekly blood work as well as to register with Sandoz Pharmaceuticals (the manufacturer of the drug). Still currently in its early stages of use, clozaril has not been approved for usage in children and adolescents.

SUPPLEMENTAL RESOURCES

Maxmen, J. S., & Ward, N. (1996). *Psychotropic drugs: Fast facts.* New York: W. W. Norton.
Weiden, P. J., Scheiffler, P. L., Diamond, R. J., & Ross, R. (1998). *Switching antipsychotic medications: A guide for consumers and families.* Arlington, VA: National Alliance for the Mentally Ill.

Cognitive Behavior Therapy

Originating in the mid-1970s, cognitive behavior therapy was designed as a means of integrating the objectivity of the then newly emerging behavior therapies with thought processes. Utilizing the basic premise that our thoughts are directly related to the manner in which we behave and experience the environment, cognitive behavior therapy views the basic task of therapy as identifying the specific relationships between thoughts and behavior, modifying these relationships as needed, and, as a result, modifying less than optimal behaviors. This approach to therapy has developed considerable popularity over the past few years in that it not only works within a short-term format, but has been shown to be effective in the treatment of a wide range of different disorders (including **Anxiety Disorders, Conduct Disorders, Mood Disorders,** and even **Eating Disorders**).

As with other behavior therapies, the first component of cognitive behavior therapy involves identifying the problematic target behavior. In so doing, this behavior is defined specifically, along with the situations during which it occurs as well as the reactions it evokes from those in the environment. The second step entails working with the person to identify the thoughts that accompany and/or precede the behavior. This can be difficult at times in that, often, these thoughts are so automatic that they are hard to identify specifically, and, when asked, the person simply replies that there are no thoughts associated with the behaviors at all!

Once the associated thoughts are identified, these thoughts (often in the form of self-talk) are examined in some detail during the therapy sessions. Specifically, the thoughts are evaluated in terms of their validity and the impact they have on the individual, as well as the impact they have on the behavior being discussed. Recognizing the relationship between specific thoughts and the behavior being discussed is the most crucial part of the therapeutic process, as it provides the rationale and basis for the remainder of the procedure.

The final step involves either modifying these thoughts or developing new thoughts to replace them. This is based upon the premise that it is indeed the pathology associated with the thought process that is problematic, thus, by changing the thought process, the problematic behavior can be addressed. As one would expect, it can be difficult to encourage a person to relinquish a thought process or to alter the way he or she thinks, as in many ways our thought process defines the manner in which we go through life. Indeed, changing our thought patterns (even if they are less than healthy!) can be an anxiety-provoking experience in and of itself.

At this point, the cognitive behavior therapeutic experience is one of experimentation in which the therapist and patient together observe how the modification of thought processes impacts upon the target behavior. Both successes and backslides are analyzed in detail to determine if thought patterns need to be further modified and/or if the originally proposed relationship between thoughts and behavior was an accurate one. Throughout, a continuing analytic process goes on reinforcing the relationship between thought and behavior, emphasizing to the patient that since he or she can certainly work to control thought patterns, behavior is similarly under his or her control.

SUPPLEMENTAL RESOURCES

Beck, A. (1976). *Cognitive therapy and the emotional disorders.* Boston: International University Press.
Gehret, J. (1996). *The don't-give-up kid and learning differences.* Fairport, NY: Verbal Images Press.

Communication Disorders

This is a diagnostic classification that encompasses those disorders in which the child/adolescent has difficulties with one or more of the aspects of language. There are four subcategories of communication disorders described in the *DSM-IV,* distinguishable according to the type of difficulty the young person has with communication: **Expressive Language Disorder; Mixed Receptive/Expressive Language Disorder;** articulation disorder; and **Stuttering.**

Clinical histories documenting developmental language disorders date back as far as the beginning of the nineteenth century. Even back then, it was recognized that some children have difficulty understanding, using, and/or expressing speech. Since then, research and clinical experience have indicated that the frequency of developmental language disorders in the general population ranges from 7% to 12%. Among children and adolescents with psychiatric diagnoses, prevalence estimates reach 15%.

SUPPLEMENTAL RESOURCES

Davis, R. D. (1994). *The gift of dyslexia.* New York: Perigee.

Featherstone, H. (1981). *A difference in the family: Living with a disabled child.* New York: Penguin.

Gehret, J. (1996). *The don't-give-up kid and learning differences.* Fairport, NY: Verbal Images Press.

Greene, L. J. (1987). *Learning disabilities and your child: A survival handbook.* New York: Ballantine.

Hamaguachi, P. M. (1995). *Childhood speech, language and listening problems—What every parent should know.* New York: John Wiley and Sons.

Kauffman, J. M., & Hallahan, D. P. (Eds.). (1995). *The illusion of full inclusion.* Austin, TX: ProEd.

Mandel, H. P., & Marcus, S. I. (1995). *Could do better.* New York: John Wiley and Sons.

Martin, K. L. (1997). *Does my child have a speech problem?* Chicago: Chicago Review Press.

McNamara, B. E., & McNamara, F. J. (1995). *Keys to parenting a child with a learning disability.* Hauppage, NY: Barrons.

Meyer, D., & Vadasy, P. (1996). *Living with a brother or sister with special needs: A book for siblings.* Seattle: University of Washington Press.

Miller, W. H. (1993). *Complete reading disabilities handbook.* West Nyack, NY: Simon & Schuster.

Rosner, J. (1993). *Helping children overcome learning difficulties.* New York: Walker.

Salvovskis, P. M. (Ed.). (1996). *Frontiers of cognitive therapy.* New York: Guilford Press.

Smith, S. L. (1991). *Succeeding against the odds: How the learning disabled can realize their promise.* New York: Putnam.

Smith, S. L. (1995). *No easy answers: The learning disabled child at home and at school.* New York: Bantam.

Treiber, P. M. (1993). *Keys to dealing with stuttering.* New York: Barrons.

Unger, H. G. (1998). *The learning disabilities trap.* Chicago: Contemporary Books.

Zionts, P. (1997). *Inclusion strategies for students with learning and behavioral problems: Perspectives, experiences and best practices.* Austin, TX: ProEd.

Comorbidity

Comorbidity refers to the situation in which one disorder is present at the same time as is another disorder. The two disorders are then said to be *comorbid* with each other. For example, it is common for depressive disorders to be present in individuals with **Obsessive-Compulsive Disorder.** In such cases, obsessive-compulsive disorder and depression would be said to be comorbid with each other. A component of studying various psychological/psychiatric disorders is having some familiarity as to which disorders tend to exhibit comorbidity with which other disorders.

Compulsions

Compulsions are repetitive behaviors that tend to be performed with the goal of reducing the anxiety associated with **Obsessions.** In cases of **Obsessive-Compulsive Disorder,** the nature of compulsions varies from person to person, specifically in regards to the particular obsessive thoughts they are designed to counteract. Compulsions can be actual observable behaviors, or they can be a nonobservable thought or behavior. Interestingly, most individuals (children, adolescents, and adults alike) suffering from obsessive-compulsive disorder are aware of the irrationality associated with the compulsions, however the anxiety stemming from the obsessions is so intense that they are reluctant to give up these compulsions that somewhat lessen their anxious feelings. According to the *DSM-IV* (American Psychiatric Association, 1994), the most common compulsions include washing, cleaning, checking, counting, repeating specific actions/behaviors, ordering, and requesting/demanding reassurance.

> *Example:* Thirteen-year-old Patti insists on washing her hands for 10 minutes after every time she (by accident) touches another person because she is afraid of catching some life-threatening disease (specifically, AIDS or cancer).

> *Example:* Eleven-year-old Jack feels he must count to fifty prior to beginning to eat anything because he believes that if he doesn't he will become sick to his stomach and throw up.

> *Example:* Seven-year-old Martha is so afraid that somebody is going to break into her house during the night and murder her parents that she gets up at least once per hour throughout the night to ensure that the doors are locked securely and that her parents are sleeping soundly.

SUPPLEMENTAL RESOURCES

Please refer to resources listed under the entry **Obsessive-Compulsive Disorder.**

Conduct Disorder

Considered to be the most common clinical problem (estimated to occur in approximately 10% of the population) in both and child and adolescent patients, a diagnosis of conduct disorder is applied when a young person repeatedly presents behavior problems involving violating the basic rights of others, or, violating age-appropriate norms and rules.

The manner in which conduct disorder presents clinically will vary as a function of developmental level as well as a function of gender. Clinical symptoms of conduct disorder in preschool-age range consist primarily of an exaggeration of developmentally predictable temper **Tantrum Behavior.** Typically, this is accompanied by general oppositional and/or negativistic behavior, poor impulse control, motor activity impairment, and inattentiveness.

> *Example:* Four-year-old Ricky is described by his parents as being out of control. Whenever he is asked to something he doesn't want to do, he screams "No" and then smashes the nearest inanimate object to the floor. When his parents attempt to restrain him, he becomes violent—hitting, punching, or flinging his arms and legs in a wild, uncontrollable manner.

Elementary school conduct disorder is seen as aggressive behavior, behavior that is more blatantly aggressive than that of conduct-disordered preschoolers. Physical and verbal aggression, both with peers and toward parents, is what is most typically observed. At this age, children with conduct disorder are likely also to begin stealing—first from the home and later from others outside of the home. They often also begin lying and cheating as well as becoming disruptive in school. In some cases, cruelty to animals is also exhibited.

> *Example:* Nine-year-old Leah has been referred to the school psychologist for her behavior problems. Besides attempting to disrupt the class on a regular basis, she has been taking personal belongings from the desks of her classmates and has been torturing the class pet guinea pig.

By the time the individual with conduct disorder reaches adolescence, physical acting out decreases in frequency; however, when it does occur, it is more intense. Truancy becomes more prevalent, as does acting out within a group context. Prevalent symptoms of adolescents with conduct disorder include vandalism, sexual acting out, and substance use/abuse. Interestingly, those adolescents whose conduct disorder had its onset in childhood tend to manifest more serious symptomatology than those adolescents whose conduct disorder had a later onset.

> *Example:* Mr. and Mrs. J. received a call from their son's high school guidance counselor, who told them that their son has not been in school for the past 3 days. The true reason for the call, however, was that the son was found spray-painting obscenities on the outside walls of a vacant building two blocks from the school. Although this was not the first time the boy had exhibited truancy, there had never been any previous reports of vandalism.

According to the *DSM-IV* (American Psychiatric Association, 1994), in order for conduct disorder to be diagnosed, the child/adolescent needs to show at least three of the following types of behaviors within a 12-month period, with symptoms in at least one of the categories occurring within the past 6 months:

> aggression to people and/or animals
> destruction of property
> deceitfulness or theft
> serious violation of rules

When to Seek Professional Help

Whereas every child/adolescent has periods of exhibiting problem behavior, conduct disorder certainly extends beyond the normally expected behavioral difficulties of childhood and adolescence. When a child/adolescent's behavioral problems are beyond the point at which the parents feel capable of controlling them, and they exceed the frequency and intensity typically expected from an individual of that age, professional treatment is best considered.

Not surprisingly, most of the treatment approaches for children and adolescents with conduct disorder are predominantly behavioral in nature. However, there is significant variability with respect to therapeutic technique, varying from those that are purely behavioral to those incorporating **Cognitive Behavioral Therapy** approaches. In addition, the format of the therapy varies, ranging from the more traditional individual therapy interventions to those that involve the whole family (as well as others in the child/adolescent's immediate environment). In yet other cases, the therapist works with the parents and/or teachers, training them to act as cotherapists for the child or adolescent.

When consulting a professional for a suspected case of conduct disorder, the parents should be prepared to provide the following information to the clinician:

- a complete description of the problematic behavior(s)
  - when the behavior began to become problematic
  - under what situations the problem behavior(s) occurs
  - how others in the immediate environment react to the problem behavior(s)
  - where the problematic behavior(s) occurs
- any changes in the child/adolescent's environment over the past year or so
- any attempts to change the child's behavior
  - the nature of these attempts
  - the outcome of these attempts
- any previous experiences with counseling/therapy

Prior to committing to a therapeutic relationship with a clinician for the treatment of conduct disorder, the parent/guardian should be comfortable with the answers to the following questions of the clinician:

- What is your experience working with individuals of this age group?
- Specifically, what is your experience working with behavioral problems of this type?
- What is your basic treatment orientation for this type of problem?
- To what extent and how will we as parents be involved in the treatment process?
- At what point in treatment can we begin to expect results?
- Are there any specific changes we should expect in the child/adolescent during the treatment process?

SUPPLEMENTAL RESOURCES

Adams, C., & Fruge, E. (1996). *Why children misbehave and what to do about it.* Oakland, CA: New Harbinger.

Bloomquist, M. L. (1996). *Skills training for children with behavior disorders.* New York: Guilford Press.

Bodenhamer, G. (1983). *Back in control.* New York: Simon & Schuster.

Canter, L. (1994). *What to do when your child won't behave.* Santa Monica, CA: Lee Canter.

Crary, E. (1993). *Without spanking or spoiling.* Seattle; WA: Parenting Press.

Fleming, D. (1993). *How to stop the battle with your child.* New York: Simon & Schuster.

Patterson, G. R. (1972). *Living with children: New methods for parents and teachers.* Champaign, IL: Research Press.

Phelan, T. W. (1995). *1-2-3 management.* Glen Ellyn, IL: Child Management.

Risso, M. J. (1999). *Little Michael's guide to raising good parents: A seven year old's view.* Buffalo, NY: Continuing Learning Publications.

Silberman, M. (1995). *When your child is difficult.* Champaign, IL: Research Press.

Confidentiality

Confidentiality refers to the principle of psychological/psychiatric ethics, which requires that all interactions between patient and professional remain completely confidential. That is to say not only is the clinician not free to share what has transpired in therapy sessions or other contacts with the patient, but the clinician cannot even share that he or she is seeing the patient professionally without the (preferably written) consent of the patient. In cases where the patient is a minor, it is usually the parent who provides the permission to disclose information.

Specifically with respect to psychologists, it is the fifth principle of the American Psychological Association's ethical standards that addresses the confidentiality of the therapeutic relationship.

> a. Psychologists discuss with persons and organizations with whom they establish a scientific or professional relationship (including to the extent feasible, minors and their legal representatives) (1) the relevant limitations on confidentiality, including limitations where applicable in the group, marital, and family therapy or in organizational consulting, and (2) the foreseeable uses of the information generated through their services.
> b. Unless it is not feasible or is contraindicated, the discussion of confidentiality occurs at the outset of the relationship and thereafter as new circumstances may warrant.
> c. Permission for electronic recording of interviews is secured from clients and patients. (APA, 1992, Principle 5.01)

The ethical standards also state that

> Psychologists have a primary obligation to take reasonable precautions to respect the confidentiality rights of those with whom they work or consult, recognizing that confidentiality may be established by law, institutional rules, or professional or scientific relationships. (APA, 1992, Principle 5.02)

It is not uncommon for confidentiality issues to be less than perfectly clear in clinical work with children and adolescents. Although confidentiality principles apply regardless of the age of the patient, some clinicians interpret the stated principles as applying only to the parents when the patient is a young child. Nonetheless, when working with younger patients, the clinician may not share information with any individual(s) not clearly concerned with the case. This issue can become complicated at times as it is a rather subjective decision at to who can justifiably be considered involved with the case. For example, while most clinicians agree that it is prudent to inform parents as to the progress and content of therapy sessions with young children, it is less clear as to how to proceed when the parents are not living together and one parent has primary residential custody.

There are also four other situations in which the rules of confidentiality are not rigidly applied, and may actually be violated:

> *Duty to warn/duty to protect:* Two famous legal decisions (known now as Tarasoff I and Tarasoff II) from the seventies and eighties, respectively, established the precedent that if the clinician has any reason to believe that the patient's behavior may be potentially dangerous to self or to others, the therapist is obligated to inform the appropriate individuals to prevent such harm from occurring.

> *Child abuse:* In situations in which the clinician suspects that a child is a victim of physical and/or sexual abuse, the clinician is obligated to make the appropriate notifications to initiate investigations as indicated.

> *Insurance/third-party payers:* Many individuals who seek professional therapy have insurance coverage such that all or a portion of the fees is reimbursable. To a varying degree, insurance companies require information about the clinical treatment in order to provide financial reimbursement. In most cases, the patient has signed a release providing permission for the provider to communicate with the insurance company. However, since without such a signature the payment would need to be provided by the patient himself or herself, the degree to which the patient actually has full choice in this matter is questionable.

> *Legal subpoenas:* In cases in which there are some legal issues associated with the patient or his or her situation, the records of the clinician may be subpoenaed by the courts.

SUPPLEMENTAL RESOURCES

American Psychological Association. (1992). *Ethical principles of psychologists and code of conduct.* Washington, DC: American Psychological Association.

Congruent Affect

Congruent affect is a term used to describe the amount of consistency between an individual's observable behavior with respect to mood and his or her verbal description of mood. That is, to what extent does the person's observable mood correspond with what one would expect it to be given the content of the person's conversation and the context of the situation? When the individual's mood is consistent with his or her verbalizations and/or the situational context, it is said that the person is exhibiting congruent affect. For example, a person speaking about a happy situation and exhibiting observable indication of happiness (i.e., smiling) would be manifesting congruent affect. Related information can be found in the entry on **Affect.**

Conjoint Therapy

This phrase refers to the actual modality of the psychotherapy, or, more specifically, which family members are actually present in the therapeutic situation. Conjoint therapy can refer to couples therapy in which both members of the couple are seen at the same time in the same session, or it can refer to a situation in which parents and children are seen at the same time in the same therapy session.

A major advantage to conjoint therapy sessions in which parents and children are seen together is that this format allows the clinician to view the dynamics of family interactions firsthand. Keeping in mind that the therapeutic situation tends to be a fairly good representation of what transpires outside of it, the conjoint format allows the therapist to observe how members of the family deal with conflict, control issues, and other emotionally laden situations. In addition, this format reveals family norms and unspoken, unwritten rules of interactions. In so doing, the therapist can view family attitudes toward authority, generational boundaries, degree of rigidity, and **Defense Mechanisms** employed, as well as what subgroups exist within the family unit. A final advantage to conjoint sessions is that they allow the child/adolescent to observe the impact his or her behaviors has on those closest to him or her.

Despite all of this, conjoint therapy is not the recommended modality for every family, as there are definitely aspects of conjoint therapy that would be disadvantageous in certain situations. In some cases, family members feel inhibited in sharing different information when the entire family is present. Further, issues of **Confidentiality** should be taken into account, as there may very well be things that family members would like to share with a therapist and which they would prefer other family members not know. Thus, in the large majority of outpatient therapeutic situations with children/adolescents (excepting, of course, sessions with those therapists who strictly adhere to the **Systems** perspective), the actual therapeutic modality assumes some combination of the conjoint format and that in which parents and children are seen separately (albeit usually by the same therapist).

Contingency Management

This is a term used in behavior therapy to refer to the planned removal and addition of **Reinforcements** to the environment. In contingency management, this adding and removing of stimuli is done as a function of the person engaging in positive or negative behaviors. For example, as a means of reinforcing and encouraging a desired behavior, something positive will be increased or added to the individual's environment with the goal of increasing the probability of this behavior reoccurring and continuing to occur.

> *Example:* Fourteen-year-old Lisa was told by her parents that she would be allowed unlimited use of the telephone in her room as long as her school academic average was at least in the "B" range.

> *Example:* Eight-year-old Alex was promised a one-dollar raise in his weekly allowance if he made it through the entire week without having any bad reports about his behavior from either child care personnel or schoolteachers.

From the opposite approach, contingency management can also be used to reduce the frequency or actually eliminate the occurrence of a less than desirable behavior. In such situations, a positive feature of the individual's environment is eliminated with the goal of the individual associating this relatively negative situation with the performance of the undesirable behavior.

> *Example:* Sixteen-year-old Jack was told by his parents that he would no longer be able to use the family car if he continued to be late to his classes and his supermarket job.

> *Example:* Nine-year-old Jessica has 15 minutes removed from her bedtime for every time her parents hear her saying a swear word or speaking vulgarly.

SUPPLEMENTAL RESOURCES

Hall, R. V., & Hall, M. C. (1990). *How to negotiate a behavioral contract.* Austin, TX: ProEd.
Hall, R. V., & Hall, M. C. (1990). *How to select reinforcers.* Austin, TX: ProEd.
Hall, R. V., & Hall, M. C. (1990). *How to use time out.* Austin, TX: ProEd.
Kazdin, A., & Dawson, K. E. (1990). *How to maintain behavior.* Austin, TX: ProEd.

Cross-Dressing

Technically, cross-dressing refers to the wearing of clothing of the opposite sex. That is to say, a male's wearing the clothing of a female or a female's wearing the clothing of male would be defined as cross-dressing. Generally, cross-dressing behavior occurs in one of three circumstances: in cases of **Gender Identity Disorder,** in cases of *transvestic fetishism,* and as part of developmentally appropriate gender role experimentation.

> *Gender identity disorder:* A common component of gender identity disorder involves wearing clothing characteristic of the opposite sex. This is part of the individual's fantasy and wish to be, indeed, a member of

the opposite sex. Oftentimes, this cross-dressing is related to stress and is reported to reduce feelings of stress and/or anxiety. Please refer to the entry on gender identity disorder for a more detailed description of the entire phenomenon.

Transvestic fetishism: In these cases, the individual engaged in the cross-dressing behavior has no desire or fantasy to be a member of the opposite sex. Rather, the individual will wear anywhere from one to several articles of clothing of the opposite sex, typically for the purpose of sexual arousal and excitement. In some cases, the person will appear as rather unremarkable, with others not even being aware that he or she is wearing clothing of the opposite sex. However, in other situations, the cross-dressing is so extensive that the individual could, indeed, be mistaken for a member of the opposite sex.

Gender role experimentation: Most children develop a sense of gender identity (i.e., the sense of being either a girl or a boy) by the age of 2 or 3. At this point, they have a firm sense of their own gender as well as its implications. After this sense of gender identity is in place (usually during the preschool or early school years), children commonly incorporate gender reversal in their make-believe play. The key here, however, is that the child maintains a firm sense of his or her own gender and never believes that he or she is truly a member of the opposite sex.

Even in those situations in which the parent is pretty much convinced that the cross-dressing behavior is simply a developmental stage, and is not diagnostic of some form of upsetting psychological/psychiatric disorder, the behavior in and of itself may certainly cause the parents considerable distress. Nonetheless, it is important for the parents not to overreact in a dramatic fashion, thereby resulting in the child not really knowing what he or she did wrong—and experiencing undue anxiety in trying to figure it out. In such innocent situations, to the child, the cross-dressing behavior is not different from other forms of make-believe play in which he or she may engage. Thus, an intense parental reaction only leaves the child confused, shocked, and worried.

A parent who wishes to actively eliminate the cross-dressing behavior (as opposed to letting it take its course and disappear on its own) best behave in such a manner that his or her reactions are not only minimally reinforcing, but not at all punishing. In addition, the parent can use his or her reactions to the cross-dressing as a vehicle to convey healthy, positive statements about the child's gender identity. Possible examples of such responses could include:

"That sure looks funny, especially since you are such a handsome/pretty boy/girl."
"It certainly is fun to pretend, isn't it?"

These responses are to be conveyed with a minimum amount of emotion, disapproval, or indication of disgust on the part of the parent. The message to the child is not that what he or she is doing as being wrong, but, rather, that of emphasizing the make-pretend component of it all.

When to Seek Professional Help

Oftentimes, parents have rather intense reactions to their children engaging in behaviors that may be indicative of some problems in **Gender Identity.** Whereas gender identity problems are indeed serious and worthy of clinical attention, more often than not, what is observed among young children is merely an example of the developmentally appropriate experimentation and make-believe play described above. One means of evaluating the clinical implications of a child's cross-dressing behavior (i.e., Is this indicative of a true case of gender identity disorder or simply normal experimentation?) is to conceptualize the situation along the dimension of a questionnaire developed in the early 1990s. Whereas a parent may not want to bombard the child with this list of questions, evaluating the child's response to questions such as these allows the cross-dressing to be put into proper perspective:

1. Are you a boy or a girl?
2. Are you (opposite of response to question 1)?
3. When you grow up, will you be a mommy or daddy?
4. Could you ever grow up to be a (opposite of the response to question 3)?
5. Are there any good things about being a boy (girl)? If yes, probe for a maximum of three responses.
6. Are there any things you don't like about being a boy (girl)? If yes, probe for a maximum of three responses.
7. Do you think it is better to be a boy or girl? Why? Probe for a maximum of three responses.
8. In your mind, do you ever think that you would like to be a girl (boy)? Can you tell me why? Probe for a maximum of three responses.
9. In your mind, do you ever get mixed up and feel not really sure if you are a boy or girl?
10. Do you ever feel more like a girl than a boy?
11. You know what dreams are, right? Well, when you dream at night, are you ever in the dream? (If yes, ask: In your dreams, are you a boy, girl, or sometimes a boy and sometimes a girl?)
12. Do you ever think that you are really a girl (boy)?
13. When you were in your mom's tummy, do you think she wanted you to be a boy or a girl? What do you think about that?
14. When you were in your mom's tummy, do you think your dad wanted you to be a boy or a girl? What do you think about that? (Zucker & Green, 1991)

SUPPLEMENTAL RESOURCES

Roberts, J. (1995). *Coping with cross dressing.* King of Prussia, PA: Creative Design Services.

Crying, Frequent

Addressing the problem of parents complaining of a child crying too frequently requires a knowledge of the developmental level of the child. Clinical implications of a frequently crying infant are certainly dramatically different from the potential clinical implications of a 7-year-old who cries frequently, of an 11-year-old who cries frequently, as well as of an adolescent or teen who seems to be crying more often than usual. Whereas the general rule of thumb (especially for an infant) is to ensure that there is no physical problem (either illness, pain, or discomfort of some sort), it is the possible psychological sources of frequent crying that will be addressed in this entry.

> *Attention seeking:* Children at all ages easily learn that crying behavior is able to get them attention. This lesson is learned early on, and it is recognized that crying can be counted upon to get the attention of not only parents and other adults in authority, but also siblings, peers, and even strangers around us. After all, who can refrain from stopping and looking at a crying child, preteen, or adolescent? While in no way would one want to curtail the expression of honest emotion (i.e., by punishing crying behavior), if it is determined that crying is done primarily for manipulative, attention-seeking purposes, this is certainly not the kind of behavior one wishes to reinforce. Thus, the two strategies to employ in such situations entail
>
> > *Selective ignoring:* Deliberately not paying attention or responding to the child/adolescent when he or she is seeking attention via crying behavior; an example of an appropriate response in this situation would be the equivalent of "I can see that you are upset and we can talk about/discuss the situation when you are calmer/stop crying," and so forth.
> >
> > **DRO:** If it has been determined that the child/adolescent cries to get the attention of others, the behavioral principle of DRO (differential reinforcement of other behaviors) can be applied; by providing the young person with what he or she wants (i.e., attention) when he or she is acting in an appropriate manner, the more appropriate behavior will then be reinforced and the connection between crying and attention will gradually be extinguished.
>
> *Anger:* It is certainly not uncommon for people of all ages to cry out of anger and frustration. While, for very young babies and toddlers, crying is the only way they know to express feelings of anger, such behavior, optimally, is not the case as we move into childhood, adolescence, and then adulthood. In these cases, expression of feelings is never to be discouraged, but rather it is the appropriate expression of feelings that must be reinforced (and when necessary, taught). Thus, in those cases in which the young person has reached the developmental level where he or she is

able to express anger appropriately, it is important that he or she be taught how to do so. Part of this teaching involves helping the child learn to distinguish between different emotions (i.e., between anger and sadness) and appropriate expression of each. Again, the message to be conveyed is that all feelings are valid and defensible in their expression, however the manner in which they are expressed plays a significant role in the manner in which they are received. Thus, accurate and appropriate expression of all feelings is preferable, whenever possible.

Sadness: Whereas crying is a very natural way to express sadness, when it reaches an extreme in either intensity or frequency, it can be potentially indicative of a clinically significant problem. Of course, such is not always the case, as crying could be merely indicative of a stressful time in the child/adolescent's life, or a simple period of emotional moodiness. However, if the chronic crying cannot be explained in either of these ways, it is recommended that the parent consider professional intervention to assess for possible depression, **Anxiety Disorder, Post-Traumatic Stress Disorder,** adjustment disorder, or **Acute Stress Disorder.**

Cyclothymic Disorder

Similar to the **Bipolar Disorders** and depression, cyclothymic disorder is a classified as a **Mood Disorder.** Specifically, cyclothymic disorder refers to the clinical situation in which the individual manifests repeated fluctuations in mood—fluctuations in mood that include both hypomanic and depressive symptoms. For a diagnosis of cyclothymic disorder to be applied, the person's symptoms must meet the full criteria for **Hypomania;** however, the depressive symptoms cannot be of an intensity, duration, or severity to meet the diagnosis of major depression. (If hypomanic episodes are alternating with episodes of full-fledged depression, the more appropriate diagnosis would be **Bipolar II Disorder.**)

In order for cyclothymic disorder to be diagnosed in children or adolescents, the *DSM-IV* (American Psychiatric Association, 1994) requires that the following criteria be met:

a. There must be several periods of hypomanic symptoms as well as several periods of depressive symptoms (that do not meet the criteria for major depressive episodes) for a period of at least one year.
b. During the one-year period mentioned above, the child/adolescent had not been without the hypomanic symptoms and depressive symptoms as described above.
c. No episodes of mania or major depression have been present during the first 2 years of this disturbance.

Since cyclothymic disorder is actually a combination of hypomania and a less severe case of depressive disorder, the reader is referred to the entries on hypomania and **Childhood Depression** for information on treatment.

SUPPLEMENTAL RESOURCES

Berger, D., & Berger, L. (1991). *We heard the angels of madness: A family guide to coping with manic depression.* New York: Quill.

Jefferson, J., & Bohn, M. (1990). *Lithium and manic depression: A guide.* Lithium Information Center, University of Wisconsin, Department of Psychiatry.

Jefferson, J., & Greist, J. (1990). *Valproate and manic depression: A guide.* Lithium Information Center, University of Wisconsin, Department of Psychiatry.

Medenwald, J. (1990). *Carbamazepine and manic depression: A guide.* Lithium Information Center, University of Wisconsin, Department of Psychiatry.

Cylert

This is the trade name for pemoline magnesium, a stimulant used for the treatment of **Attention Deficit Disorder** in children over the age of 6 years. Typically administered once per day, Cylert is available in 18.75 mg, 37.5 mg, and 75 mg tablets. The usual starting dosage for treatment of ADD is 18.75 mg daily. (In obese or otherwise unusually large children, the initial dosage is usually 37.5 mg.) The initial dose is typically increased weekly until the optimal daily dosage (ranging from 37.5 mg to 112.5 mg) is reached. For some children, Cylert is better tolerated than the other psychostimulants (e.g., Ritalin) and tends to have less of a stimulant effect. If either Ritalin or dextroamphetamine is not effective, there is a 25% chance that Cylert will be effective. However, if use of any of the other stimulant medications result in a severe tic/movement disorder or psychotic symptoms, most clinicians will advise against the use of Cylert. Onset of the positive effects of Cylert occurs within 3 to 4 hours after administration, with a duration time of 12 to 24 hours.

With respect to side effects, Cylert reduces appetite and delays sleep onset in approximately 30% of children. However, it is noteworthy that Cylert causes anorexia, growth suppression, and cardiovascular problems less frequently than do the other stimulant medications. Further, of the stimulant medications utilized in the treatment of attention deficit disorders, Cylert has the lowest potential for addiction. Liver function testing (LFT) is required with Cylert, as this drug can cause a chemical hepatitis.

SUPPLEMENTAL RESOURCES

Johnston, H. (1990). *Stimulants and hyperactive children: A guide.* Lithium Information Center, University of Wisconsin, Department of Psychiatry.

Maxmen, J. S., & Ward, N. (1996). *Psychotropic drugs: Fast facts.* New York: W. W. Norton.

Rosenberg, D. R., Holttum. J., & Gershon, S. (1994). *Textbook of pharmacotherapy for child and adolescent psychiatric disorders.* New York: Brunner/Mazel.

Werry, J. S., & Aman, M. G. (1993). *Practitioner's guide to psychoactive drugs for children and adolescents.* New York: Plenum.

D

Day Care–
Dysthymic Disorder

Day Care

Controversy around the relative advantages and disadvantages of day care abound throughout both the professional and lay literature. Aside from the concerns about the competence of the day care facility and staff, there are issues as to the value of day care even if it is in a professional, competent, developmentally appropriate, stimulating setting. The basic issue revolves around the previously universally accepted fact that being raised by one's own parents is superior to being raised by another; thus, no matter how professionally the day care program is run, what the child receives is, by definition, inferior to what would be received if he or she were at home with parents.

Assuming that the day care environment is optimal, there are indeed psychological advantages to having a child in a day care situation. While even the best day care environment cannot substitute for good parenting, the day care situation provides the child with the following benefits that an exclusively at-home environment cannot:

Interaction with a wide variety of people: Exposes the child to interpersonal interactions with individuals outside of the family.

Interaction with peer group: Allows the child to develop interpersonal skills with those similar in age.

Exposure to a different environment: Allows the child to be exposed to an environment other than home and neighborhood—an environment where the rules, customs, and general atmosphere may be different.

Separation from parents: Helps the child learn to function in a situation separate from parents for a certain period of the day.

Of course, enrollment in a day care program is not necessary for the child to receive the aforementioned benefits. However, many parents who are perfectly able to care for their children on a full-time basis enroll them in day care for the reasons mentioned above, whereas others maintain full-time child care at home and expose children to the named situations via other means.

SUPPLEMENTAL RESOURCES

Auerbach, S. (1991). *Keys to choosing child care.* New York: Barrons.
Fox, I. (1996). *Being there: The benefits of a stay at home parent.* New York: Bantam

Death, Child's Conceptualization of

In most cases, a child is aware of the concept of death (and its permanency) around the age of 6 years. Children usually conceptualize death as something that happens to "old people"—as a means of both making it more concrete to themselves and of defending against their own anxiety. After all, if death happens only to the elderly, this mysterious occurrence cannot happen to them. (Actually, it is not at all uncommon for children to repeatedly ask their parents if they are old—again, as a means of reassurance that their parents will not abandon them and die.)

Another common characteristic is the child's attempt to provide a rational explanation for death. As a result, children often draw illusory correlations between various occurrences and a person's death. For example, a child may say that a person died because the last time they were together the child did not kiss him or her good bye. Or, the child may say that the reason a person died is that the doctor did not do his or her job adequately. All of these conclusions in some way reassure the child so that he or she does not have to deal with the anxiety associated with the unpredictability of death once these "rules" are established. The negative aspect of such an approach is that the child ultimately directs his or her anger toward others or even toward the self as he or she develops concepts of blame for the death.

When someone close to the child dies, he or she is forced to confront personal fears about death, and, in some cases, to challenge his or her own beliefs about it. Death evokes feelings of abandonment by parents (who will take care of me if mom or dad dies?), fears about one's own death, as well as fears of "who will die next?" Behaviorally these feelings are often expressed in terms of blatant **Anxiety,** a clingyness to family members, **Nightmares** or **Night Terrors,** as well as symptoms of depression. Anniversary reactions are often observed wherein the child manifests symptoms around the time of year the death occurred, after being virtually symptom free. In addition, at times one will see an attempt at identification with the deceased. In such cases, the child will assume one or more mannerisms or behaviors of the deceased in an attempt to "keep them alive."

SUPPLEMENTAL RESOURCES

Brown, L. K., & Brown, M. (1996). *When dinosaurs die.* Boston: Little, Brown.
Gellman, M., & Hartman, T. (1999). *Lost and found.* New York: Morrow Junior Books.
Greenlee, S. (1998). *When someone dies.* Atlanta: Peachtree.
Grollman, E. A. (1990). *Talking about death.* Boston: Beacon.
Hegart, M. (1988). *When someone very special dies.* Minneapolis, MN: Woodland Press.

MacGreggor, C. (1999). *Why do people die?* Secaucus, NJ: Carol Publishing Group.
Rofes, E. E. (1985). *The kids' book about death and dying.* Boston: Little, Brown.
Simon, N. (1986). *The saddest time.* Morton Grove, IL: Albert Whitman.

Defense Mechanism

The phenomenon of the defense mechanism stems from the psychoanalytic work of **Sigmund Freud.** It derives from a concept referred to as the *pleasure principle,* which, loosely translated, states that it is natural for human beings to do everything in their power to eliminate or lessen feelings of anxiety. Defense mechanisms are psychological manipulations, if you will, designed to do just that—reduce the amount of anxiety the individual is experiencing. The individual unconsciously distorts his or her perception of reality so the source of the anxiety is altered to appear less threatening and anxiety provoking. Defense mechanisms in and of themselves are neither adaptive nor maladaptive. We all utilize them to some extent, and, for the most part, our lives are better because of them. However, when defense mechanisms are used to an extreme, the person's perception of reality can be distorted to the extent that symptoms of a psychological/psychiatric disorder are manifested.

Included among the most common psychological defense mechanisms are the following:

Denial: Denial is considered to be at the core of all of the other defense mechanisms, and is, therefore, the most generic. Denial simply refers to any seeming refusal or inability to accept the objective truth.

> *Example:* The mother of 13-year-old Bonnie was severely injured in an automobile accident. As Bonnie sat with her family in the intensive care unit waiting room of the hospital, she kept saying "it's really not that bad, she'll be fine."

Repression: Also referred to as selective forgetting, repression refers to the inability of a person to remember entire, or parts of, situations that are anxiety provoking. Repression is especially common in traumatic situations in which accurate and complete memories of details would cause extreme anxiety.

> *Example:* Twenty-one-year-old Sarah knows that she was sexually molested by a neighborhood man during her early elementary school years. However, she cannot remember any of the details of what the perpetrator actually did to her.

> *Example:* Last month, 11-year-old Jason was badly injured when his bike was run off the road by an intoxicated driver. Although Jason did not suffer any head injuries, he is unable to remember anything about the accident (e.g., when it happened, where it occurred, etc.) except that he was riding his bike.

Regression: Regression refers to a situation in which a person exhibits behaviors characteristic of an earlier stage of life. As with other defense mechanisms, these symptoms typically occur in response to perceived stress.

> *Example:* Threatened by the birth of his new baby brother, 4-year-old Brandon has lately began to wet the bed at night, requests to use a baby bottle, and crawls on the floor rather than walking.

> *Example:* Whenever 11-year-old Bessie has an exam in school, she sucks her thumb (as she did when she was a toddler).

Reaction formation: This defense mechanism involves a person acting in a manner virtually opposite to the way he or she really feels so as to convey a more socially appropriate impression and/or to avoid experiencing the feelings (i.e., guilt) associated with acknowledging that less than positive feelings are being experienced.

> *Example:* Twelve-year-old Jennifer truly despises one of her classmates—Pat. However, since Pat is considered by everyone else in her school to be so nice, and because she is generally well liked, Jennifer cannot bring herself to admit her negative feelings toward Pat to any of her classmates (or even to herself!). Thus, Jennifer goes out of her way to be nice to Pat and to praise her whenever she is talking with her other classmates.

> *Example:* Nine-year-old Bart is extremely upset by the behavior of his alcoholic father. When drunk, his father becomes verbally abusive, and often will throw and break inanimate objects. Bart was referred to his guidance counselor by his teacher, and, when asked about his father's situation, he replied, "I'm used to Dad's drinking…it doesn't bother me at all.… In fact, I kind of enjoy the excitement."

Deferred Imitation

This phrase refers to the situation in which an individual performs a behavior to which he or she has been exposed at a previous time. However, the key issue here is that the behavior was actually observed some period of time earlier (often as long as 6 to 8 months ago). Thus, the unique aspect of this phenomenon is not the actual imitation of the behavior itself, but rather the time lapse between the observance of the behavior and the actual performance of it. This is especially prevalent in toddlers who often surprise their parents by demonstrating a behavior to which they had been exposed several months ago and evidenced no signs of actually learning at the time of exposure.

The actual behavior that is performed via deferred imitation is determined more as a function of the original person who performed it, rather than the nature of the behavior itself. It has been established that younger children tend to choose models whom they view as being kind and/or somewhat powerful. (Note that it is not the actual kindness or power that is crucial here, but rather the child's perception of the model as being so.) Thus, it is rather common for young children to look to television characters as models—observing the manner in which they act, or a specific behavior in which they engage, then performing that same behavior several months later.

> *Example:* Two-year-old Jeffy recently has begun to ask others for hugs and will spontaneously hug members of his family, seemingly for no reason. This is rather unusual as nobody in his family is physically affectionate, nor has Jeffy been this affectionately demonstrative before. Once this situation was probed, it was found out that, twice a day in day care, Jeffy watches *Barney*—a television show that features and reinforces open expression of physical affection. (What is especially interesting is that Jeffy has been in day care for 6 months, but has only recently begun to manifest this behavior.)

Delusion

Often a component of **Schizophrenia,** delusions refer to a mode of thinking, or a more general thought pattern, that significantly distorts reality. These beliefs tend to be fixed and, oftentimes, aside from the delusions, a person's manner of thinking and relating is intact. When the delusions are not considered to be bizarre in content (as they most often are in cases of schizophrenia), and the delusions are not present in conjunction with any other symptoms of schizophrenia, a diagnosis of *delusional disorder* can be applied.

Delusions vary according to their content, with the major different types of delusions being as follows:

> *Grandiose type:* Delusions in which the person believes that he or she has great power, worth, wealth, identity and/or knowledge; at times individuals with grandiose delusions believe that they have some special relationship with a famous person; also referred to as *megalomania.*
>
> > *Example:* Jon tells everybody that he is really the reincarnation of Jesus Christ.
>
> *Persecutory type:* Belief that either someone close to the individual or the individual himself or herself is being mistreated in some unfair manner; the most common type of delusion.
>
> > *Example:* Jeff believes that the reason he continues to fail his exams at school is that all of the teachers and the school administration are out to get him.

Erotomanic type: Belief that another person (usually someone of a higher status) is sexually attracted to the individual; individuals with this type of delusion tend to live rather isolated lives.

> *Example:* Barry believes that the lead singer in the rock group Spice Girls is really in love with him.

Jealous type: Belief that one's sexual partner is unfaithful.

> *Example:* Beth is convinced that her boyfriend has been sleeping with all of the girls in the high school senior class.

Somatic type: Belief that the individual has some (usually serious) medical condition.

> *Example:* Richard is sure that he has AIDS, although his HIV test repeatedly comes back negative.

Heutoscopy: Belief that one has a double who is impersonating him or her.

> *Example:* Ed is convinced that he has a double who is committing various serious crimes around the country. As a result, Ed lives in fear of the police coming to his home to arrest him.

Capgra's syndrome: belief that familiar people in the individual's life have been replaced by impostors.

> *Example:* Jim is convinced that his parents are not really his parents but rather imposters who have been placed in his home to torture him.

The major type of treatment intervention for delusions tends to be **Antipsychotic Medication.** However, there can be major problems with treatment compliance, as oftentimes the physician and medication become incorporated into the person's delusional system. Further, since, by definition, people with delusions believe that they are absolutely true, it is difficult for them to seek treatment to begin with, as they perceive no need.

When psychotherapy is employed as a treatment intervention, it is crucial that a trusting relationship develop between clinician and patient. Since the delusional beliefs often become so much of the person's way of life, it takes considerable trust of the therapist to even consider modifying the delusional belief system. The therapist treating the delusional individual should not challenge the beliefs immediately; however, at no point does he or she indicate agreement with or acceptance of the delusional belief structure.

Dependent Personality Disorder

Dependent personality disorder is one of the **Personality Disorders** diagnosed in the *DSM-IV.* As with most of the personality disorders, dependent personality disorder is primarily manifested in adults. Consideration of developmental factors is especially important here, as the symptoms of dependent personality disorder are actually normal and characteristic of children and young adolescents at various developmental stages. Indeed, if one were to fail to take such developmental factors into account, a vast number of young children would meet the clinical criteria for this disorder.

A major dynamic underlying the behavior of those with dependent personality disorder is a strong feeling of a need for approval, love, and support from those around them. Thus, the behavior of an individual with dependent personality disorder is such that he or she will do everything possible to avoid the perceived rejection and eventual abandonment by another. What is observed then is extreme agreement (often to the point of submissiveness), passivity, and a seeking of reassurance and advice from others. Part of this behavior stems from feeling insecure and incompetent about making decisions, whereas another determining factor stems from the person's anxiety about being rejected for making an unpopular decision. Finally, as would be expected, individuals with dependent personality disorder become quite anxious at the thought of being alone—either for a prolonged period of time (as in being without a significant relationship) or for a brief period of time (as in being left alone while a loved one takes a vacation). This, too, stems from a similar dynamic of lack of confidence wherein the dependent individual truly feels as if he or she *needs* another individual in order to function in day-to-day life.

According to the *DSM-IV* (American Psychiatric Association, 1994), at least five of the following criteria must be met in order for a person to be diagnosed with dependent personality disorder:

1. Has difficulty making day-to-day decisions without an unusual amount of advice and reassurance from others that he or she is making the right decision.
2. Looks to others to assume responsibility for most major areas of his or her life.
3. Will avoid expressing disagreement with others because of fears of anger and eventual abandonment.
4. Low self-confidence makes it difficult to initiate projects or to engage in activities independently.
5. Will go to extremes to obtain compliments from others, as they are viewed as reassuring—even if this involves doing aversive things and being taken advantage of.
6. Feels uncomfortable or helpless when alone.
7. Upon the ending of a relationship, will desperately seek another relationship as a replacement.
8. Is phobically preoccupied with fears of being left alone to care for one's own needs. (pp. 668–669)

Treatment for dependent personality disorder, as is true with the majority of the other Personality Disorders, is primarily psychotherapeutic in nature. Again, as with the other personality disorders, this therapy tends to be long-term, requiring a considerable amount of time to develop a therapeutic relationship between therapist and patient, then a relatively lengthy time in order to accomplish significant therapeutic improvements.

SUPPLEMENTAL RESOURCES

Masterson, J. F. (1988). *The search for the real self: Unmasking the personality disorders of our age.* New York: Free Press.
Millon, T., & Everly, G. S. (1985). *Personality and its disorders: A biosocial learning approach.* New York: John Wiley and Sons.

Depersonalization Disorder

An example of one of the **Dissociative Disorders,** depersonalization disorder is characterized by difficulties with the individual's sense of self and reality. While this is occurring, individuals are well aware of the perceptual distortion as being such (i.e., they know that these sensations are not based in reality), yet their experience is that of feeling as if they are in a dream, feeling basically unreal, and/or feeling as if they are separate from their physical bodies. Especially interesting is that in most cases, the person suffering from depersonalization disorder proceeds through day-to-day activities relatively normally, however, experiencing intense anxiety while doing so.

Brief feelings of depersonalization occur in the life experience of many adults as well as children. However, depersonalization to the degree that it is severe enough to constitute a true clinical disorder is considerably less common. Causes of depersonalization disorder are varied, ranging from the purely psychological to those that are more physiologically based such as brain tumors, substance usage, epilepsy, and various hormonal abnormalities. Symptoms tend to come on suddenly, and, most often, ages of onset range between 15 and 30 years of age.

For this disorder to be diagnosed, the *DSM-IV* (American Psychiatric Association, 1994) requires the following diagnostic criteria to be met:

A. One repeatedly experiences being detached from one's train of thought or one's body.
B. Person maintains an accurate sense of reality while experiencing these symptoms.
C. These symptoms of depersonalization result in impairment in the person's ability to function in day-to-day life.
D. Depersonalization symptoms do not occur exclusively during the course of some other psychological/psychiatric disorder. (p. 490)

Unfortunately, an extensive database does not exist regarding the treatment of depersonalization disorder. Drug treatments are employed when there is an underlying psychological/psychiatric process (such as **Schizophrenia** or anxiety), however, there are certainly no specific psychopharmacological interventions for the treatment of depersonalization disorder. Similarly, specific psychological interventions are not available either, excepting those designed to address the trauma or anxiety at the basis of the depersonalization symptoms.

Depressed Parents

When a parent is experiencing depression, it is only natural that his or her ability to parent optimally is impaired. By simple definition, the symptoms of depression preclude persons from being able to take care of themselves in the way they should, so, it is only natural that a depressive disorder would interfere with optimal parenting.

The first thing to keep in mind is that the person who depressed is not able to make decisions optimally. Thus, it is wise for a depressed parent to have another trusted adult help with decision making in terms of caring for the children. While acknowledging the need for such help is difficult in and of itself, actually taking advantage of it may be even more difficult. Whereas this help is certainly necessary, it is similarly necessary to ensure that the depressed parent maintain as much control and responsibility over the parenting as is possible. This will allow the relationship between parent and child to remain relatively intact, and, it will not damage the adult's already fragile sense of self-esteem by indicating there is one *more* thing that he or she is unable to do on his or her own. Further, once the depression is under control, it allows for a less dramatic transition for the children.

Depending, of course, on the severity of depression (as well as the developmental level of the child) it is advisable, if at all possible, that the parent explain the situation to the child. Again, being careful to present an explanation consistent with what the child can understand, the parent is the best one to explain to the child what is going on, as well as the resulting changes that will be occurring in the child's life. In so doing, it is important to reinforce to the child that the parent will continue to be available to the child for most things, and that this current situation is merely temporary. Some parents find it useful to present this within an illness model so they are able to use the metaphor completely with examples of symptoms, seeking professional help, having treatment (which may involve hospitalization, medicine, and other professional appointments) and, then, getting better.

When considering what elements of parenting to delegate to another, there are certain basic rules to follow.

> *To whom should parenting tasks be delegated?* Whenever possible, parenting tasks that need to be temporarily delegated are best delegated to the other parent. When such is not feasible, the general principle should be delegation to the adult with whom the child is most familiar and/or comfortable. If there is more than one person who would be willing to accept a given responsibility, it is often useful to ask the child/adolescent's preference.

What parenting tasks should be delegated? There is a basic twofold concept to be kept in mind in determining which parenting tasks are to be delegated. Delegate those chores of parenting that cause the depressed parent the most stress and those tasks that would cause the child the least stress if they are actually delegated to someone else for a brief period of time. Often, such tasks tend to be trivial, menial jobs that are time-consuming and annoying, but probably don't have much emotional significance for the child. Examples of such chores include driving carpools, grocery shopping, packing of lunches, and the like.

Whatever tasks are temporarily performed by someone else and whoever it is who performs them, it is crucial that every effort be made to have the child understand that this is a temporary situation, and that in no way is it a punishment or rejection of the child.

It is similarly important for the parent to try to put his or her needs in the forefront, possibly in some ways equal to or above those of the child. Keeping in mind the psychological adage that in order to take care of another one needs to care for himself or herself, the depressed parent should attempt to avoid feeling guilty regarding what he or she is not providing for the child. Rather, it should be recognized that in many ways, obtaining and adhering to appropriate treatment for the parental depressive condition teaches the child some very valuable lessons. Specifically, by observing such behavior, the child is taught the value in seeking professional treatment when necessary, as well as the relationship between following prescribed treatment and getting well. By observing such a process in action (and having it pointed out), the child also is provided with an optimistic view of illness, treatment, and recovery.

SUPPLEMENTAL RESOURCES

Knowles, J. J. (1994). *What of the night: A journey through depression and anxiety.* Fort Erie, Ontario: Magpie Publishing.
Marsh, D. T., & Dickins, R. (1997). *How to cope with mental illness in your family.* New York: Putnam.

Depression Self-Rating Scale

First released in 1981, the Depression Self-Rating Scale (DSRS) is actually a young people's version of the commonly used Zung Depression Scale for adults. Designed as a self-report measure, it instructs the child/adolescent to respond to a series of 18 statements—indicating for each, how often he or she has felt the way the statement describes over the past seven days. In addition, the scale provides an opportunity for the respondent to indicate the severity of the symptomatology being experienced. A later version of the DSRS, released in 1985, also includes items assessing feelings of hopelessness as well as the child/adolescent's capacity to experience empathic feelings.

Derealization

Derealization is a dissociative symptom, typically associated with one of the **Dissociative Disorders** or with **Schizophrenia.** It is similar to **Depersonalization;** however, while in depersonalization the individual feels unrealistically disconnected with his or her body, in derealization the person reports feeling unrealistically disconnected with people, things, or occurrences in the environment. Worded another way, symptoms of depersonalization tend to be internally focused whereas symptoms of derealization tend to be more externally focused. Oftentimes, derealization brings on the feeling that the world has changed in an anxiety-provoking manner. Treatment of derealization symptoms tend to focus on the source of the derealization, treating the cause(s) or the underlying disorder as a means of treating the derealization.

Desipramine

Desipramine is one of the **Tricyclic Antidepressant** drugs (also marketed under the trade names of norpramin and pertofrane). In addition to being used for depressive disorders, desipramine is known to be prescribed for a multitude of different diagnoses including **Post-Traumatic Stress Disorder,** trichotillomania, **Obsessive-Compulsive Disorder,** cocaine-related disorders, **Bulimia,** and **Panic Disorder.** For children and adolescents, the list of diagnoses for which desipramine is prescribed is expanded to include **Attention Deficit Hyperactivity Disorder, Enuresis,** and **Mood Disorders,** as well as those mentioned above. It is important to note, however, that despite the widespread use of desipramine (and other tricyclic antidepressants), their FDA approval for use in individuals younger than 12 years is limited to the treatment of **Enuresis.**

Available in 10 mg, 25 mg, 50 mg, 75 mg, 100 mg, and 150 mg tablets, initial dosages of desipramine for adolescents start low and eventually increase to somewhere between 25 and 100 mg per day. As is true for many of the other tricyclic antidepressants, it may take up to 3 weeks of treatment before positive effects are noticed. The potential negative side effects of desipramine are consistent with those of the other medications in this group. Please refer to the entry tricyclic antidepressants for a detailed discussion of these side effects in young people.

SUPPLEMENTAL RESOURCES

Breggin, P. (1991). *Toxic psychiatry.* New York: St. Martin's Press.

Maxmen, J. S., & Ward, N. (1996). *Psychotropic drugs: Fast facts.* New York: Norton.

Norden, M. J. (1996). *Beyond Prozac.* New York: HarperCollins.

Rosenberg, D. R., Holttum, J., & Gershon, S. (1994). *Textbook of pharmacotherapy for child and adolescent disorders.* New York: Brunner/Mazel.

Werry, J. S., & Aman, M. G. (1991). *Practitioner's guide to psychoactive drugs for children and adolescents.* New York: Plenum.

Developmental Arrest

Developmental arrest refers to the situation in which an infant, child, or adolescent does not mature in the manner in which one would normally expect. Specifically, the child's development in one or more areas does not proceed beyond a certain point to reach the expected level of development characteristic of most children. Rather, the development proceeds along and then ceases—it is arrested at a certain stage and does not continue to proceed. (As a means of contrast, it should be noted that it is not developmental arrest that typically occurs in cases of **Mental Retardation.** In such situations the individual's development will usually occur normally, however more slowly than normally expected.)

Developmental Disorders, Specific

Until the 1940s, specific developmental disorders (also referred to as developmental learning disorders) were considered to be virtually synonymous with **Mental Retardation.** Children who had severe academic problems were classified as being emotionally disturbed, socially or culturally disorganized, and/or mentally retarded. However in the mid-1940s, a new conceptualization was offered, based primarily on an **Etiological** approach.

In consideration of the possibility that these children might suffer from academic difficulty because of neurological impairments, these disorders were soon conceptualized as deriving from some form of brain damage. Thus, these children then came to be considered brain damaged, and diagnoses of *minimal brain damage* and, later, *minimal brain dysfunction* were applied. Subsequent classification schemes labeled these disorders in terms of the major skill deficits they presented. The most recent classifications use the term "learning disability," focusing on the specific academic deficits.

For further description of this diagnostic category, refer to the entry **Learning Disorders.**

Developmental Toxicity

Developmental toxicity refers to a problem that is potentially associated with the prescription of psychiatric medications to children and adolescents. Specifically, in some cases there can be a negative interaction between the drug and the progression of normal developmental process(es). In other words, the drug interferes with one or more processes of development, thereby impeding those processes. The extent to which any drug affects a young person in a developmentally toxic manner is variable. This depends upon the drug itself, the age of the child (both chronological and developmental), the dose of the drug, the dosing interval of the drug, and the manner in which the drug is metabolized by the body. In addition, there is considerable variation among individuals of the same age.

SUPPLEMENTARY RESOURCES

Werry, J. S., & Aman, M. G. (1991). *Practitioner's guide to psychoactive drugs for children and adolescents.* New York: Plenum.

Dexamethasone Suppression Test (DST)

The Dexamethasone Suppression Test is a psychiatric screening test designed to help diagnose cases of major depressive disorder. In addition to being used to assess possible cases of depression, the DST is also used to monitor a depressed person's response to treatment. Based on the premise that a malfunction of the hypothalamic-adrenal-pituitary axis is indicative of the individual experiencing stress, the procedure entails the individual being given dexamethasone by mouth with his or her plasma cortisol level then measured 8 hours, 16 hours and 23 hours later. Whereas a normal DST does not necessarily indicate an absence of clinical depression, the general consensus is that the DST is anywhere from 45 to 70% accurate in diagnosing cases of depression.

Dexedrine

This is one of the **Stimulant** medications that is approved for treatment of **Attention Deficit Disorder** as well as obesity in children over 3 years of age. Indeed, Dexedrine is currently the only amphetamine regularly used to treat attention deficit disorder, as well as the only stimulant medication that has approval for use in children as young as 3 years. Thus, for children younger than 6, it is considered to be the standard psychopharmacological intervention for attention deficit disorder.

Available in 5 mg orange-colored tablets as well as in sustained-release capsules (of 5, 10, and 15 mg dosages), Dexedrine is typically administered twice per day, with the initial dosages ranging from 2.5 mg daily (for younger children) to 5 mg daily (for older children). Dosages are slowly increased (titrated) until ideal levels have been reached, with the eventual maximum dose usually not exceeding 40 mg per day (for children 6 years and older). It is typically recommended that this drug be administered early in the morning (30 to 60 minutes prior to breakfast), with subsequent dosages at 4- to 6-hour intervals. The child should not take Dexedrine within 6 hours of bedtime, especially with the sustained acting formulas.

Side effects of Dexedrine are similar to those seen in other stimulants and are described in detail in the entry stimulants.

SUPPLEMENTARY RESOURCES

Johnston, H. (1990). *Stimulants and hyperactive children: A guide.* Lithium Information Center, University of Wisconsin, Department of Psychiatry.
Maxmen, J. S., & Ward, N. (1996). *Psychotropic drugs: Fast facts.* New York: Norton.

Werry, J. S., & Aman, M. G. (1991). *Practitioner's guide to psychoactive drugs for children and adolescents.* New York: Plenum.

Dextroamphetamine

This is the generic name for the psychostimulant marketed as **Dexedrine.**

Diagnostic Interview for Children and Adolescents

This is an assessment instrument that was designed originally for use as a research instrument. Able to be used for children and adolescents, it is composed of three sections. The first is a 19-question interview that is administered to the parent and child at the same time. The second component is given to the child alone and is composed of 247 items to which the child must respond. Finally, the third component of the Diagnostic Interview for Children and Adolescents is observational in nature, in which the child's actual behaviors and responses in certain situations are directly observed by the clinician.

Diaries

From middle childhood through the teenage years, diaries tend to be relatively popular with young people (more often females than males). Over the past several years, with the popularization of books designed for journalizing, the written recording of life experiences and feelings has become a common behavior for adults as well. Of course, the goals of the diaries kept, as well as the content within them, is largely determined by the developmental, psychological, and emotional level of the person writing.

For most preteens and teens, diaries serve as a medium through which they can express some feelings, and, equally as frequently, record the happenings of the day. The happenings recorded tend to be focused on interpersonal interactions between friends, and discussion of people to whom they feel some attraction. In addition, arguments and frustrations around interactions with parents also serve as popular subjects of the writings found in these diaries. Whereas the content that is actually recorded can appear trivial and silly to more mature readers, the process of being able to write of these happenings complete with the associated feelings serves an important function for the writer.

One of the major psychological functions served by diary keeping is that the writer feels as if he or she can express herself or himself without limitations imposed by the possibility of the writing being read by others. For that reason, it is important for parental figures to refrain from reading a diary except under only the most extreme of circumstances. While parents will indicate that they are tempted to read diaries in an attempt to know what their child is *really* feeling, or what the child is actually doing with friends, such behavior is often more troublesome than it is worth. First, if a parent feels as if reading the child's private writings is the only way he or she can be made aware of what the child is experiencing emotionally, there is certainly a problem in the parent/child relationship. Similarly, if the situation between parent and child is such that the only way the parent is comfortable with respect to the validity of his or her information about the child's activities is via reading the diary, again, this is indicative of problems that need to be addressed. Secondly, as indicated above, a major function served by this diary writing is feelings of freedom in being able to write confidentially. A parent reading the diary without the child's expressed approval not only removes that advantage of diary writing from the child, but, perhaps more significantly, wreaks havoc on feelings of trust in their relationship.

In sum, a child or adolescent keeping diaries and/or journalizing, in and of itself, tends to be a psychologically healthy experience. For those cases in which parents have serious concerns about what is written by the child/adolescent, this is more of a problem with the child/adolescent's overall behavior and/or the relationship with the parents than it is indicative of the behavior of writing itself. Intense curiosity or anxiety on the part of the parent with respect to what is contained in the child/adolescent's private writings should be taken as a sign of potentially more global problems in the behavior patterns of the child/adolescent and the relationship within the family, and, as such, should be addressed accordingly. In such cases, focusing merely on what is written in the diary or journal is an example of the proverbial missing of the forest for the trees.

Diazepam

Diazepam is the generic name for benzodiazepine valium. The reader is referred to the entry on **Valium** for a complete description.

Differential Diagnosis

This is a clinical concept utilized to refer to determining an accurate diagnosis in a particular situation. Specifically, the process of differential diagnosis is used to determine which (usually of two) different diagnoses is most applicable to a given clinical case. There are many psychological/psychiatric disorders that have similar symptoms. Indeed, there are some cases in which the symptoms of two different disorders are actually overlapping, and it is difficult to determine with certainty which of the two diagnoses would more appropriately apply. For example, a child can be observed to have difficulties paying attention and sitting still in class. Such a symptom profile, in and of itself, could be indicative of (at the very least) **Attention Deficit Disorder,** various **Anxiety Disorders, Depression,** and/ or a **Manic** or **Hypomanic** episode. Needless to say, such a situation has powerful treatment implications as well as more general implications for parental, school, and clinical management of the case.

For the above reasons, the issue of differential diagnosis is an important one. Thus, there are both formally documented as well as less formally acknowledged criteria that are used to distinguish between similarly appearing symptom profiles. Whenever relevant, the most commonly used diagnostic manual in the United States (the *DSM-IV*) provides criteria for differential diagnosis for its entries. It explains how to distinguish between different disorders in which there is symptom overlap, and what to look for in order to make the correct diagnostic decision. In addition, clinical experience as well has developed its own rules and norms to help resolve differential diagnostic concerns. Both the more formal differential diagnostic criteria delineated in diagnostic manuals as well as those based more upon clinical experience are delineated in this book as the specific diagnostic categories are described.

SUPPLEMENTAL RESOURCES

Hamstra, B. (1995). *How therapists diagnose.* New York: St. Martin's Press.

Differential Reinforcement of Other Behavior (DRO)

This is a method utilized in behavioral therapy approaches, typically employed to eliminate an undesirable behavior (or behavior pattern). Rather than working exclusively through the process of **Extinction** (refer to this entry below), DRO aims not to merely eliminate a target behavior, but to do so by reinforcing the occurrence/performance of an alternative (presumably more desirable) behavior. As with many principles in psychology, DRO is closely related to a commonly used process—that of addressing a problem behavior by distraction (i.e., showing the individual some other phenomenon to take his or her attention away from the behavior to be eliminated) rather than simple punishment.

It is important to note, however, that the process of DRO goes beyond distraction in that it incorporates the actual reinforcement of a more preferable behavior. Oftentimes, the nature of the behavior to be reinforced is such that it cannot be performed at the same time as the less desirable target behavior. Thus, as the preferred behavior is being reinforced (and the probability of it occurring is thereby increased), the target behavior is gradually being extinguished.

> *Example:* Five-year-old Tess, a child with moderate **Mental Retardation,** recently began exhibiting signs of trichotillomania (compulsive hair pulling). Over the past 6 weeks or so, whenever Tess is watching television or enjoying one of her favorite videos, she begins to compulsively pull out her eyebrows and eyelashes. Once her parents had discovered

the pattern of her behavior (i.e., that she does this only during television and video times), their family psychologist recommended the use of DRO. Tess has always enjoyed playing with *koosh* balls, specifically pulling on the rubberized prongs. Now, when Tess begins to settle in to watch television or a video, her parents provide her with one of her koosh toys, and encourage her to play with it. As long as Tess is occupied with her koosh, she is unable to pull at her eyelashes or eyebrows.

Example: Seventeen-year-old Brian behaves rather poorly at family social gatherings. Rather than interact with his cousins and older relatives, Brian typically isolates himself in a corner of the room and hides behind a magazine or newspaper that he finds around. Now, whenever Brian initiates or participates appropriately in a conversation at these gatherings, his parents subtly reinforce him verbally (so as not to embarrass him) in an attempt to replace the withdrawn behavior with more appropriate social interaction.

SUPPLEMENTARY RESOURCES

Hall, R. V., & Hall, M. C. (1980). *How to select reinforcers.* Austin, TX: ProEd.
Hall, R. V., & Hall, M. C. (1980). *How to use planned ignoring.* Austin, TX: ProEd.
Hall, R. V., & Hall, M. C. (1980). *How to use systematic attention and approval.* Austin, TX: ProEd.
Hall, R. V., & Hall, M. C. (1980). *How to use time out.* Austin, TX: ProEd.
Kazdin, A., & Dawson, K. E. (1980). *How to maintain behavior.* Austin, TX: ProEd.

Disorder of Written Expression

Disorder of written expression is one of the diagnoses under the more general category of Learning Disorders (previously referred to as **Academic Skill Disorders**). Formerly called developmental expressive writing disorder, this disorder is diagnosed when there are problems with writing abilities, specifically when the individual writing abilities are significantly lower than what would be expected considering the individual's age, developmental level, educational level, and/or IQ. As a result, this inability to write at the expected level interferes with the person's ability to function in academic, social, and (potentially) work settings.

Such a disorder usually is diagnosed around the second grade when the child is first asked to use writing in a substantial level in his or her school work. Common symptoms that initially alert the parents and/or teachers of a potential problem in this area include unusually poor or messy handwriting as well as difficulties composing grammatically correct sentences and paragraphs. Formalized assessment is typically used to confirm the presence of the disorder. Unfortunately, however, assessment instruments designed to specifically diagnose the presence of disorder of written expression are not as well developed as for the other learning disabilities. Thus, assessment often consists of comparing the individual's performance on certain tasks with what is expected from one at his/her developmental level. The performance is evaluated based upon multiple samples of the individual's spontaneous, creative writing as well as that from dictation. Symptoms of disorder of written expression are generally grouped into one of three categories: grammatical difficulties, phonological (sound) problems, and problems with visuospatial perception. The grammatical difficulties can involve the order of the words, incorrect omissions, additions or substitutions of pronouns, verbs, adverbs, prepositions, or any other type of word for the correct word. Phonological symptoms involve the transposition, omission or incorrect substitution of a sound or syllable. Finally, the third type of symptoms entail the deletion, inversion, substitution and/or substitution of letters in the individual's writing.

Treatment modalities for disorder of written expression usually assume one of two forms. In the first, the child is involved in an individualized program of writing instruction, the program focusing exclusively on the child's particular area of difficulty. The second type of treatment intervention entails the use of special provisions in the child/adolescent's classroom setting. Examples of such provisions include the assistance of note takers, use of laptop or notebook computers/typewriters, and altering the actual academic demands placed upon the child in an attempt to minimize the amount of writing required.

When to Seek Professional Help

Typically, the symptoms of disorder of written expression first become evident during the early elementary school years, when the child is first required to utilize writing to any significant degree in his or her work. Whereas the child's teacher is usually the one who brings the symptoms to the attention of the parents, there are indeed instances where the parents notice that their child's writing ability is not consistent with his or her ability in other areas. Or, in yet other circumstances, the parents recognize their child's avoidance of school assignments that involve writing.

For those cases in which the parents suspect the presence of one or more symptoms of disorder of written expression, they should contact the child's teacher and/or school psychologist. The teacher would be able to confirm if these symptoms are manifested in the school environment as well, and if so, the school psychologist would be able to perform a more thorough evaluation to assess if a diagnosis of disorder of written expression is indeed indicated.

SUPPLEMENTAL RESOURCES

Kaye, P. (1995). *Games for writing*. New York: Noonday Press.

Mandel, H. P., & Marcus, S. I. (1995). *Could do better*. New York: John Wiley.

McNamara, B. E., & McNamara, F. J. (1995). *Keys to parenting a child with a learning disability*. New York: Barrons.

Rosner, J. (1993). *Helping children overcome learning difficulties*. New York: Walker.

Smith, S. L. (1991). *Succeeding against the odds: How the learning disabled can realize their promise*. New York: Putnam.

Smith, S. L. (1995). *No easy answers: The learning disabled child at home and at school*. New York: Bantam.

Unger, H. G. (1998). *The learning disabilities trap*. Chicago: Contemporary Books.

Dissociation

This is a term describing the phenomenon wherein a single mental process (or group of mental processes) is somehow separated from the remainder of the person's psychological functioning. Occurring with this separation is the absence of the typical interrelationships between the separated mental process and the other aspects of psychological functioning. Involved aspects of psychological functioning usually include consciousness and/or identity. Early writings (from the mid-1930s) describe the dissociative process as follows:

> ...dissociation is the separation of the mind or consciousness by a splitting off of one (sometimes more) component or system of ideas, the personality or remainder of the mind being unable to exert any control over the split off portion. (Strecker & Ebaugh, 1935)

In children and adolescents, such a phenomenon is usually brought on by a traumatic event or the witnessing of such an event. The theory behind such an occurrence is that the individual observes something that is incredibly upsetting and, as a result, needs to psychologically protect himself or herself from the intense anxiety invoked by the trauma. Thus, the young person somehow psychologically dissociates, or separates, from the event by altering cognitive process so as to lessen the intensity of the impact of the event. Such mechanisms of dissociation range from the rather common "I'm not going to think about it" approach to the more extreme cases of actual amnesia for the event and/or assumption of a total change in identity or lifestyle. Such extreme examples of dissociation include cases of multiple personality, fugue state, **Depersonalization,** and **Dissociative Disorder.**

It is important to note, however, that the phenomenon of dissociation is observed not only in the traditional cases of the dissociative disorders, but also in other diagnostic categories as well. Specifically, it is not uncommon for dissociative symptoms to be observed in cases of **Post-Traumatic Stress Disorder,** as well as **Acute Stress Disorder.**

> *Example:* Thirteen-year-old Joyce had been sexually molested on a continuous basis by her uncle from the time she was 8 years old. Not only is Joyce unable to remember the actual incidents of abuse, but she reports not knowing her uncle and, at family gatherings, claims that this is a man she has never met.

> *Example:* Louie observed both of his parents being violently murdered in the family home. Although this horrible event occurred approximately 2 years ago, the 8-year-old child is still suffering the consequences. Although he is able to describe what happened in some detail, the child speaks of the event as if he were not involved as directly. Specifically, he tells the story and says "that wasn't me, though…it was another kid named Louie."

Example: When Jon was a young boy (from age 3 through 5 years), an elderly neighbor would repeatedly engage in oral sex with him. Now, at age 14, Jon complains of a total lack of feeling in his penis, experiencing complete numbness when he masturbates.

Dissociative Disorder

This term refers to a classification of disorders, all of which are characterized by **Dissociation** as their primary symptom. The *DSM-IV* includes the following diagnoses in this classification: dissociative amnesia (involving a sudden, intense loss of memory), dissociative fugue (involving sudden, unexpected traveling behavior often accompanied by a loss of memory for a major portion of the person's life), dissociative identity disorder (involving the presence of two or more identities in the same person), and depersonalization disorder (involving the sense of being separate from or apart from one's own self).

In 1993, the American Psychiatric Association published a diagnostic interview designed to detect the presence of symptoms of one or more of the dissociative disorders. This instrument, called the Structured Clinical Interview for *DSM-IV* Dissociative Disorders (abbreviated SCID-D), provides the opportunity for the clinician to rate the patient in terms of the presence/severity of the five major dissociative symptoms (corresponding to the major diagnostic categories of dissociative disorders):

Amnesia: Loss of memory for some portion of what has transpired in the past.

> *Example:* The Peterson family lost all of their belongings in a seriously destructive house fire. Although 12-year-old Caitlin was the member of the family who first noticed the fire and warned the rest of the family, she cannot remember any details of the incident. Further, she reports that the only way she knows that a fire did indeed occur is that her belongings are gone and that others have told her about the incident.

Depersonalization: Feeling of separation from one's own self, experiencing one's body as not being one's own, feeling of being unreal, feeling of being an outsider observing oneself.

> *Example:* Eleven-year-old Amanda talks about being in school, but feeling as if she is not really there. Specifically, she describes the sensation of feeling as if she is watching herself go through the motions of participating in school activities, but not really feeling as if she herself is involved. Amanda reports, "It's almost as if I'm not really me."

Derealization: feeling of separation from the people and things in one's environment.

Example: Fifteen-year-old Phyllis reports experiencing her home (where she has lived since she was born) as a strange place. She says that things don't seem the same, and at times she feels as if people have come in and changed everything so that nothing is the same as she remembered it.

Identity confusion: The feeling of not knowing who one is.

Example: Ten-year-old Lester repeatedly walks around, confused and anxious, repeating "I don't know who I am."

Identity alteration: A sense of major change in the way one thinks about oneself, often to the degree of assuming one or more alternate identities.

Example: At times, 18-year-old Andrea will speak in a totally different voice and assume a different personality and demeanor. When she does this, she does not respond to her name and insists that she be called Genevieve.

Divorce

The psychological and emotional impact upon parents who are engaged in the divorce or separation process is incredibly intense, to say the least. As a result, the adults' ability to attend to their children's psychological needs can easily become compromised. Indeed, this is through no fault of the parents, but, rather a basic fact of the human condition—that it's difficult to take care of someone else emotionally when you are feeling extremely needy in that area yourself. The major focus of this entry, then, is not to provide pessimistic statistics about the viability of marriage or what to do to maintain a marriage's longevity. Rather, the information here is designed as a guide or checklist to help the divorcing parent through common difficult parenting issues at this time in their life.

Several important points are to be emphasized (and reemphasized) when informing the child about the parents' decision to divorce. If at all possible, it is optimal for both parents to be involved in this initial discussion so that the child recognizes that despite the marital separation, there is not to be a separation in parenting. The following guidelines provide suggestions in addressing certain points—suggestions that will help ease the journey on the sometimes rocky road along which this initial conversation often travels.

Cause of the divorce: Repeatedly emphasize that in no way did the child, or anything the child did, play a role in the decision to divorce. Point out that the decision to separate has to do with the parents deciding it would be better if they lived separately, that they have had trouble getting along (ask the child if he or she has noticed), that the marriage is no longer working, and so on. The crucial issue here is that the child is given an explanation consistent with her or his understanding and that he or she in no way feels responsible for the situation.

Parenting issues: The child needs to be informed/reminded that both of the parents will remain active in the parenting process. Emphasize that the child will be seeing both parents on a regular basis (especially the one who will not be living with the child) and explain the arrangements for telephone and face-to-face contact. Do whatever is possible to convince the child that he or she is not being divorced.

Both during the process of divorce and after the divorce is taking place, it is likely that parents will be faced with further, more detailed questions from the child. In responding to these queries, two factors are to be utilized as guiding principles. First, questions are to be answered in a manner consistent with the child's understanding. The child's comprehension of the answers needs to be checked often, as a child will act as if he or she understands, but in reality does not. Second, the parent needs to remember that it is perfectly appropriate to not answer certain questions. Parents are to recognize that it is all right to tell a child that a particular question deals with an adult issue and therefore will not be answered at this time. Finally, it is also acceptable, when relevant, to respond to a child's question with a simple "I don't know."

As this emotionally trying process moves along, it is common for one or both parents to feel lonely, isolated, and so forth. After all, one of the primary adult confidantes in the parent's life is gone, and despite the anger and hostility, there is bound to be an empty feeling in one's heart. Although such feelings may get quite intense at times, it should be remembered that your child is a child—not your best friend. Maintain a parent–child relationship. There will be a natural tendency (on the part of parent and child alike since both have lost an important relationship) to use each other as a substitute for the other parent.

Child as confidante: It is easy to fall into the trap of telling the child all the ins and outs of the divorce process. To whom else is the parent closer, after all, and shouldn't the child know the truth? Whereas the answers to these questions are certainly in the affirmative, there needs to be definitive boundaries in terms of what is shared between parent and child. Informing the child of every misdeed committed by the other parent serves no valid purpose. Further, it confuses the child even more (Why would mom/dad do that to mom/dad? Why would mom/dad say that about mom/dad?). Also, as is true with many aspects of the parenting process, although the child is entitled to truthful information, some things are indeed better left unsaid. Toward these ends, parents need to be alert to any indication that they are violating the boundaries of the parent–child relationship by treating it more like a friendship among equals.

Mother as father/father as mother: All too commonly, the primary custodial parent (out of feelings of guilt and anger, among other things) tries to compensate for the perceived separation from the other parent. In so doing, the primary custodial parent attempts to assume both parental roles, in most cases ineffectually. Although the motivation is typically positive, it is not advised for any parent to attempt to be both mother and father. The forced quality of such behavior is perceived by the child, resulting in confusion, anxiety (about yet another change at home), and a decrease in general parenting efficacy.

More so than in other cases, situations involving divorce are so highly individualized that no two cases can be commented upon with the same generalities. The issues addressed above, however, do tend to surface with some regularity. The Supplementary Resources below provide referrals to other commonly encountered dilemmas.

SUPPLEMENTARY RESOURCES

Deutsch, F. M. (1999). *Halving it all: How equally shared parenting works.* Cambridge, MA: Harvard University Press.

Garndner, R. A. (1991). *The parents book about divorce.* Cresskill, NJ: Creative Therapeutics.

Girard, J. W. (1987). *At Daddy's on Saturdays.* Morton Grove, IL: Albert Whitman.

Ross, J. A., & Corcan, J. (1996). *Joint custody with a jerk.* New York: St. Martin's.

Royko, D. (1999). *Voices of children of divorce.* New York: Golden Books.

Shulman, D. (1996). *Coparenting after divorce.* Sherman Oaks, CA: Winnspeed Press.

Stern, Z., & Stern, E. (1997). *Divorce is not the end of the world—Zoe and Evans coping guide for kids.* Berkeley, CA: Tricycle Press.

Stinson, K. (1984). *Mom and dad don't live together anymore.* Buffalo, NY: Firefly Books.

Sullivan, S. A. (1992). *The father's almanac.* New York: Doubleday.

Thomas, S. (1997). *Parents are forever: A step by step guide to becoming coparents after divorce.* Longmont, CA: Springboard.

Thomas, S., & Rankin, D. (1998). *Divorced but still my parents: A helping book about divorce for children and parents.* Longmont, CA: Springboard Publications.

Wolf, A. E. (1998). *Why did you have to get a divorce and when can I get a hamster: A parent's guide to parenting through divorce.* New York: Nonnday Press.

Draw a Person Test

This is a projective assessment instrument that was originated in the early 1950s. Still used today, the Draw a Person Test is one of the most commonly used projective instruments in clinical practice, especially with children and young people. Extremely simple in its delivery, it involves asking the person being tested to "draw a person." Following the completion of the drawing of the initial figure, the individual is next instructed to draw a person of the opposite gender (to the original drawing). Based upon the size of the components of the drawing, the order in which different parts of the drawings are actually completed, the amount of slanting and overall shading, the clinician is able to propose various hypotheses about the personality dynamics of the subject.

Whereas the actual conclusions drawn and hypotheses proposed based upon the drawings depend upon the scoring system utilized, there are certain basic relationships of drawing to personality dynamics to which most clinicians who utilize this test adhere. For example, disproportionately large hands represent a tendency toward acting out behaviors while short arms are interpreted as a tendency to inhibit impulses. Similarly, a small figure is correlated with insecurity and/or depression, whereas large figures are usually interpreted as representing expansiveness. Further, the gender of the drawings is also considered to be clinically significant. In the large majority of cases, when asked to "draw a person," the individual first draws a human figure of the same gender. For example, when a figure of the opposite gender is drawn first, the clinician investigates further into possible concerns about **Gender Identity** issues.

A variation of the Draw a Person Test is the equally popular *House Tree Person* test. Also a projective instrument, this test instructs the child/adolescent to draw a house, then a tree and then a person. Similar to the interpretive style utilized in the Draw a Person Test, in the House Tree Person Test various characteristics of each of the drawings are examined and analyzed yielding hypotheses about the individual's personality. For example, the presence and/or number of windows on the house, the manner in which the trunk of the tree is depicted, as well as the placement of the drawings on the sheet of paper are all believed to have interpretive significance.

SUPPLEMENTAL RESOURCES

Gardner, H. (1980). *Artful scribbles: The significance of children's drawings.* New York: Basic Books.
Oster, G. D., & Gould, P. (1987). *Using drawings in assessment and therapy: A guide for mental health professionals.* New York: Brunner/Mazel.

DSM

This is an abbreviation or an acronym for the *Diagnostic and Statistical Manual.* Now in its fourth major edition (referred to as the *DSM-IV),* the *DSM* serves as the primary source for diagnostic information on psychiatric/psychological disorders in the United States. This manual contains descriptions and diagnostic criteria for all of the psychological/psychiatric disorders. In addition, when relevant, it indicates how the clinical presentation of the disorder varies as a function of developmental level. Information on **Differential Diagnosis** is also provided when relevant. Designed to be used with a multiaxial format, the *DSM-IV* has provisions for every patient to receive a diagnosis along five major axes: Axis I: clinical disorders and other conditions that may be a focus of clinical attention; Axis II: personality disorders, mental retardation; Axis III: general medical conditions; Axis IV: psychosocial and environmental problems; and Axis V: global assessment of functioning.

Each individual diagnosis is given a numerical code, usually a three-digit number with two digits to the right of the decimal point (taking the form of XXX.XX). The different diagnoses are grouped according to the following major categories: disorders usually first diagnosed in infancy, childhood or adolescence; delirium, dementia, and amnestic and other cognitive disorders; mental disorders due to a general medical condition not elsewhere classified; substance-related disorders; schizophrenia and other psychotic disorders; mood disorders; anxiety disorders; somatoform disorders; factitious disorders; dissociative disorders; sexual and gender identity disorders; eating disorders; sleep disorders; impulse-control disorders not elsewhere classified; adjustment disorders; personality disorders; and other factors that may be a focus of clinical attention.

S U P P L E M E N T A L   R E S O U R C E S

Barron, J. W. (Ed.). (1998). *Making diagnosis meaningful: Enhancing evaluation and treatment of psychological disorders.* Washington, DC: American Psychological Association.

Hamstra, B. (1995). *How therapists diagnose.* New York: St. Martin's Press.

LaBruzza, A. L., & Mendez-Villarrubia, J. M. (1994). *Using DSM-IV: A clinician's guide to psychiatric diagnosis.* Northvale, NJ: Jason Aronson.

Rapoport, J. L., & Ismond, D. R. (1996). *DSM-IV training guide for diagnosis of childhood disorders.* New York: Brunner/Mazel.

Reid, W. H., & Wise, M. G. (1995). *DSM-IV training guide.* New York: Brunner/Mazel.

DSM-PC

This is an acronym for the *Diagnostic and Statistical Manual for Primary Care (DSM-PC) Child and Adolescent Version,* a publication designed to make the **DSM** more useful and more user friendly for practitioners. Published by the American Psychiatric Association (the publishers of the *DSM*), it was composed by child psychologists, pediatricians, as well as child psychiatrists. Not only does it provide information about diagnoses, but it supplements the material in the *DSM* with information on parental concerns, **Psychosocial Issues,** managed care, and how to make appropriate referrals to mental health professionals, when necessary.

S U P P L E M E N T A L   R E S O U R C E S

Please refer to resources under the *DSM* entry.

Dysphoria

This is a rather general, generic term to refer to a state of unhappiness, sadness, feeling ill at ease. Dysphoria (or dysphoric affect) incorporates full-blown depressive disorders as well as the less severe **Dysthymic Disorders.** In addition, dysphoria is also used to describe the mood of individuals who are angry/irritable as well as those who are noticeably anxious.

Dysthymic Disorder

Dysthymic disorder is one of the mood disorders in which the individual manifests symptoms similar to those in depression, however, these symptoms are not as severe. The *DSM-IV* defines the person with dysthymic disorder as characterized by a depressed or irritable mood during the majority of the day ("for more days than not") for at least a one-year period. Two or more of the following symptoms are present in dysthymic disorder: disturbance in eating patterns; disturbance in sleeping pattern; low energy or fatigue; low self-esteem; poor concentration and/or difficulty making decisions; feelings of hopelessness. Further, in order for dysthymic disorder to be diagnosed in children and adolescents, the individual could never have been without these symptoms for more than 2 months at any given time. As one would expect, the symptoms of dysthymic disorder impact significantly on the child/adolescent's ability to achieve optimal functioning in school, family, and other interpersonal situations.

A major distinction between dysthymic disorder and major depressive disorder is that dysthymic disorder tends to be more characterological, more a part of the individual's personality. Indeed, dysthymic disorder can be conceptualized as an approach to life, a demeanor, a way of being. Children and adolescents with dysthymic disorder are described by those around them as seeming to never be happy. Whereas depressed young people have symptoms that are can usually be identified as beginning (and hopefully ending) at a prescribed point in time, those with dysthymic disorder are usually perceived as "always having been this way." It is possible, however, when dysthymic disorder has been present in a child or adolescent for one year, for a major depressive episode to subsequently develop.

When to Seek Professional Help

Similar to cases of depressive disorder, if a parent observes any combination of the above symptoms in his or her child for any period of time, and these symptoms cannot be linked to a specific environmental event, it is recommended that the child be evaluated by a mental health professional. Since dysthymic disorder tends to be more characterological in nature, it can be more resistant to treatment than the depressive disorders. For that reason, then, it is important that treatment be sought as early on in the progress of the disorder as possible.

Questions to Ask the Clinician

- Is my child/adolescent depressed or is this a case dysthymic disorder?
- What factors did you use in coming to the above conclusion?
- Would medication be helpful in the treatment?
- What type of therapeutic approach do you feel would be most useful?
- How is the family supposed to react when my child/adolescent acts in a symptomatic manner? Should we try to talk him or her out of it, or would it be better for us to try to ignore such behavior?

- When can we expect to see some improvement in symptoms, and what type of changes can we expect to observe initially?
- To what extent will the parents and other family members be involved in the therapeutic process?

Example: Nine-year-old Alton has been having problems with his schoolwork lately. Previously an honor student in his early years, he has been barely passing since the second half of last year. When asked about this change, all Alton can say is that he has a difficult time concentrating and paying attention. In addition, the school guidance counselor reports that Alton has become quite withdrawn and isolated from his peers. Previously one of the more popular boys in his grade, he now tends to sit by himself during free periods, and becomes irritable when approached by other children.

E | Eating Disorders–Extrapyramidal Side Effects

Eating Disorders

Eating disorders is a diagnostic classification in the current edition of the *DSM* (*DSM-IV*) that includes the disorders of **Anorexia Nervosa, Bulimia,** and eating disorder not otherwise specified (NOS). For descriptions of anorexia nervosa and bulimia, the reader is referred to those entries. Eating disorder NOS refers to any form of irregular eating behavior that causes the individual clinically significant distresss, yet does not meet the diagnostic criteria of anorexia nervosa or bulimia. However, it is not at all uncommon for individuals diagnosed with eating disorder NOS to exhibit symptoms similar to those seen in anorexia or bulimia. For example, binging, purging, excessive fasting, and so forth can be manifested in a given individual without the individual showing all of the symptoms of some other eating disorder. In such cases, a diagnosis of eating disorder NOS is applied.

Echolalia

Echolalia refers to the imitating or repeating of the speech of others. In echolalia, the individual will repeat the syllable, word, phrase, or even sentence recently heard spoken (even if it was not spoken to him or her directly). Whereas this is most commonly considered to be a symptom of some type of **Schizophrenia** or **Psychotic Disorder,** it is important to note that elementary-aged school children often find exhibiting the echolalia like behavior most entertaining, especially when those around them find it most obnoxious! Thus, when evaluating the clinical implication of echolalia-like symptoms in children and preadolescent, it is crucial not to overpathologize typical childlike attempts at annoyance or attribute undue clinical significance to it. In sum, if the child does not exhibit any other symptoms characteristic of a schizophrenic or psychotic process, it is probably safe to assume that the echolalia does not warrant clinical concern.

> *Example:* Six-year-old Nan and her friends are having some behavioral problems in their first-grade class. Apparently, they have gotten into the

habit of repeating the last two words of every sentence their teacher says. This results in distracting the rest of the class, causing an outbreak of laughter in the classroom, and generally disrupting the learning process.

Echopraxia

Usually a symptom of **Catatonic Schizophrenia,** echopraxia refers to the symptom in which the person imitates or mirrors the movements of another person, and does so repeatedly.

Elavil

Elavil is the trade name for the **Antidepressant** drug **Amitriptyline.** Please refer to the entry amitriptyline for information.

Electra Complex/Conflict

This is a concept that originated in the psychoanalytic theories of **Sigmund Freud.** Closely related to the **Oedipal Complex,** the Electra Complex refers to the phenomenon wherein a female child experiences some variation of romantic feelings toward her father. Although the original conceptualization of the Electra Complex focused on sexually based feelings, the concept has been expanded to incorporate any form of romantic or intimate feelings experienced by a daughter toward a paternal male figure (i.e., not always the father).

Occurring during the Freudian phallic stage of development, the Electra Complex typically occurs somewhere around 3 and 6 years of age. During this time, the young girl struggles with conflicts around her feelings toward both of her parents. The theory explains that, although the child is close with her mother, the positive feelings are tempered by jealous feelings deriving from the child's budding romantic feelings toward her father. As the child begins to experience romantic or otherwise intimate feelings toward her father, she views her mother as a rival for the father's affections—oftentimes perceiving the mother as achieving the type of relationship with the father that she is unable to have. Typically, this results in the expression of some form of negativity (of varying intensity) toward the mother, as well as some seemingly inappropriate positive feelings (again to varying intensities) toward the father. Even though the majority of clinicians and developmental theorists do not adhere to Freudian theory unconditionally, most do acknowledge the universality of the experience of the Electra Conflict as a normal developmental milestone.

Example: Six-year-old Jennifer has recently become rather "mouthy" and defiant with her mother. Whenever her mother asks her to do something, or tries to reinforce some limits with Jennifer, the child puts up an argument. At times, the argument reaches the point of a full-blown temper tantrum. In addition, Jennifer's behavior toward her father has also changed. Although previously able to be characterized as "Mommy's little girl," Jennifer now makes "I Love You" cards and presents for her father almost every day. On family outings, she insists on sitting next to her father, and, whenever he is around, she wants her father (as opposed to her mother) to help her with various tasks.

Encopresis

Encopresis refers to the repeated (voluntary or involuntary) passing of feces into places considered to be inappropriate. For some individuals, the disorder is due to constipation that results in what is called *overflow incontinence,* yielding the inappropriate behavior with bowel movements. However, in other situations, there is no medical evidence of constipation or a history thereof. Within both of these groups, there are two types of encopresis: **Primary** encopresis, in which the individual has never manifested adequate control of his/her bowel movements; and **Secondary** encopresis, in which the individual has demonstrated the ability to control his or her bowel movements for at least one year, but has then regressed. Research indicates that approximately half of the cases of encopresis are primary, and half are secondary.

The actual symptoms of encopresis can be variable. In some cases, a child who is perfectly able to control his or her bowel movements deliberately expels or places feces in inappropriate locations. In such situations, the encopresis is best conceptualized as means of expressing anger, frustration, rebellion, and/or stress. More often than not, these feelings are relevant to some aspect of the family dynamics. Thus, it is recommended that the family unit be examined in terms of recent changes or upheavals that may be impacting upon the child/adolescent. In such situations, identifying these issues, discussing them with the child, and then making necessary modifications will impact upon the encopresis.

> *Example:* Over the past 6 months or so, 8-year-old Jeff has been having bowel movements in inappropriate places. Specifically, the fecal matter shows up in his mother's bedroom closet, or in the corner of his mother's bathroom. When confronted with this behavior, Jeff admits to doing this, however manifests little if any remorse. As a matter of fact, he typically storms away from his mother, stomps up the stairs, and remains in his bedroom for several hours after he has been accused. It is especially significant that Jeff's encopresis began soon after his parents were separated and his father moved out of the house. Indeed, during arguments, Jeff frequently accuses his mother of chasing his father out of the family.

In other cases of encopresis, the child actually has no or very limited control of his or her bowel movements. Such cases can usually be distinguished from those described in the previous paragraphs as, in this group, the individual typically manifests intense shame and embarrassment regarding the symptoms. He or she will try to deny the fact that this inappropriate voiding is occurring, may try to blame other family members, and may hide, wash, or otherwise destroy soiled clothing in an attempt to eliminate any evidence. Clearly, from a clinical perspective, such a situation presents a rather different situation from the child who is attempting to express some negative feelings via the encopretic behavior.

When to Seek Professional Help

One of the first (and most important) tasks in seeking help for encopresis is the determination of the cause of the symptoms. In addition to having a physical examination to assess if the source of encopretic behavior is predominantly medical or psychological, it similarly needs to be determined whether the encopresis is the primary disorder, or if it is a secondary symptom of another psychological disorder. For example, children/adolescents who have been diagnosed with **Mental Retardation, Attention Deficit Disorder, Oppositional Defiant Disorder,** various **Anxiety Disorders, Psychotic Disorders,** and **Mood Disorders** have been known to exhibit encopresis. In these cases, however, the encopresis is secondary (i.e., is a result of) to the other diagnosis. As such, it is the main diagnosis that needs to be treated prior to addressing the encopretic symptoms.

Assuming that a thorough medical examination has revealed the primary cause of the encopresis to be psychological, the parent should be prepared to provide the following information to the clinician at the initial appointment:

- When were the symptoms of encopresis first noticed?
- What is the best estimate as to when they actually began?
- How long has the child been completely toilet trained?
- Were there any unusual occurrences during the first toilet training period?
- How often do the symptoms of encopresis occur?
- What is the child/adolescent's attitude toward the encopresis?
- How have the parents and other family members reacted to the encopresis?
- Have there been any significant family events within the recent past?
- Have you noticed any other changes in the child within the recent past?
- What types of interventions have been tried to stop the encopresis?

Questions to Ask the Treating Clinician

- Is the encopresis the major disorder, or is it secondary to another diagnosis?
- If it is secondary, what is the primary diagnosis?
- Will the treatment be primarily individual, or do you plan on involving other family members?
- What type of therapeutic approach will you be using?
- During the early phases of treatment, what types of changes can be expected (positive and negative)?
- When would it be reasonable to expect to see some improvement?

- How should the rest of the family react when inappropriate bowel movement is discovered?
- What can be done at home to speed up the treatment process?

Endep

This is a brand name of the **Tricyclic Antidepressant Amitriptyline.** This drug is also marketed as **Elavil.** Please refer to these entries for a more detailed description of this drug.

Enuresis

Enuresis is the term used to describe the repeated (involuntary or intentional) discharge of urine in inappropriate places by an individual who would be expected to have control of his or her urinary output. In approximately 80% of the cases, the enuresis is classified as **Primary,** in that the child/adolescent has never had a consistent pattern of long-term urinary control. The remaining cases are classified as **Secondary,** in that the child/adolescent has had periods of being symptom free for at least 6 months, and then resumed the enuresis. Yet another means of classifying the enuresis is by the time of day at which the inappropriate urination occurs. In *nocturnal enuresis* (the most common variation), the enuresis occurs only at night while in *diurnal enuresis,* the symptoms occur only during the daytime. Of course, some children/adolescents have symptoms of enuresis in both the daytime and night hours. Enuresis, especially nocturnal enuresis, is surprisingly common. Indeed, it is estimated that 25% of boys (of all ages) experience some form of nocturnal enuresis at some point in their life. The frequency decreases with age, as by age 10, the estimate goes down to 3% for boys and 2% for girls.

As with the diagnosis of **Encopresis,** appropriate treatment depends upon the actual cause of the disorder. Without a doubt, a thorough medical examination should precede the initiation of any psychological treatment regimen, to rule out any possible medical factors. Similarly, if the symptoms of enuresis are actually secondary to some other psychological problem/disorder, it is important to address the primary issues first. Indeed, for each individual case, it must be determined if the enuresis is a result of psychological difficulties, or is actually the cause of them! Generally, treatment for enuresis itself entails behavioral therapies, psychopharmacological (drug) interventions, family therapy, or (most often) some combination of the three.

The drug therapies for enuresis primarily involve the use of the drug **Imipramine (Tofranil).** This antidepressant was first used in the treatment of enuresis some 30 years ago, and, research reports that it is effective for approximately 50% of the cases. In addition, the antienuretic effect of Imipramine tends to occur rather rapidly. However, its efficacy is certainly not complete in that it is known to be rather short lived, and certainly not permanent. Further, one must consider the possibility of side effects with the use of Imipramine, the most common ones being anxiety, a general nervousness, sleep problems, and some gastrointestinal problems. Also, Imipramine is not recommended for the treatment of enuresis in children under the age of 6 years. Other **Antidepressants** that are used (albeit less commonly) in the treatment of enuresis include **Clomipramine (Anafranil)** and **Desipramine (Norpramin).** Finally, it should be noted that some physicians will prescribe **Diazepam** (valium) as a treatment for enuresis when the antidepressants are ineffective, or for some reason are not tolerated (Green, 1995).

Regardless of the choice of drug therapy employed for enuresis, it is generally acknowledged (primarily because of the short-lived nature of the effects as well as concern about potential negative side effects of the medications) that drug therapy is best used (if used at all) in conjunction with some form of behavioral treatment. The majority of these psychologically oriented treatments involve the entire family, and, generally, they fall into one of two categories: (1) **Urine Alarm Training** and (2) retention control procedures. Urine Alarm training was first introduced (as the bell and pad technique) in the 1930s, and continues to be utilized today as a component of various different treatment regimes for enuresis. It involves a moisture-sensitive device that sounds an alarm as soon as the child begins to wet the bed. Retention-control procedures are based on the premise that individuals with enuresis have an impaired ability to retain urine. Thus, the procedure entails daily practice in which the child ingests large amounts of fluid and practices retaining the urine for increasingly longer periods of time. Although not especially effective as a single-treatment modality, retention-control procedures are often useful adjuncts to other behavioral methods.

SUPPLEMENTAL RESOURCES

Arnold, S. (1997). *No more bedwetting.* New York: John Wiley.
Houts, A. C. (1990). *Bedwetting: A guide for parents and children.* Boston: C. C. Thomas.
Mills, J. C. (1989). *Sammy the elephant and Mr. Camel.* Washington, DC: American Psychological Association.
Mack, A. (1989). *Dry all night: The picture book technique that stops bedwetting.* Boston: Little, Brown.
Schaefer, C. E., & Digeronimo, T. F. (1997). *Toilet training without tears.* New York: Putnam.

Erections

Erection of the penis represents the observable manifestation of sexual excitement or sexual arousal in males. Typically occurring a very short time after the actual sexual stimulation is initiated, erections result from the tissues of the penis rapidly filling with blood (referred to as *vasocongestion*). As a result, the erect penis appears to be larger and more firm than the penis would typically appear in its flaccid state. However, it is certainly possible for a male to be sexually aroused without the presence of an erection.

The process of erection begins early in life, with studies indicating that infant boys experience erections several months prior to birth, as well as then even in the first few moments following birth. Similarly, it is common for infant boys to have erections while they are nursing—seemingly responding to the feeling of being held close and cuddled. Further, it is not at all uncommon for an infant to have an erection when playing with his genitals. Thus, it is not surprising then that by the time a little boy is 2 or 3 years old he is able to articulate the connection between manipulation of his penis, positive feelings, and the erectile response. By the middle of the eleventh year, most boys begin to experience noticeable growth in their genitals. Whereas the speed with which this development proceeds varies, most boys have genitals of adult size and shape by the time they are 15 years of age.

The manner in which the parents respond to the child/adolescent's discovery of his erectile capabilities is crucial in setting the stage for the young person's subsequent sexual behavior and overall attitudes toward his own sexuality. From a very early age, a child is sensitive to parental reaction, and becomes especially sensitive when he is looking for guidance as to the normalcy and/or direction of his own reactions. Thus, while parents need to convey their own feelings regarding the morality of genital stimulation as well as to when and where it is appropriate, privacy issues, and so forth, it is also important that the parents communicate the fact that the body is not dirty or vulgar, and that when evoked in the appropriate context (i.e., to be determined by the value system of the parents), neither is the erectile response. In sum, messages given to the child by the parents around this issue should be couched in terms of appropriateness (thereby educating within the context of parental values) rather than in terms of right and wrong (thereby imposing messages of guilt and punishment).

SUPPLEMENTARY RESOURCES

Madaras, L. (1988). *The what's happening to my body book for boys.* New York: New Market.

Erikson, E.

Erik Erikson (1902–1994) was a psychoanalyst who specialized in working with children and young people. Studying under the tutelage of **Anna Freud,** Erikson was considered to be unique for his era in his application of psychoanalytic principles to children. Although he wrote various famous works (including *Gandhi's Truth, Insight and Responsibility, Identity: Youth and Crisis,* and *Young Man Luther),* he is perhaps best known for his book *Childhood and Society,* in which he proposed the eight stages of the human life cycle. Erikson conceptualized each of the eight stages in terms of a specific conflict triggered by the physical and psychological changes characteristic of the specific age. According to Erikson, it is the resolution of the conflict at each given age level that results in growth, moral development, and the consequent ability to move on to confront the conflicts of the subsequent stages of life. In contrast, the inability to resolve one or more of the conflicts characteristic of any of the given stages results in psychological problems and overall maladjustment (to various degrees). Those stages along with their associated conflicts are as follows:

1. Trust versus mistrust   Birth–18 months
2. Autonomy versus shame and doubt   18 months–3 years
3. Initiative versus guilt   3 years–5 years
4. Industry versus inferiority   5 years–13 years
5. Identity versus identity confusion   13 years–21 years
6. Intimacy versus isolation   21 years–40 years
7. Generativity versus stagnation   40 years–60 years
8. Integrity versus despair   60 years–death

SUPPLEMENTAL RESOURCES

Coles, R. (1970). *Erik H. Erikson: The growth of his work.* Boston: Little, Brown.
Evans, R. (1967). *Dialogue with Erik Erikson.* New York: Harper & Row.
Schein, S. (Ed.). (1987). *Erik Erikson: A way of looking at things.* New York: Norton.

Etiology

This term refers to the cause or causes of a given illness, behavior, or diagnosis. More often than not, the manner in which the etiology is conceptualized is crucial in determining the type of treatment that is employed. For the most part, theories about the etiology of a given psychological/psychiatric disorder can be divided into two major categories: (1) those that promote biological factors as the primary cause, and (2) those that promote more psychological issues as the primary cause.

Theories of etiology that fall into the first category include those that explain the problem by neurological, biochemical, or structural abnormalities. Indeed, the multitude of "chemical imbalance" theories so popular in our culture over the past few years are prime examples of physiologically based theories of etiology. (In addition, those approaches that look to contributions of genetics and heredity as primary explanations for various disorders can also be classified as biological. However, most practitioners believe that the majority of behaviors actually represent an interaction between genetic and environmental factors.)

Approaches to etiology that are more psychological in character place less of an emphasis on the biological workings of the organism in question and, instead, focus more on environmental factors. Such factors could include anything and everything from the manner in which the child was parented as an infant, to the stressors the child has experienced or is currently experiencing, to what behaviors he or she was inadvertently reinforced for, to the particular psychological stage of development, to the pattern of interaction/communication within the family unit.

As indicated above, the manner in which the etiology of a symptom or a disorder is conceptualized has significant implications for the manner in which it is treated. For example, one would not bring a child for psychotherapy if it was believed that the target symptoms were due to a chemical imbalance. Similarly, one would not consult a psychiatrist for medication if it was believed that the symptoms to be treated were due to an inconsistent parenting style. Although it may seem trivial to some, the impact of beliefs about etiology cannot be overemphasized as, for the majority of the psychological problems of children and adolescents, there is no universal belief about the nature of the causal factors. Specifically, diagnoses involving anxiety, hyperactivity, **Attention Deficit,** and **Depression** are among the disorders that currently emit the most controversy in terms of etiological theory and their impact on treatment modality.

Exchange of Information

This phrase refers to the sharing of information regarding what has transpired in a therapy session and/or in psychological treatment. Whereas such information is certainly to be considered confidential, there are indeed situations in which it may be appropriate to convey all or some portion of this information to individuals who are not directly involved in the therapeutic process. For example, exchange of information commonly occurs between/among various clinicians, different family members, school personnel, legal professionals, and so forth.

In the majority of cases involving adult patients, this sharing of information is contingent upon a written consent from the patient to do so. That is to say, should a patient desire any aspect of his or her clinical treatment be shared with another, a written consent indicating this wish is given to the treating professional, who, in turn, then is responsible for ensuring that the specified information gets conveyed to the designated party. Although the treating clinician may, at times, provide input as to his or her feelings as to the clinical appropriateness of sharing the information, for the most part, the decision to share portions of the clinical file—or the file in its entirety—belongs to the patient.

Needless to say, the issue as to whether to exchange clinical information is considerably different when dealing with children/adolescents. Age and/or developmental level often preclude the patient from being able to make an informed decision as to the appropriateness of sharing information from the clinical file. Similarly, the clinical issues specific to the treatment of adolescents further complicate issues of sharing clinical information. Concerns with respect to trust and betrayal also influence decisions whether to exchange information from the patient's file with another professional or family member.

Although one cannot depend upon the child or adolescent in every case to make an informed decision that would be in his or her best interest, there are indeed situations in which the parents are not the optimal individuals upon whom to depend to make a decision in the child/adolescent's best interest. Examples of such situations include those in which there are questions of child abuse and/or custody disputes in which one or both parents have their own agendas that may compromise their making decisions in the best interest of the child/adolescent. It is in cases of this nature that the judgment of the clinician working with the young person comes into play. Specifically, the Ethical Principles of the American Psychological Association (which are intended to guide the professional behavior of all practicing psychologists) state that, when working with an individual who is too young, or at a developmental level that precludes his or her being able to make informed decisions about treatment, it is incumbent upon the treating psychologist to act in the individual's best interest. This principle, while certainly relevant to the exchange of information regarding the child/adolescent's clinical treatment, is not always as clear cut in its actual operation as it may seem.

> *Example* Ten-year-old Karin is being seen by a psychologist for problems in school performance. After three sessions, the psychologist suspects that Karin may be suffering from some **Attention Deficit** problems and would potentially benefit from a trial of Ritalin or imipramine. When this information was shared with Karin's parents, they refused to sign the consent to share this information with Karin's pediatrician (or any other medical professional in town). Her parents explained that Karin's father works in an accounting firm that has several medical clients, and, therefore, does not want individuals in the local medical community to be aware of Karin's attention deficit problems.

> *Example:* Currently, there is a custody battle going on between the divorced parents of six-year-old Matt. The law guardian (who is assigned to represent the best legal interests of the child) is requesting that Matt's clinical records from his treating counselor be sent to the court. However, Matt's mother does not want to sign a consent to release this information because she is afraid that some of the descriptions will place her in a less than positive light.

Thus, as is true with most ethical issues, the decision as to how to proceed is frequently not as concrete and clear as one might assume. Rather than being a situation of simply following ethical principles, it often becomes more a case of the manner in which the principles are interpreted as applying to a specific clinical case.

Expressive Language Disorder

Children with expressive language disorder are characterized by difficulties in their abilities to express themselves verbally via conventional language. Unlike cases of **Developmental Disorder,** symptoms of expressive language disorder do not primarily involve the actual pronunciation of words or syllables. Rather, children with expressive language disorder manifest symptoms that appear to be more cognitive in nature, specifically reflecting difficulties in conceptualization and expression of spoken language. The clinical presentation varies considerably, both in terms of severity as well as in terms of the actual symptoms exhibited. For example, the child may show:

Limitations in vocabulary: The child may speak using a vocabulary that appears to be less advanced that would be expected from a child of his or her developmental level.

Difficulties with word retrieval: Often referred to as the "tip of the tongue" phenomenon, the child may be speaking and stop in mid-sentence because of inability to recall the appropriate word.

Poor word substitution: At times related to the aforementioned difficulties with word retrieval, a child with expressive language disorder may use an inappropriate word as a substitute for a word he or she has trouble retrieving. As a result, the communication becomes impaired as the flow is interrupted and/or it is difficult to understand.

Grammatical problems: The grammar used by a child with expressive language disorder can appear to be less sophisticated than would be normally expected in a child of the given developmental age.

Strange word combinations: Beyond the problems with grammatical structure, a child with expressive language disorder may put words together in an odd manner, again compromising the degree of understanding by others with whom he or she is communicating.

Inappropriate changing/focusing on topics: Largely because of their difficulties in expressing their thoughts adequately, children with expressive language disorder will often switch topics in mid-conversation, often appearing as if they are unable to concentrate on any given subject for a prolonged period of time.

Incorrect ordering of words: When children with expressive language disorder speak, their speech may have a curious quality associated with it due to their mixing up the order of the words in phrases and sentences.

According to the current diagnostic criteria, in order for expressive language disorder to be diagnosed, the above problems must be sufficiently severe that they interfere with social communication, academic, and/or occupational achievement.

SUPPLEMENTAL RESOURCES

Hamaguachi, P. M. (1995). *Childhood speech, language and listening problems: What every parent should know.* New York: John Wiley.

Martin, K. L. (1997). *Does my child have a speech problem?* Chicago: Chicago Review Press.

McNamara, B. E., & McNamara, F. J. (1995). *Keys to parenting a child with a learning disability.* New York: Barrons.

Meyer, D., & Vadasy, P. (1986). *Living with a brother or sister with special needs: A book for siblings.* Seattle: University of Washington Press.

Rosner, J. (1993). *Helping children overcome learning difficulties.* New York: Walker.

Smith, S. L. (1991). *Succeeding against the odds: How the learning disabled can realize their promise.* New York: Putnam.

Smith, S. L. (1995). *No easy answers: The learning disabled child at home and at school.* New York: Bantam.

Unger, H. G. (1998). *The learning disabilities trap.* Chicago: Contemporary Books.

Extinction

Extinction (also referred to as *planned ignoring*) is a term that has its origins in **Behavior Therapy.** It refers to the elimination of a (usually undesirable or aversive) behavior by the removal of one or more **Reinforcements** previously associated with the performance of the behavior in question. In other words, since behavioral theory maintains that the performance of any behavior is a function of that particular behavior being reinforced, it further postulates that the removal of such reinforcement can be used to eliminate or extinguish the performance of the behavior.

Thus, if there is an undesirable behavior that a parent wishes a child to stop, it would be common for a behaviorally oriented therapist to recommend the following steps: (1) identify the nature of the target behavior in as specific terms as possible, (2) determine what reactions from others are reinforcing the behavior, and (3) plan how to remove those reinforcing stimuli from the environment. It is this removal of the reinforcing consequences in conjunction with the subsequent elimination (or at least lessening in frequency) of the target behavior that comprises the phenomenon known as extinction.

Example: Whenever 4-year-old Jesse goes to a grocery store, he begins to scream as soon as he and his parents approach the checkout counter. In an attempt to stop the screaming behavior, his parents immediately take a chocolate bar from the checkout display and purchase it for the child. Although the parents perceive buying the candy as helping to quiet the child and end the **Tantrum Behavior,** in reality, they are actually reinforcing the tantrums (as the child has learned that by screaming at the end of a grocery shopping trip, he will be reinforced by a treat). Once this process was pointed out to Jesse's parents, they were instructed to take Jesse to the car immediately upon his beginning his tantrums. By reacting to this tantrum behavior with a negative consequence (taking the child to the car) as opposed to reinforcing it with a positive consequence (buying the child a candy bar), the parents were able to eventually extinguish the tantrum behavior.

Example: Twelve-year-old Jared has begun to use four-letter swear words on a fairly regular basis. This has become rather disturbing to his parents, and whenever he uses one of these words, his mother reacts in horror—clearly extremely offended. A school psychologist pointed out to Jared's parents that a dramatic, shocked, horrified reaction may indeed be reinforcing Jared's swearing, as this may be precisely what he wants. Thus, it was suggested that this reinforcing reaction be removed from the situation, and rather than acting upset and shocked, his parents calmly institute a certain amount of television/VCR restriction for each four-letter word uttered. After two weeks of removing the reinforcing stimuli (i.e., the parents' dramatic reaction) from the situation, the swearing behavior was extinguished.

SUPPLEMENTAL RESOURCES

Hall, R. V., & Hall, M. C. (1980). *How to use planned ignoring.* Austin, TX: ProEd.

Extrapyramidal Side Effects

Extrapyramidal side effects are a group of side effects that tend to occur with the use of high-potency **Neuroleptics.** (High-potency neuroleptics are antipsychotic medications that are relatively strong and therefore require a smaller dosage for the same intensity of therapeutic effect.) Generally speaking, the more potent the antipsychotic, the fewer its side effects. However, a major exception to this rule are the extrapyramidal side effects, which are both more intense and more frequent in the higher-potency neuroleptics.

The major categories of extrapyramidal symptoms include: *dystonia,* **Akathisia, Rabbit Syndrome, Parkinsonism, Tardive Dyskinesia,** and **Neuroleptic Malignant Syndrome.** Since each of these side effects will be described in detail in its own individual entry, they are merely mentioned here. The reader is referred to the separate entries for a thorough explanation of each.

SUPPLEMENTAL RESOURCES

Gorman, J. M. (1997). *The essential guide to psychiatric drugs.* New York: St. Martin's Press.

Rosenberg, D. R., Holttum, J., & Gershon, S. (1994). *Textbook of pharmacotherapy for child and adolescent psychiatric disorders.* New York: Brunner/Mazel.

Weiden, P. J., Scheifer, P. L., Diamond, R. J., & Ross, R. (1998). *Switching antipsychotic medications: A guide for consumers and families.* Arlington, VA: National Alliance for the Mentally Ill.

F Failure to Thrive–Freud

Failure to Thrive

Failure to thrive is a term associated with depression as it is manifested in infants. Infants who have symptoms of failure to thrive show evidence of poor care, a delay in psychosocial development, as well as a failure to achieve the expected gains in weight. Yet another component of the failure to thrive phenomenon is referred to as *sensory motor deprivation*. This more short-term syndrome results in the infants having a sad, flat facial expression along with an irritable tone to the cry. Such infants make prolonged eye contact without incorporating the usual brightness in facial expression. Language development is delayed and there is a virtual elimination of any type of social smiling. This can be accompanied by pathological eating behaviors, delays in cognitive development, an increase in the amount of sleep required, as well as an increased number of physical illnesses.

Family Therapy

Family therapy refers to therapeutic interventions in which two or more members of the family are actually involved in the therapy session. Although the roots of family therapy date back to the early twentieth century, this approach has only recently been used in the treatment of children and adolescents. Whereas a 1983 survey of child psychiatrists (Silver & Silver, 1983) reported that practicing child psychiatrists spend little time doing any form of family therapy, a more recent review of the literature identified at least ten different schools of family therapy including: Bowen approaches, systemic therapy, family psychoeducational treatment, Eriksonian family therapy, structural family therapy, strategic family therapy, contextual therapy, brief family therapy, and symbolic experiential family therapy. Even today, no single approach to family therapy has been demonstrated to be empirically superior to others, overall.

Although this wide range of different theoretical approaches to family therapy and its accompanying wide range of different modalities preclude the conceptualization of family therapy as a single entity, what unites these approaches is a pervasive belief in the value of seeing the family together as well as a belief in the importance of examining interpersonal relationships among family members. When family therapy was first introduced, family therapists assumed an *environ-*

mentalist perspective in their work—minimizing the importance of focusing on an identified patient and, instead, looking at the family as an ever changing system. As the field matured and individual practitioners integrated their own theoretical perspectives into their work, however, the practice of family therapy began to incorporate a multitude of theoretical orientations.

The general process of family therapy involves an assessment of the overall functioning of the family as a unit. With the unit itself viewed as the identified patient, the child or adolescent with the problem is not considered to be the major source of the family's difficulties. However, the initial assessment has one of its major goals the determination of how the young person's difficulties relate to the family's overall level of functioning. Thus, the family therapist sees as his or her goal the analysis of the family dynamics and, in turn, the determination of the relationship between this particular family system and the symptoms being observed.

There are several advantages to family therapy as a general intervention. As indicated above, in a family therapy format, no single member of the family is identified as the patient or the one with the problem. With the family conceptualized as the patient, it is less likely that a given family member feels stigmatized with a label of having a psychological/psychiatric problem. A second advantage to a family therapy approach is the increase in the amount of information made available to the treating clinician. Not only is he or she potentially exposed to explanations and interpretations of family life from a variety of different perspectives (i.e., those of everybody in the family), the therapist is also able to observe the interpersonal interaction patterns between and among different family members. This latter ability allows the clinician not only to see how the various members interact with each other, but also to validate the perceptions of the various family members in terms of what is reported. Data obtained from child, parents, as well as other family members can be evaluated in terms of their accuracy, and with respect to implications of any overall patterns of distortion.

There are, however, some potential disadvantages to family approaches. First, the presence of other individuals can affect what is shared by other family members. While this may result in an inhibition of spontaneity, it could also manifest itself in the opposite manner wherein one family member acts in a more dramatic fashion in an attempt to gain attention, or to demonstrate a point. Despite the fact that this could obviously distort the data somewhat, many family therapists believe that such a phenomenon actually provides the clinician with more data, as he or she is able to observe the manner in which the different family members react in the presence of each other.

Other critics of family therapy believe that, in a family situation, the presence of the other family members may detract from the attention paid to and the necessary clinical focus on the young person. They go on to say that, in such cases, the therapeutic value of the situation may be lower than in the cases in which the child or adolescent is seen alone. Again, however, the validity of this criticism has a lot to do with the specific situation. There are indeed cases in which individual therapy may be clearly indicated. For example, if a child is severely depressed or if there is an adolescent who has significant trust issues with parents, there is certainly justification for individual sessions (at least initially). However, as in the above case with the distortion of data, a seasoned clinician is often able to utilize a child who has been forced into the background, for example, as valuable clinical data to be utilized in the actual intervention. Consider the following clinical example:

> *Example:* The Dickinson family consulted a therapist because of their 10-year-old son's recent behavior problems at home. Apparently over the past several weeks, this previously mild-mannered young man has been exhibiting violent outbursts in which he will swear and, at times, throw things. At the first meeting with the entire family, the therapist recognized that the parents and the older sister did virtually all of the talking (this occurring while the parents were also attending to a new-born infant 2 months of age). The 10-year-old was unable to get a word in, and it became clear to the therapist that this type of interaction is probably similar to what transpires at home. After a bit of probing, the therapist offered the interpretation that the 10-year-old acts so belliger-ently because he feels as if he would not be listened to or noticed other-wise. The 10-year-old agreed, and a discussion then ensued as to how this problem could be remedied.

In conclusion, then, family therapy (as is true of any given therapeutic inter-vention) is not appropriate for all families, nor is it appropriate for all types of pre-senting complaints. However, even for those cases in which family therapy is best supplemented by some type of individual work (in terms of psychopharmacolog-ical interventions or individual psychotherapy) with the child or adolescent, there are extremely few cases for which family therapy does not have the potential to be helpful. Indeed, it requires the (at least superficial) cooperation of the other family members, as well as the willingness of the therapist to work within a family for-mat. Assuming that those two prerequisites are met, however, family therapy typ-ically does have the potential to be clinically helpful to all parties involved.

SUPPLEMENTAL RESOURCES

Annunziata, J., & Kram, P. J. (1994). *Solving your problems together: Family therapy for the whole fam-ily.* Washington, DC: American Psychological Association.

Borcherdt, B. (1996). *Making families work and what to do when they don't: Thirty guides for imperfect parents of imperfect children.* Binghamton, NY: Haworth Press.

Carlson, R. (1998). *Don't sweat the small stuff with your family.* New York: Hyperion.

Eastman, M. (1994). *Taming the dragon in your child: Solutions for breaking the cycle of family anger.* New York: Wiley.

Freeman, D. S. (1981). *Techniques of family therapy.* Northvale, NJ: Jason Aronson.

Minuchin, S. (1984). *Family kaleidoscope.* Cambridge, MA: Harvard University Press.

Nicholaus, B., & Lowrie, P. (1997). *The mom and dad conversation piece.* New York: Ballantine Books.

Wahlroos, S. (1995). *Family communication.* Chicago: Contemporary Books.

Whitaker, C. (1989). *Midnight musings of a family therapist.* New York: W. W. Norton.

Fear of the Dark

Fears are a natural part of childhood development, even to the extent to which certain fears are characteristic of children at different ages. Specifically, fear of the dark is an especially common fear—seen quite frequently in children between the ages of 1 and 5 years. As with other fears, it can vary in intensity from child to child, and even within the same child. Whereas fear of the dark is certainly not to be considered pathological, nor is it to be the object of a parent's punishment or ridicule, there are times where parents feel uncomfortable in accepting the fear as it is. In other cases, parents feel as if they do not know the appropriate way to respond to the child's fear of the dark. Again, they do not want to be rejecting; however, neither do they want to encourage the fearful behavior. Finally, there are those cases in which the parents are ready to work with the child to help him or her conquer this fear of the dark, but they are uncertain as to how to proceed.

How to React to a Child's Fear of the Dark
Accept the fear as real: Although there may indeed be no real, objective danger inherent in a dark environment, it must be acknowledged that, from the child's perspective, his or her fears and anxieties are real and valid. Thus, the first step is ensuring the child that you are aware of what he or she is experiencing, and that you respect how frightening it must feel. This is crucial because, especially as the child gets older, there may be some embarrassment about having this fear, and, as a parent, in no way do you want to contribute to it. Remember, although the reason for the fear may not be objectively valid, the fear being experienced certainly is.

Encourage discussion: Work with your child (within the confines of his or her developmental level, of course) to discuss the fearful feelings. Have the child explain to you what the fear feels like, in what situations it's worse and in what situations it's better, when the fear began, and so forth. The more information you can have about the fear from the child's own perspective, the better position you are in to be of meaningful assistance. Further, the mere act of your questioning the child, and actually paying attention to his or her answers, conveys a level of respect and caring that is invaluable.

How to Help Your Child Overcome the Fear of the Dark
Timing is crucial: Prior to attempting to help your child overcome a fear of the dark, it is essential that the child is ready to do this. If the child is for some reason not receptive to working on overcoming his or her fear, any attempts made by the parents would indeed be futile. Most of the time, however, when a child is resistant to working on overcoming a fear, it is because of one of two reasons: Either the child is obtaining some type of secondary gain or benefit from exhibiting the fear (e.g., if

I say I'm afraid of the dark, I can sleep in my parents' bed, etc.), or the child is actually fearful of the process of attempting to conquer the fear. If the former is relevant, the parent need only work to remove the reinforcing elements from the fearful situation. Should the latter be relevant, some simple reassurance from the parent is necessary that this will proceed exclusively according to the directions of the child. In other words, working with the child will not follow the premise of throwing the water-fearful child into the pool! Inform the child that you will work very gradually with him, at his own pace, and, he will *never* be forced into doing anything he doesn't want to do.

Getting into specifics: Ask the child to verbalize precisely what it is he or she fears about being in the dark; use this information to formulate the plan of action in terms of addressing directly the true object of the child's fear.

Evaluate rationally: In talking with the child, evaluate the extent to which the child perceives his or her fear as rational; in other words, does the child recognize that his fears are not entirely based in reality, or are the objects of the child's fear very real to him or her? The child's perception of the actual reality of his or her fears plays a significant role in the manner in which the parents address the attempts to deal with the fear.

Safe object: For young children, oftentimes allowing them to bring a toy, charm, trinket, or other such good luck or "safe" object along with them into the feared situation can be helpful; even going so far as to encourage a fantasy conversation between the child and the object, with one reassuring the other of the safety of the situation can be a useful intervention.

Gradual exposure: When introducing the child to exposure to the feared situation, it is necessary to do so in such a way to (1) maximize the child's chances of having a successful experience (i.e., being able to complete the identified task), and to (2) allow the child to feel in control of the experience. Keeping these two short-term objectives in mind when working with a child to confront a fear of the dark, constructing the exercises within the context of very small steps is certainly advisable; for example, a possible first-exposure exercise may be as simple as standing outside the door of a dark room holding the child's hand; although seemingly trivial, the experience of success in such a situation gives the child the courage to attempt subsequent steps; examples of other possible exposure exercises to address a fear of the dark include:

- Standing in a well-lit room with the child and then gradually turning off one light at a time (or using the dimmer switch) until the room is dark; at each step reassuring the child that nothing has changed in the room (i.e., in terms of safety) except for the degree of darkness.

- Having the child stand in a dark room with the parent immediately outside the room; then with the door to the room only partially ajar; then with the door to the room closed; then with the parent standing at increasingly further distances away from the room.
- Sitting in a dark room with the child and holding him or her on your lap; then reducing the physical contact to holding hands; eventually reducing to standing next to the child; and then standing at the other side of the room without any physical contact.

(None of the above exercises is foolproof, nor is any one purported to be relevant for all children who suffer from a fear of the dark. However, they are presented to provide ideas and general direction as to how parents can proceed to address such an issue with a child who fears the dark.)

Feeding Disorder of Infancy or Early Childhood

This is a relatively new diagnostic category, first published in the newest revision of the *Diagnostic and Statistical Manual (DSM-IV)*. It is used to replace three older diagnostic categories (reactive attachment disorder, nonorganic failure to thrive, and psychosocial dwarfism), the symptoms of which have been acknowledged since the early 1900s. The major symptom of this disorder is described by the *DSM-IV* as being the failure of a child 6 years old or younger to eat properly and/or gain weight over at least a 1-month period. A significant loss of weight over such a time frame would also meet the criteria for a diagnosis of feeding disorder of infancy or early childhood. If the aforementioned symptoms are due to a lack of available food, some other psychological disorder, or some medical disorder, a diagnosis of feeding disorder of infancy or early childhood is not made.

Feminine Behavior in Boys

Please refer to entry **Gender Identity Disorder.**

Flat Affect

Flat affect is a descriptive term used when an individual shows virtually no range or variation in his or her observable emotion. In other words, regardless of the topic of conversation or the environmental stimuli, the individual manifests the same **Affect,** which, often can be described as no affect at all. Flat affect is often characteristic of **Schizophrenia** and other **Psychotic Disorders** as well as of various depressive disorders. For further information, especially in terms of contrast with other forms of manifestation of affect, the writer is referred to the entry on affect.

Fluoxetine

This is the generic name for the drug **Prozac.** Please refer to that entry for description.

Fluphenazine

This is the generic name for the antipsychotic (neuroleptic) drug marketed as **Pro-lixin.** Please refer to that entry for description.

Fluvoxamine Maleate

This is the generic name for the drug marketed as **Luvox.** Please refer to that entry for description.

Four A's

This is a phrase coined by Eugen Bleuler in the early part of the twentieth century as he attempted to describe and characterize the symptoms of **Schizophrenia.** The Four A's refer to four fundamental symptom patterns that are seen in individuals suffering from schizophrennia. Bleuler was specific in noting that, although non-schizophrenic individuals also manifest such symptoms, schizophrenic individuals manifest these symptoms to a more severe degree. Thus, it is not the presence of the Four A's that distinguishes the schizophrenic process, but rather the intensity of their manifestation.

These four symptom clusters are identified by Bleuler as follows:

1. *Fragmented and discontinuous associations in thinking:* Referring to the cognitive symptoms of schizophrenia; specifically, this first of the Four A's describes irregularities in speech and thought marked by a lack of obvious connectedness, poor flow of ideas, and a thought process that just doesn't make sense.

2. *Autistic behavior and thinking:* Here Bleuler was referring to the overall self-absorption and reality distortion (in terms of both reality contact and perceptual distortions) observed in schizophrenic individuals; specifically **Delusions** and the various types of **Hallucinations** would fit into this category.

3. *Abnormal affect:* Affect of schizophrenic individuals is typically characterized as being impaired in either its intensity, quality, or range; problems with the intensity characteristic of schizophrenia include unusual exaggeration or dampening of emotional expression; impairment in quality refers to some schizophrenics' inappropriate expression of affect—often expressing emotion that seems almost opposite to what one would expect the person to express in the given situation; finally, common range of affect problems in schizophrenic individuals in-

clude **Blunted Affect, Flat Affect,** or some other form of affect of a restricted range wherein the individual seems to react virtually uniformly to all situations.

4. *Ambivalence:* Refers to the common perception that schizophrenic individuals seem to be less concerned about various matters than one would expect, as well as the perception that schizophrenic individuals have a difficult time making decisions.

Freud, Anna

The daughter of the well-known psychoanalyst **Sigmund Freud,** Anna Freud (1895–1982) focused her work on the study of the psychological development of, development of psychopathology in, and doing psychotherapy with the child. Although she certainly did not completely discount the importance of unconscious process, Anna Freud emphasized the necessity of focusing on children's observable behavior. Similar to the work of her father, Anna Freud's writings talked about the conflicts and tensions characteristic of the various life stages, specifically stating that each stage of development has its own tasks that need to be accomplished. Anna Freud even went on to discuss the importance of the child's role within the family itself, emphasizing the role of the family as it impacts on the young person's healthy or pathological development.

With respect to psychological problems, Anna Freud believed that psychopathology stems from the inability of the child to accomplish the appropriate tasks of development at the necessary times. Believing that there are two types of psychological problems, Anna Freud made the distinction between those disorders that are a function of developmental disturbances versus those that are due to internal conflict. Specifically, Anna Freud classified the psychological/psychiatric problems of children as falling into the following categories: psychosomatics, neurotic symptoms, psychotic/delinquent symptoms, borderline symptoms, personality disorders, hypochondriasis, inhibited or destructive symptoms, infantile symptoms, symptoms resulting from organic causes, delays/failures in development, fears/anxieties, school failures, failures in social adaptation, and aches/pains.

SUPPLEMENTAL RESOURCES

Coles, R. (1992). *Anna Freud.* New York: Addison Wesley Longman.
Freud, A. (1965). *The writings of Anna Freud.* New York: International Universities Press.

Freud, Sigmund

Viewed as the father of psychoanalysis, Sigmund Freud (1856–1939) was an Austrian scientist who believed that the key to psychological function was to be found in the physiological processes of the brain. With a career transcending the boundaries of medicine, hypnosis, neurology, psychology, and psychoanalysis, Freud's work was influenced by the major scientific names of his day. He is best known for his work on the classification of **Defense Mechanisms,** theories of the structure of the mind, as well as his belief in the importance of unconscious processes.

Although he never worked directly with children himself, Sigmund Freud's best-known work relevant to children is his theories regarding psychological development. Referred to as his theory of *psychosexual development*, Freud proposed human development as consisting of five consecutive stages through which every human being must pass (in sequence) in order to mature into a psychologically healthy adult. If, for some reason, an individual is unable to complete the prescribed tasks of any given stage, the individual is said to be *fixated* at that particular stage. According to Freud, it is the specific stage at which this fixation occurs that determines the nature of an individual's personality, or, in pathological cases, psychological disorder. These stages are defined according to the body part that is the focus of the child's sensual gratification. This theory postulates that the child's erogenous zones change as the child matures, with this timely movement from one erogenous zone to another indicating psychological health and maturity.

Psychosexual theory defines the mouth as the primary source of gratification during the first 18 months of life. The nature of the baby's experience during this *oral stage* will determine crucial aspects of adult personality. For example, a baby whose oral needs are consistently frustrated will engage in aggressive oral behaviors such as biting, loud crying, and screaming. Indeed, this may continue into adulthood with the tendency to express anger verbally through sarcasm, yelling, and swearing. Such adults also have a difficult time trusting others (because of the betrayal associated with infant feeding needs). Finally, according to Freudian theory, these adults also use their teeth in aggressive oral activities such as chewing ice, biting a popsicle (rather than sucking on it), and/or habitually chewing on nonedible things. On the other hand, an infant who experiences this oral stage as excessively pleasurable and satisfying is said to develop into an *oral dependent* personality. Characteristics of such an individual include frequent eating (which can lead to obesity), appearing extremely dependent and psychologically needy, as well as engaging in a variety of compulsive oral habits (e.g., thumb-sucking, insertion of various nonfood objects into the mouth, and sucking on hard candies).

From 18 months until approximately 3 years of age, Freudian psychosexual theory proposes that the child is confronted with two interrelated phenomena. First the child is beginning to recognize his or her control over the process of having a bowel movement, this behavior a possible source of pleasure. Second, the parents are approaching the stage in which they are attempting to control that very process via instruction in toilet training. Power struggles that evolve during this *anal stage* lay the framework for the child's attitudes toward authority and control once he or she becomes an adult. Individuals whose anal period experiences were extremely strict and limiting will mature into what Freud referred to as *anal retentive* personalities. These adults tend to focus on details, rigidly adhere to rules, are compulsively neat and orderly, and tend to be extremely frugal with financial matters. In contrast, Freud proposed that those whose experiences during this stage of development were rather unstructured and free from rules will tend to mature into *anal expulsive* personalities. These anal expulsive types tend to be messy and disorganized. Rebelling against authority, anal expulsive individuals resent rules and regulations and are generally careless with their money. According to this theory, then, adequate resolution of anal stage issues results in a mature adult, with appropriately moderate approaches to finances, organization, and authority.

Between the ages of 3 and 5 years, the child deals with the issues of the third stage of psychosexual development—the *phallic stage.* At this time, the child directs erotic energies toward the genitalia (the penis in boys, the clitoris in girls), and masturbation becomes a more or less regular activity. In addition, it is during this stage that the child's conceptualization of the parents changes. Up until the phallic stage, the child perceived the parents as a single caretaking unit. However, during the phallic stage the child begins to develop a sense of **Gender Identity** via identification with the same-sex parent. As a result, it is during the phallic stage that the boy or girl experiences the **Oedipal** or **Electra** conflicts, respectively. Successful resolution of the conflicts inherent in the phallic stage prepares the individuals for fulfilling heterosexual relationships later in life.

Following the phallic stage, psychosexual theory predicts entry into the *latency stage* of development. From about 6 to 12 years of age, there is no specific erotic focus in the child's life. Rather, the sexual urges are attenuated somewhat and he or she learns to channel sexual energies into more socially acceptable activities. For example, an anally fixated second grader may choose to engage in sculpting with clay rather than playing with his feces. Similarly, a third grader who is orally aggressive may develop a strong preference for crunchy foods or gum chewing rather than biting everyone who angers her.

Around 12 years of age (upon reaching puberty), the preadolescent enters the *genital stage* of development. At this point, psychosexual theory predicts that the preteen embarks on a quest to fulfill his or her reproductive needs. The erotic focus returns to the genital area—back to the penis for the male, but requiring a shift from the clitoris to the vagina for the female. The maturing individual is thereby preparing for the eventual formation of a mature marital relationship.

In sum, then, a major portion of Freud's work focuses on the development of the child and the basic principle that the child must successfully complete all five psychosexual stages in order to become a psychologically healthy adult.

SUPPLEMENTARY RESOURCES

Balmary, M. (1982). *Psychoanalyzing psychoanalysis.* Baltimore, MD: John Hopkins University Press.
Elder, C. R. (1994). *The grammar of the unconscious.* University Park, PA: Penn State Press.
MacMillan, M. (1997). *Freud evaluated.* Cambridge, MA: MIT Press.
Osborne, R. (1993). *Freud for beginners.* New York: Writers and Readers Press.

G   Gender Identity–Group Therapy

Gender Identity

Gender identity refers to an individual's sense of being male or female. For most children, this develops somewhere between the ages of 2 and 3 years, at which time the child can express a knowledge and/or awareness that "I am a girl" or "I am a boy." This ability of correctly identifying one's own gender, however, is only a preliminary step in development of a complete sense of masculinity or femininity. In his now classic work, *Sex and Gender,* Robert Stoller (1968) views the development of gender identity as being a function of contributions of several different sources, including physical characteristics, cultural norms, psychosocial experiences, and family values around what is considered to be appropriate for males and females.

It is crucial to note that gender identity has very little, if anything, to do with a person's sexual orientation (i.e., whether he or she is homosexual, heterosexual, or bisexual). Although often confused as being closely related, an individual's gender identity only refers to his or her sense of being male or female. Sexual orientation (in terms of preference for the gender of the sexual partner) is not an issue of gender identity.

Gender Identity Disorder

Gender identity disorder refers to the condition in which the young person's sense of being male or female is distorted. More specifically, the individual believes that he or she is wrongly labeled with respect to gender. In other words, boys with gender identity disorder believe that they are truly females, and girls with gender identity disorder believe that they are truly males. As one would expect, this belief system causes such individuals a great deal of psychological distress.

Actual clinical symptoms of gender identity disorder of childhood typically first occur during the preschool years. Both boys and girls usually begin to show gender preference around the age of 3 or 4 years (at times as young as 2 years of age). In a young boy, the first signs of problems with gender identity usually consist of **Cross-Dressing,** a strong preference for traditionally feminine toys, or an actual insistence that he is in fact a girl. For little girls, the first symptoms typically involve a preference for rough and tumble play, a dislike of traditionally feminine clothing, as well as an insistence that she receive (or that she actually has) a penis.

As time progresses, a child with gender identity disorder grows to identify increasingly with the characteristics of the opposite sex. Although most such children are intellectually aware of their true gender (i.e., whether he or she is a boy or a girl), this knowledge of gender can appear to be rather unstable in certain cases.

Girls with gender identity disorder work hard to appear as masculine as possible, both in their appearance as well as in their behavior. As indicated above, they express an intense dislike for traditional feminine clothing; they attempt to involve themselves in activities considered to be typical of boys; and they may even alter their walk, speech, and other aspects of their demeanor. Indeed, some girls with gender identity disorder will even go so far as to attempt to urinate standing up, or to insert objects into their undergarments to give the appearance of having a penis. The following eight characteristics are considered common in a fully developed case of gender identity disorder in girls (Zucker and Green, 1991):

1. expressed desire for or insistence on being a boy
2. verbal or behavioral expressions of anatomic dysphoria (unhappiness with sexual organs or other body parts)
3. dislike of traditional feminine clothing
4. preference for male roles in fantasy play
5. preference for stereotypical male play and activities
6. behavioral display of masculine mannerisms
7. preference for boys as playmates
8. strong interest in rough and tumble play

Example: Five-year-old Jenna is having a difficult time in her kindergarten class. She insists on playing with the boys, and when the teacher instructs the class to divide itself according to boys and girls, Jenna consistently goes over to the boys' group. The problem came to a head last week when Jenna was found in the little boys's bathroom, attempting to urinate standing up.

Boys with gender identity disorder will tend to wear feminine clothing to varying degrees, and similarly engage in feminine fantasies, especially in play. They will express a preference for girls as play companions and will prefer to engage in behaviors that are considered to be traditionally feminine. Similar to girls with gender identity disorder, boys with this disorder may attempt to feminize their walk, voice, and other aspects of their appearance and behavior (at times going so far as to attempt to hide their penises). Zucker and Green (1991) list the following eight characteristics of a fully developed case of gender identity disorder in boys:

1. expressed desire for or insistence on being a girl
2. verbal or behavioral expressions of anatomic dysphoria (dislike and/or dissatisfaction with sexual organs or other body parts)
3. frequent dressing in female clothing
4. preference for female roles in fantasy play

5. preference for stereotypical female play and activities
6. display of feminine mannerisms
7. preference for girls as playmates
8. avoidance of rough and tumble play

> *Example:* Six-year-old Ricky enjoys playing house with the little girls in the neighborhood. When he does so, Ricky insists upon being the mommy or the little girl. In so doing, he dresses up in feminine clothing (at times, even stuffing his shirt so that it looks as if he has developed breasts). When his parents ask him if he enjoys pretending to be a girl, Ricky responds indignantly, "I *am* a girl."

By the time the individual reaches middle childhood or early adolescence, the cross-gender behavior interferes significantly with peer relationships as well as with relationships with family and teachers. Whereas masculine behavior in girls is tolerated in our culture more readily than is feminine behavior in boys, cross-gender behavior in general can cause significant discomfort for those in the young person's surroundings. As a result, sufferers of gender identity disorder are forced to deal with the less than positive reactions of others to their symptoms, in addition to the psychological discomfort associated with the disorder itself.

As alluded to in the entry on **Gender Identity,** the presence or absence of gender identity disorder has very little (if anything) to do with the young person's sexual orientation (i.e., gender preference for sexual partner). The sexual orientations of individuals who have been diagnosed with gender identity disorder in childhood run the gamut from heterosexual, to bisexual, to homosexual.

When to Seek Professional Help

When looking at cases in which gender identity disorder may be expected, it is crucial to take issues of development into account. Indeed, there are certain situations in which a little boy or little girl appears to assume the role of the opposite sex, and it is simply a developmental stage that is clearly temporary. Most children develop a sense of gender identity by age 2½, at which time they seem to have a firm sense of being either a boy or a girl (as well as its implications). However, after this sense of gender identity is in place, many children do incorporate gender reversal in their make-believe play. The key distinction between this type of behavior and true gender identity disorder is that, even in the height of the make-believe play, the child is well aware of his or her true gender and does not actually believe that he or she is a member of the opposite sex.

In addition, it is important to take into account that there is a form of feminine dressing in boys, usually limited to the wearing of undergarments or hosiery. This behavior is typically not accompanied by identification with the female gender role, but rather is used to serve a consoling, comforting function for the child. Similarly, in girls, there are cases of "tomboyism" that seem to mirror many of the symptoms of gender identity disorder. Again, however, there is not the insistence of being a boy, nor is there the identification with the masculine sex role that is present in true gender identity disorder.

Whereas reassurance from a mental health professional can often be curative in and of itself, prior to seeking treatment for gender identity disorder, the parents should attempt to ensure that the observed symptoms are not simply part of a normally expected developmental stage. Further, the insistence that the child/adolescent is imprisoned in a body of the wrong gender or some type of insistence that he or she is really a member of the opposite sex (outside of fantasy play) are important symptoms to diagnose the presence of this disorder. If professional help is deemed to be necessary (even at a consultative level), the parent should be prepared to answer the following questions:

1. At what age did the child first indicate an awareness of his or her correct gender?
2. When did the cross-gender behavior first begin?
3. What is the exact nature of the cross-gender behavior? (In other words, what does the child do that prompted seeking of treatment?)
4. What is the reaction of the family and others in the child's environment when he or she performs this cross-gender behavior?
5. Is the child closer with the parent of the same sex or the parent of the opposite sex?
6. How does the parent of the same sex rate in terms of traditional sex role behaviors?
7. Who are the child's closest friends?
8. In what types of activities does the child prefer to engage?
9. Has the child verbally expressed any opinions about his or her body parts or those of others?
10. What is the child's preferred mode of dress?

Treatment for gender identity disorder will usually consist of individual psychotherapy with the child, often in some combination with therapeutic work with the family. Depending upon the nature of the specific case, **Behavior Therapy** may also be incorporated into the treatment program. The following questions would be appropriate to ask the treating clinician after the initial examination of the child:

1. Do you see this as a case of true gender identity disorder, a developmental phase, or simply a case of "innocent" cross-gender behavior? On what basis are you making your decision?
2. Does my child really believe that he or she is a member of the opposite sex, or, does he or she wish it so?
3. Does this appear to be a behavioral issue or something more deep-seated?
4. How troubled is my child by his or her cross-gender preferences? What is the the implication of this?
5. How are members of the family supposed to act when the child engages in cross-gender behaviors?

6. What should the parents say if the child insists that he or she is a member of the opposite sex?
7. Is this something for which it is reasonable to expect a cure within a short-term time frame?
8. What modes of therapy will you be using?
9. How will my child react to therapy? Will he or she react as if there is nothing wrong and therefore resist attempts to modify cross-gender behavior?

Generalized Anxiety Disorder

Generalized anxiety disorder (GAD) involves as its primary symptom excessive anxiety and worry, along with a difficulty controlling this worry. Accompanying the anxiety and worry are some combination of the following: restlessness, being easily fatigued, difficulty concentrating, irritability, muscle tension, and/or sleep disturbance. When an individual suffers from generalized anxiety disorder, the anxiety, worry, and/or physical symptoms are severe enough to cause clinically significant distress or impairment in life functioning.

When a child or adolescent suffers from generalized anxiety disorder, he or she tends to seek constant reassurance of positive outcomes as well as of personal abilities and worth. Although these young people often give an impression of being unusually mature for their age, this is really a facade in an attempt to mask feelings of insecurity. Children with generalized anxiety often feel as if adults (and authority figures in general) are extremely critical, and their reactions and interpersonal communication reflect this perception. They feel as if their performance is never "good enough," and, as a result, go along through life in a state of almost constant tension.

Young people with generalized anxiety disorder are often viewed by others as constant worriers who seem unusually serious in their approach toward life. They often ask multiple questions in an attempt to obtain reassurance, as they have a difficult time dealing with any type of unpredictability and uncertainty. Unlike many of the other **Anxiety Disorders,** the anxiety shown in generalized anxiety disorder tends to be rather pervasive and constant as opposed to a response to a specific stimulus. It is interesting to note that specific symptoms of generalized anxiety disorder vary as a function of the age of the child/adolescent. Younger children more often show additional symptoms of **Separation Anxiety Disorder** and/or **Attention Deficit Disorder** in conjunction with the generalized anxiety disorder symptoms, whereas adolescents tend to show symptoms of **Depression** and/or **Phobias** along with the symptoms of generalized anxiety disorder.

Treatment for generalized anxiety disorder usually consists of some combination of individual psychotherapy, **Family Therapy, Behavior Therapy,** and drug therapy. The majority of the behavioral treatments used to treat generalized anxiety disorder in children and adolescents focus on the direct reduction of the experience of anxiety. Relaxation training, progressive muscle relaxation, and **Systematic Desensitization** to anxiety-provoking thoughts and situations are all used to help the child/adolescent learn techniques to control the symptoms of anxiety. **Cognitive Behavioral** techniques are also utilized as a treatment method, showing the young person the relationship between their thoughts and their anxiety symptoms, and providing them with techniques to control intrusive symptoms. More traditional individual and family therapy approaches are designed to increase the young person's tolerance of everyday situations that are seen as anxiety provoking. In addition, the therapist will work to help the child modify his or her way of thinking (again utilizing cognitive behavioral approaches) to eliminate perfectionistic attitudes, self-defeating values, and generally increase assertiveness.

> *Example:* Twelve-year-old Rhonda is having a difficult time concentrating in school as well as in social situations. She appears to be constantly preoccupied and always has a worried appearance. Although there are no behavior problems either at home or at school, Rhonda is repeatedly asking for reassurance that she hasn't done anything wrong and that everything will be all right. When asked what she means by that, she simply replies, "…you know, everything, that's all." In addition, over the past several months, Rhonda has been having a difficult time sleeping at night, reporting frequent awakenings and then being unable to fall back asleep.

When to Seek Professional Help

Although there are several young people who can rightfully be described as serious, perfectionistic, and/or worriers, they certainly do not all meet the clinical criteria to be diagnosed with generalized anxiety disorder. Indeed, some children/adolescents (and adults as well) simply seem to take life a bit more seriously than do others, and that is a fact of life. However, for some individuals, it goes beyond a mere serious approach to living, and transcends the boundary of almost constant worry, perfectionism, and need for repeated reassurance. When, for individuals in this latter group, the anxiety is so severe that it interferes with day-to-day functioning for any extended period of time, then professional help is recommended. As with the other anxiety disorders, generalized anxiety disorder is very treatable—and, in most cases, within a relatively short-term format. At the time of the first appointment, the parent (or child, if he or she is able) should be able to provide the clinician with the following information:

1. What is the specific nature of the symptoms about which you are concerned?
2. When were these symptoms first noticed?
3. Was anything significant going on in the young person's life or in the family at or around the time the symptoms first appeared?
4. What types of situations tend to make the symptoms worse?
5. Are there any times when the symptoms appear to improve at all? If so, when do these times occur?

6. Is there anyone else in the family who suffers or has been diagnosed with any other form of anxiety disorder (or any other psychological disorder, for that matter)?
7. Has the young person shown any signs of any other psychological disorder within the recent or remote past?

Questions to Ask the Treating Clinician

1. What do you perceive as being the primary diagnosis?
2. Is there any other anxiety disorder also present here?
3. What do you view as being the major source of the anxiety?
4. How do you think generalized anxiety disorder is best treated?
5. How much experience have you had in treating generalized anxiety disorder in young people?
6. What approach(es) will you be using in treating this disorder?
7. Will any family members be involved in the treatment sessions and, if so, who and to what degree?
8. How should family members react when the child/adolescent shows symptoms of anxiety at home?
9. Are there any special instructions to provide for the child/adolescent's teachers and/or school personnel?
10. When can some improvement first be expected?

SUPPLEMENTAL RESOURCES

Babior, S., & Goldman, C. (1996). *Overcoming panic, anxiety and phobias: New strategies to free yourself from worry and fear.* Duluth, MN: Pfeifer-Hamilton.
Bourne, E. J. (1995). *The phobia and anxiety disorder workbook.* New York: New Harbinger.
Greist, J., Jefferson, J., & Marks, I. (1986). *Anxiety and its treatment.* Washington, DC: American Psychiatric Press.

Genogram

Originated by family therapist Murray Bowen, a genogram can be conceptualized as somewhat of a psychologically detailed family tree. Going back as many generations as is feasible, the genogram traces the siblings and ancestry of an individual, paying particular attention to interpersonal relationships and psychological/psychiatric history. Once constructed, the clinician uses the genogram with the individual to determine patterns and trends, especially as they relate to the presenting complaint.

SUPPLEMENTAL RESOURCES

McGoldrick, M., & Gerson, R. (1985). *Genograms in family assessment.* New York: W. W. Norton.

Group Therapy

Although children and adolescents have been treated in groups for a long time, group therapy, as it is conceptualized today, was not utilized with young people to any significant degree in the United States until approximately 20 years ago. Currently one of the most popular therapeutic interventions in treating adolescents, group therapy is now used to treat a wide variety of different diagnostic categories.

Perhaps even more so than individual therapy, group therapy provides the clinician insight into the manner in which the patient interacts with the world. Similarly, group therapy reveals how the child or adolescent interacts with peers as well as with other adults. Yet another advantage of group work is that, with peers around, a child or adolescent may feel less inhibited about sharing information that could be potentially more awkward in a one-to-one situation with an adult. However, probably the most valuable characteristic of group therapy is its ability to provide the young person with the opportunity of recognizing that his or her problems are not unique and do not reflect some internal weirdness.

What actually transpires in a group therapy situation is largely a function of the therapeutic orientation of the clinician as well as the type of group being run. Groups vary according to how homogeneous or heterogeneous they are. That is to say, some groups are homogeneous (uniform) around one or more given dimensions. In these groups, all of the members fit a certain age group, are of the same gender, and/or experience similar problems. The dimension along which the group chooses to be homogeneous plays a large factor in terms of the actual character of the group. For example, a group can consist of children of alcoholic parents (but the children can be of various ages), adolescents who have experienced a serious loss, or even children who fit a certain diagnostic category or are experiencing similar symptoms. Most groups are homogeneous along at least one dimension, yet they may vary considerably along others. As an illustration, specialized groups tend to focus on symptoms, situation, or diagnostic category, but may vary considerably along the dimensions of age, psychological functioning, and overall developmental level.

In some situations, group therapy is combined with family therapy and parent training. **Parallel Groups** involve parent groups that meet separately from the child/adolescent groups. Oftentimes, these parallel groups meet at the same time as do the groups for the young people to alleviate possible transportation problems. *Merged groups* (usually for younger children) involve the parents meeting in group sessions at the same time together with their children. Finally, some therapists work with more than one family (parents and children) at a given time in a single group. These combined groups work well for families with similar problems—as a means of learning from each other as well as providing peer support.

As with all of the other therapeutic interventions, group therapy is not for everybody and can have its potential disadvantages. First, there are some patients as well as some problems that do not lend themselves to group treatment. Whereas most diagnostic categories as well as most children and adolescents can, at some time during their treatment, benefit from group interventions, group therapy is certainly not always the optimal intervention. Many times, children are too easily intimidated or too psychologically disturbed to participate meaningfully in a group therapy situation. In situations such as these, group therapy participation can even hinder the optimal progression of treatment. For such cases, individual treatment is usually employed at the outset, with plans for group therapy to be added at a later date, if clinically indicated.

SUPPLEMENTAL RESOURCES

Kaplan, H. I., & Sadock, B. J. (Eds.). (1993). *Comprehensive group therapy (3rd ed.).* Baltimore: Williams & Wilkins.

H Haldol–Hypomania

Haldol

Haldol is an **Antipsychotic** drug approved for use in the treatment of **Psychotic Disorders** and of **Tourette's Disorder.** In addition, in cases wherein psychotherapy interventions have been proved to be ineffective, and in cases wherein drug interventions other than antipsychotic medications have also been ineffective, the package insert for Haldol indicates the suitability of Haldol for the treatment of severe behavioral problems in children. It specifically indicates that this drug can be used for "…combative, explosive hyperexcitability (which cannot be accounted for by immediate provocation)" as well as for the short-term treatment of certain cases of **Attention Deficit Disorder.** Again, referring to the package insert, Haldol is recommended for children diagnosed with attention deficit disorder who suffer additionally from conduct problems manifesting "impulsivity, difficulty sustaining attention, aggressivity, mood lability and poor frustration tolerance."

It is important to note that Haldol has not been approved for children under the age of 3 years, no matter what the clinical status. Dosages for children from age 3 through 12 years usually begin with 0.5 mg per day, with increases of 0.5 mg occurring every 5 to 7 days. This increase continues at this rate until the drug reaches therapeutic level, the actual dosage depending upon the weight of the child (usually 0.05–0.15 mg/kg/day). Haldol can take the form of tablets, a concentrate solution, or an injectable solution (referred to as haloperidol decanoate).

SUPPLEMENTAL RESOURCES

Breggin, P. (1991). *Toxic psychiatry.* New York: St Martin's Press.
Maxmen, J., & Ward, N. (1996). *Psychotropic drugs: Fast facts.* New York: Norton.
Rosenberg, D. R., Holttum, J., & Gershon, S. (1994). *Textbook of pharmacotherapy for child and adolescent psychiatric disorders.* New York: Brunner/Mazel.
Werry, J. S., & Aman, M. G. (1993). *Practitioner's guide to psychoactive drugs for children and adolescents.* New York: Plenum.

Hallucinations

Hallucinations are defined as distortions in sensory experience which are severe enough to alter an individual's perception of reality. Hallucinations assume various

183

forms including **Auditory Hallucinations,** visual hallucinations, tactile hallucinations, and olfactory hallucinations. For a more detailed description of hallucinations, the reader is referred to the entry on **Schizophrenia**—the disorder of which hallucinations are often a symptom—and the entry on auditory hallucinations, the most common type of hallucination.

Haloperidol

Haloperidol is the generic name of the anitpsychotic (neuroleptic) drug marketed as **Haldol.** Please refer to that entry for a detailed description of this drug.

Homework Problems

In the majority of cases when a child or adolescent has problems submitting or completing homework assignments, the issue with the homework is typically a symptom rather than the actual problem itself. Indeed, there are various factors that have the potential of contributing to homework problems, and it is the specific factor in each case that needs to be addressed before the actual homework issue can be truly solved. By confronting the homework issue directly without paying heed to what may be causing the problem(s), one is simply putting a Band-Aid on a possibly enormous wound—and not an especially efficient Band-Aid at that!

As an aid to determining the possible cause, it is useful to examine the specific nature of the homework problem. There are two dimensions that tend to be especially useful in this regard. First, is the homework problem more or less universal (occurring in every subject), or is it specific to one or two subjects? Secondly, is the homework problem due to the child/adolescent not completing the assignment, or is it due to the child/adolescent completing the assignment but simply not submitting it to the teacher?

One subject or several? If the young person's homework difficulties are with one subject, it is probably safe to assume that there is a problem with the given subject. Such a difficulty can range anywhere from difficulty with the subject matter itself, some type of problem with the teacher, or some other issue with one or more other students in the class. If, however, the homework problems transcend over all but certain subjects, information can be gleaned by deciphering patterns among the subjects that are problematic versus those that are not. Again, such patterns can focus around the nature of the subject matter, teacher issues, or issues with one or more students in the class.

Doesn't complete versus doesn't submit: The student who completes his or her homework but, for some reason, doesn't submit it presents quite a different picture diagnostically from the student who doesn't complete the work. Indeed, students in the "nonsubmit" group are relatively few and far between, and parents need to be wary of the student who claims the work has been completed, but simply not submitted. If such is determined to be really the case, then the reasons for not submitting the work need to be explored. These usually stem from disorganization or feelings of shame/embarrassment about the quality of the work. For those students who simply do not complete the homework at all, issues of intellectual limitations, problems with concentration and/or attention span, anger at parents, teachers, or other authority figures, depression, or some **Anxiety Disorder** all need to be investigated as possible causes.

Once the basic facts are determined, the parent is ready to proceed to attempt to determine the true source of the homework difficulties. Although this will be done primarily via actual discussion with the student, there will need to be a certain amount of psychological detective work on the parents' part as well. To help guide the parents on their way, the following questions are provided as a framework or a starting point:

- When did the problems with homework first begin?
- How long was it from the time the problems began and the parents became aware of the problems?
- How did the parents become aware of the homework problems?
- Prior to the current problems with homework, how was the child's overall school performance?
- Is the child feeling okay physically? (In other words, could this be due to a medical problem?)
- To what extent is the homework difficulty an issue of organizational problems?
- Has anything unusual been going on in the child's life or in the child's family around the time the homework problems began?
- Have there been any other changes noticed in the child's behavior?
- Does the child exhibit signs of any other psychological problem? depression? anxiety? behavior problem?
- What is the child's reaction to being confronted about the homework problem?
- How does the child explain the homework problem in his or her own words?
- Can the teacher or other school personnel provide any insight into the child's homework problem (in terms of other school behavior?)
- Has there been any conflict between the child and parents for which the homework problem is serving as a means to express anger?
- What is the child's response when asked what he or she feels should be done to remedy the situation?
- How does the child respond to suggestions from others as to what should be done to remedy the situation?

Determining the answers to these questions will help the parent begin to formulate a treatment plan to address the situation. By more specifically identifying the nature of the problem, and then attempting to determine what the homework difficulties are actually symptomatic of, the parents will be in a better position to determine whether or not professional help is necessary.

SUPPLEMENTAL RESOURCES

Radenich, M. C., & Schumm, J. S. (1997). *How to help your child with homework: Every caring parent's guide to encouraging good study habits and ending the homework wars.* Secaucus, NJ: Childswork/Childsplay.

Silverman, S. H. (1995). *Kids don't come with instruction manuals—No more homework headaches.* Secaucus, NJ: Childswork/Childsplay.

Schneider, M. F. (1994). *Help—My teacher hates me.* New York: Workman.

Homosexuality

Homosexuality refers to the sexual orientation of an individual, specifically that of sexual attraction to members of one's own sex. In most cases, homosexuality begins in early childhood but is not openly acknowledged (if at all) until late adolescence or early to mid-adulthood. Nonetheless, most male homosexuals report recognizing an attraction to those of the same sex prior to reaching puberty. From the time of the publication of the 1973 edition of the *DSM* by the American Psychiatric Association, homosexuality has not been considered by mental health professionals as sexually pathological or dysfunctional. Rather, it is conceptualized as a normal variant of human sexual expression. Thus, the idea of perceiving homosexuality as some sort of psychological or psychiatric disorder that necessitates treatment is not a valid concept. Indeed, a chapter on doing **Group Therapy** with homosexuals, written in a mid 1990s psychiatric text reads as follows: "The presence of homosexuality does not appear to be a matter of choice; the expression of it is a matter of choice."

Estimates with respect to the frequency of practicing homosexuals varies considerably. As far back as the famous studies by Kinsey in the forties, it was reported that 10% of men were homosexual, with only 5% of women being homosexual. Even in those studies, however, Kinsey reported that over one third of adults had experienced at least one homosexual experience in their lifetime. Thus, although these figures may be outdated, what remains consistent, even in the more recent studies (which tend to cluster around 10% for a prevalence figure for homosexuality in general) is the discrepancy between those who identify themselves as being homosexual, and those who have experienced some homosexual activity in the past.

Young people who identify themselves as homosexual typically engage in significant psychological struggles. Whereas sexuality, in and of itself, is a difficult concept for a young person to grapple with, feeling as if one's sexuality is different from the majority of those around can only intensify matters. Concerns about normality versus abnormality, being ridiculed by one's peers, and parental and familial reaction all contribute to the sources of anxiety experienced by youth coming to terms with their homosexuality. Indeed, the psychological struggles are certainly not limited to the young person himself or herself. The *homophobic* society in which we live has resulted in a generation of parents who are quite likely to experience their own concerns about having a homosexual son or daughter. It is difficult for a parent to react in a manner that is optimal for the child when he or she is struggling with his or her own personal issues around the child's sexual orientation.

Because of these reasons, it is typically helpful for the entire family to seek some type of professional intervention. There are professionals who are expert in helping individuals and families come to terms with sexual orientation issues, and, although we are not talking about some form of diagnosable psychological or psychiatric disorder, the struggles inherent in such a situation typically benefit from some outside assistance. The nature of the issue is so personal and emotionally laden that working with a professional who has extensive experience dealing with such matters is often necessary.

Initial sessions tend to be individual in format and are geared toward helping the young person identify and then come to terms with his or her sexual preferences. As these individual sessions are transpiring, at times it is useful for the parents to meet with a therapist (usually the same one) separately from their child. Most of the time, these parent sessions involve providing general information about sexual orientation, as well as providing a forum in which the parents can express their feelings regarding their specific child. These sessions are necessary, as the parents need an opportunity to express themselves freely without worries about the effect their comments will have on their offspring. Subsequent sessions will involve parents and other family members as the therapist and young person deem appropriate. These latter sessions will allow an open expression of feelings, concerns, and anxieties.

SUPPLEMENTAL RESOURCES

Alexander, C. J. (1997). *Growth and intimacy for gay men: A workbook.* Binghamton, NY: Haworth Press.

Owens, R.E. (1998). *Queer kids: The challenges and promise for lesbian, gay and bisexual youth.* Binghamton, NY: Haworth Press.

Hypomania

Hypomania is very similar to **Mania** in presentation, however it is somewhat less severe in terms of duration as well as intensity of the symptoms. In order for a manic episode to be diagnosed, the *DSM-IV* (American Psychiatric Association, 1994) requires that the following diagnostic criteria must be met:

A. Elevated, expansive, or irritable mood for at least 4 days.
B. During the above 4-day period, at least three of the following has been present:
1. Inflated self esteem or grandiosity: Person feels as if he or she can do virtually anything, without the normally expected consequences.
2. Noticeably decreased need for sleep.

3. Talking is increased in frequency, volume, with a sense of the person's speech seeming pressured.
4. Content of speech gives impression that it is "all over the place" and person reports feeling that thoughts are racing.
5. Person is easily distracted.
6. Person appears to be always moving, sometimes in a goal-directed fashion, and sometimes not.
7. Engaging in pleasurable activities seemingly without any awareness of the potential consequences.

C. Symptoms result in impairment in functioning.
D. Impairment in functioning is observed by others.

For information on the treatment of hypomanic symptoms, please refer to the entry on mania.

SUPPLEMENTARY RESOURCES

Berger, D., & Berger, L. (1991). *We heard the angels of madness: A family guide to coping with manic depression.* New York: Quill.

Jefferson, J., & Bohn, M. (1990). *Lithium and manic depression: A guide.* Lithium Information Center, University of Wisconsin, Department of Psychiatry.

Jefferson, J., & Greist, J. (1990). *Valproate and manic depression: A guide.* Lithium Information Center, University of Wisconsin, Department of Psychiatry.

Medenwald, J. (1990). *Carbamaxepine and manic depression: A guide.* Lithium Information Center, University of Wisconsin, Department of Psychiatry.

I Idolization–Interview Schedule for Children

Idolization

Often to the chagrin of parents, teachers, and other authority figures, children and adolescents often take it upon themselves to engage in the process of idolization. That is to say, they identify a person or group of people (real or fantasy) with whom they choose to identify, imitate, and, to varying degrees, put on a pedestal. This idolization can take the form of actually identifying with the idolized figure (ranging in intensity from dressing similarly, to mimicking the style of verbalization, to asking to be "called" by the name of the idolized figure, to actually attempting to act like the figure).

As indicated in the entry on **Modeling,** younger children tend to choose figures to idolize whom they perceive as being kind and/or powerful. Thus, when younger children engage in idolization, it is typically not as aversive to their parents because the objects of their idolization tend to be figures of whom adults do not necessarily disapprove. However, between the ages of 18 months and 3 years, it is similarly likely for the children to choose television characters to idolize. As children mature into the school years, it seems to become more important for the object of the idolization to be their age or older, and to be similar to them in as many ways as possible—especially gender. It is at this time when boys will look to sports figures and male rock stars and girls tend to look to fashion models, female performers, and, for some girls, female sports figures.

As the child approaches adolescence, it is often the case that the purpose of idolization assumes a different role. Specifically, as the child approaches his or her preteen and teen years, he or she tends to look for an object of idolization who possesses the qualities the adolescent perceives himself or herself as lacking. Thus, the shy, withdrawn adolescent may look to a flamboyant entertainer or the most popular classmate to idolize. Similarly, the overweight teen is likely to look to the slim, athletic classmates or popular magazine images to idolize. Adults seldom find this behavior especially problematic until the teen reaches the point where he or she either looks to inappropriate people as role models (e.g., the adolescent who is repeatedly picked on by classmates beginning to idolize someone who is extremely physically aggressive) or the teen seems to relinquish his or her own sense of identity in an attempt to idolize some other figure.

Whereas a certain amount of idolization is common during childhood, and especially during adolescence, as with any other behavior, when the idolization reaches extreme proportions it can approach being psychologically unhealthy and, certainly, troublesome for the parents and other family members. Of course, the process of idolization, in and of itself, is certainly not indicative of some major psychological crisis. However, in those cases in which the idolization is carried out to an extreme, this is usually indicative of some deeper psychological issue. Indeed, by looking at the type of person or the type of behavior the young person chooses to idolize, one can obtain some insight as to what is going on for the young person psychologically.

For example, as indicated above, it is often the case that much can be revealed about the child/adolescent's psychological issues by looking at whom he or she chooses to idolize. In those cases in which it is not blatantly obvious, one need only ask the young person why he or she is so fond of this particular individual or type of behavior. One way or the other, the adult will eventually decipher that the choice of idolization object is certainly not random. To varying degrees, this choice typically reflects how the particular young person "wants to be," and, sheds some light as to how he or she perceives himself as being (i.e., more specifically, in what areas he or she is currently lacking or deficient).

The extent to which the parent can determine details about the object being idolized provides valuable information about the young person's psychological struggles. More specifically, answers to the following questions can prove helpful in this endeavor:

- What is it in particular that the young person has chosen to idolize?
  - Is it a specific behavior observed in various people?
  - Is it an entire range of behaviors observed in a single person?
- How does the young person perceive what is being idolized?
  - How does he or she perceive others reacting to what is being idolized?
  - How does he/she perceive the lifestyle of those who engage in the behavior that is being idolized?
- How does the person and/or behavior being idolized differ from the young person's normal behavior?

Determining the answers to these questions will help to decipher the dynamics behind the idolization process. In so doing, the adult will be able to help the child identify (and possibly even articulate) crucial psychological issues so that they can be addressed directly.

Imaginary Friends

Having imaginary friends is a common aspect of childhood in that many children of preschool and kindergarten age speak of imaginary playmates, siblings, pets, family members, and adventures. These are in no way in and of themselves to be considered pathological, hallucinatory, or indicative of some severe **Psychotic Disorder**. Indeed, when pressed (not that this is always necessarily a good idea!), the child will admit that these characters are indeed imaginary, make-pretend, or otherwise not real. Unfortunately (but understandably!), parents often pressure the child to admit this to reassure themselves that the child is not mentally ill. It is noteworthy, however, that this can turn into a power struggle with the child somehow sensing that it is important to the parent that he or she admit that the characters are not real, and therefore refusing to do so.

Imaginary friends are quite valuable in obtaining insight as to what is going on for the child psychologically at any given time. Similar to the information gleaned when observing the content and the manner in which a child plays, imaginary friends provide considerable insight into the child's psychological processes. The imaginary friends—in terms of who they are, how they treat the child, how the child treats them, and how they behave—provide insight into the child's wishes, desires, fears, and anxieties. As with other forms of fantasy, the child uses the imaginary friends as a vehicle to exercise various emotional and psychological needs such as anger, practicing of interpersonal skills, sharing of fears, creating of situations that will turn out the way he or she wants them to, feelings toward parents and others in his or her life, as well as how he or she would like life to be and/ or how he or she fears life will be.

The parents should look at the presence of imaginary friends as an opportunity to view what is psychologically transpiring for the child. By taking the time to listen closely to the child's descriptions of the imaginary friends and their activities, the parent can initiate some therapeutic interaction with the child in terms of the deeper meaning behind what is being said. For example, when talking with the child about the imaginary friend (or friends for that matter!), answers to some of the following questions may prove insightful:

- Why do you think the imaginary friend said that?
- Why do you think the imaginary friend did that?
- Do other people like the imaginary friend? Why or why not?
- Do you think the imaginary friend is happy, sad, angry, or scared?
- Why does he or she feel that way?
- Have you ever felt that way? (Be cautious with such questions; oftentimes, the child uses the imaginary friend to express aspects of himself or herself with which he or she is uncomfortable; if the adult brings the child into the conversation before he or she is ready, the child may shut down and terminate the interaction.)
- What do you think we could do to make the imaginary friend feel better?

Imipramine

Imipramine is one of the more commonly prescribed **Tricyclic Antidepressants** and, of this groups of drugs, it is the one most frequently used in treating young people. Approved for the treatment of depression in adolescents as well as adults, imipramine is also used as a pharmacological intervention for **Enuresis, Attention**

Deficit Disorder, and various **Phobias** and **Anxiety Disorders.** Aside from use in the treatment of enuresis (in which imipramine can be used for children as young as 6 years of age), imipramine is not recommended for children under the age of 12 years.

The actual dosage schedule for imipramine depends on the diagnosis as well as the target symptoms being addressed. In cases of adolescent depression, the initial dosage ranges from 30–40 mg with gradual increases (often up to 100 mg). As a treatment for enuresis, 25 mg one hour before bedtime is the recommended dosage. Should this not be effective after one week, an increase to a maximum of 50 mg should then be tried. If the child is over the age of 12, a maximum dosage of 75 mg can be considered. There is no established dosage schedule with respect to the usage of imipramine in the treatment of attention deficit disorder, phobias, or anxiety disorders. Imipramine comes in two primary forms: tablets and capsules. However, the capsules are stronger in potency and are therefore recommended for dosage regimens of once daily dosing. Because of the greater potential for side effects in the capsules, they are not advised for children and young people.

The primary concern with respect to negative side effects of imipramine focuses around cardiovascular problems. In addition, it has been reported that, in some cases, imipramine increases the probability of seizure activity. Thus, children and adolescents with known cardiovascular problems or tendencies toward seizure activity are advised against the use of imipramine (as well as the other tricyclic antidepressants).

SUPPLEMENTAL RESOURCES

Breggin, P. (1991). *Toxic psychiatry.* New York: St. Martin's Press.
Maxmen, J., & Ward, N. (1996). *Psychotropic drugs: Fast facts.* New York: Norton.
Rosenberg, D. R., Holttum, J., & Gershon, S. (1994). *Textbook of pharmacotherapy for child and adolescent psychiatric disorders.* New York: Brunner/Mazel.
Werry, J. S., & Aman, M. G. (1993). *Practitioner's guide to psychoactive drugs for children and adolescents.* New York: Plenum.

Implosive Therapy

Implosive therapy is a form of behavior therapy typically used to treat **Anxiety Disorders,** specifically **Phobias.** Originated by Stamfl in the early sixties, implosive therapy involves having the person imagine contact with the phobic object. Based upon the assumption that phobic avoidance is predicated on the avoidance of anxiety, implosive therapy works by actually attempting to prevent the individual from avoiding the phobic object. This is done via vivid sensory imagery that is designed to *desensitize* the individual to exposure to the phobic object via imagination so that, theoretically, he or she will be able to confront the phobic stimulus in reality. Images are presented in a hierarchical fashion, "imploding" the individual with the image thought to be the least anxiety provoking first, and gradually increasing the anxiety level associated with the images presented. The crucial aspect of this process is that the individual experience his or her anxiety, not flee (metaphorically or physically) from the anxiety, and then recognize that no negative consequences will result.

In their early work on implosive therapy, Stamfl and Lewis (1967) outlined the eight areas that tend to be the focus of implosive therapy sessions. According to these pioneers of the implosive therapy process, such themes are present (in one form or another) in virtually every case treated:

Orality: ideas and fears of being physically harmed, usually in a gruesome manner

Anality: images and fears of becoming humiliated or otherwise embarrassed by having a bowel movement in a social or otherwise inappropriate situation

Sexuality: images or fears of having one's genitals harmed, being raped, or otherwise sexually assaulted

Aggression: images or fears of expressing anger in an inappropriate manner or with an inappropriate intensity

Rejection: fears of being abandoned, insulted, or otherwise rejected

Loss of impulse control: loss of control of angry or sexual impulses

Guilt: feelings of having committed some unpardonable wrong

Physical symptoms of anxiety: fears of experiencing panic symptoms

Despite the hypothetical validity associated with the implosive therapy procedure, currently, this mode of therapy is not used very frequently. Rather, in the treatment of phobic disorders, some form of **Cognitive Behavior Therapy** is the technique of preference, or, if exposure therapy is utilized, it is done in a real-life situation as opposed to imaginary exposure.

Incongruent Affect

This is a term used to describe the quality of **Affect** expressed by an individual. When affect is described as incongruent, what is being conveyed is that the affect does not appear to be consistent with the content of the situation. For example, an individual who is telling about the death of a loved one is laughing heartily as he talks. Yet another example would be an individual telling of a positive, satisfying experience but exhibiting severe symptoms of anxiety and/or anger as she speaks.

The key element here is that it is the observer who is judging the affect to be inconsistent, incongruent. What that means, then, is that the individual expressing this incongruent affect is clearly experiencing the situation in a manner different from that of the observer. Thus, one can conclude that, in most such cases, one of the parties is perceiving reality differently from the other! This could be a situation wherein the individual is actually experiencing **Hallucinations** of some form, or simply a situation in which the perception of reality is otherwise altered. In any case, it is clear why incongruent affect is often considered a symptom of **Schizophrenia** or some other **Psychotic Disorder.** However, the psychotic disorders are certainly not the only situations in which incongruent affect can appear. Indeed, depression, **Dissociative Disorder,** and substance abuse disorders all have incongruent affect as a common symptom.

When considering the case of incongruent affect, it is important to recognize that the issue of congruence extends beyond appropriateness between the observed affect and the content of the conversation. Incongruence of affect is also a relevant concept with respect to the mood reported by the child/adolescent (e.g., the individual reports feeling in a certain way, but his or her affect is not consistent with what is reported), the physical appearance of the patient (in terms of clothing, facial gestures, body language), and overall behavior and speech (in terms of delivery, articulation, wording chosen, etc.). The extent to which the expressed affect is deemed incongruent as well as the areas (both quantity and quality) in which the incongruence appears are all significant in assessing the presence and severity of pathology.

Individual Psychotherapy

Individual psychotherapy remains the most common treatment format with adults as well as with young people. In most, if not all such sessions, the primary interaction remains between the clinician and the identified patient. When utilizing this approach, the clinician treats the child or adolescent as the patient and assumes that clinical progress can occur with the primary contact limited to individual sessions. Clinicians who use this approach do not deny the importance of obtaining data from parents, other family members, or school personnel. However, the young person is conceptualized as the patient, and, the primary clinical interactions are with him or her.

This format of doing therapy has the advantage of metacommunicating to the child/adolescent that he or she is deserving of the clinician's sole attention. It also allows the child to privately share information with the clinician. Of course, the major disadvantage of this format is that the clinician has limited opportunity to observe interaction patterns between the child and the parents, as well as relatively limited opportunity to validate information that the child provides.

Individuation

Individuation is a term used to refer to the development of an adult relationship with one's parents as well as the development of a sense of personhood as an adult separate and apart from the rest of the world—more specifically, separate and apart from one's parents. Developed from a psychoanalytic concept (specifically that of *separation–individuation)*, individuation is often presented as being opposite to the phenomenon of *enmeshment*—an unhealthy connection with one's parents, to an extent beyond which one would expect at the given developmental stage, and intense enough to impede psychologically healthy development and growth. Oftentimes, individuation is conceptualized as the elimination of a feeling of oneness between parent and child—both on the part of the parent as well as on the part of the child.

SUPPLEMENTAL RESOURCES

Ashner, L., & Meyerson, M. (1997). *When parents love too much.* Center City, MN: Hazelden.
MacArthur, D. (1996). *The birth of a self in adulthood* New York: Jason Aronson.
Neuharth, Dan. (1998). *If you had controlling parents.* New York: HarperCollins.

Infantile Autism

Infantile autism is a term originated by Leo Kanner in his 1943 paper "Autistic Disturbance of Affective Contact." This being the first time **Autistic Disorder** as such was acknowledged as a diagnosis, Kanner described the symptoms of eleven children who he believed were suffering from the early stages of **Schizophrenia.** It is interesting that, although Kanner based his observations upon a very small sample, his conclusions as to the characteristic symptoms of infantile autism do not differ significantly from the description of autistic disorder held today. Indeed, Kanner wrote of these children as being characterized by impaired spontaneity, problems in interactions with others, monotonous repetition of certain noises or words, problems with language development, and difficulties adjusting to change.

Informed Consent

Informed consent refers to an individual's agreement to engage in a process of therapy, assessment, or research with the understanding that the consent is based upon a thorough understanding of what is going to transpire. That is to say, the understanding is as extensive as it can be considering the developmental, psychiatric, and intellectual level of the individual involved. This process of informed consent is mandatory prior to engaging anybody in treatment, research, or assessment. Indeed, informed consent is a crucial element of all professional interactions with a psychologist or other mental health professional.

However, although the concept of informed consent is a rather simple one in and of itself, the issue becomes a bit more complicated when young people are concerned. The extent to which a child or adolescent is capable of providing informed consent is not always clear. The *Ethical Principles* of the American Psychological Association emphasizes the necessity of the person's ability to fully understand the research, assessment, or therapeutic procedure(s). However, if psychological, intellectual, or developmental factors prevent the individual from providing informed consent, it is incumbent upon the treating professional to ensure that any intervention is in the person's best interest. Ethical standards demand that the clinician offer the individual an explanation of any and all services proposed, whether therapeutic, research. or diagnostic in nature. When working with children or adolescents, the clinician is supposed to explain the assessment of therapeutic procedures in a manner appropriate to the person's developmental level. When such an explanation is not feasible, the therapist may obtain informed consent from a representative of the child—usually a parent, teacher, or some other responsible party. It is the responsibility of the treating clinician, however, to ensure that the choice of this representative is also in the young person's best interest.

SUPPLEMENTAL RESOURCES

American Psychological Association. (1992). *Ethical principles and standards.* Washington, DC: American Psychological Association.

Insomnia

Insomnia is a general term referring to either problems with initiating sleep (i.e., falling asleep) or maintaining sleep (i.e., as evidenced by frequent wakening during the night). Causes of insomnia can be either physical (e.g., pain, dietary factors, hormonal problems, aging, various diseases, substance use/abuse) or more psychological in nature (e.g., depression, grief reaction, general worry, anxiety, **Post-Traumatic Stress Disorder, Schizophrenia,** environmental changes).

In the current edition of the *DSM* (American Psychiatric Association, 1994), insomnia is classified under the category sleep disorders. The manual distinguishes between insomnia that occurs independently of any other psychological/psychiatric disorder (e.g., primary insomnia) and those cases of insomnia related to an Axis I or Axis II disorder. In general, the *DSM-IV* requires that the insomnia be present for a period of at least 1 month, and that the actual disturbance in sleep results in impairment in the individual's functioning (even if this impairment is largely a function of fatigue during the day due to lack of sleep).

Occasional bouts of insomnia are not at all uncommon and often occur as a response to situational anxiety. In such situations, the following can be helpful interventions for children, adolescents, and adults alike:

Regular sleep time: Establishing of a regular time to go to bed each night and to awaken each morning, keeping loyal to that schedule.

Stimulus control: Rearrange the sleep area (even if it involves only moving a picture around or changing the quilt on the bed); this extinguishes the connection between the environment and being unable to sleep properly.

Bed is for sleeping: Limit the use of the bed itself to sleep; again, by not using the bed for reading, watching television, playing board games, and the like, the person begins to develop an association between the bed and its being a place for sleep.

Limit/eliminate daytime naps: Sleeping during the day can decrease a person's need/desire for sleep at night; further, sleeping during the day in an environment outside of the "designated bed area" can also hinder the process of association described above.

Limitations on caffeine: Restrain from ingesting beverages or foods containing caffeine before bedtime.

Develop a bedtime ritual: The consistency of performing the same behaviors prior to going to bed creates a routine that can be relaxing in and of itself, and therefore support a restful sleep.

Relaxation training: Include some form of formalized relaxation in the bedtime ritual; this can be an instructional relaxation tape, a structured exercise, or a simple behavior that the person happens to find relaxing.

Food intake: Avoid eating large quantities of food or elaborate meals prior to bedtime.

Conversation: Avoid discussing topics immediately prior to bedtime that have the potential of being anxiety provoking or contentious.

SUPPLEMENTAL RESOURCES

Coren, S. (1996). *Sleep thieves.* New York: Free Press.
Eberlein, T. (1996). *Sleep—How to teach your child to sleep like a baby.* New York: Pocket Books.
Ferber, R. (1985). *Solve your child's sleep problems.* New York: Simon & Schuster.
Gottlieb, S. (1993). *Keys to children's sleep problems.* New York: Barrons.

Intelligence Quotient (IQ)

Technically, the term *Intelligence Quotient* (abbreviated IQ) refers to the figure obtained when an individual's intelligence score (on a certain measure) is divided by the average intelligence score (on that same measure) for others of his or her age. Originally, the most common manner of calculating this ratio was by dividing the person's *mental age* (as determined by testing) by the person's *chronological age* (i.e., how old the person is). Over the past several years, however, the phrase Intelligence Quotient has come to be associated with the specific score an individual receives on a standardized test designed to measure the ambiguous concept known as intelligence.

One of the earliest such tests to measure intelligence in children was the Stanford-Binet Intelligence Scale. Still in use today in a revised form, the test is designed to assess intelligence of people aged 2 to 24 years. This was the first test that presented the concept of IQ—the ratio of mental age to chronological age.

Currently, the most commonly used measures to assess intelligence in children are the two age-appropriate versions of the Wechsler Intelligence Tests: the Wechsler Primary and Preschool Intelligence Scales–Revised (referred to as the WPPSI-R) and the Wechsler Intelligence Scale for Children–3 (referred to as the WISC-III). Both of these tests yield three major IQ scores: one that represents the child's overall verbal abilities (the Verbal IQ–VIQ), one that represents the child's overall performance (or nonverbal) abilities (the Performance IQ–PIQ), and a third called the Full Scale IQ (FSIQ), which is a combination of the verbal and performance IQ scores. In turn, each of the Verbal and Performance IQ Scores is composed of scores on various subscales that tap different aspects of verbal and nonverbal skills, respectively. (Thus, analyses of the child's scores on these different subscales can provide information about the child's relative strengths and weaknesses within each area.)

Although there is considerable flexibility, generally speaking, an IQ score of 100 on both of the Wechsler tests is considered to be average with the following breakdowns:

70 and below	mental retardation range
70 to 80	borderline intellectual functioning
80 to 90	low average range of intellectual functioning
90 to 109	average range of intellectual functioning
110 to 119	high average range of intellectual functioning
120 and above	superior range of intellectual functioning

SUPPLEMENTAL RESOURCES

Serebriakoff, V. (1996). *Self administered IQ tests for children.* New York: Barnes & Noble Books.

International Classification of Diseases (ICD)

This manual contains the diagnostic system most commonly used in Great Britain and Europe. Published by the World Health Organization, it provides diagnostic guidelines and information on **Differential Diagnosis** for each diagnostic category listed. Although the volume containing the classification of the mental and behavioral disorders is designed to correspond as closely as possible with the *DSM-IV*, the current edition of the *International Classification of Diseases* (now the tenth one, therefore entitled the *ICD-10*) lists more diagnostic categories specific to children and adolescents than does the *DSM-IV*. Indeed, the *ICD-10* lists fourteen major diagnostic categories in addition to mental retardation, each category containing several subcategories. The major diagnostic categories listed in the *ICD-10* relevant to young people are as follows:

Mental retardation
Disorders of psychological development
Specific developmental disorders of speech and language
Specific developmental disorders of scholastic skills
Specific developmental disorder of motor function
Mixed specific developmental disorders
Pervasive developmental disorders
Hyperkinetic disorders
Conduct disorders
Mixed disorders of conduct and emotions
Emotional disorders with onset specific to childhood
Disorders of social functioning with onset specific to childhood and adolescence
Tic disorders
Stereotyped movement disorders

SUPPLEMENTAL RESOURCES

World Health Organization. (1992). *The ICD-10 classification of mental and behavioral disorders: Clinical descriptions and diagnostic guidelines.* Geneva, Switzerland: World Health Organization.

Interview Schedule for Children

This is a semistructured interview that is used to assess the presence of various psychological disorders in children. It is important to note that the Interview Schedule for Children (ISC) was designed primarily for research purposes as opposed to being designed for actual clinical practice. Designed to be used with young people ranging from 8 to 17 years of age, the ISC is administered separately to the parent and the child (with each administration lasting approximately 1 hour). The first part of assessment with this instrument consists of a rather general exploratory interview designed to glean information about the general nature of the young person's symptoms. Considerably more structured, the second part of the ISC consists of a series of questions addressing the frequency and severity of various symptoms, asking the rater to respond along a nine-point scale.

L Labeling Effects–Luvox

Labeling Effects

The phrase *labeling effects* refers to the potential implications of providing an individual with a diagnosis, placing an individual in a given classification, and/or otherwise labeling an individual in some manner or another. The theory behind labeling effects is based upon the fact that the mere act of giving a person a label of some type, in and of itself, influences the manner in which the person behaves. The actual impact of the label can be either positive or negative, and can be either consistent with or opposite to the implications of the actual label itself.

Closely related to the concept of *expectancy effect*, labeling effects derive from the expectations of society as well as the expectations of the individual in terms of how someone with this specific label *should* behave. Thus, once there is awareness of the specific category, the individual is either treated differently, expects to be treated differently, and/or acts differently. At times this is a conscious, deliberate action, whereas at other times it is entirely unconscious. For example, one common example of the application of labeling effects focuses on the issue of diagnosis. Many people believe that by labeling a young person with a psychological/psychiatric diagnosis, the stigma associated with this can cause the child/adolescent to suffer additional difficulties virtually unrelated to the actual symptoms themselves. Thus, the diagnosis itself becomes a self-fulfilling prophecy, and the child engages in behaviors because he or she feels as if society expects it.

> *Example:* Nine-year-old Manny was recently informed that he will be assigned to the resource room for help with his troubles in mathematics. Previously a child who was motivated and hard working, Manny's attitude toward his mathematics schoolwork seems to have changed. His mother reports him giving up easily on math problems, saying, "I'm no good in math…even the school says so…what's the use in trying?"

As indicated above, however, labeling effects can also work in a positive direction, and often in a manner contrary to what one would initially think.

> *Example:* Thirteen-year-old John was falsely accused of cheating in his science class. He performed unusually well on an exam (for which he studied extensively), and his teacher accused him of copying the an-

swers from the "A" student who sits in front of him. Feeling that he is now labeled as a "Cheat," John is determined to perform equally well on all subsequent tests to prove his teacher wrong and to validate his honesty.

Learned Helplessness

Developed by Martin Seligman, learned helplessness is a clinical concept that has its origins in experimental research. The concept of learned helplessness was discovered when dogs were experimentally exposed to a situation wherein they were administered electric shocks, but were unable to do anything to escape. It was observed that these dogs eventually appeared to give up; that is, they stopped making any attempt to avoid the shock when they learned that they were actually helpless in doing so. Further, eventually this giving up behavior began to generalize to other situations in the dogs' lives and they assumed an overall helpless demeanor.

After this phenomenon was recognized, some believed that it served as a valid model for human depression. Proponents of such a model of clinical depression point out that, when an individual is in an aversive situation, and perceives himself or herself as having no way out or no way to control the negative aspects, the person eventually resigns to the situation and stops trying to change it. A classic example of such a case would be the child who has been having difficulty with his school subjects his entire life who eventually gives up, saying "I'm stupid" and then resigns himself to a life of failure.

Learning Disorders

Formerly referred to as **Academic Skill Disorders,** this is a classification of diagnoses in the current edition of the *DSM (DSM-IV)* that includes the following disorders: **Reading Disorder, Mathematics Disorder, Disorder of Written Expression,** and **Learning Disorder Not Otherwise Specified (NOS).** For a specific description of each of these disorders, the reader is referred to the particular entry.

SUPPLEMENTARY RESOURCES

Fisher, G., & Cummings, R. (1995). *When your child has LD (learning differences).* Minneapolis, MN: Free Spirit.

Gehret, J. (1996). *The don't-give-up kid and learning differences.* Fairport, NY: Verbal Images Press.

Mandel, H. P., & Marcus, S. I. (1995). *Could do better.* New York: John Wiley.

McNamara, B. E., & McNamara, F. J. (1995). *Keys to parenting a child with a learning disability.* New York: Barrons.

Rosner, J. (1993). *Helping children overcome learning difficulties.* New York: Walker.

Smith, S. L. (1991). *Succeeding against the odds: How the learning disabled can realize their promise.* New York: Bantam.

Smith, S. L. (1995). *No easy answers: The learning disabled child at home and at school.* New York: Bantam.
Unger, H. G. (1998). *The learning disabilities trap.* Chicago: Contemporary Books.

Learning Disorders Not Otherwise Specified (NOS)

This is a diagnosis in the **Learning Disorders** category designed to incorporate those individuals with some type of learning disorder, yet, a learning disorder that does not meet the diagnostic criteria of **Reading Disorder, Mathematics Disorder** or **Disorder of Written Expression.** A diagnosis of learning disorder NOS is applied to those individuals who have problems in all of the above three content areas, or individuals who have problems in any combination of the aforementioned content areas but who do not meet the criteria required for one of the more specific diagnoses.

Listening to the Child or Adolescent

In actuality, interacting with a child or adolescent is not all that different from having a meaningful interaction with an adult, as the same basic principles apply. It is crucial to pay attention to verbal and nonverbal cues, to be aware of what is being *said* not merely of what is being verbalized, and to interact on a level compatible with both parties' ability to understand. With respect to listening to the child or adolescent, again, there is not much that is significantly different from listening to an adult. Certain applied principles vary somewhat as a function of age and developmental level. However, as these principles are reviewed below, it is clear how easily they could be applied to any interpersonal interactions, employing only minor variations:

> *Listen first at a pure content level:* At times, in our attempt to be helpful and understanding, we tend to assume that there is some hidden meaning to what is verbalized. Whereas this is certainly the case in some instances, it is always advisable to pay attention to the surface (superficial) content of what is being said. Indeed, even if there is some hidden deeper meaning to the communication, what is *actually* said is a good indication of what the child/adolescent wants you to hear.

> *What is really being said here:* After you code the actual verbalization, it is necessary to determine if what is being physically heard is consistent with the true meaning of the communication. It is crucial not to engage in mind reading behaviors here (no matter how well the listener thinks he or she knows the young person), but rather to attempt to confirm impressions of what is actually transpiring. The best way to do this is to

formulate some hypotheses, and then test them out—either directly or indirectly.

> *Formulation of hypotheses:* In order to determine whether what is being said is actually what is *really* being said, answers to the following questions can be helpful:
>
> - Is the young person's body language consistent with what he or she is actually verbalizing?
> - Does the young person appear to be satisfied when you respond to him or her on a surface level?
> - Based upon the content of the conversation, would there be any reasons for the young person to feel uncomfortable articulating his feelings directly?
> - Would there be any other thing that the young person would be trying to say?
>
> *Testing of hypotheses:* When testing the hypotheses of what you think the child/adolescent is really saying, it is important to do so in a respectful, cautious manner. Even if your theories about what is being said are completely accurate, it is important not to bring them into the conversation in a definitive, headstrong manner. After all, there is a reason that the child/adolescent is not being direct in his or her communication, and these feelings need to be respected. Thus, when introducing your hypotheses about what is being conveyed, it best be done delicately. The following are approaches that can be helpful in this matter:
>
> - Comment on the inconsistency between what the young person is saying and what you are observing, how you would expect him or her to act, or whatever it is that appears to be inconsistent between what is being verbalized and what you believe is being experienced; preface your comments with a "diffusing" statement such as "I may be wrong but…," "It seems weird to me that…," "Could it be that…," or "Some people…." A major goal here is to minimize the possibility of putting the young person on the defensive and/or having him or her feel forced into divulging something.
> - Present your comments in the framework of an observation as opposed to a definitive statement of fact.
> - Always frame your comment in such a way that the child/adolescent has the opportunity to maintain/retain his or her esteem and sense of dignity.

Keep in mind whenever you listen (or otherwise interact) with a child or adolescent that he or she has the best sense of what is going on psychologically for him or her (even if he or she does not opt to face these issues directly at the current time). Thus, when interacting with a young person, you as an adult can learn the most by simply listening. (Indeed, at times, young people do not want advice, comments, etc., but rather simply a nonjudgmental ear!) When in doubt in terms of how to respond, the best option follows the dictum "less is more." Rather than feel pressured to respond verbally, it is best for the adult to listen carefully, acknowledge what is being said, and allow the young person's communicative style to direct the flow of conversation.

SUPPLEMENTARY RESOURCES

Faber, A., & Mazlish, E. (1982). *How to talk so kids will listen and listen so kids will talk.* New York: Avon.
Henkart, A. F., & Henkart, J. (1988). *Cool communication.* New York: Berkeley Press.
Risso, M. J. (1999). *Little Michael's guide to good parents: A seven year old's view.* Buffalo, NY: Continuing Learning.

Lithium

Considered to be the primary line of treatment for adults with **Bipolar Disorder,** lithium has also been approved for use in the treatment of young people with bipolar disorder as long as they are 12 years of age or older. However, it is interesting to note that there continue to be investigations as to the potential use of lithium in younger children with respect to the treatment of bipolar disorder as well as other diagnoses. Specifically, research is investigating the usage of lithium in the treatment of depression, aggressive behaviors, and various behavior problems—especially in those children whose parents have shown a positive response to lithium themselves. In sum then, although lithium currently has FDA approval only for the treatment of bipolar disorder in individuals 12 years of age and older, the following diagnoses are currently being investigated as possible indications for lithium use: **Encopresis,** aggression/violent behavior, depression, **Cyclothymia, Attention Deficit Hyperactivity Disorder, Bulimia, Alcoholism** and various **Personality Disorders.**

Available in 300 mg tablets, 300 mg capsules, 300 mg and 450 mg controlled-release tablets, and in a lithium citrate syrup (with 8 mEQ/5 ml dosage equaling one 300 mg tablet), lithium dosage usually begins with a range between 150 and 300 mg/day. Dosage increases are to be gradual, determined as a function of serum level checks (to determine lithium level). It is recommended that serum levels be obtained 5 days after the first dose, and then obtained 5 days after every increase. It is interesting to note that, because of the way lithium is metabolized, the drug reaches therapeutic levels more quickly in children than in adults. Further, as a function of their metabolizing of the drug, it is not uncommon for children and adolescents to require higher dosages of lithium (per body weight) than would adults.

A major issue with lithium treatment (and a major reason for needing to perform the aforementioned serum levels on a regular basis) is the potential for the drug to reach a toxic level in the child/adolescent's bloodstream. What makes this especially prevalent in cases with lithium is that the level at which it becomes toxic is not that different from the level necessary for the drug to be therapeutic. Further, since there is no established treatment for lithium toxicity, preventive measures are required. Symptoms of lithium toxicity include gastrointestinal distress, tremors, sedation, slurred speech, and coordination problems. If allowed to proceed unaddressed, lithium toxicity can be fatal. When symptoms of lithium toxicity occur, the lithium treatment should temporarily cease, serum levels should be obtained, and the drug resumed only after 24–48 hours (and then, at a lower dosage).

Separate and apart from the potentially dangerous occurrence of lithium toxicity, there are negative side effects that are relatively common early on when beginning treatment with lithium. Included among these early side effects are tremors, weight gain, headaches, gastrointestinal problems, frequent urination, frequent thirst, and nausea. Because of the manner in which the body metabolizes the drug, thyroid functioning and kidney functioning need to be monitored regularly throughout the treatment to assess for potentially dangerous effects.

SUPPLEMENTAL RESOURCES

Breggin, P. (1991). *Toxic psychiatry.* New York: St Martin's Press.

Jefferson, J., & Bohn, M. (1990). *Lithium and manic depression: A guide.* Lithium Information Center, University of Wisconsin, Department of Psychiatry.

Maxmen, J., & Ward, N. (1996). *Psychotropic drugs: Fast facts.* New York: Norton.

Rosenberg, D. R., Holttum, J., & Gershon, S. (1994). *Textbook of pharmacotherapy for child and adolescent disorders.* New York: Brunner/Mazel.

Werry, J. S., & Aman, M. G. (1993). *Practitioner's guide to psychoactive drugs for children and adolescents.* New York:Plenum.

Loose Associations

Loose associations are a type of verbal and/or thought process in which the person jumps from subject to subject without any meaningful transition or connection among the former topics, current topics, and subsequent topics. Considered to be a form of *derailment*, when a person is exhibiting loose associations, the flow of conversation can be barely understandable to the listener. Whereas interacting with someone who is exhibiting loose associations can leave the listener somewhat confused and bewildered as to the process/direction of the conversation, the person who is manifesting the loose associations appears to be totally unaware of any aspect of his or her speech that is unusual. Most often, the presence of loose associations occurs in cases of severe thought disturbance, as is present in **Schizophrenia,** and less frequently in **Manic** and **Hypomanic Episodes.**

Example: Nineteen-year-old Estelle responded as follows to her parents when they asked her how she was enjoying her first semester of college: "College, oh, college is okay. I enjoy the classes and the professors as they tend to be intellectually stimulating, as is the vibrator I recently purchased but there was no service plan and sure enough it broke after one week…at which time my paper for my language arts course is due…so, I have to learn the updated version of my word processing program…. They're all such money hungry capitalists…"

Loxapine

This is the generic name for the antipsychotic (neuroleptic) drug **Loxitane.** Please refer to that entry for a description of the drug.

Loxitane

Loxitane (**Loxapine**) is an antipsychotic drug, a member of the chemical family of the dibenzoxazepines. According to the manufacturer, it is to be used only in individuals over the age of 16 years. Available in capsules, oral concentrate, and intramuscular injection, the initial recommended dosage for loxitane is usually 10 mg twice per day, to be increased gradually to the therapeutic level of 60–100 mg per day. **Extrapyramidal Side Effects** are among the most common side effects of loxitane.

SUPPLEMENTARY RESOURCES

Gorman, M. J. (1997). *The essential guide to psychiatric drugs.* New York: St. Martin's Press.
Maxmen, J., & Ward, N. (1996). *Psychotropic drugs: Fast facts.* New York: Plenum.
Weiden, P. J., Scheifler, P. L., Diamond, R. J., & Ross, R. (1998). *Switching antipsychotic medications: A guide for consumers and families.* Arlington, VA: National Alliance for the Mentally Ill.

Luria Nebraska Neuropsychological Battery

This is a collection of tests designed to assess an individual's **Neuropsychological** functioning. Specifically, this battery is designed to determine if indeed there is any neurophysiological pathology present, and, if so, the precise nature of it. Based upon the techniques developed by neuropsychologist Alexander Luria, the subtests in the Luria Nebraska battery include tests of speech, writing, reading, touch, rhythm, expressive and receptive speech, motor skills, as well as general intellectual ability. In addition, the Luria Nebraska battery is designed such that the test results can be interpreted in terms of strengths and weaknesses relative to the abilities of the left and right side of the brain.

SUPPLEMENTAL RESOURCES

Adams, R. L., Parsons, O. A., Culbertson, J. L., & Nixon, S. J. (Eds.). (1996). *Neuropsychology for clinical practice.* Washington, DC: American Psychological Association Press.

Luvox

Luvox is one of the newer medications in the class of **Selective Serotonin Reuptake Inhibitors.** Currently it is approved only for individuals 18 years and older, and then only for the treatment of the symptoms of **Obsessive-Compulsive Disorder.** Available in 50 mg and 100 mg tablets, an initial dosage of 50 mg is usually prescribed for bedtime, with dosages gradually increased as clinically indicated.

SUPPLEMENTAL RESOURCES

Gorman, J. M. (1997). *The essential guide to psychiatric drugs.* New York: St. Martin's Press.

Nordern, M. J. (1996). *Beyond Prozac.* New York: HarperCollins.

Rosenberg, D. R., Holttum, J., & Gershon, S. (1994). *Textbook of pharmacotherapy for child and adolescent disorders.* New York: Brunner/Mazel.

M
Major Tranquilizers–
Mood Disorders

Major Tranquilizers

This term is used synonymously with **Antipsychotic Medications.** Although the term is somewhat out of date, it is still used occasionally—specifically as a means of contrasting antipsychotic medications with those medications used to lessen anxiety symptoms (those referred to as *minor tranquilizers*). For more specific information on this class of medications, please refer to the entry on antipsychotic medications.

Mania

The term *mania* refers to a disorder of mood, which can be conceptualized as the polar opposite of **Depression.** Mania is often characterized as happiness carried to a pathological extreme with manic individuals manifesting expansive, overly dramatic affect and **Overproductive Speech** (also referred to as *pressured speech*). According to the *DSM-IV* (American Psychiatric Association, 1994), the following criteria must be met in order for a manic episode to be diagnosed:

A. A period of elevated, expansive or irritable mood lasting at least one week.
B. During the above period, at least three of the following are observed. If only irritability is observed, at least four of the following must be observed:
  1. unusually high self-esteem or grandiosity
  2. decreased need for sleep
  3. appearing more talkative than usual, often with an apparent pressure to keep talking
  4. sense that one's thoughts or ideas are racing
  5. easily distracted
  6. sense of the person always being moving or an increase in activity
  7. extreme involvement in pleasurable activities, which have the potential for dangerous consequences
C. The above symptoms are severe enough to cause impairment in day-to-day functioning. (p. 332)

With respect to mania in young people, the clinical presentation depends upon the age of the child/adolescent. Manic symptoms of children aged 9 years or younger tend to be more along the lines of irritability and **Affective Lability.** As the child gets older, the manic symptoms are characterized more by paranoia, extreme happiness and/or excitement, as well as grandiose ideas. Adolescents with manic symptoms present rather similarly to adults with such symptoms, with a greater prevalence of the extreme mood fluctuations often seen in adult cases of **Bipolar Disorder.**

It is important to be aware that there are several disorders that present similarly to manic disorders shown in young people, especially younger children. The most common disorders with which mania can be confused are listed below:

Attention Deficit Disorder: Children with attention deficit disorder tend to manifest lower self-esteem, whereas those with manic symptoms show a more grandiose sense of self and often an inflated self-esteem; also, attention deficit disorder has an earlier age of onset than do manic symptoms.

Conduct Disorder: In cases of conduct disorder, there is not the rapid, pressured speech pattern that is characteristic of manic disorder; in addition, cases of conduct disorder do not have the grandiosity that tends to be present in manic episodes.

Schizophrenia: The early histories of those with manic disorder differ considerably from those with the schizophrenic disorders; in cases of schizophrenia, early histories tend to be characterized by strange, isolated, or bizarre behavior.

Professional Treatment

The primary mode of treatment for manic disorder is pharmacological in orientation. Although **Lithium** is the drug most commonly used, it has not been approved by the FDA for children under the age of 12 years. Nonetheless, lithium has often been used in children as young as 5. Interestingly, the recommended dosage for these children is almost the same as that recommended for adults. However because of the potential danger of lithium toxicity, regular blood tests and physical exams are necessary before as well as during the treatment regimen.

SUPPLEMENTARY RESOURCES

Berger, D., & Berger, L. (1991). *We heard the angels of madness: A family guide to coping with manic depression.* New York: Quill.

Jefferson, J., & Bohn, M. (1990). *Lithium and manic depression: A guide.* Lithium Information Center, University of Wisconsin, Department of Psychiatry.

Jefferson, J., & Greist, J. (1990). *Valproate and manic depression: A guide.* Lithium Information Center, University of Wisconsin, Department of Psychiatry.

Medenwald, J. (1990). *Carbamazepine and manic depression: A guide.* Lithium Information Center, University of Wisconsin, Department of Psychiatry.

Masturbation

Technically, the behavior of masturbation refers to self-manipulation of one's genitals for the purpose of sexual pleasure. (It should be noted that there is a variation of masturbation, referred to as *psychic masturbation,* in which the individual achieves sexual pleasure and often reaches orgasm merely by the use of fantasy without any direct physical stimulation.)

It is generally acknowledged that masturbation is a normal human behavior, with even infants engaging in sexual self-stimulation. By the age of 15 months, babies of both sexes regularly masturbate, and begin to become aware of the association between the genital stimulation the resulting pleasurable feelings. Once the child approaches puberty, hormonal factors contribute the increase in sexual desire, and the resulting increase in the frequency of masturbatory activity.

How to react to childhood masturbation: When deciding how to react to a child's masturbation, the parent needs to take two things into account: (1) the parental value system that he or she wishes to impose, and (2) the manner in which the child is likely to internalize the message in terms of his or her own self-esteem, guilt, and other aspects of the child's psychology. No matter what the parental value system, it is not recommended that the parent react in a dramatic, hysterical, or otherwise emotional fashion. The message conveyed to the child needs to be done in a rational, factual tone—devoid of judgment or punishment. The child should matter of factly be informed that masturbation is a natural behavior, and then informed as to how the family perceives the behavior. Finally, it is important that the child be informed under what circumstances masturbation is deemed appropriate.

Comment upon the behavior, not upon the child: As with other behaviors in which a child may engage that evoke less than completely positive reactions, it is important that conversations about that behavior (especially relevant to its acceptability) focus on the behavior, not on the child. In other words a clear distinction must be made between the appropriateness of the child and the appropriateness of the masturbatory behavior. All possible assurances must be undertaken so that the child does not receive the message that there is somehow something wrong with him or her (psychologically, physically, morally) because of the masturbating.

Adolescent masturbation: With the hormonal fluctuations accompanying adolescence, masturbation often becomes a frequent activity. Still, despite its frequency, adolescents often experience significant shame and embarrassment regarding the activity. Part of this is due to their overall discomfort and lack of familiarity with sexuality in general, while another contributing factor is the adolescent's ambivalence about the masturbatory process. This can be addressed by acknowledging and respecting the adolescent's psychological position, providing him or her with accurate information, and, to the extent that the relationship will tolerate, address specific concerns directly.

SUPPLEMENTAL RESOURCES

Madaras, L. (1988). *The what's happening to my body book for boys.* New York: Newmarket Press.
Madaras, L. (1988). *The what's happening to my body book for girls.* New York: Newmarket Press.

Mathematics Disorder

Previously referred to as developmental arithmetic disorder, mathematics disorder is a diagnosis used when the child's mathematical ability is (1) significantly below his or her capabilities in other academic areas, and (2) significantly below that which would be expected for the child's overall developmental level. As with the other **Academic Skill Disorders,** assessment is performed via a series of standardized intelligence tests. Although a diagnosis of mathematics disorder is usually precipitated by school personnel, parents who have concerns about their child's mathematics ability relative to performance in other subjects can request testing from the school or from a private psychologist.

Because there are so many skills required in the mathematical process, there are various ways in which mathematics disorder can manifest itself. The *International Classification of Diseases (ICD-10)* lists the following symptoms as characteristic of children and adolescents with mathematics disorder:

- failure to understand the concepts underlying particular mathematical operations
- lack of understanding of mathematical terms of signs
- failure to recognize numerical symbols
- problems carrying out standard mathematical manipulations
- difficulty in understanding which numbers are relevant to the mathematical problem being considered
- difficulty in properly aligning numbers or in inserting decimal points or symbols during calculations
- poor spatial organization of mathematical calculations
- inability to learn multiplication tables satisfactorily

Again, should a parent observe any combination of these symptoms to an intensity beyond what would be expected from a child of the given developmental level (and relevant to abilities and skills in other areas), it is recommended that formalized testing be performed to determine if a diagnosis of mathematics disorder is warranted. As with the other learning disabilities, treatment interventions would focus on special educational programs aimed at facilitating the development of the specific mathematical skills that are deficient.

S U P P L E M E N T A L   R E S O U R C E S

Greene, L. J. (1997). *Learning disabilities and your child: A survival handbook.* New York: Ballantine.

McNamara, B. E., & McNamara, F. J. (1995). *Keys to parenting a child with a learning disability.* Hauppage, NY: Barrons.

Smith, S. L. (1991). *Succeeding against the odds: How the learning disabled can realize their promise.* New York: Putnam.

Smith, S. L. (1995). *No easy answers: The learning disabled child at home and at school.* New York: Bantam.

Unger, H. G. (1998). *The learning disabilities trap.* Chicago: Contemporary Books.

Zahler, K. A. (1998). *50 simple things you can do to raise a child who loves math.* New York: Macmillian.

Mellaril

Mellaril is an antipsychotic medication that is also FDA approved for the treatment of explosive behaviors and some forms of **Attention Deficit Disorder** in children over 2 years of age. Specifically, Mellaril is considered to be a possible intervention when a child/adolescent is exhibiting physically aggressive behaviors or explosive episodes, as well as in cases of attention deficit disorder in which the child shows symptoms of impulsivity, aggression, **Affective Lability,** attention problems, and/or poor frustration tolerance.

Available in 15 mg, 25 mg, 50 mg, 100 mg, 150 mg, and 200 mg tablets, Mellaril is also available in a concentrate form as well as in a suspension form. For children 12 years of age and under, the dosage ranges anywhere from 0.5 mg/kg/day to 3 mg/kg/day. Even in older children and adolescents, the maximum recommended dosage in 800 mg/day. Sedation and **Anticholinergic Side Effects** are among the most common side effects of Mellaril.

S U P P L E M E N T A L   R E S O U R C E S

Breggin, P. (1991). *Toxic psychiatry.* New York: St Martin's Press.

Gorman, J. M. (1997). *The essential guide to psychiatric drugs.* New York: St. Martin's Press.

Maxmen, J., & Ward, N. (1996). *Psychotropic drugs: Fast facts.* New York: Norton.

Werry, J. S., & Aman, M. G. (1993). *Practitioner's guide to psychoactive drugs for children and adolescents.* New York: Plenum.

Mental Illness in the Family

When there is some form of psychological/psychiatric illness in a child/adolescent's immediate family, there are several issues that need to be addressed. Understandably, with much of adult attention being focused on caring for the impaired family member (whether adult or young person) and tending to basic family needs, oftentimes the emotional and psychological need of the other children in the family tend to be overlooked. Whereas every case is certainly different, there are certain common issues that characterize the emotional struggles of young people who belong to a family in which another member (or members) suffers from some form of mental disorder:

Denial: Because the thought of having a family member suffering from a psychological or psychiatric disorder can be so anxiety provoking for a child, there is a natural tendency to deny that such is the case and to act as if everything is all right. Actually, there may even be some magical thinking involved in this behavior, believing that by acting "as if," the problem may actually cease to exist. Whereas a certain amount of denial may be necessary (and even healthy) at the very early stages to help the child get through the shock, supportive adults will eventually have to help the child gently break through his defenses of denial and begin to face the issues at hand.

What will happen to me? At the root of the young person's concerns is a fundamental worry about his or her safety and well-being. Having a basic awareness that an adult is necessary to care for him or her, mental illness in the family evokes strong concerns as to who will serve in that role. Specifically, if it is a parental figure who is suffering from the illness, the child has concerns that one of his or her primary caretakers is no longer able to serve the caretaking function in the same manner. On the other hand, if it is a sibling, the child's "who will take care of me" worries are activated by the fact that the caretaking adults' energies are being directed primarily to the psychologically troubled sibling. In turn, this brings on feelings of worry whether there will be any caretaking energy left for the healthy child.

Will this happen to me? As the child observes what is transpiring, it is only natural that he or she experience concern as to whether the same type of disorder can overtake him or her. At a level that is consistent with the child's understanding, it should be explained that everybody gets sick, and that this is simply a different kind of sickness. While no guarantees should be offered, a useful intervention can be reassurance that the child has not exhibited any symptoms of this illness, and, as such, evidences no signs of "coming down with it" in the immediate future.

What do I tell other people? With respect to what to tell others, the child should be encouraged to respond to others' inquiries in the manner that he or she finds most comfortable. Keeping in mind the family's preferences around the matter of sharing information, it best be emphasized to the child that what is transpiring in the family is nothing to be ashamed of, or from which to feel embarrassment. Indeed, everybody becomes sick at some time in life, and this is simply an example of that. However, there are issues around privacy and what type of information is appropriate to share with which people. At this point, the adult(s) should integrate the family's preferences with what the child feels comfortable sharing with others in providing suggestions as how to handle people's inquiries, and what information to volunteer.

How do I talk to the mentally ill family member? Answers to questions such as this need to consider the child's developmental level (in terms of being able to understand certain psychiatric/psychological symptoms) as well as the actual clinical condition of the family member in question. To the extent to which it is possible, it is recommended that the child be encouraged to interact with the impaired family member in as normal and natural a way as possible, but to be prepared for the chance of a less than usual type of response. It is at this time that an adult figure can be most useful in explaining the response of the ill family member in terms that the child can understand, emphasizing that the response was more a function of the mental disorder than it was of the family member's feelings toward the child.

SUPPLEMENTAL RESOURCES

Marsh, D. T., & Dickins, R. (1997). *How to cope with mental illness in your family.* New York: Putnam.
Marsh, D. T. (1998). *How to cope with mental illness in your family.* Fort Erie, Ontario: Magpie.
Woolis, R. (1992). *When someone you love has a mental illness.* Fort Erie, Ontario: Magpie.

Mental Retardation

Mental retardation is conceptualized as a condition, as opposed to a disease that is curable or treatable. Individuals diagnosed with mental retardation are quite variable in their presentation as a function of the degree to which they are impaired. Indeed, whereas an individual with mild mental retardation can have a mental age expectancy as high as that of a 12 year old, individuals with profound mental retardation can require complete institutionalization because of a total inability to complete the basic of tasks. Estimates of the frequency of mental retardation in the general population range from 1% to 3% (with the most commonly accepted figure being 2.3%). Interestingly, in the lowest socioeconomic classes, the prevalence ranges from 10% to 30%. At all levels of mental retardation, there is a predominance of males, with an overall ratio of approximately 1.5 to 1.

Over the years, several classifications systems have been employed for mental retardation. The first such classification system was proposed in 1905 classifying the mentally retarded into four basic categories: backward/mentally feeble, moral imbecile, idio-imbecile, and idiot. This system remained in effect until the first official classification system for mental retardation was published by the American Association on Mental Retardation in 1921. In this system, three classifications (all based on IQ scores) were offered: moron, imbecile, and idiot. The first edition of the *Diagnostic and Statistical Manual,* published in 1952, classified mental retardation along the lines of mental deficiency. By the 1960s, mental retardation was regarded as having a developmental basis with classification systems incorporating functional level into their criteria. Five levels of mental retardation were defined: borderline, mild, moderate, severe, and profound. Then, in the 1970s, the category of borderline mental retardation was eliminated with a diagnosis of mental retardation requiring an IQ below 70, as well as problems with adaptive functioning (i.e., impairment in at least two of the following skill areas: home living, social skills, self-direction, community functioning, self-care, and health and safety). Currently, the *DSM* and the **American Association of Mental Retardation** retain a four-level classification system (Mild, Moderate, Profound, Severe). Whereas an IQ of 70 remains the cutoff score for a diagnosis of mental retardation, both systems allow IQ scores as high as 75 if the adaptive functioning is sufficiently impaired.

The only generalizations that can be offered with respect to the clinical presentation of the mentally retarded individual pertain to functional level and overall clinical progression. Generally, the progression of mental retardation is strongly influenced by environmental factors. The child's progression through the developmental milestones is not deviant, but rather delayed. That is to say, the child will manifest most of the developmental milestones in a nonremarkable manner; however, these milestones will be achieved at a later age than would be normally expected. Further, although the normal sequence of developmental stages is indeed observed, in most cases there is a definite limit to the degree of achievement reached.

Individuals with a diagnosis of *mild mental retardation* tend to have a rather childlike, dependent demeanor. By adulthood, most are able to achieve an academic level roughly comparable to that of sixth grader. With few, if any, distinguishing physical features, individuals with mild mental retardation are often able to hold simple jobs, marry, and enjoy productive social lives. In terms of verbal development, speech patterns are usually unremarkable, although there is characteristically an impoverished bank of information. These individuals are able to live in the community, usually in the lower socioeconomic class, and are able to manage their own finances with minimal assistance.

The next level of severity is *moderate mental retardation.* By adulthood, moderately mentally retarded people have attained an academic level roughly equivalent to that of a second grader. These individuals are able to talk, but usually with some impairment (lisps, poor pronunciation, awkward speech patterns). Their social skills are severely limited, yet, with some training, they can become mostly independent with respect to their own personal hygiene. The typical individual with moderate mental retardation is able to work in a sheltered workshop with limited task assignments. As adults, most moderately mentally retarded people live in supervised settings and are able to manage only small amounts of money.

Severe mental retardation manifests its symptoms early in the child's life. Motor development is severely impaired, as is verbal development. Many children with severe mental retardation never learn to speak. Tasks of personal hygiene require supervision, so individuals with severe mental retardation need to live in highly structured and supervised settings. With a maximum academic level of first grade, as adults they are unable to perform any type of formal job. Abilities are limited to simple tasks such as dumping of trash, drying dishes, using coin machines, and bringing a shopping list to a store. Even these tasks need to be performed under close supervision.

Finally, individuals diagnosed with *profound mental retardation* often suffer from some form of neurological deficit as well. They exhibit significant impairment in both cognitive as well as social abilities to such a severe degree that they may appear to be virtually unaware of their environment and surroundings. Speech, if it is present at all, is severely limited. Thus, profoundly mentally retarded individuals require special care, and may need to be restrained to beds to prevent injury to self or others.

Since, as mentioned above, mental retardation is not an illness, nor a psychiatric or psychological disorder, it does not make sense to talk about treatment for mental retardation. Rather, appropriate interventions to accommodate the individual's limitations are instituted, among these including modifications in living situations, altering the traditional educational format, and development of vocational opportunities. Despite the appropriateness and necessity of these interventions, they are not accurately conceptualized as treatments. Indeed, they do not alleviate any symptoms, as the mental retardation and its ramifications remain unchanged.

Nonetheless, it should be noted that both behavior therapy and psychopharmacological interventions are utilized with mentally retarded individuals. These interventions are modified to correspond with the individual's mental and functional levels, and are used primarily to reduce the symptom patterns of **Secondary** psychological or psychiatric disorders. Indeed, any individual who is mentally retarded can suffer from other psychological or psychiatric disorders as well. In their *Comprehensive Textbook of Psychiatry*, Szymanski and Kaplan present eight guidelines for treating psychopathology in mentally retarded individuals. These can be used by parents and caretakers as foundations upon which to evaluate the care given to the mentally retarded child/adolescent by clinicians:

1. Perform a comprehensive diagnostic assessment.
2. Design a comprehensive treatment program, considering all of the patient's needs—not merely the disruptive behaviors.
3. Address causative factors.
4. Choose psychiatric treatment approaches on the basis of best benefit/risk ratio.
5. Establish target behaviors and measures to monitor them.
6. Ensure caregivers' understanding of and agreement with the treatment plan.
7. Monitor adverse effects of treatment.
8. Adhere to all ethical principles.

SUPPLEMENTAL RESOURCES

Kaufman, S. Z. (1995). *Retarded ISN'T stupid, mom*. Duarte, CA: Hope Press.
Smith, R. (1993). *Children with mental retardation: A parent's guide*. Bethesda, MD: Woodbine House.

Methylphenidate

This is the generic name for the psychostimulant marketed as **Ritalin.** Please refer to that entry for a description.

Minuchin, S.

Salvatore Minuchin is known for his contribution to the practice of **Family Therapy,** specifically the approach to family therapy known as the *structural family systems approach.* Refer to the entry on family therapy for a more detailed description of Minuchin's work.

Mixed Receptive/Expressive Language Disorder

Previously referred to as developmental receptive language disorder, this diagnosis falls in the classification of **Developmental Language Disorders.** Typified by problems in the actual understanding of language, there is considerable variation as to the degree of severity. As one would expect, the children with the more severe symptoms tend to be diagnosed earlier in life than do those with milder forms of the disorder. Finally, it should be noted that many children with the diagnosis of mixed receptive/expressive language disorder meet the diagnostic criteria for **Expressive Language Disorder** as well.

The actual symptoms of mixed receptive/expressive language disorder may occur in any or all of the various aspects of language. Actual language usage, grammar, vocabulary, and/or the ordering of words are all potential areas of impairment. Diagnosis of this disorder is made when the scores obtained from a battery of individually administered standardized tests of language development are substantially below those obtained on measures of nonverbal intellectual skills. Such a diagnosis is typically made by the school as a result of standardized testing and/or of problems observed in completing verbal aspects of the schoolwork. The school will usually initiate interventions, which tend to assume the form of special help, resource room, and individual instruction (depending upon the precise nature of the child).

SUPPLEMENTAL RESOURCES

Gehret, J. (1996). *The don't-give-up kid and learning differences.* Fairport, NY: Verbal Images Press.

Greene, L. J. (1987). *Learning disabilities and your child: A survival handbook.* New York: Ballantine.

Hamaguachi, P. M. (1995). *Childhood speech, language and listening problems: What every parent should know.* New York: Wiley.

Mandel, H. P., & Marcus, S. I. (1995). *Could do better.* New York: Wiley.

Martin, K. L. (1997). *Does my child have a speech problem?* Chicago: Chicago Review Press.

McNamara, B. E., & McNamara, F. J. (1995). *Keys to parenting a child with a learning disability.* New York: Barrons.

Rosner, J. (1993). *Helping children overcome learning difficulties.* New York: Walker.

Smith, S. L. (1991). *Succeeding against the odds: How the learning disabled can realize their promise.* New York: Putnam.

Smith, S. L. (1995). *No easy answers: The learning disabled child at home and at school.* New York: Bantam.

Unger, H. G. (1998). *The learning disabilities trap.* Chicago: Contemporary Books.

Modeling

Modeling is a type of learning that occurs by one person simply observing the target behavior being performed by another person. Also referred to as *vicarious learning,* modeling can occur without the individual ever actually engaging in the target behavior—simply by observing another. First proposed in the 1960s by Albert Bandura, modeling was identified when it was observed that children can learn various behaviors without ever having been reinforced in any way. In other words, a child observes another individual (referred to as a *social model*) performing a given behavior, and, at some point, demonstrates mastery of that behavior.

Whereas **Reinforcement** is not believed to be necessary for modeling to occur, reinforcement does play a role in terms of which learned behaviors are actually performed. For example, a child may learn several different behaviors via the modeling route; however, he or she is more likely to perform (and continue to perform) those behaviors for which he or she perceives himself or herself as being reinforced.

It is also interesting to note that research has shown various developmental factors influencing the choice of models. For example, younger children tend to choose models whom they perceive as being kind, or whom they perceive as having a certain amount of authority or power. Thus, it is common for a young child to model the behavior of an adult who was especially kind to him or her, as well as to model the behavior of a teacher or parent. Similarly, it is common for children between the ages of 18 months and 3 years to view television characters as models. Yet, as children mature into the school years, it becomes more important for them for the model to be at least their age, and to be similar to them in as many ways as possible (especially with respect to gender).

Common Models for Various Developmental Stages
Preschool children: teachers, parents, clergy, television heroes, grandparents, relatives, cartoon characters

> *Example:* Four-year-old Richie attempted to bounce down the stairs of his house because he saw the Road Runner do something similar on television.

> *Example:* Three-year-old Jenna runs up to any child she sees (whether she knows him or not), hugs him, and then says, "Will you be my friend?" Although her family has always taught her to be wary of strangers, Jenna has been modeling her behavior after Barney (the purple dinosaur on television).

School children: children in higher grades, older siblings, another child in his or her own class whom the child perceives as similar in certain attributes

> *Example:* Eight-year-old Beth has taken to putting on her sister's lipstick, blush, and eye makeup before going out of the house. This behavior has recently developed, specifically since Beth's sister has been allowed to wear makeup to school.

> *Example:* Ten-year-old Steven is pestering his parents to have his one ear pierced since his 18-year-old brother came home from college with an earring. When his parents insist that Steven is too young, he draws a design on his ear that closely resembles the shape of his brother's earring.

SUPPLEMENTARY RESOURCES

Striefel, S. (1980). *How to teach through modeling and imitation.* Austin, TX: ProEd.

Monoamine Oxidase Inhibitors

This is a class of **Antidepressants** that work by inhibiting the function of the enzyme monoamine oxidase (thus their name). This class of medication is typically prescribed to treat depression in adults who have not responded well to other forms of antidepressant therapy. Currently, the monoamine oxidase inhibitors are FDA-approved only for individuals 16 years of age and older; however, experimental studies are being conducted to investigate their potential use in the treatment of childhood **Depression** (for ages under 16), **Anorexia, Bulimia, Borderline Personality Disorder** without depression, **Attention Deficit Hyperactivity Disorder,** and various **Anxiety Disorders.**

To avoid the danger of a hypertensive crisis, individuals who are taking monoamine oxidase inhibitors need to avoid food rich in the chemical tyramine, as well as the usage of amphetamines, **Tricyclic Antidepressants,** caffeine, and many other drugs. Thus, it is crucial to note that because of the necessity of dietary restrictions when using this class of medication, as well as interaction with so many other drugs, the use of monoamine oxidase inhibitors is quite uncommon in children.

SUPPLEMENTAL RESOURCES

Breggin, P. (1991). *Toxic psychiatry.* New York: St. Martin's Press.

Gorman, J. M. (1997). *The essential guide to psychiatric drugs.* New York: St. Martin's Press.

Maxmen, J., & Ward, N. (1996). *Psychotropic drugs: Fast facts.* New York: Norton.

Rosenberg, D. R., Holttum, J., & Gershon, S. (1994). *Textbook of pharmacotherapy for child and adolescent psychiatric disorders.* New York: Brunner/Mazel.

Shulman, K. I., Walker, J. E., MacKenzie, S., & Knowles, S. (1989). Dietary restriction, tyramine, and the use of monoamine oxidase inhibitors. *Journal of Clinical Psychopharmacology, 9,* 397–402.

Werry, J. S., & Aman, M. G. (1993). *Practitioner's guide to psychoactive drugs for children and adolescents*. New York: Plenum.

Mood Disorders

Mood disorders is a diagnostic category which incorporates those disorders which have either some form of **Depression** and/or **Mania** as their primary symptoms. In the current edition of the *DSM* (the *DSM-IV*), the **Bipolar Disorders** as well as the various depressive disorders are included in this diagnostic category.

N | Nail Biting–Nortriptyline

Nail Biting

The habitual biting of one's (finger)nails is a rather common habit that can begin as early as 1 year of age. With respect to frequency of occurrence, nail biting tends to increase in the early childhood years and then to decline around age 12. Whereas some cases are so severe as to cause physical damage (i.e., to the cuticles, to the fingers themselves), most cases of nail biting are not that severe, and are made worse by cases of stress, anxiety, and/or boredom.

Oftentimes, when nail biting occurs in school-aged children, the behavior is more aversive to the adults around the child than it is to the child himself or herself. Exceptions to this occur when the child is taunted or somehow made fun of by his or her peers as a result of the nail biting, but even then it is more the reaction of others than the actual nail biting itself that is troublesome to the child. Again, while some of the more severe cases require professional intervention, most cases of common nail biting in children can be addressed with some sensitivity on the part of the parental figure(s).

Perform a behavioral assessment of the behavior: Keep a record (either written or visual) as to when the child engages in the nail biting behavior. When is it more frequent and when is it less frequent? Are there any times when the child does *not* bite his or her nails? What kinds of situations increase the frequency and intensity of the nail biting?

Address the source: By using the information gained above, see if there are any noticeable patterns in the child's nail biting behavior; by examining these patterns, try to determine with the child *why* he or she bites the nails; there will not be one answer to this question, but a general trend can be noted; should it be recognized that the child tends to engage in nail biting due to boredom, anxiety, worry, stress, and the like, these issues best be addressed directly; determine what situation is causing the child to experience these feelings, then work with him or her to develop more adaptive ways of coping.

Less is more: In some cases, it is best not to try too hard to remedy the nail biting behavior; placing too heavy an emphasis on it can in many cases make things worse; especially in situations where the behavior is primarily motivated by anxiety, placing undue emphasis on needing to stop could intensify the anxious feelings; at times, the most important task of the parent of a nail biter is to determine when to leave well enough (even if it's not so well enough) alone, and when and how to intervene sensitively.

Navane

Navane (**Thiothixene**) is an antipsychotic drug used to treat the symptoms of **Schizophrenia** and other **Psychotic Disorders.** It is approved only for individuals over the age of 12 years. In the less serious cases, the initial dosage recommended is 2 mg (three times per day) with eventual increase to 5 mg (three times per day) when indicated. More severe cases require an initial dosage of 5 mg (twice daily) with an eventual increase to 20–30 mg/day. Navane is available in 1 mg, 2 mg, 5 mg, 10 mg, and 20 mg capsules as well as concentrate and intramuscular injections. **Extrapyramidal Side Effects** are especially common with the use of Navane.

SUPPLEMENTAL RESOURCES

Gorman, J. M. (1997). *The essential guide to psychiatric drugs.* New York: St. Martin's Press.
Maxmen, J., & Ward, N. (1996). *Psychotropic drugs: Fast facts.* New York: Norton.
Rosenberg, D. R., Holttum, J., & Gershon, S. (1994). *Textbook of pharmacotherapy for child and adolescent psychiatric disorders.* New York: Brunner/Mazel.
Werry, J. S., & Aman, M. G., (1993). *Practitioner's guide to psychoactive drugs for children and adolescents.* New York: Plenum.

Nefazodone

This is the generic or trade name for the medication **Serzone.** Please refer to that entry for a description of the drug.

Negative Reinforcement

This is a common concept associated with **Behavior Therapy,** yet a frequently misunderstood one. Although negative reinforcement is often considered to be synonymous with **Punishment,** nothing can be further from the truth. A basic principle of behavior therapy is that **Reinforcement** of any type is designed to *increase* the probability of the target behavior occurring, while **Punishment** is designed to *decrease* the probability of the target behavior occurring. Negative reinforcement works by removing a negative behavior or terminating a negative event following the occurrence of a desired behavior. In other words, in negative reinforcement, rather than a positive characteristic being added to the environment following the performance of a desired behavior, a negative characteristic is removed from the environment following the performance of the desired behavior. (Again since both of these conditions increase the probability of that desired behavior occurring, they are both considered to be reinforcing.)

Example: A child continues to tantrum in a grocery store until her mother buys her the candy bar she wants; that is, the aversive behavior of tantruming is removed from the mother's environment once the mother performs the desired behavior—buying the candy bar.

Example: Mr. and Mrs. Robertson agreed that one of them will follow their 12-year-old son around to classes until he improves his in-class behavior; that is, being accompanied by a parent during class is embarrassing for the 12-year-old; once his behavior becomes more appropriate, the annoyance of his parents following him around will be removed.

Negative Symptoms

This phrase dates back to the 1980s when T. J. Crow proposed a classification system to distinguish among different types of schizophrenic patients. As part of this attempt at classification, two types of symptoms were described: *Type I* (or positive) symptoms and *Type II* (or negative) symptoms. According to this classification scheme, Type I schizophrenic patients have more positive symptoms, whereas Type II schizophrenic patients have more negative symptoms. In addition, research indicated that Type I patients tend to respond more favorably to treatment than do Type II patients. Whereas the positive symptoms of schizophrenia include the more flagrant ones such as bizarre behavior, **Loose Associations,** and **Hallucinations,** negative symptoms of **Schizophrenia** include **Flat,** or **Blunted, Affect,** poor personal hygiene, social withdrawal, and **Anhedonia.**

SUPPLEMENTAL RESOURCES

Watkins, J. (1996). *Living with schizophrenia: A holistic approach to understanding, preventing, and recovering from "negative" symptoms.* Melbourne, Australia: Hill of Content.

Neuroleptic

This is a term used as synonymous with "antipsychotic." Thus, neuroleptic medications are antipsychotic medications. (It should be noted that the term "**Major Tranquilizer**" is also used to describe this class of medications.)

Neuroleptic Malignant Syndrome

Neuroleptic malignant syndrome refers to a phenomenon consisting of a collection of severe side effects resulting from the use of **Neuroleptic** medication. Thus, this syndrome is observed most frequently in individuals with some form of **Schizophrenia,** as these are the individuals who most commonly utilize such medication. According to the *DSM-IV* (American Psychiatric Association, 1994), neuroleptic malignant syndrome occurs more frequently in males than in females and is estimated to occur in 0.07%–1.4% of individuals who are exposed to **Antipsychotic** medications.

Although the primary symptoms of neuroleptic malignant syndrome include muscle rigidity (stiffness) accompanied by an increased temperature (ranging from 99–100 degrees to greater increases reaching 106 degrees), there are other symptoms characteristic of this syndrome. Specifically, the research criteria proposed for neuroleptic malignant syndrome by the American Psychiatric Association in the *DSM-IV* require two or more of the following symptoms in addition to the muscular rigidity and elevated temperature:

> diaphoresis
> dysphagia: difficulties in eating
> tremor
> incontinence
> changes in consciousness level (ranging from confusion to coma)
> mutism
> tachycardia: rapid heart rate
> fluctuations in blood pressure
> leucocytosis
> muscle injury as indicated by laboratory tests

Although some people develop neuroleptic malignant syndrome after taking the same antipsychotic medication for several months, most individuals develop the syndrome within 4 weeks after initiating treatment with a neuroleptic. Symptoms resolve, however, after discontinuation of the medication, with the average amount of time being 2 weeks after stopping the medication.

Neuropsychology

Neuropsychology is a subsepeciality within the field of clinical psychology that focuses on the specific relationship(s) between the brain and behavior. In so doing, neuropsychologists study and assess brain dysfunctions, especially as they impact on psychological and cognitive functioning, as well as upon behavior in general. Neuropsychologists operate by using various specialized assessment techniques (such as the **Luria Nebraska,** for example) in addition to interpreting other more common psychological assessment instruments (such as the **Wechsler Intelligence** tests) in a more cognitively-oriented manner. The eventual goal of a neuropsychological assessment is to provide suggestions for interventions in the areas of direct treatment and/or rehabilitation.

Neuropsychologists are consulted when it is suspected that an individual's psychological/psychiatric symptoms are (at least partially) due to pathology (in terms of structure or function) of the brain. Thus, neuropsychologists are often consulted in cases of head trauma/injury, **Attention Deficit Hyperactivity Disorder,** dementia, multiple sclerosis, Parkinson's disease, substance abuse, learning disabilities, and stroke.

SUPPLEMENTAL RESOURCES

Adams, R. L., Parson, O. A., Culbertson, J. L., & Nixon, S. J. (Eds.). (1996). *Neuropsychology for clinical practice: Etiology, assessment, and treatment of common neuropsychological disorders.* Washington, DC: American Psychological Association.

Neurotransmitters (Neurohumors)

Neurotransmitters are chemical substances whose function it is to carry messages from one nerve cell (or *neuron*) to another. Although there are three major categories of neurotransmitters: (1) biogenic amines, (2) amino acids, and (3) neuropeptides, it is the neurotransmitters in the first group that are believed to have the most relevance for psychological and psychiatric disorders. Such relevant neurotransmitters included within the biogenic amine group include *dopamine, serotonin,* and *acetylcholine.*

Nightmares

Nightmares are defined as being relatively long, scary, anxiety-provoking dreams from which the person awakens feeling frightened. Most of the time, the person has a rather detailed, vivid memory of the dream and is able to recount much of it in good detail. Although nightmares can occur at any time of night, they almost always take place when the person is in the deepest (*rapid eye movement* or *REM)* phase of sleep, and usually after being in this stage of deep sleep for a long period of time. Nightmares are relatively common, with approximately one half of all adults reporting experiencing occasional nightmares, especially during periods of stress.

The current edition of the *DSM* (American Psychiatric Association, 1994) lists the following criteria as being required for a diagnosis of nightmare disorder:

A. Repeatedly waking up from the major sleep period with a detailed memory of a long and extremely frightening dream or dreams. Themes of such dreams usually involve threats to security, survival, and/or self-esteem.

B. When the person awakens from this dream, he or she is virtually immediately oriented and alert.

C. Both the actual experience of the dream as well as the disturbance resulting from the dream cause impairment in day-to-day functioning.

D. The nightmares do not occur secondary to another mental disorder. (p. 583)

In the most extreme cases, **Benzodiazepines** are prescribed for the treatment of nightmares, however they can usually be dealt with without the use of such medication. When nightmares occur in children, it is usually as a response to a stressful real life event, or as a response to an especially frightening movie, video, or television show. By the parent discussing the content of the dream with the child, providing considerable reassurance of his or her safety, and repeating that "it is scary but it is just a dream," the child is often able to return to sleep rather soon thereafter. However, in cases where the nightmares appear to be somewhat persistent, the parent should talk with the child when he or she is awake (the next day or soon thereafter) and discuss the details of the dream's content. By so doing, it will be possible to determine what is causing these nightmares, so that the anxiety or fear around that specific issue can be addressed more directly.

SUPPLEMENTAL RESOURCES

Coren, S. (1996). *Sleep thieves.* New York: Free Press.
Eberleen, T. (1996). *Sleep—How to teach your child to sleep like a baby.* New York: Pocket Books.
Ferber, R. (1985). *Solve your child's sleep problems.* New York: Simon & Schuster.
Gottlieb, S. (1993). *Keys to children's sleep problems.* New York: Barrons.
Lobby, T. (1990). *Jessica and the wolf.* New York: Magination Press.

Night/Sleep Terrors

Night/sleep terrors are different from nightmares in many ways. First, they typically occur in the first third of night (within the first 1 or 2 hours of sleep) and almost always are accompanied by a scream, cry, and/or some other manifestation of intense anxiety. Especially common in children (with estimates ranging between 1% and 6%), sleep terrors tend to be more common in boys than in girls. During the sleep terror, the person will jolt up in bed with a panicked expression on his or her face—at times awakening immediately. In some cases, the person will remain awake, but in a disoriented state. However, more often than not, the individual will fall back asleep and completely forget the episode upon awakening.

The *DSM-IV* (American Psychiatric Association, 1994) lists the following as diagnostic criteria for the diagnosis of a case of *sleep/terror disorder:*

A. Repeated abrupt awakening from sleep—incident usually beginning with a panicked scream.

B. Indications of intense fear and anxiety during each episode.

C. Individual appears to be relatively unresponsive to attempts at reassurance.

D. Neither a dream nor the actual occurrence is remembered by the person.

E. The night terror causes significant impairment in the person's day-to-day functioning.

F. Occurrence of night terrors is not due to direct effects of a substance or a general medical condition. (p. 587)

Although, in extreme cases (on occasion), a prescription of **Valium** is prescribed, most cases of night terrors are dealt with without any professional intervention. When professional consultation is utilized, the most common approach involves exploration of anxieties in the person's life that may be the source of the night problems, planned awakening of the person prior to the time that the episodes tend to occur, or some combination thereof.

SUPPLEMENTARY RESOURCES

Coren, S. (1996). *Sleep thieves.* New York: Free Press.
Eberleen, T. (1996). *Sleep—How to teach your child to sleep like a baby.* New York: Pocket Books.
Ferber, R. (1985). *Solve your child's sleep problems.* New York: Simon & Schuster.
Gottlieb, S. (1993). *Keys to children's sleep problems.* New York: Barrons.

Nortriptyline

Nortriptyline is the generic name for the **Antidepressant** marketed under the name of **Pamelor.** Please refer to that entry.

O   Obesity–Overproductive Speech

Obesity

Defined as a condition characterized by a person's body weight exceeding 20% of the standard weight listed in the traditional height/weight tables, obesity is estimated to occur in anywhere from 5% to 20% of children and adolescents. The first step in addressing a condition of obesity is that of determining if there is any physiological basis for the condition. Endocrine (e.g., thyroid) abnormalities, excessive water retention, and problems with sugar metabolism (e.g., diabetes) are but three of the various physical problems that could have obesity as a primary symptom.

Once physical problems are ruled out as a precipitating cause of the obesity, the psychological factors need to be addressed. Determining the underlying dynamic behind the excessive intake will allow the problem to be addressed at the root, rather than focusing on the obesity—which is most likely merely a symptom of some more primary difficulty.

Determine eating patterns: By keeping a diary of all food ingested as well as what time of day it is ingested, one will be able to determine what the nature of the eating difficulty is. For example, is the issue one of overeating at certain times of day, is it one of overeating under certain circumstances, is the problem one of compulsive eating, or, is the primary problem one of eating the wrong foods? Once the main issue with respect to eating patterns is determined, it can be addressed directly.

Dynamics behind the eating behavior: Based upon the information gleaned from the diary mentioned above, the next step is to determine the psychological reasons behind the excessive food intake. Does the child eat as a way to lessen anxiety, relieve boredom, relieve depression, or to sabotage his or her appearance for some reason? Individual, group, or family therapy can be used to address these underlying psychological concerns if the parent feels unable or unsuccessful addressing these issues within the context of family discussions.

Self-esteem issues: The majority of young people who deal with issues of obesity—and even of being generally overweight—also are struggling with psychological issues around self-esteem and self-image. Oftentimes, however, these issues around self-esteem are either masked (with the child overtly giving the impression "this doesn't bother me") or tend to be manifested in a less than obvious manner. For example, a female child who has been sexually abused may overeat in order to sabotage her appearance so that she will not be attractive to other men or to the perpetrator. Another example would be a child who overeats because he is convinced it doesn't matter anyway because he would never be attractive regardless. A final example would be those individuals who hide behind their obesity as a reason for their lack of popularity because of their resistance or anxiety about facing other more substantive issues. Regardless of the specifics, self-esteem plays a major role and needs to be addressed in every case of obesity.

While there are many options for professional treatment of overweight children and adolescents, it is crucial that the parent choose an option that addresses the source of the overeating, not just the overeating itself. **Individual Therapy, Family Therapy, Group Therapy,** camps, inpatient programs, and working with a nutritionist and/or dietician are just a few of the choices available.

SUPPLEMENTAL RESOURCES

Kano, S. (1989). *Making peace with food*. New York: Harper Row.
Normandi, C. E., & Roark, C. (1998). *It's not about food*. New York: Grosset Putnam.

Obsession

An obsession, a major symptomatic component of most cases of **Obsessive-Compulsive Disorder,** is an image, thought, emotion, idea, impulse, or feeling that is perceived to be intrusive and recurrent. Obsessions tend to be anxiety provoking, and, as such, commonly result in the individual developing ritualistic behaviors (**Compulsions**) in an attempt to lessen that anxiety. Further, most of these obsessions tend to be emotionally charged and, as such, being so repetitive and intrusive, are perceived by the individual as being at the very least unpleasant, and, at the very worst, interfering in the individual's ability to function in day-to-day life. Examples of common obsessions include concerns about germs/contamination, doubts about a behavior performed previously, feeling a need to have objects arranged in a particular order, and morbid or sexually vivid images. The *DSM-IV* describes obsessions as having the following characteristics:

1. Causing anxiety and stress.
2. Obsessions are not excessive worries about real-life problems.
3. Obsessions cause such anxiety or stress that the individual tries to suppress them with some other thought or behavior.
4. Person who is experiencing these obsessions recognizes that the thoughts and images are a product of his or her own mind as opposed to being somehow externally imposed.

For clinical examples of the different types of obsessions as well as a discussion of the treatment of them, please refer to the following related entries: **Obsessive Child Spectrum, Obsessive-Compulsive Disorder,** and **Compulsions.**

Obsessive Child Spectrum

In a 1985 article in the *American Journal of Psychotherapy,* a specialist in childhood **Obsessive-Compulsive Disorder** published a list of obsessive-compulsive symptoms that are observed in children. What makes this list especially interesting is that the author presents these symptoms as ranging from those obsessive symptoms considered to be normal and age appropriate to those symptoms that warrant clinical attention. Such an approach allows one to conceptualize childhood obsessive-compulsive symptoms as falling along a continuum with some being unremarkable, others being clinically significant, and still others lying somewhere in between.

This list of obsessive symptoms, from the least severe to the most clinically significant, reads as follows:

1. ritualized collective play, as in games with repetitive chanting or rigidly repetitive ritualized behavior

   Example: Eight-year-old Beth enjoys playing outdoors with her friends. She especially enjoys playing "Mother, may I?," a movement game in which each child is required to ask "Mother, may I?" prior to advancing toward the goalpost.

2. phase-appropriate rituals, such as seen in 2- or 3-year olds and again in pubescent children, needing everything "just so"

   Example: Prior to going to bed, 3-year-old Teddy insists that his parents walk around his bedroom with him, ensuring that his stuffed animals and toy soldiers are in their appropriate places on his toy shelf.

3. ritualized solitary play—for example, compulsive play with action figures, cards, and mechanical toys

   Example: Twelve-year-old Jodi spends hours playing solitaire on the computer whenever she has free time.

4. obsessive collecting

   Example: Nine-year-old Harold is so preoccupied with his coin collection that it seems that talking about his coin collection is all he is interested in doing. Whenever his parents take him to a mall or on a vacation, his first task is to check the phone book to locate the nearest coin/hobby store.

5. circumscribed interests, such as being "nuts" about rockets, meteorology, or television call letters to the exclusion of all other concerns

   Example: Since the movie *Godzilla* was released, 12-year-old Barry has become totally obsessed with the Godzilla theme. He sees the movie twice every weekend (once on Saturday and once on Sunday) and he uses his remaining spending money to purchase all available Godzilla merchandise. At times, when he is supposed to be working on his school assignments, his parents will find him in his room virtually studying his Godzilla items.

6. obsessive character

   Example: Twelve-year-old Jennifer seems to overanalyze virtually everything—from the most trivial to that which is relatively important, it doesn't matter. Everything is a major issue for her and she does not complete necessary tasks because she repeatedly obsesses over how to proceed.

7. secondary obsessions

   Example: Eleven-year-old John has been diagnosed with a degenerative muscular disease. Since the diagnosis was confirmed, John spends much of his time obsessing as to whether he was diagnosed properly and whether the doctors involved in his case are competent.

8. obsessions related to or combined with other disorders

   Example: Sixteen-year-old Jeff has been diagnosed with major **Depression** and has been prescribed **Prozac** as part of his treatment. His parents, however, have noticed that Jeff has begun to manifest obsessive symptomatology focusing on his Prozac. For example, he will ask his mother three times (prior to taking each dose) if she believes that this is *really* going to help. Further, Jeff spends a lot of time alone, seemingly deep in thought. When asked what he is thinking about, he replies "I'm just wondering if Prozac is the right medication for me."

9. obsessive-compulsive neurosis (primary OCD)
   A. compulsive rituals: cleaning (akin to phobics)

      Example: Twelve-year-old Caitlin has been having academic trouble because, her teachers report, she is constantly late for all of her classes. Apparently, Caitlin spends so much time in the school bathroom washing her hands after each of her classes, she ends up being anywhere from 5 to 10 minutes late for the following class.

   B. compulsive rituals: checking

      Example: Prior to leaving the house, 8-year-old Adam insists that his parents accompany him on a "safety tour" around the entire home, making sure every electrical appliance is turned off. Adam also demands that this tour is repeated twice (for a total of three times) "just to make sure we don't miss anything."

   C. obsessions driven by fear

      Example: Ever since hearing of a teacher from his school being injured in a car accident, 12-year-old David is obsessed with getting into some type of collision every time he rides in a car.

D. obsessions driven by guilt

Example: Six-year-old Christina just began going to religion classes. Her teacher began explaining to the children about heaven, hell, and the afterlife. The entire belief made quite an impression on Christina, and now she obsesses about possibly doing something wrong and then feeling extremely guilty about it (repeatedly saying, "I don't want to be bad, I don't want to be bad").

E. obsessions driven by shame

Example: Thirteen-year-old Ricky has been masturbating every evening before going to sleep. He is now obsessing over whether or not he is destined to go to hell as a result of his behavior.

Obsessive-Compulsive Disorder

Classified as one of the **Anxiety Disorders,** obsessive-compulsive disorder has two major components to its symptomatic presentation: **Obsessions** and **Compulsions.** These two symptom classes are related in that the obsessions are actually intrusive, upsetting thoughts which result in the individual utilizing certain behavior patterns (i.e., the compulsions) to deal with them. Thus, the repetitive, ritualistic compulsions are actually performed in an attempt to help the individual cope with the anxiety elicited by the obsessive thoughts. (For a more thorough description of obsessions and compulsions, please refer to the individual entries.)

The *DSM-IV* requires the presence of either obsessions or compulsions in order for obsessive-compulsive disorder to be diagnosed. In addition, however, the obsessions and/or compulsions must be causing marked distress, be time-consuming, or somehow otherwise interfere with the individual's day-to-day routine. Yet another required criterion for diagnosis of obsessive-compulsive disorder (although exceptions are made in the case of children) is that, at some stage during the clinical course of the disorder, the person must be able to acknowledge the abnormality of the obsessions and/or compulsions.

Although the symptoms of obsessive-compulsive disorder in children and adolescents are virtually identical to those observed in adults, it is important to recognize that many of the so-called symptoms of this disorder are actually relatively common at various developmental stages. For example, by the age of 2 years or so, many children insist that certain rituals be carried out, especially around the issues of eating, bedtime (refer to entry on **Bedtime Rituals**), bathing, and separation from parents. By the time the child reaches age 4, many of these rituals have lessened (although the bedtime rituals seem to remain or even to intensify). Through the school years, ritualized play with rather elaborate rules, superstitious behaviors, hobbies involving "collections," and/or intense preoccupations with certain activities or sports idols predominate as well. From some perspectives, these are considered to be normal developmental progressions consistent with maturing levels of cognitive skills. These developmental "obsessive-compulsive-like" behaviors tend to differ, however, in content and intensity from true obsessive-compulsive behaviors. Indeed, most simple childhood rituals lessen or even disappear by age 8, whereas true symptoms of obsessive-compulsive disorder tend to intensify after age 7. Yet another significant difference is that the rituals characteristic of normal development generally enhance socialization, whereas the symptoms of true obsessive-compulsive disorder actually impede optimal socialization. (For an illustration of the differences between developmentally appropriate obsessive-compulsive symptoms and the true obsessive-compulsive disorder, refer to the entry on the **Obsessive Child Spectrum.**)

With respect to the actual content of the obsessive thoughts, the most common is that of violence (sometimes with sexually oriented themes), cleaning, checking, counting, exactness, symmetry, religious themes, and bodily functions. Whereas the typical age of onset for obsessive-compulsive disorder is between 3 and 5 years of age, the child's embarrassment and shame about symptoms, coupled with the adults' tendency to consider the symptoms as being part of a developmental stage, combine to delay the diagnosis until the symptoms can no longer be hidden or dismissed.

Oftentimes, obsessive-compulsive disorder is classified into different subtypes, primarily as a function of the observable symptoms. Although multiple symptom types are the most common, the disorder is often classified according to the following types of observable symptoms: (1) cleaning compulsions, (2) checking compulsions, and (3) primary obsessive disorder.

> *Cleaning compulsions:* This is considered the most common of the compulsive rituals manifested in obsessive-compulsive disorder. Here, the individual is concerned about some type of contamination (be it dirt, germs, or sexual impurity) that he or she feels a need to limit contact in some way and/or feels a need to engage in compulsive washing to alleviate contamination as described above.
>
>> *Example:* Twelve-year-old Amelia takes an unusually long time to sort the family laundry. She refuses to touch either her father's or her brother's underpants, and if her hands do come into contact with them, she rushes to the bathroom and washes her hands for 15 minutes to make sure they are clean.
>
> *Checking compulsion:* Individuals who engage in checking compulsions typically have anxiety that some terrible (often life-threatening) occurrence will transpire. In an attempt to prevent the horrible act from taking place, and to lessen the anxiety about it occurring, the obsessive-compulsive sufferer will repeatedly check locks, placement of dangerous objects, sources of fire/heat, and/or the safety of individual objects or people for reassurance.
>
>> *Example:* Fifteen-year-old Alan has a ritual that he completes exactly five times prior to leaving his home. He checks all electric appliances (to make sure they are unplugged), and all locks as

well as all windows to make sure they are secured. Alan then counts the number of knives and sharp objects in the kitchen so he will know if any are missing when he returns home.

Primary obsessive disorder: Studies indicate that somewhere around 15% of obsessive-compulsive sufferers do not manifest the ritualistic behaviors (i.e., compulsions) but experience only the obsessive thoughts. These obsessive thoughts are intrusive to the extent that their content is upsetting, and that the obsessive-compulsive individual reports feeling unable to control them. In fact, these people often report that these intrusive thoughts frequently "control" them. The content of these thoughts is so upsetting because they typically are focused on aggressive, sexual, or otherwise offensive themes.

Example: Sixteen-year-old Beth reports being troubled by repeated images of her stabbing, shooting, or otherwise murdering her 9-year-old brother.

In terms of incidence and frequency, obsessive-compulsive disorder occurs twice as often in boys as in girls. In addition, boys show an earlier age of onset. It is also noteworthy that current incidence figures hover around 1% of all child psychiatric inpatients (and 0.2% of all clinical populations). However, when looking at these figures, it's important to keep in mind that the tendency of children/ adolescents to hide their obsessive-compulsive symptoms (due to shame and embarrassment) coupled with the tendency of parents to dismiss obsessive-compulsive symptoms as being due to a developmental stage result in these figures most likely being a significant underestimate of the true frequency of this disorder.

Many theorists explain obsessive-compulsive disorder in children and adolescents as being biological in nature. Variants along this theme include neurological, neurochemical, and/or genetic mechanisms to explain the onset of this disorder. For example there are neurological studies of individuals with obsessive-compulsive disorder that seem to support some involvement of the frontal lobes of the brain as being causal. Results of other studies are interpreted as supporting the involvement of the neurotransmitter serotonin. Thus, it has become common for drug therapies for obsessive-compulsive disorder to involve use of the **Selective Serotonin Reuptake Inhibitors** (although this type of treatment has yielded contradictory results). In terms of genetic approaches, data indicate that one fourth of obsessive-compulsive patients do indeed have a family history of obsessive-compulsive disorder. Although modeling could play a role in this trend, since the specific symptoms exhibited by the child and the parent (or other relatives) are different, it is the general consensus that this clustering in families is more a function of genetic factors.

Whereas biological factors may indeed play a factor in the symptoms of obsessive-compulsive disorder, it is the position of this author that biology does not provide the entire story. Rather, while the various biological factors mentioned above may create a biological predisposition to developing obsessive-compulsive disorder (i.e., provide a biological environment that is conducive for the symptoms to develop), psychological factors are not to be overlooked. More specifically, obsessive-compulsive symptoms can be viewed as an attempt for the individual to obtain control over a life that is perceived to be overwhelming. Oftentimes, when an obsessive-compulsive sufferer is interviewed in detail, it becomes evident that he or she perceives one or more aspects of his or her life as being overwhelmingly out of control. Usually this involves major life areas, the effects of which tend to transcend into various aspects of life functioning. Thus, in an attempt to feel "in control over something," the individual focuses on one or a few areas and develops rules, if you will, that are followed compulsively, thereby providing the person with a (usually false) sense of control over (at least) that aspect of his or her life. Refocusing one's attention to the target of the obsessive thoughts (which is believed to be controllable by following the established rules) allows the person to feel more in control of this single aspect of his or her life and, as a result, of life in general.

> *Example:* Six-year-old Debbie has been quite upset since her father divorced her mother and moved out of the family home. Since that time, she has been manifesting some strange symptoms. For example, before she leaves her bedroom for any reason (as well as before she goes to bed at night), she will go over to each of her toys and touch them two times with her index finger. Further, if Debbie perceives any of her toys to be out of place, she will carefully rearrange as necessary so that she feels the toy is in the correct position. When asked by her mother about this behavior, Debbie replies, "I just want to make sure they are all here."

Treatment for obsessive-compulsive disorder in children is quite variable in terms of modality and efficacy. This variation is as much a function of the **Theoretical Orientation** of the clinician as it is a function of the young person's developmental level. The drug-oriented therapies tend to utilize the **Selective Serotonin Reuptake Inhibitors** (antidepressants that block the body's uptake of the **Neurotransmitter** serotonin), whereas the more psychologically oriented therapies tend to use more behaviorally oriented methods. In the majority of cases in which drug treatment is used to treat this disorder in young people, it is supplemented by some form of psychological intervention (in either individual or family format).

As mentioned above, drug treatment is typically with the chemical goal of inhibiting the reuptake of the neurotransmitter serotonin. However, there are reports in the clinical literature of successful treatment of obsessive-compulsive disorder with virtually every type of **Antidepressant.** Indeed, initially **Anafranil** was the first such medication used for the treatment of this disorder and, therefore, this **Tricyclic Antidepressant** is currently the best researched psychopharmacological treatment for obsessive-compulsive disorder. In addition to the other tricyclic drugs, **Prozac, Luvox, Zoloft,** and **Serzone** have all been utilized recently as treatments. Although not especially frequently, **Lithium, Monoamine Oxidase Inhibitors** as well as some **Antipsychotic** agents have all been employed as potential psychopharmacological treatments for obsessive-compulsive disorder.

SUPPLEMENTAL RESOURCES

Dornbush, M. P., & Pruitt, S. K. (1998). *Teaching the tiger: A handbook for individuals involved in the education of students with Attention Deficit Disorders, Tourette Syndrome or Obsessive Compulsive Disorder.* Duarte, CA: Hope Press.

March, J. S., & Mulie, K. (1995). *OCD in children and adolescents: A cognitive behavioral treatment manual.* Secaucus, NJ: Childswork/Childsplay.

Moritz, E. K., & Jablensky, J. (1996). *Blink, blink, clop, clop: Why do we do things we can't stop?* Secaucus, NJ: Childswork/Childsplay.

OCD Information Line: 1-800-639-7462 (NEWS-4-OCD) OCD Website: http://www.ocdresource.com

Steketee, G., & White, K. (1990). *When once is not enough: Help for obsessive compulsives.* Oakland, CA: New Harbinger.

Oedipus/Oedipal Conflict

The Oedipus conflict is a concept from **Sigmund Freud's** psychosexual theory, stemming from the Greek myth of Oedipus. The story tells of a young man who falls in love with his mother, becomes jealous of his father, and eventually kills him. According to Freud, during the *phallic stage* of development, boys experience a somewhat similar conflict to that of the protagonist in the Oedipus myth. Specifically, the boy is experiencing positive feelings toward his mother (often with sexual overtones), and as such perceives his father as a rival for his mother's affections. During the Oedipus conflict, Freud proposes that it is a developmental task of the boy to resolve his feelings of anger and jealousy toward his father and to somehow translate these negative feelings into a sense of identification with the father as a male role model. Freudian theory dictates that such a transition is necessary for the boy to develop healthy heterosexual relationships as an adult and to mature psychologically overall.

Related information can be found in the following entries: Freud, S. and **Electra Conflict.**

Oppositional Defiant Disorder

Interestingly, some investigators conceptualize the history of American child psychiatry as the history and diagnosis of children with oppositional defiant disorder. Although this is probably somewhat of an exaggeration, since the diagnosis focuses around problematic behavior patterns in the child or adolescent, it is certainly fair to say that this diagnosis is relatively common (with estimates of frequency ranging between 2% and 20% of the general population). Indeed, children/adolescents with oppositional defiant disorder are characterized by an overall pattern of defiant, hostile, and oppositionally negativistic behavior—this behavior most often directed toward adults in authority positions (i.e., usually teachers and/or parents.).

Whereas symptom presentation varies considerably among individuals with oppositional defiant disorder, what is usually seen is exaggerated versions of the typical problems expected of a child/adolescent of the given age group. Generally, young people with oppositional defiant disorder exhibit a chronic defiance of requests, rules, or demands set forth by adults. At times, these children/adolescents seem to be purposefully intent on annoying others with their behavior. However, this behavior tends to be more passive in character, typically not involving overtly aggressive physical acting out.

No single area of oppositional behavior predominates in individuals with oppositional defiant disorder. Indeed, the most recent edition of the *Diagnostic and Statistical Manual (DSM-IV)*, requires that there be a pattern of "negativistic, hostile and defiant behavior lasting at least six months" for the diagnosis to be applied. More specifically, this behavior can be defined by any combination of four of the following characteristics: frequent loss of temper; frequent arguing with adults; frequent defiance or refusal to comply with adults' requests/rules; frequent deliberate annoyance of others; frequent blaming of others for his or her mistakes or misbehavior; frequently easily being annoyed by others; frequent anger and resentfulness; and frequent spitefulness or vindictiveness. The *DSM-IV* specifically states that these behaviors must be perceived as occurring more frequently than would be typically observed in a child/adolescent of comparable developmental level, and that these behaviors must to occur at a severity that compromises functioning.

As with other diagnoses, there is some rather predictable variation as a function of the developmental level of the individual. For example, when symptoms of oppositional defiant disorder appear at an early age, the parents often describe the child as being bad or tough. As one would expect, such a perception initiates a cycle in which the parents' approach toward the child is altered, thereby affecting the child's subsequent behavior. Sometimes, the major issue of behavioral opposition is that of noncompliance with parental requests or demands. With a pattern of forgetting or not hearing what the parent has to say, the child/adolescent with oppositional defiant disorder will provoke adults who, in turn, will respond with punitive and hostile behavior. The process then continues with the young person with oppositional defiant disorder blaming others for the ensuing problems, and then losing control.

Interpersonally, children and adults with oppositional defiant disorder have considerable difficulty. They typically report feeling victimized by those in authority as well as by their peers. Generally viewing the world as being unjustly critical and punitive, they feel repeatedly attacked, and, as a result, generally suffer from low self-esteem. Also characteristic of the behavior of oppositional defiant disorder children/adolescents is a self-sabotaging approach to disagreements and power struggles. It can appear as if the issue of "winning" an argument or power struggle takes on a life of its own, with the individual with oppositional defiant disorder ending up losing something he or she wants, simply to be perceived as victorious in the power struggle.

As indicated above, the symptoms of oppositional defiant disorder are often exaggerations of the type of behavior that is characteristic of the particular developmental stage the child or adolescent is in. Thus, it is important that therapists, parents, and teachers alike differentiate cases of true oppositional defiant disorder from those situations in which the child or adolescent is simply manifesting behavior difficulties characteristic of a specific developmental stage. Those individuals with a valid diagnosis of oppositional defiant disorder differ from those who exhibit the expected parenting challenges (of the **Terrible Twos** or adolescence, for example) in terms of both the quality and the severity of the symptoms seen.

Theories regarding the **Etiology** or cause of oppositional defiant disorder are varied. Whereas the traditional psychoanalytic approaches look to problems with toilet training as an explanation, the more behavioral theories see the disorder as being caused by parental unintentional reinforcement of the oppositional behavior. This reinforcement is most often in the form of attention and/or yielding to the child's wishes—usually out of frustration or desperation. Then, once such a pattern is established, the child/adolescent soon learns to obtain what he or she wants by acting in this (oppositional) manner.

When to Seek Professional Help

Potential cases of oppositonal defiant disorder are probably among the most difficult in terms of determining whether professional help is indicated. It can be hard to differentiate the typical behavioral acting out (characteristic of the so-called terrible twos, for example) from that which is clinically more significant. Indeed, when a parent is experiencing behavioral problems with a child it is not at all uncommon for parental reluctance to label the child with a psychological/psychiatric diagnosis (e.g., oppositional defiant disorder) to cope with the frustration inherent in such behavioral difficulties.

As is often the case, the major guideline in determining whether to seek professional intervention should be the degree to which the behavior(s) in question interfere(s) significantly with the family's functional level. A further, and possibly more significant, guideline would be the degree to which the parents feel out of control with respect to the child's behavior. Oftentimes, this latter criterion is not directly related to the severity of the acting out behavior itself, but rather is more closely related to the parental figure's perception of his or her control over the behavior and its impact. Clearly, it is when the parents feel as if they no longer have control over the child's behavior, but, more accurately, when the child's behavior has control over the functioning of the family, that professional help is warranted.

In many cases of oppositional defiant disorder, the majority (if not all) of the therapy occurs with the clinician working with the parents. Of course, this is not to say that it is the parents' fault, so to speak, that the child is exhibiting the behavior, but, rather, that by providing the parents some modified techniques with respect to interaction with the child, the problematic behavior can be alleviated. Indeed, in most situations, the clinician requests that the initial meeting be with the parents alone with the therapist (i.e., without the child present). In other such cases, therapeutic work assumes other variations in format, including working individually with the child, with the child together with parents, and/or at times with the entire family.

Regardless of the therapeutic modality, the primary orientation of therapy for oppositional defiant disorder is behavioral in nature. Toward that end, the parent should be prepared to have the following information available for the clinician during the first session so an appropriate treatment intervention can be designed.

- A detailed description of the problematic behavior that needs to be addressed.

- A history of when the behaviors began, as well as any variation in the behavior since they first began.

- Description as to when the problematic behavior(s) occur(s)—especially in terms of whether there is any variation in the behavior as a function of where the child is and/or who is present in the child's environment.

- Detailed description of the things the parents have tried in an attempt to modify the undesirable behavior; in addition the parents should be able to provide the clinician with information with respect to

  - how the child reacted to these attempts.
  - if the targeted behavior changed at all as a result of these attempts (i.e., if it improved or became worse).
  - the consistency with which these attempts were applied (i.e., did one parent apply these techniques more successfully and/or regularly than did the other parent? Were these techniques applied in all situations?).

- How individuals in the child's environment react when the child engages in his/her oppositional behaviors.

Information obtained from the answers to the above questions provides the clinician with the necessary structure to construct a meaningful treatment plan to address the child's oppositional behavior. The therapeutic approach is usually primarily behavioral in nature and, as alluded to above, involves the parental figures in fundamental roles. More specifically, the parents are taught how to behave in such a manner so as not to inadvertently reinforce the oppositional behavior but, rather, reinforce more adaptive, desirable behavior patterns. The clinician works with the parental figures to identify patterns of reinforcement and to instruct them as to how to redirect the child's oppositional behaviors and to impose appropriate, effective consequences.

The reader is encouraged to refer to the entry on **Conduct Disorder** for related information on treatment approaches.

SUPPLEMENTAL RESOURCES

Adams, C., & Fruge, E. (1996). *Why children misbehave and what to do about it.* Oakland, CA: New Harbinger.

Barkley, R. A., & Benton, C. M. (1998). *Your defiant child: 8 steps to better behavior.* New York: Guilford Press.

Bloomquist, M. L. (1996). *Skills training for children with behavioral disorders.* New York: Guilford Press.

Bodenhamer, G. (1983). *Back in control.* New York: Simon & Schuster.

Fleming, D. (1993). *How to stop the battle with your child.* New York: Simon & Schuster.

Forehand, R., & Long, N. (1996). *Parenting the strong willed child.* Chicago: Contemporary.

Riley, D. A. (1997). *The defiant child: A parent's guide to oppositional defiant disorder.* Dallas, TX: Taylor Publishing.

Organic Pathology

A somewhat outdated term, organic pathology was used to refer to those disorders having their **Etiological** basis (cause) in physiological sources. The term *organic* was commonly used to describe pathologies resulting from brain anomalies, strokes, seizures, and the like.

Overanxious Disorder

Overanxious disorder of Childhood is a diagnostic category used in previous editions of the *DSM*, but no longer included in the currently utilized *DSM-IV* (American Psychiatric Association, 1994). This disorder was characterized by constant worry on the part of the child, a worry so pervasive that although it impeded upon the quality of the child's day-to-day functioning, oftentimes the child would be unable to articulate precisely what it was that he or she was anxious about. As indicated above, this diagnostic category is no longer included in the *DSM-IV*, but rather it has been incorporated into the **Generalized Anxiety Disorder** diagnosis.

Overcorrection

Overcorrection is a behavioral procedure used as a means of eliminating a less than desirable behavior. The process involves requiring the child to perform extreme variations of corrective behaviors in order to demonstrate the process of righting the undesirable behavior. Motives underlying overcorrection are multiple in purpose: First, engaging in the overcorrective process tends to be less than enjoyable, so the process of overcorrection serves somewhat as a form of **Punishment.** Second, the specific behavior in which the child is asked to engage in the process of overcorrection serves as a means of reinforcing what the appropriate behavior should be.

> *Example:* When he is angry, 10-year-old Johnny defecates on the floor and then proceeds to smear his feces. As a means of employing overcorrection, his parents make him not only clean the floors and wall but also wash both areas with a disinfectant for 10 minutes each.

Example: Eleven-year-old Jeff and his friends have taken to writing obscenities on the wall of the middle school boys' room. When they are caught engaging in that behavior, the principal makes them clean up the graffiti, then choose one other bathroom in the school, and clean those walls as well.

SUPPLEMENTAL RESOURCES

Azrin, N. H., & Besalel, V. A. (1980). *How to use overcorrection.* Austin, TX: ProEd.

Overproductive Speech

Also referred to as *pressured speech,* this is one of the major symptoms of **Manic** and of **Hypomanic** episodes. Overproductive speech refers to the person's rapid speed of talking as well as the sense that the person just could not tolerate not talking. Thus, the person with overproductive speech will not only speak rapidly, but will speak almost incessantly—seeming to jump from one topic to the others. Further, the listener has the sense that the person with overproductive speech would be impossible to interrupt. In addition, as the overproductive speech becomes more intense, it also increases in volume and becomes more difficult to understand. At times, the speech appears to almost feed off of itself as the individual incorporates puns, rhymes, and **Loose Associations.**

P

Pamelor–Punishment

Pamelor

Pamelor is the trade name for the **Tricyclic Antidepressant Nortriptyline.** Although it is one of the more potent drugs of this grouping, its **Anticholinergic** side effects are generally classified as being moderate in intensity. Although Pamelor is approved for the treatment of depression in adults and adolescents, its safety has not yet been established for use with children. Nonetheless, studies are currently being conducted evaluating the usage of Pamelor in the treatment of children with depression as well as with children with **Attention Deficit Disorder.**

Available in 10, 25, 50, and 75 mg capsules, as well as a 10 mg/5 ml oral solution, dosage for depression treatment is usually titrated to result in serum levels between 75–100 mg/ml, with a typical daily dose ranging from 0.5–2.0 mg/kg. Because of the potential side effects of the **Tricyclic Antidepressant** group, careful monitoring needs to be employed when using Pamelor.

SUPPLEMENTAL RESOURCES

Gorman, J. M. (1997). *The essential guide to psychiatric drugs.* New York: St. Martin's Press.
Maxmen, J., & Ward, N. (1996). *Psychotropic drugs: Fast facts.* New York: Norton.
Rosenberg, D. R., Holttum, J., & Gershon, S. (1994). *Textbook of pharmacotherapy for child and adolescent psychiatric disorders.* New York: Brunner/Mazel.
Werry, J. S., & Aman, M. G. (1993). *Practitioner's guide to psychoactive drugs for children and adolescents.* New York: Plenum.

Panic Attack

As a major symptom of many of the **Anxiety Disorders,** panic attacks refer to a "discrete period of intense fear or discomfort that is accompanied by at least 4 of 13 somatic or cognitive symptoms" (American Psychiatric Association, 1994). The experience of a panic attack is often so intense and anxiety provoking in and of itself that oftentimes a person develops secondary symptoms as a result of his or her fear of fear, that is, in an attempt to avoid experiencing the panic attack itself. Included among the physical symptoms that can be present in a panic attack are the following: sweating, trembling or shaking, a sense of choking, chest pain or heaviness, nausea or other forms of abdominal distress, dizziness, lightheadedness, feeling of numbness or tingling, chills or hot flashes, shortness of breath, blushing, heart palpitations, pounding heart, and accelerated heart rate. Common cognitive or psychological symptoms associated with panic disorder include **Derealization,** fear of losing control, fear of going crazy, fear of social embarrassment, fear of dying, **Depersonalization,** and overall fear of the impact of the physical symptoms themselves.

SUPPLEMENTAL RESOURCES

Babior, S., & Goldman, C. (1996). *Overcoming panic, anxiety and phobias: New strategies to free yourself from worry and fear.* Duluth, MN: Pfeifer-Hamilton.

Bourne, E. J. (1995). *The phobia and panic disorder workbook.* New York: New Harbinger.

Eisen, A. R., Kearney, C. A., & Schaefer, C. E. (Eds.). (1995). *Clinical handbook of anxiety disorders in children and adolescents.* Northvale, NJ: Jason Aronson.

Husain, S. A., & Kashani, J. H. (1992). *Anxiety disorders in children and adolescents.* Washington, DC: American Psychiatric Press.

White, E. Z. (1995). *An end to panic.* Oakland, CA: New Harbinger.

Panic Disorder

Panic disorder is a diagnosis characterized by the presence of **Panic Attacks.** These panic attacks appear to the individual (and those around him or her) to be spontaneous, unexpected, and to come out of nowhere. A major feature of panic disorder is the so-called fear of fear, or the subsequent concern about experiencing panic attacks in the future. Because the experience of the panic attack is so frightening and unpleasant, the person with panic disorder often develops a concern about panic attacks happening again, as well as concern regarding possibly dangerous implications of the panic attacks. Frequently, the panic disorder sufferer expresses concerns about passing out, having a heart attack, going "crazy," losing control of his or her bowels, and so forth. In addition, there are also commonly concerns on the part of panic disorder sufferers in terms of how others may perceive them when they are experiencing the panic symptoms.

The *DSM-IV* describes two types of panic disorder—one in which **Agoraphobia** is also present and another in which there is an absence of agoraphobia symptoms. In the former type of panic disorder, the individual specifically avoids situations out of fear of a panic attack occurring. These individuals define certain conditions as safe (either by virtue of the environment itself, the location of the environment in terms of access to escape, and/or in terms of being accompanied by a "safe" person), and limit their travel to those designated locations.

When to Seek Professional Help

In cases of panic disorder, especially with children, there is seldom a question as to whether to seek professional treatment. Due to the nature of panic disorder symptoms, both the sufferer and those around him or her tend to have little ambivalence or confusion about seeking treatment. What is crucial, however, is to ensure that treatment is with a professional who has not only an expertise in working with young people but also an expertise in treating panic disorder in children and adolescents.

With respect to treatment modality, treatment for panic disorder involves some type of drug therapy, **Cognitive Behavior Therapy**, or a combination of these two approaches. Since, when pharmacological methods are used to treat panic disorder, the most popular ones are in the group of the **Selective Serotonin Reuptake Inhibitors (SSRI)** and most of these drugs have not been approved for young children, the cognitive approach is usually the initial line of treatment. The approach works by first identifying the thoughts that the person experiences prior to, during, and after the panic symptoms. Next, these thoughts are examined in terms of their validity and rationality, and interpreted in terms of the potentially panic-inducing effects they have on the individual. The final component of the cognitive behavior process for panic disorder involves replacing the maladaptive thoughts with healthier ones, then working with the child/adolescent to learn to employ the more adaptive thoughts during periods of anxiety and panic. Overall, this tends to be a rather short-term therapy (varying, of course, according to the individual) and works best with patients who are relatively verbally articulate.

Questions to Ask the Clinician

- What has been your experience in treating young people with panic disorder?
- What mode of therapy will you be using? (Should the response not be cognitive behavior therapy ask for further explanation.)
- To what extent and in what manner will the parents (and other family members) be involved in the therapy process?
- Do you feel medication will be indicated, and, if so, by whom will that be be prescribed?
- What will the actual therapy sessions consist of?
- At what point will it be reasonable to expect some improvement?

SUPPLEMENTAL RESOURCES

Please refer to the entry **Panic Attacks.**

Parallel Group Therapy

This is a form of group therapy often utilized with parents, children, adolescents, and families. The term *parallel group* refers more to the actual format of the groups than to the therapeutic orientation of the therapist. Parallel groups refer to the situation in which both the child/adolescent and one (or both) parent(s) attend(s) group therapy at the same time, but in separate groups. At times the parent and child groups focus on similar topics; at other times, the groups are set up so that the adults and young people focus on different issues.

Parasuicide

This is a term used to refer to suicide attempts or gestures that do not result in the person's actual death. Thus, in cases of parasuicide, the person may be injured seriously, or the attempt may result in psychiatric hospitalization. However, that which defines a parasuicide is the fact that the individual who engaged in the self-injurious behavior did not die.

Parent-Induced Anxious Attachment

This is a theoretical concept designed to explain the development of various **Anxiety Disorders** in children and adolescents. Combining the psychodynamic and **Behavioral** theoretical orientations, those who support theories of parent-induced anxious attachment propose that, either consciously or unconsciously, some parents actually encourage their child to exhibit behaviors that reflect and/or result in an overdependence on one or both parents. Usually this is manifested behaviorally in symptoms of **Separation Anxiety Disorder** or some other form of pathological attachment in which the child becomes intensely anxious at the thought or actualization of separation from the parental figure. Potential psychological explanations for the parents' behavior include the parent possibly suffering from an anxiety disorder himself or herself and/or the parent not resolving some of his or her own separation issues. Thus, by reinforcing the child's anxiety symptoms, the parent is (most likely unintentionally) creating a situation that meets his or her own psychological needs, although at the expense of the child.

> *Example:* When bringing 5-year-old Jesse to kindergarten on the first day, his mother told the teacher (in front of Jesse) the following: Jesse doesn't like to be away from his mommy, so today may be a very difficult day for both of you!

Parent Training

Based upon the premise that the actual time spent with a child in a therapy session is, in reality, a very small percentage of his waking hours, the concept of parent training was derived in order to teach parents (or other responsible adults) the skills necessary for them to act as surrogate therapists for their children. By accompanying the children to the actual therapy sessions and observing the techniques of the professional therapist, the parents are able to gradually learn to model behaviors and interventions that would be therapeutic for their particular child. In addition, the professional therapist will often meet with the parents separately, instructing them in more detail, answering any questions they may have, and continuing to meet with them on a regular basis to address any problems that may arise as the treatment progresses.

SUPPLEMENTAL RESOURCES

Schaefer, C. E., & Briesmeister, J. M. (Eds.). (1991). *Handbook of parent training: Parents as co-therapists for children's behavior problems.* New York: John Wiley.

Parkinsonism (Neuroleptic Induced)

This syndrome is a side effect of some **Neuroleptic** medications, most frequently affecting female, elderly patients. As the term implies, the symptoms are very similar to those manifested in Parkinson's disease and develop within a few weeks of starting or increasing the dosage of a neuroleptic medication. Neuroleptic-induced Parkinsonism is also a possibility when medication used to reduce **Extrapyramidal Side Effects** is decreased or withdrawn. Once these symptoms develop, the common approach to treatment entails reducing the dose of the antipsychotic medication, introducing (or increasing the dosage of) a medication designed to address extrapyramidal side effects, and/or actually changing the neuroleptic medication being used.

According to the *DSM-IV,* (American Psychiatric Association, 1994) one or more of the following symptoms are necessary for the diagnosis of neuroleptic-induced parkinsonism:

1. Parkinsonian tremor
2. Parkinsonian muscular rigidity
3. **Akinesia**

Paroxetine Hydrochloride

This is the generic name for the drug marketed as **Paxil.** Please refer to that entry for description.

Paxil

Paxil is one of the so-called *novel* or *atypical antidepressants* which promotes itself as having generally fewer side effects than **Prozac** (the first of this group of drugs). In children and adolescents, it typically begins to take effect within 2 to 3 weeks; however, it can take as long as 6 to 8 weeks for a clinical response to be noted. It is important to note that with respect to child and adolescent treatment, there are no FDA established indications for the use of Paxil. However, its use for the treatment of the following disorders in young people is currently being investigated: depressive disorders, **Attention Deficit Hyperactivity Disorder, Obsessive-Compulsive Disorder, Panic Disorder, Anorexia Nervosa, Bulimia, Borderline Personality Disorder** and **Post-Traumatic Stress Disorder.**

Pemoline Magnesium

This is the generic name of the psychostimulant marketed as **Cylert.** Please refer to that entry for description.

Personality Disorders

Personality disorders (also referred to as *characterological disorders)* comprise one of the diagnostic classifications that are diagnosed along Axis II of the *DSM-IV.* Since these diagnoses refer to actual disorders in personality, symptoms of personality disorders tend to be rather chronic and pervasive, and are typically not especially bothersome to the person manifesting them. Indeed, it is rather uncommon for individuals with personality disorders to seek professional help on their own unless they perceive themselves to somehow be forced (i.e., by a significant other, by the law, by an employer, etc.). When an individual with a personality disorder does indeed consult a professional for treatment, the treatment tends to be rather prolonged and long-term due to the chronicity of the symptoms as well as the individual's poor insight into the fact that he or she has any form of psychological problem.

As a diagnostic classification, the personality disorders are divided into three major clusters. Those people with disorders that are included in Cluster A are usually perceived by those who interact with them as being strange, eccentric, or otherwise weird. Included in Cluster A are the disorders of paranoid personality disorder, schizotypal personality disorder, and schizoid personality disorder. Individuals with personality disorders from Cluster B are viewed by others as being extremely emotional and dramatic. Cluster B personality disorders include **Antisocial Personality Disorder, Borderline Personality Disorder,** histrionic personality disorder, and narcissistic personality disorder. It is generally believed at this point that Cluster B personality disorders have a strong genetic component to their **Etiology.** Finally, Cluster C personality disordered individuals convey to the rest of the world a feeling of pervasive fear and anxiety. These Cluster C disorders include **Avoidant Personality Disorder, Dependent Personality Disorder** and **Obsessive-Compulsive** personality disorder.

SUPPLEMENTAL RESOURCES

Masterson, J. F. (1988). *The search for the real self: Unmasking the personality disorders of our age.* New York: Free Press.
Millon, T., & Everly, G. S. (1985). *Personality and its disorders: A biosocial learning approach.* New York: John Wiley.

Pervasive Developmental Disorders

This is a classification of diagnoses which, according to the *DSM-IV* are "characterized by severe and pervasive impairment in several areas of development: reciprocal social interaction skills, communication skills, or the presence of stereotyped behavior, interests, and activities" (American Psychiatric Association, 1994, p. 65). Diagnoses included in this category are **Autistic Disorder, Rett's Disorder, Childhood Disintegrative Disorder, Asperger's Disorder,** and pervasive developmental disorder not otherwise specified. This last category is applied when a child exhibits symptoms of one or more of the aforementioned pervasive developmental disorders, but the symptoms do not meet the diagnostic criteria for any single diagnosis in this category.

Phobic Disorders

It is generally acknowledged that fears are a normal developmental feature of childhood and adolescence. Indeed, certain fears are considered to be characteristic of different ages. Dulcan and Popper (1991) write that loss of physical support, loud noises, and large rapidly approaching objects tend to frighten infants from birth until 6 months of age. When babies are from 7 to 12 months old, they tend to be frightened by strangers. Storms, animals, darkness, and separation from parents frighten children during their preschool years, whereas monsters, ghosts, and other such fantasy figures are the focus of fears during the school years.

Whenever the anxiety component or the resulting avoidant component of fear interferes with the child's optimal day-to-day functioning, and whenever the fear is out of proportion to the actual danger of the situation (and not developmentally appropriate), a diagnosis of phobia or phobic disorder is considered. The phobia is characterized as a *specific phobia* when there is a specific stimulus that evokes the phobic response in the child. In all cases of phobia, when the individual is exposed to the phobic object, or there is even a chance of the individual coming into contact with the phobic object, there is an almost predictable anxiety reaction—often to the intensity of a **Panic Attack.** The intensity and discomfort of such a reaction result in the individual attempting to avoid such an experience in the future. As a result, the person develops an avoidance response to the phobic stimulus as well as *anticipatory anxiety* regarding coming into contact with the phobic stimulus in the future. As would be expected, these components combine to result in a dramatic impairment in the person's day-to-day functioning.

Theories of the **Etiology** of phobic disorders in children and adolescents can be divided into four major categories: (1) psychodynamic perspectives (i.e., those based upon the theoretical orientation of **Sigmund Freud**), (2) **Behavioral** perspectives, (3) genetic perspectives, and (4) psychophysiological perspectives.

Psychodynamic perspectives: Conceptualize phobias as being the result of misdirected or displaced sexual or aggressive energies.

Behavioral perspectives: View development of phobias within the framework of **Classical Conditioning** and **Modeling** behaviors.

Genetic perspectives: Based upon data that indicate that children with phobias often have parents or other first-degree relatives who also suffer from phobic disorders.

Psychophysiological approaches: Postulate that individuals with phobic disorders have more sensitive nervous systems (specifically the *autonomic nervous system)*, which results in the more frequent activation of the fear/anxiety response.

Professional Treatment

Professional consultation is best sought whenever a child or adolescent's phobias or fears significantly impede the quality of his or her life. Further, when the parent is of the opinion that the fears are not only out of proportion to the actual danger of the situation but are also beyond what is normally expected for a young person of that stage of development, it is wise to seek treatment.

Unlike the case of many of the other **Anxiety Disorders** of childhood and adolescence, it is generally agreed that the most effective treatments for phobic disorders are behavioral or **Cognitive Behavioral** in orientation. These treatments fall into four major treatment modalities: (1) **Systematic Desensitization,** (2) modeling, (3) operant models, and (4) cognitive behavior therapy.

Systematic desensitization: After being trained in relaxation methods, child is taught to pair relaxation response with exposure to the phobic stimulus.

Modeling: Involves having the child/adolescent view other individuals actually confronting the phobic stimulus and reacting without anxiety.

Operant conditioning: Child is reinforced for not avoiding the phobic object and reacting without anxiety when exposed to it.

Cognitive behavior therapy: Works with patient to identify maladaptive thoughts that result in phobic reactions and symptoms.

When Seeking Professional Treatment

When a decision has been made to consult a mental health professional for the treatment of a young person's phobic disorder, as with other diagnostic categories, investigate the professional's experience with respect to treating phobias in the specific age group. Although there are some limitations as a function of the child's developmental level, the general consensus is that some form of cognitive behavior therapy is the treatment of choice for phobic disorders. Thus, it is recommended that, when choosing a professional to treat the phobic disorder, his or her inclination to utilize cognitive behavioral techniques be investigated, as should his or her experience in using such techniques with children. Whereas some form of exposure to the phobic stimulus (either real or imagined) is a component of virtually all types of therapy for phobic disorders, the parent should also question the professional as to how he or she does this. To the extent to which it is possible, the child should be consistently given the message that he or she has control over the exposure situation at all times, and that at no time will he or she be forced into doing anything before he or she is ready. It is important to keep in mind that the child need not be traumatized for the treatment to be successful.

SUPPLEMENTAL RESOURCES

Babior, S., & Goldman, C. (1996). *Overcoming panic, anxiety, and phobia: New strategies to free yourself from worry and fear.* Duluth, MN: Pfeifer-Hamilton.
Bourne, E. J. (1995). *The phobia and anxiety disorder workbook.* New York: New Harbinger.
White, E. Z. (1995). *An end to panic.* Oakland, CA: New Harbinger.

Phonological Disorder

Phonological disorder, previously referred to as *articulation disorder,* is characterized by the inability to accurately produce certain sounds of speech at a level appropriate to the child's expected developmental capability. At times the child will distort certain sounds, omit other sounds, and substitute one sound for another. In addition, the child will also demonstrate an overall general inability to articulate properly. Initially, the speech of children with phonological disorder is not substantially different from the distortions commonly heard in young children who are just learning to speak. Thus, prior to considering a diagnosis of phonological disorder, it is important for the clinician to take the child's developmental level into account.

There is a great deal of variation with respect to severity and general presentation of the symptoms of phonological disorder. A lot of this variation depends on the developmental stage of the youngster, as well as the intensity of symptoms. Children who are younger or who are more severely affected will show problems in pronouncing those sounds of language that are characteristic of early language development (for example, pronouncing of d, n, t, and b). On the other hand, children with milder cases have trouble only with the more complicated sounds. Thus, the severity of the disorder is directly related to the number of different sounds the child has trouble articulating. A diagnosis of phonological disorder requires that the difficulties with speech be severe enough to interfere with the child's ability to communicate and day-to-day functioning.

SUPPLEMENTAL RESOURCES

Hamaguachi, P. M. (1995). *Childhood speech, language and listening problems: What every parent should know.* New York: John Wiley.

Martin, K. L. (1997). *Does my child have a speech problem?* Chicago: Chicago Review Press.

McNamara, B. E., & McNamara, F. J. (1995). *Keys to parenting a child with a learning disability.* New York: Barrons.

Rosner, J. (1993). *Helping children overcome learning difficulties.* New York: Walker.

Smith, S. L. (1991). *Succeeding against the odds: How the learning disabled can realize their promise.* New York: Putnam.

Smith, S. L. (1995). *No easy answers: The learning disabled child at home and at school.* New York: Bantam.

Physical Abuse

Childhood physical abuse is problematic on several levels. First, of course, there is the physical pain and potential danger associated with the physical process itself. Second, there is the multitude of psychological, psychiatric, and emotional problems that frequently develop as consequences of being a victim of childhood physical abuse. Finally, there is the fact that those who are abused tend to become perpetrators of abuse—either later in life or concurrently (with their victims being smaller, younger, more vulnerable than they).

Interestingly, it is more frequently the mother than the father of the child who is the perpetrator of physical abuse. Further, studies indicate that there are certain characteristics of children that seem to make them more prone to being victims of physical abuse. Specifically, children with intellectual handicaps, physical handicaps, who have been born prematurely (with premature children accounting for 50% of all those reported to be abused), and those who cry a lot—in other words, those children who are perceived by their parents as being more demanding than average—are more likely to be victims of physical abuse. A 1992 study published by the National Committee for the Prevention of Child Abuse reports that of those children reported to be physically abused, 32% are under the age of 5 years, 27% are between 5 and 9 years old, 27% are between 10 and 14 years, and 14% are between 15 and 18 years of age (Kaplan & Sadock, 1996).

In the majority of cases of child physical abuse, the parents are not evil or malicious individuals who operate with the intention of severely harming their child. Rather, the typical situation is one of frustration, problems with anger control, and a general lack of adequate parenting skills. In addition, many of the parents who physically abuse their children were indeed abused themselves by their parents and are relatively unaware of the consequences and pathology of their behavior.

Child victims of physical abuse manifest the entire gamut of psychological disorders ranging from the relatively common to the most severe. Whereas, in some such children, the psychological ramifications of the physical abuse is blatantly obvious (e.g., anxiety, depression, extreme aggression), in other children, the psychological effects are somewhat more subtle. Quite often, the child experiences a considerable amount of shame, embarrassment, and guilt over being the victim of such abuse and, as such, will go to rather extreme efforts to prevent others from finding out.

SUPPLEMENTAL RESOURCES

Ennis, G., & Black, J. (1997). *It's not okay anymore—Your personal guide to ending abuse, taking charge, and loving yourself.* Oakland, CA: New Harbinger.

Rickard, V. (1998). *The learning about myself (LAMS) program for at-risk parents: Learning from the past, changing the future.* Binghamton, NY: Haworth Press.

Trickett, P. K., & Schellenbach, C. (Eds.). (1998). *Violence against children in the family and the community.* Washington, DC: American Psychological Association.

Wilson, K. J. (1997). *When violence begins at home: A comprehensive guide to understanding and ending domestic violence.* Alameda, CA: Hunter House.

Woht, A., & Kaufman, B. (1995). *Silent screams and hidden cries: An interpretation of artwork by children from violent homes.* New York: Brunner/Mazel.

Physician's Desk Reference (PDR)

The *Physician's Desk Reference* is an annual edition published by the Officers of Medical Economics, Inc. It contains detailed descriptions of all prescription drugs (and photographs of many), including information regarding for what conditions they are most commonly prescribed, common dosages, clinical situations for which they should not be prescribed, and common side effects as well as less common side effects. While the *PDR* itself is the primary reference in this series, it should be noted that there are other similar annually published references in the same series including the *PDR For Non-Prescription Drugs* and the *PDR for Ophthalmology*.

Pica

Pica is described as the repeated eating of nonnutritive (nonfood) substances. It is considered to be one of the most unusual eating disorders (in terms of characteristic symptoms) of childhood and adolescence. The name *pica* is derived from the Latin word for magpie, a bird that ingests a wide variety of different substances. Children with pica are likely to eat approximately three different nonfood items, among the most common being leaves, grass, sticks, insects, buttons, hair, string, cloth, plants, stones, crayons, pieces of plaster or paint, clothing, sand, animal droppings, and pebbles. Surveys indicate that the majority of children diagnosed with pica are under 6 years of age, with a peak in incidence around age 2. In order for pica to be diagnosed, the *DSM-IV* (American Psychiatric Association, 1994) requires that the behavior continue for at least a 1-month period, that the behavior be beyond what would expect at the child's developmental level, and that the eating behavior is not culturally based. Data indicate that between 10% and 20% of all children will manifest symptoms of pica at some time in their lives.

Theories of **Etiology** with respect to pica are rather varied. Those based on animal models propose dietary deficiencies as a major factor (specifically deficiencies of iron, zinc, or calcium). Approaches that are more psychodynamic in nature explain pica as being the result of unresolved feelings of parental abandonment, with the child using the ingestion of various substances as a defense against the anxiety associated with these feelings. Finally, other theorists look to the fact that pica has been found to be associated with families in which there was emotional and/or physical neglect or abuse by the parents.

Professional treatment for pica revolves around a combination of education of the parents with respect to nutrition, appropriately stimulating play activities for the child, and more behaviorally oriented techniques including **Differential Reinforcement, Overcorrection** procedures, as well as **Contingency Management.** It is important that even if a parent only suspects pica that it be brought to the attention of a treatment professional. Quite frequently, children with pica are brought for treatment of other conditions, and unfortunately the pica symptoms themselves are overlooked.

Placebo

A placebo is some type of inert treatment (a medication, therapy intervention, and so on) that has a curative effect simply because the patient *expects* the treatment to be effective. Worded another way, there is no actual curative component to a placebo treatment. However, the placebo closely resembles the true treatment (often complete with identical side effects) and the patient has the expectation that the intervention will be effective, which results in the placebo having an effect on the target symptom.

Example: Following the death of her grandmother, 7-year-old Althea had a difficult time sleeping at night. In conjunction with her counseling, Althea's pediatrician prescribed a small dose of Benadryl to help her sleep at night. Six months later, Althea completed her therapy, but felt that she could not fall asleep without the aid of the Benadryl. So when it came time to fill her next prescription, her pediatrician instructed the pharmacy to give Althea a bottle of sugar pills which looked exactly like her Benadryl pills and that resulted in the child having some dryness in her mouth (a side effect of Benadryl). Althea was able to sleep just fine and after 3 weeks of the placebo medication, Althea was able to sleep without any pills at all.

Example: Dr. Smith is doing some research to evaluate the effectiveness of a new medication for **Attention Deficit Hyperactivity Disorder.** Her research protocol involves giving one-half or her subjects the new drug and the other half of her subjects a placebo. The placebo was designed by a drug company to look exactly like the true medication and to have side effects similar to that of the true medication.

Play Therapy

Although play therapy is typically considered a psychodynamic approach, its use is certainly not restricted to practitioners who operate within that framework. In a 1993 chapter (Brems, 1993) the three general goals of play therapy were listed as follows: (1) establishment of a trusting, special relationship between therapist and child; (2) providing of data to the clinician in terms of allowing the expression of feelings, the acting out of fears, and allowing the expression of emotions that may be perceived as forbidden under other circumstances; and (3) providing the environment that would facilitate healing. Play therapy is believed to be effective in that in operates within a format with which the child is comfortable. By meeting the child on his or her own turf, so to speak, many of the anxieties associated with the traditional psychotherapy situation are alleviated.

Because play is generally acknowledged to be one of the natural developmental tasks of childhood, it is a modality through which children can express themselves easily. It is not uncommon for a child who is uncomfortable verbalizing feelings to clearly express these feelings through play. Indeed, play represents how the child interacts in the outside world. His or her approach toward dolls, army figures, puppets, and so on reveals to the therapist the quality of the child's interpersonal interactions. Finally, the play modality, with its varying amount of the component "let's pretend," allows the child to work with threatening psychological issues without directly taking responsibility for them.

The famous psychologist **Erik Erikson** summarizes play therapy and its functions as follows:

> Modern play therapy is based on the observation that a child made insecure by a secret hate or fear of the natural protectors of his play in the family and neighborhood seems able to use the protective sanction of an understanding adult to regain some play peace. Grandmothers and favorite aunts may have played that role in the past; its professional elaboration of today is the play therapist. The most obvious condition is that the child has the toys and adult for himself, and that sibling rivalry, parental nagging, or any kind of sudden interruption does not disturb the unfolding of his play intentions. (Erikson, 1994)

Depending upon the specific clinical situation as well as the developmental level of the child, play therapy can assume varying prominence in the treatment of a child or adolescent. That is to say, in some cases it comprises virtually the entire therapeutic protocol, wherein in other cases it comprises only a small portion.

SUPPLEMENTAL RESOURCES

Alixine, V. M. (1993). *Play therapy.* New York: Ballantine.

Gil, E. (1991). *The healing power of play: Working with abused children.* New York: Guilford Press.
Nemiroff, M. A., & Annunziata, J. (1990). *A child's first book about play therapy.* Washington, DC: American Psychological Association.
Schaefer, C., & Kaduson, H. (Eds.). (1994). *The quotable play therapist.* Northvale, NJ: Jason Aronson.

Pornography

It is not at all uncommon for adolescents to be attracted to pornographic materials, often much to the dismay of the parent and other adults. Whereas, in a small minority of cases, the adolescent's use of pornography for sexual stimulation is problematic in its compulsive nature, in most cases adolescents look to pornography for education about sexuality. For other adolescents, the pornography is used in masturbatory activity—again, as a means of experimenting with different aspects of sexuality in an interpersonally safe, nonthreatening situation. After all, when using pornography, the adolescent (who is insecure about his or her sexuality) does not have to be concerned with rejection, being judged inadequate, or the complexities of true interpersonal intimate contact.

Despite the relative commonality of adolescent pornography usage, it is considerably upsetting to many parents (the degree of the upset a function of the parental attitude toward pornography). Especially when the pornography is of a homosexual nature or contains violent themes, parents become concerned as to how to address the situation. While they certainly want the adolescent to cease this behavior, issues of embarrassment and trust (i.e., how did the parents find the pornography to begin with?) all contribute to making the initiation of such a discussion difficult.

Important points to keep in mind when confronting the adolescent regarding his or her suspected use of pornography are as follows:

- Be as honest as possible with respect to why you suspect pornography usage.
- Be careful not to speak negatively of the adolescent's sexual urges, needs, but rather discuss only how he is expressing them; acknowledge that he indeed has sexual needs that need to be expressed.
- Discuss the difference between compulsive masturbation and masturbation in general.
- Explain your attitude toward pornography and why you perceive it to be a less than positive thing.
- Come to an agreement with the adolescent as to what types of materials are permitted in the home and what types are not.
- Discuss with the adolescent what you consider more appropriate options for expressing his or her sexuality; remember, you cannot ask someone to give up a behavior without arranging for another behavior to meet the same needs.
- Discuss with the adolescent what is going to be done with the pornographic materials.

Positive Reinforcement

Positive reinforcement is defined as any stimulus that, when added to the environment, increases the probability of a target behavior occurring. Synonymous with the concept of reward, positive reinforcement involves adding a positive, desirable element to the environment in an attempt to encourage the performance of a certain behavior. Thus, the traditional star charts, providing an allowance contingent on the completion of chores, and giving the child a special gift for an excellent report card are all examples of applications of positive reinforcement.

The manner in which positive reinforcement is delivered can vary considerably. For example, is the reinforcement delivered every time the desired response occurs, or only certain times? If it is the latter, on what schedule is the reinforcement delivered? There are various different reinforcement schedules, the most common of which are described below:

Continuous reinforcement: Every performance of the desired response is followed by reinforcement.

Example: Every time 6-year-old Johnny says "please" or "thank you" at the appropriate time, his mother gives him a penny.

Intermittent reinforcement: Not every performance of the desired response is followed by reinforcement.

Ratio schedules: Rather than having every incidence of the desired response be reinforced, the desired response is reinforced only after it is correctly performed a certain number of times.

Example: For every 2 days of good reports from the babysitter, 4-year-old Rena is given a treat from the "treat box."

Interval schedules: Rather than having the reinforcement be contingent on the number of correct responses, it comes after a certain amount of time since the last reinforcement.

Example: Mr. Hitchcock's third-grade class is allowed 10 minutes of computer game time at 11:00 and 2:00 every day.

SUPPLEMENTAL RESOURCES

Hall, R. V., & Hall, M. C. (1980). *How to select reinforcers.* Austin, TX: ProEd.

Post-Traumatic Stress Disorder

Classified under the more general category of **Anxiety Disorders,** post-traumatic stress disorder (PTSD) is characterized by reactions to a traumatic event (or set of traumatic events) in which there is repeated reexperiencing of the event (via dreams, images, recollections, and associations to environmental cues viewed as similar or related); avoidance of stimuli that are perceived by the sufferer to be associated with the trauma; as well as increased levels of arousal. Should these symptoms last longer than 3 months, the post-traumatic stress disorder is characterized as *chronic,* whereas if the symptoms have lasted less than 3 months, the post-traumatic stress disorder is characterized as *acute.* It is most commonly found in children and elderly people who have experienced traumatic events, with the disorder being less frequently seen in middle-aged adults.

The current version of the *DSM* (American Psychiatric Association, 1994) requires the following criteria for a diagnosis of *post-traumatic stress disorder:*

A. Exposure to a traumatic event in which the person's response involved intense fear, helplessness, horror, or agitated behavior in children
B. Reexperiencing of the traumatic event in at least one of the following ways:
   1. recurrent recollections of the event, often manifested by children via repetitive play with themes similar to the trauma
   2. repeated dreams or nightmares of the event
   3. reenactment of the trauma in actuality or cognitively
   4. distress in response to exposure to cues that are perceived to be related to the traumatic event
   5. physiological reactivity to the cues described in (4)
C. Avoidance of stimuli associated with the trauma as well as numbness as indicated by at least three of the following:
   1. avoidance of feelings and conversations associated with the trauma
   2. avoidance of activities and people that remind person of trauma
   3. inability to remember aspects of the trauma
   4. diminished interest in activities
   5. feelings of separation from others
   6. restricted **Affect**
   7. sense of a shortened future
D. At least two of the following symptoms of increased arousal:
   1. sleep problems
   2. anger issues
   3. problems concentrating
   4. hypervigilance
   5. exaggerated startle response (pp. 427–428)

For children, symptoms of post-traumatic stress disorder usually begin with anxiety-provoking dreams or **Nightmares** of the traumatic event, which eventually develop into more generic nightmares. In other situations, children will reenact the trauma in their play as well as in their fantasy life.

Professional Treatment

Although treatment for PTSD may involve the use of medication (usually one of the **Selective Serotonin Reuptake Inhibitors**), the primary component of treatment for this disorder is psychotherapy. The content of the therapy will vary according to the

Therapeutic Orientation of the clinician as well as according to the specific needs of the patient. Regardless, the therapy process usually assumes a model based upon crisis intervention, with the initial steps aimed at development of appropriate coping mechanisms to allow acceptance of the traumatic event. **Behavior Therapy** and/or **Cognitive Behavior Therapy** is then employed to help the individual develop skills to attenuate and eventually eliminate the symptoms associated with the disorder.

The specific manner in which the clinician proceeds is a function of the traumatic event, the patient's clinical condition, as well as the preferences of the clinician. Thus, when seeking professional treatment, it is important to determine the clinician's experience in working with the specific form of trauma, especially in young people. Assuming the experience level is acceptable, the therapist should be questioned in terms of how he or she plans to proceed, especially with respect to the elimination of symptoms.

SUPPLEMENTAL RESOURCES

Bean, B., & Bennett, S. (1993). *The me nobody knows: A guide for teen survivors.* New York: Lexington Books.

Davis, L. (1990). *The courage to heal workbook.* New York: Harper & Row.

Flannery, R. B. (1998). *PTSD: The victim's guide to healing and recovery.* New York: Crossroad.

Poverty of Content

Poverty of content is characteristic of the speech of some individuals with **Schizophrenia.** It describes a situation wherein a schizophrenic person may speak for a considerable period of time, but actually have very little content to his or her speech. Thus, despite the fact that the individual is speaking an appropriate amount or for an appropriate period of time, the actual information being imparted is minimal. Oftentimes, the speech of individuals exhibiting poverty of content is vague, difficult to understand, and characterized by stereotyped, meaningless phrases.

Practice Effects

Practice effects refers to the impact that the experience of taking a given test has on the results of taking the same or similar test another time. Specifically, does the person's experience in taking the test previously result in any impact on his or her scores on subsequent administration of the same test? In many cases, memory of the questions, a "learning to learn" phenomenon (in which repeatedly performing the same task in and of itself results in improved performance), and/or somehow procuring information between administrations in terms of what the test is attempting to assess can all impact upon the individual's performance on future administrations of the test.

> *Example:* When 7-year-old Jeff was brought to a private psychologist for an intellectual assessment, the psychologist was not aware that Jeff had recently been tested with the **Wechsler Intelligence Test** by his school psychologist just last week. As the private psychologist began the testing, Jeff proudly stated, "I did this before in school." Once the test was scored, it was found that Jeff scored significantly higher on the performance scales of the intelligence test the second time he took it. When the private psychologist wrote the report, he explained this discrepancy in scores as being due to *practice effects.*

Premorbid

Premorbid is an adjective utilized to describe symptoms that appear or occur prior to the actual diagnosis of the specific full-blown disorder. For example, there are certain symptoms known to be indicative of the future development of certain psychological/psychiatric illnesses. Such symptoms are known as premorbid symptoms of that particular disorder. The term *premorbid* is also used to refer to those characteristics in an individual that exist prior to the development of any symptoms. Thus, it is common to talk about a *premorbid personality,* referring to an individual's personality prior to the development of the symptoms of a specific disorder.

Pressured Speech

This term is synonymous with **Overproductive Speech.** Refer to that entry.

Primary

This is an adjective used to describe symptoms or a disorder. When a symptom or a disorder is described as primary, the meaning is that the symptom is not a result of some other condition or disorder. For example, if a person is said to have primary depression, that is meant to imply that the depression is the major disorder and the depressive symptoms are not a result of anxiety or some other disorder.

Procrastination

When a young person engages in behaviors of procrastination, it is usually due to one of four underlying factors: (1) depression, (2) anxiety, (3) oppositional tendencies, or

(4) organizational deficits. When a child presents with problems of procrastination, in order to correct the behavior, the underlying basis for it must first be determined.

Depression: One of the common symptoms of depression is a general loss of motivation and an inability to become productively engaged in day-to-day activities. Thus, if the child/adolescent is showing any other signs or behaviors consistent with depression, the presence of depression should be considered as a real possibility, and appropriate actions should be taken. (Refer to the entry **Childhood Depression.**)

Anxiety: It is common for all of us to avoid situations and experiences that cause us anxiety. When a child exhibits behaviors of procrastination, it is important to first evaluate the nature of the procrastination. In other words is the child generally a procrastinator, or does he or she only procrastinate around certain activities? If the situation is closer to the latter, the specific situations around which the child procrastinates need to be examined. Quite often, it is determined that specific situations are those that cause the child anxiety, and, as a result, he or she opts to avoid them. Common examples include a child with a problem with math who procrastinates doing his math homework, or a child who is afraid of the dark procrastinating doing her chore of cleaning the basement. As in the case of depression as described above, in such a case the anxiety needs to be addressed in order for the procrastination to be addressed.

Oppositional behavior: The source of procrastination in a child (or adult, for that matter) can be a passive-aggressive way of expressing anger at the person or people who require that the specific behavior be done. Yet another facet of this same dynamic is the child who, for various reasons, simply does not want to engage in the particular behavior, so procrastinates as a way of avoiding doing it. Common situations that fit this explanation include the child who will clean his room or empty the dishwasher "in a few minutes," or the preteen who will make plans to visit her relatives "in a few days." In such cases, the best approach is to address not only the situations that the young person is attempting to avoid, but also the fact that putting off what we do not enjoy is not an optimal way to deal with the situation. Finally, it is important that the child does not perceive his doing the task as being especially important to the parental figures (as not completing the task would then be an optimal way of getting back at them), and that the child learn from the procrastinating experience that there are consequences to not completing tasks in a timely fashion.

Disorganization issues: Some children procrastinate simply because of problems with organizing their time, materials, and tasks. While this is characteristic of children with **Attention Deficit Disorder,** problems with organization are certainly not limited to individuals with this diagnosis. Once the exact nature of the organizational problems are identified, the parents can help the child address these issues in a nonpunitive manner. Oftentimes, a trip to the local office supply store to purchase a minimum order (including perhaps a planner, an assignment book, folders, etc.) along with continual guidance from the parents as to how to utilize these materials can be sufficient to provide major inroads into organizational problems.

Prodromal Symptoms

Prodromal symptoms refer to those symptoms that are evident prior to the person manifesting a full-blown case of a given psychiatric illness. Many clinicians, therefore, conceptualize prodromal symptoms as warning signs of the development of a clinical condition. Prodromal symptoms vary not only from diagnosis to diagnosis but also from individual to individual.

Example: Mr. and Mrs. Sanderson know that whenever their 13-year-old son begins sleeping during the days and not sleeping at all at night, he is about to have an onset of his **Obsessive-Compulsive Disorder.**

Example: Eleven-year-old Jessica has been withdrawing from her friends, seemingly showing no interest in socialization activities at all. Her parents recognize these behaviors from past experience as indicating that she is about to have another depressive episode.

Professional Help, Locating

Locating professional help for a child or adolescent with an emotional, psychological, or psychiatric problem can be one of the more challenging tasks a parent may ever have to face. In addition to the issues raised whenever one seeks professional help for a problem, additional issues complicate the situation when the type of help sought extends beyond the traditional medical. Once the decision to seek professional help has been made, however, the basic principles involved do not differ significantly from those employed in seeking professional assistance in any other matter of life. Still, feelings of shame, embarrassment, and anxiety (on the part of the child as well as the other family members) tend to complicate the matter considerably.

Type of Professional

Unlike seeking help for your child's medical problem (where the parent seeks out a physician of some type), there are several options available when it comes to seeking out professional consultation for an emotional, psychological, or psychiatric disorder. Professionals of several different disciplines offer assessment and treatment for the various psychopathologies, and, at times, choosing the appropriate type of professional can seem a monumental task in and of itself. The following can serve as a rather generic guide in terms of the different types of professionals who provide such services and how they compare along various dimensions.

Psychiatrist: This is a medical doctor who has chosen to specialize in the field of psychiatry. Psychiatrists are able to prescribe medication, and many of them utilize drug therapy as their primary mode of intervention. If you opt to go to a psychiatrist, it is important to find out if he or she is willing to provide regular psychotherapy and/or behavior therapy to supplement the medication. If not, investigate his or her willingness to work with whatever other professional you choose.

Psychologist: The credentials required to call oneself a psychologist vary from state to state. Whereas in some states the individual needs to have completed a doctoral degree and passed a licensing examination, in other states completion of a bachelor's degree is sufficient. Although there is a movement within some professional groups of psychologists to obtain prescribing privileges, at the present time, few psychologists are able to prescribe medication. Psychologists work primarily via individual, group, and family therapy. Psychologists (unlike any of the other professionals mentioned) are schooled in various assessment techniques and are able to perform different types of diagnostic testing.

Social worker: A social worker can have either a bachelor's degree or a master's degree. (Some social workers do have doctoral degrees, but they are usually working in an academic setting.) Masters level social workers receive a certain amount of general training, and then choose to specialize in a field of social work. Social workers who have chosen psychiatric social work tend to have received considerable training in various psychotherapeutic modalities. In addition, social workers tend to be skilled in issues regarding community resources, potential short-term and long-term placement sites, and family interventions. Again, since they are not medical professionals, social workers are unable to prescribe medication.

Counselors and psychotherapists: The terms *counselor* and *psychotherapist* are unprotected terms in most states. What that means is that virtually anybody can legally be called a counselor or a psychotherapist without any required amount of training. This is not to imply that professionals with such titles are untrained, unethical phonies. Indeed, many of the most competent mental health professionals with whom I have come into contact operated under one of these two titles. However, when considering the services of a professional in one of these unprotected titles, it is crucial that the parent do a bit more investigation into credentials.

This discussion of the different professional disciplines is not at all meant to imply that one discipline provides superior services (or inferior services, for that matter) to any other. What is significant here is the individual, not the professional discipline with which the individual is affiliated. Both you and your child/adolescent need to feel comfortable with the professional, and, quite honestly, the professional needs to feel equally comfortable with you and your child/adolescent. Whereas comfort level and overall rapport can only be determined after actual face-to-face interaction, there are certain screening questions that can help with the initial screening process. It is recommended that the following information be obtained from as many different clinicians as possible prior to scheduling the first appointment so an informed decision can be made. Remember, you are the consumer searching for the ideal "product" for your child. As such, you are entitled to this information and need not be apologetic about asking for it.

Questions to Ask Prior to Scheduling the First Appointment

- What experience have you had treating this particular problem in young people of this age?
- What do you anticipate will be the formats used (individual, family, parent, group) in treatment?
- What are the primary therapeutic techniques you tend to use when you treat this problem?
- How will we (as parents) be informed of the child/adolescent's progress?
- What measures do you take to ensure confidentiality? Who will have access to my child's file?
- What arrangements are there if we need to contact you in between appointments? What is the charge for these contacts?
- What provisions are made should we need to contact you in an emergency situation?
- Do you accept our insurance coverage? If so, who completes the necessary forms? What portion of the fee billed will I be responsible for? What information about the treatment will be shared with the insurance company?

SUPPLEMENTAL RESOURCES

Bush, R. (1995). *A parent's guide to child therapy.* Northvale, NJ: Jason Aronson.

Kahn, M. (1997). *Between therapist and client.* New York: Freeman.

Masi, D., & Kuettel, R. M. (1998). *Shrink to fit: Answers to your questions about therapy.* Deerfield Beach, FL: Health Communications.

Vaughan, S. C. (1998). *The talking cure—Why traditional talking therapy offers a better chance for long term relief than any drugs.* New York: Owl.

Projective Testing

This is a type of testing which has its theoretical foundations in **Psychoanalytic** schools of psychotherapy. Projective testing is built around the premise that crucial aspects of personality functioning operate at an unconscious level. Thus, projective tests provide a minimal amount of stimulus or structure in the test setting. The goal of projective tests is to provide the test subject with a "blank slate" upon which to *project* his or her own feelings.

More specifically, the most popular projective tests being used today involve presenting some type of ambiguous visual stimulus to the subject and then asking the subject to talk about the stimulus freely. This stimulus can range from vague, abstract inkblots characteristic of the **Rorschach** test to more structured photographs and drawings of people characteristic of the Thematic Apperception Test (TAT) and the Children's Apperception Test (CAT).

Still other types of projective testing assume another approach. Rather than asking the child or adolescent to respond to pictures, they may ask the child to complete the beginnings of sentences or to draw something specific (refer to the entry **Draw a Person Test**), usually a self portrait, a family portrait, a house, a tree, or some combination of these items. As with the other projective testing approaches, the child or adolescent is provided with minimal instructions so that the young person is able to *project* his or her psychological issues with minimal interference from the examiner.

Prolixin

Prolixin is the brand name of the **Antipsychotic** medication *fluphenazine hydochloride*. Relative to other antipsychotic medication, it is considered to have moderate sedative and **Anticholinergic Side Effects** and to be very high in its **Extrapyramidal Side Effects.** Prolixin has not been approved for use in children under the age of 12 years, and, unlike some of the other antipsychotics, there is not evidence that it is useful in treating behavioral problems in **Mentally Retarded** individuals. Prolixin is available in tablets (1.0, 2.5, 5, and 10 mg), a liquid form, an oral concentrate, as well as in an injectable form. For young people, the manufacturer recommends an initial daily dose ranging from 2.5 to 10 mg.

SUPPLEMENTAL RESOURCES

Gorman, J. M. (1997). *The essential guide to psychiatric drugs.* New York: St. Martin's Press.
Maxmen, J., & Ward, N. (1996). *Psychotropic drugs: Fast Facts.* New York: Plenum.
Rosenberg, D. R., Holttum, J., & Gershon, S. (1994). *Textbook of pharmacotherapy for child and adolescent psychiatric disorders.* New York: Brunner/Mazel.
Werry, J. S., & Aman, M. G. (1993). *Practitioner's guide to psychoactive drugs for children and adolescents.* New York: Plenum.

Prozac

Prozac (or **Fluoxetine** hydrocholoride) is one of the **Selective Serotonin Reuptake Inhibitors** indicated for the treatment of **Obsessive-Compulsive Disorder** and

Depression in older adolescents (at least 18 years of age) and adults. Nonetheless, studies abound in the clinical literature reporting successful treatment of children and adolescents with **Anxiety Disorders, Attention Deficit Disorder, Tourette's Disorder,** obsessive-compulsive disorder and **Depressive Disorders** with Prozac. Although FDA approval has not been obtained, Prozac is prescribed for individuals under the age of 18, usually at a dosage approximating 20 mg.

SUPPLEMENTAL RESOURCES

Fieve, R. R. (1994). *Prozac: Questions and answers for patients, families, and physicians.* New York: Avon.
Sachs, J. (1997). *Nature's Prozac.* Paramus, NJ: Prentice Hall.
Salzman, B. (1996). *The handbook of psychiatric drugs.* New York: Owl.
Wurtzel, E. (1995). *Prozac nation.* New York: Berkley Publishing Group.

Pseudohallucination

A pseudohallucination is an imaginary sensory experience that does not meet the criteria for true **Hallucinations.** Pseudohallucinations are characteristic of young and middle childhood and should not be considered to be indicative of **Schizophrenia** or other pathological process.

Psychiatric Medication, Children on

At some time in their lives, most children have been treated with prescription drugs for various childhood maladies. However, even the most psychologically/ psychiatrically disturbed children are not automatically treated with psychiatric medication as a first line of treatment. The majority of pediatric clinicians regard psychopharmacological interventions as adjuncts to psychotherapy in the treatment of young people. Generally speaking, practitioners consider drugs only when the symptoms are chronic, or when psychotherapeutic interventions appear to be ineffective.

One reason for this relative reluctance to prescribe psychiatric medications for children is that pharmaceutical companies rarely fund investigation of the use of their products with children. Dosages for the majority of psychiatric medications are not as well established for children and adolescents as they are for adults. This is a potentially problematic situation in that medications can interfere with various developmental processes in the physical, cognitive, psychological, behavioral, or growth spheres (refer to entry on **Developmental Toxicity**).

Pharmacokinetics—the manner in which a drug is metabolized by the various systems of the body—are difficult to anticipate when dealing with children and adolescents. Drug therapy in and of itself is age dependent because growing tissue may metabolize the drug in different ways. Interestingly, children often require larger dosages in proportion to body weight than would adults because they have a more rapid metabolism. Thus, although an initial dosage is often too low to be effectively therapeutic, any increases need to be gradual as the clinician watches for negative side effects as well as positive responses.

Once the clinician has decided that psychopharmacological intervention may be appropriate, the child and his or her family must be involved in the final decision. Parents need to be informed of the need for drug therapy in terms that both the parents and child can understand. Information is required regarding the reason for the choice of the specific drug, the dosage (amount and schedule), results that can be expected as well as when they can be expected, and, finally, the most likely side effects. (The clinician and the parent need to decide together whether to explain potential side effects to the child. Sometimes an explanation of side effects decreases anxiety by letting the young person know what to expect, while, in other cases, the anticipatory anxiety can lead to noncompliance with the treatment regimen.)

Questions to Ask the Clinician

- What features of my child's clinical condition led you to consider medication?
- Will medication be instead of psychological treatment or will it be an adjunct to treatment?
- What factors contributed to choosing this particular drug? What are its relative advantages and disadvantages when compared with other drugs used to treat the same disorder?
- Is this drug FDA approved for treatment of this disorder in children my child's age?
- What has been your experience in using this drug to treat this disorder in children the age of my child?
- What will be the initial dosage regimen?
- What side effects can be expected at the beginning and how will they change as treatment progresses?
- Is there a way to alter the dosage schedule to minimize side effects interfering with the child's day-to-day activities?
- At what point during treatment can we expect to begin to see some positive changes?
- After what period of time without positive changes will we consider changing to another medication?

SUPPLEMENTAL RESOURCES

Rosenberg, D. R., Holttum, J., & Gershon, S. (1994). *Textbook of pharmacotherapy for child and adolescent psychiatric disorders.* New York: Brunner/Mazel.

Werry, J. S., & Aman, M. G. (1993). *Practitioner's guide to psychoactive drugs for children and adolescents.* New York: Plenum.

Psychoanalytic Approach

The psychoanalytic approach to doing psychotherapy refers to any of the approaches based upon the work of **Sigmund Freud** and his followers. Focusing on psychological functioning rather than behavior, psychoanalytic theory was developed primarily through the clinical observation of young people with psychological problems (although, interestingly, Sigmund Freud himself never worked with children directly!). Although the majority of current clinical work with children and adolescents generally involves some form of **Behavioral** approaches, the psychoanalytic school continues to exert a powerful influence. In addition to the work of Sigmund Freud, who pioneered the psychoanalytic model, other figures who have contributed significantly to the application of the psychoanalytic model to work with children include **Anna Freud,** Melanie Klein, D. W. Winnicott, and **Erik Erikson.**

Psychodynamic Psychotherapy

Psychodynamic psychotherapy is a term used to refer to any form of psychotherapy that incorporates the principle that there is an underlying motive or dynamic behind an individual's behavior. The premise is further extended to the corollary that understanding the underlying dynamic (be it conscious or unconscious) associated with a person's behavior is crucial to addressing the behavior and, when relevant, treating the pathology.

Psychogenic

The term psychogenic is an adjective used to describe a symptom or condition that is believed not to have an organic, physical, or biological basis or **Etiology.** Rather, when a symptom or condition is described as psychogenic, the implication is that its basis is primarily (if not solely) psychological in nature. It should be noted, however, that the term *psychogenic* is not used as often as it used to be because in the current conceptualization of psychopathology, in most cases, the etiological foundation is believed to be a combination of psychological and physiological factors.

Psychosocial

Psychosocial is an adjective used typically used to describe **Etiology,** indicating that a symptom, disorder, treatment, or factor is more environmental than biological in nature. For example, psychosocial theories of treatment or human behavior focus more on interpersonal influences than they do on biochemical ones. As the field of child and adolescent psychology/psychiatry has developed, however, it has become increasingly clear that the dichotomy of psychosocial versus biological is really a false one, since most issues in this field are a melding of both of these influences.

Psychotic Disorders

Technically, the term *psychotic disorders* refers to any form of psychological/psychiatric disorder in which an individual's perception of reality is severely altered. The most common of the psychotic disorders, of course, is **Schizophrenia** in which **Hallucinations** and **Delusions** are prominent symptoms. However, schizophrenia is by no means the only psychotic disorder, as other psychotic disorders exist that do not meet the diagnostic criteria for schizophrenia. Included among these other psychotic disorders included in the *DSM-IV* are *shared psychotic disorder* (in which the individual picks up or shares one or more psychotic symptoms exhibited by another), *delusional disorder* (in which the individual has at least 1 month of delusional thinking without any other symptoms of schizophrenia being present), *brief psychotic disorder* (any form of psychotic disorder that lasts somewhere between 1 day and 30 days), *psychotic disorder due to a general medical condition* (in which the person exhibits psychotic symptoms that are judged to be the result of some medical condition), *substance induced psychotic disorder* (in which the person exhibits psychotic symptoms that are judged to be the result of substance abuse, exposure to some toxic substance, or medication) and *psychotic disorder not otherwise specified* (in which psychotic symptoms are evidenced, but none of the aforementioned diagnoses apply).

Puberty

Technically, the term puberty refers to the developmental phase in individuals beginning with the development of *secondary sex characteristics* (e.g., voice changes, growth of body hair, growth of facial hair, breast development, etc.) and continuing for approximately 2 to 3 years thereafter, with puberty beginning and ending approximately 2 years earlier for girls than it does for boys. Hormonal systems that have been present since birth become activated with the onset of puberty, thus the changes in the adolescent's sexual drive, sexual organs, body appearance, and, at times, level of aggression.

In girls, the first sign of puberty is usually the development of breasts. Growth of pubic hair as well as a general growth spurt tends to precede the onset of menstruation. For boys, the first visible signs of puberty are usually an increase in penis size and the growth of pubic hair. This is followed by hair growth under the arms and expansion of pubic hair. The final changes in the boy are usually the voice change and growth of facial hair (Offer & Boxer, 1991).

SUPPLEMENTAL RESOURCES

Brown, L. K., & Brown, M. (1997). *What's the big secret?* Boston: Little, Brown.
Harris, R. H. (1994). *It's perfectly normal.* Cambridge, MA: Candlewick.
Madaras, L. (1998). *The what's happening to my body book for boys.* New York: New Market.
Madaras, L. (1998). *The what's happening to my body book for girls.* New York: New Market.

Punishment

Punishment is a concept from behavioral theory and is defined as any stimulus or behavior introduced into the environment with the end effect of decreasing the frequency of a target behavior. As would be expected, in most cases punishment involves some negative or aversive behavior or condition that is unpleasant enough so that the individual will cease to engage in the target behavior in an attempt to avoid the punishment. Examples of common punishments include grounding a teenager for unacceptable behavior, withdrawing television privileges from a school-aged child for failure to do homework, and giving a toddler time out for misbehaving.

The actual effectiveness of punishment (as opposed to reinforcement) has been a much researched topic. Various aspects of punishment (including its timing, the nature of the punishment, etc.) have been researched in terms of their impact on the effectiveness of the punishment in eliminating the target behavior. Further, the ethical issues and psychological effects in the administration of punishment (specifically, physical punishment such as **Spanking**) currently are major areas of controversy among parents as well as professionals.

R Rabbit Syndrome–Rumination Disorder

Rabbit Syndrome

Please refer to the entry on **Parkinsonism.**

Reading Disorder, Developmental

Also referred to as *dyslexia* and *specific reading disability*, this disorder is characterized by impairment in the individual's ability to read. More specifically, reading disorder entails problems in reading comprehension as well as in the ability to recognize words. When the child with reading disorder reads aloud, he or she shows unusually slow speed as well as distortions, substitutions, and omissions of words and phrases. In order for this diagnosis to be applied, the child's reading achievement (as measured by an individually administered standardized test) must be substantially below that which is expected "given the person's chronological age, measured intelligence, and age-appropriate education" (American Psychiatric Association, 1994) and this impairment must interfere significantly with day-to-day activities and academic achievement.

The term "treatment" with reference to the various developmental disorders is really a misnomer. While none of these disorders can be cured in the true sense, it is crucial to note that the specific symptoms of the various learning disorders (including reading disorder) respond positively to appropriate interventions. In cases of reading disorder, the educational approaches are redesigned to maximize use of the child's assets, with the eventual goal of teaching the child to improve his or her skill of employing associations between sounds and letters.

SUPPLEMENTAL RESOURCES

Gehret, J. (1996). *The don't-give-up kid and learning differences.* Fairport, NY: Verbal Images Press.

Greene, L. J. (1987). *Learning disabilities and your child: A survival handbook.* New York: Ballantine.

Hamaguachi, P. M. (1995). *Childhood speech, language and listening problems: What every parent should know.* New York: Wiley.

Kauffmann, J. M., & Hallahan, D. P. (Eds.). (1995). *The illusion of full inclusion.* Austin, TX: ProEd.

Mandel, H. P., & Marcus, S. I. (1995). *Could do better.* New York: Wiley.

McNamara, B. E., & McNamara, F. J. (1995). *Keys to parenting a child with a learning disability.* Hauppage, NY: Barrons.

Miller, W. H. (1993). *Complete reading disabilities handbook.* West Nyack, NY: Simon & Schuster.

Rosner, J. (1993). *Helping children overcome learning difficulties.* New York: Walker.

Smith, S. L. (1991). *Succeeding against the odds: How the learning disabled can realize their promise.* New York: Putnam.

Smith, S. L. (1995). *No easy answers: The learning disabled child at home and at school.* New York: Bantam.

Unger, H. G. (1998). *The learning disabilities trap.* Chicago: Contemporary Books.

Zahler, K. A. (1998). *50 simple things you can do to raise a child who loves to read.* New York: Macmillian.

Also refer to references in the entry, **Learning Disorders.**

Rebound Effects

Rebound effects are defined as the exacerbation or worsening of symptoms following the administration of a psychiatric medication prescribed to treat those very symptoms. For example, a child prescribed **Ritalin** for symptoms of **Attention Deficit Disorder** may exhibit an increase in his hyperactivity 5 hours after taking the drug. Usually, rebound effects can be addressed by altering the dosage schedule of the drug. When that is not effective, another drug in the same category is usually prescribed.

Reciprocal Inhibition

Reciprocal inhibition is a behavioral principle that is frequently used in **Behavior Therapy** when *in vivo* exposure is utilized. The basic premise of reciprocal inhibition is that if an individual experiences feelings incompatible with anxiety during exposure to an anxiety-producing situation, eventually the connection between anxiety and that situation will be eliminated, and, as a result, the situation in question will no longer be anxiety producing for the person. When principles of reciprocal inhibition are utilized with children, eating is often employed as the response behavior incompatible with anxiety.

> *Example:* Ten-year-old Brittany is phobic of dark rooms. Her therapy has reached the point at which her therapist is going to begin in vivo exposure to darkness by working with Brittany through spending some time in the therapy room when the lights are out. Using the principles of reciprocal inhibition, the therapist instructs Brittany to eat a Milky Way chocolate bar (her favorite candy) as she enters the dark room and remains in it. The idea behind this is that Brittany will begin to associate sitting in a dark room with the pleasant feeling of eating her favorite snack. This association will replace Brittany's association of sitting in a dark room with anxiety (as the pleasant feelings associated with eating are incompatible with anxiety).

Regression

The term regression refers to an individual's behaving in a manner characteristic of an earlier stage in his or her development. The two major uses of the term deal with (1) a decompensation or worsening during a psychological/psychiatric illness, and (2) utilization of regression as a defense mechanism.

> *Decompensation or worsening during a psychological/psychiatric illness:* When a person's symptoms increase in intensity, frequency, and/or number, or a person is showing some improvement in symptomatology and then the symptoms worsen, this is characterized as regression.
>
> > *Example:* After 3 weeks of therapy for a depressive disorder, 11-year-old David seemed to show significant improvement. He began to socialize again with his friends, developed a more regular sleeping pattern, and overall appeared to be in a better mood. However, 7 weeks into therapy, many of his symptoms seemed to return.
>
> *Regression as a defense mechanism:* Some people, when they are under stress or experiencing anxiety, attempt to cope by acting in a childlike manner. This can include individuals who cry easily, yell and scream (similar to a child's temper tantrum), or assume a helpless, dependent posture.
>
> > *Example:* Four-year-old Alix began to wet the bed and crawl around the house like a baby when his parents brought home the newly adopted 6-month-old baby.

Reinforcement

Reinforcement is any stimulus or behavior that, when applied, increases the probability of another event occurring. For a more detailed discussion of reinforcement, refer to related entries on **Positive Reinforcement, Negative Reinforcement,** and **Punishment.**

Response Cost

This is a procedure utilized in **Contingency Management** approaches that involves fining the child for performance of an inappropriate behavior.

> *Example:* Every time 11-year-old Richard swears, his parents deduct one dollar from his weekly allowance.

> *Example:* Five minutes is taken off of 6-year-old Barry's bedtime for each time the baby-sitter has to ask him to do something more than once.

Response Prevention

Response prevention is a behavioral technique that involves exposing the patient to symptom-eliciting stimuli but not allowing him or her to engage in the usual response. Also referred to as *flooding*, examples of this procedure could include (1) exposing a person to an object of which he or she is phobic, and preventing him or her from fleeing the situation; (2) creating a situation in which a person with **Obsessive-Compulsive Disorder** would typically engage in a compulsive ritual, and not allowing that ritual to take place; and (3) putting mittens on a child who is a chronic nail biter when she is in a situation in which she would typically bite her nails.

Retention Control Training

Retention control training refers to a variety of procedures used to treat the symptoms of **Enuresis.** Based on the premise that children and others with enuresis have an impaired ability to retain their urine, retention control procedures involve daily practice in which the child (with the assistance and support of parental figures) drinks large amounts of fluid, and then practices retaining the urine for increasing periods of time. Urine retention training is not considered a treatment to be used as the sole modality, but it can be effective as an adjunct to other treatment methods for enuresis.

Rett's Disorder

Not even identified as a formal diagnosis until 1966, Rett's disorder (or Rett syndrome) is a **Pervasive Developmental Disorder** with both cognitive and behavioral symptoms. Since Andreas Rett's 1966 paper describing 22 girls with a characteristic pattern of neurological symptoms, several hundreds of such patients have been identified.

Rett's disorder is a neurological disorder that assumes a progressive clinical course. Symptom presentation varies throughout, largely as a function of the patient's age and the stage of the disease process. As a result, the progress of the disease is conceptualized as having four stages:

Stage 1: Also referred to as the *early onset stagnation period;* typically manifests itself sometime between 6 and 18 months of age; no specific symptoms are associated with this stage; developmental milestones can be completed but are often delayed.

Stage 2: Occurs somewhere between 1 and 4 years of age; characterized by a regression of abilities already acquired as well as personality changes; mental deficiency first appears and child loses ability to communicate verbally.

Stage 3: Referred to as the *pseudo stationary period;* can last for several years (or even decades); regression in neuromotor skills but some restitution of ability to communicate; continued ability to walk.

Stage 4: Marked by a loss of the ability to walk; patient completely dependent upon a wheelchair; neuromuscular weakness and overall neurological impairment.

The prevalence of Rett's disorder is estimated to be 1 per 10,000 to 15,000. Although Rett's disorder was initially considered to be limited to females, a few male sufferers have been identified. Treatment of Rett's disorder involves psychoeducational therapies, as well as supportive family interventions. In addition, medical intervention is often required to address the physical symptoms. In some cases, physical therapy and exercise also play a significant role in treatment.

Risperidone

Risperidone (or Risperdal) is one of the newer **Antipsychotic Medications,** classified in the group known as the *atypical antispychotics.* Chemically, drugs in this class differ from the traditional antipsychotic medications in that these newer drugs exert action not only on dopamine systems, but also on serotonin systems (dopamine and serotonin both being **Neurotransmitters).** As an antipsychotic, risperidone primarily exerts its effects on the **Negative Symptoms** of schizophrenia, and is advantageous over many of the more traditional antipsychotic medications as it has fewer **Extrapyramidal Side Effects.** Available in 1 mg, 2 mg, 3 mg, and 4 mg tablets, risperidone is not recommended for individuals under the age of 16 years.

SUPPLEMENTAL RESOURCES

Weiden, P. J., Scheifler, P. L., Diamond, R. J., & Ross, R. (1998). *Switching antipsychotic medications: A guide for consumers and families.* Arlington, VA: National Alliance for the Mentally Ill.

Ritalin

Ritalin (or **Methylphenidate)** is one of the most popular psychiatric drugs prescribed for children and adolescents. A member of the class of drugs known as **Stimulants,** Ritalin in the most commonly prescribed drug for the treatment of **Attention Deficit Disorder.** Although treatment of attention deficit disorder is the most common use for Ritalin, it has also been approved for the treatment of narcolepsy. Approved for usage in children 6 years old and older, initial dosages are usually around 5 mg, with the maximum daily dosage being 60 mg. Whereas Ritalin peaks in terms of effect between 1 and 2½ hours after administration, positive effects can be seen as soon as 20 minutes after taking the medication. Thus, the most popular administration times tend to be prior to leaving for school in the morning and then again during the lunch break. It is also noteworthy that Ritalin has been known to have **Rebound Effects** wherein the child's symptoms intensify as the drug wears off. Ritalin is also now available in time-release capsules, which can prolong its effectiveness for 8 to 10 hours.

The two most common negative side effects of Ritalin treatment include **Insomnia** and seizures; however, the empirical data are contradictory in terms of the frequency of these occurring as a result of treatment with Ritalin. When, however, treatment with Ritalin results in untoward side effects, or the rebound effect cannot be managed by altering the dosage schedule, **Tricyclic Antidepressants** (especially **Imipramine)** tend to be the next line of pharmacological treatment. Although imipramine does not have FDA approval for the treatment of attention deficit disorder, it is generally considered to be the drug of first choice if treatment with ritalin (or other stimulants) is not successful.

Despite the generally impressive effects of psychopharmacological intervention in the treatment of attention deficit disorder, this form of treatment clearly has its limitations. Pelham and Hinshaw (1992) list three negative effects of drug treatment, specifically the use of stimulants, in cases of attention deficit disorder: (1) This type of treatment does not work for all individuals, and even in those for whom stimulants are effective, there are clear limitations to the results that can be expected in terms of interpersonal and academic functioning. (2) The beneficial effects are observed only during those times when the drug is at a certain level in the individual's system. Thus, there is a limited period during which the child can benefit from the intervention without administration of subsequent dosages. (3) The empirical studies currently available do not support improvement and/or efficacy on a long-term basis.

SUPPLEMENTAL RESOURCES

DeGrandpre, R. (1999). *Ritalin nation.* New York: W. W. Norton.
Diller, L. H. (1998). *Running on Ritalin.* New York: Bantam.
Hunter, D. (1995). *The Ritalin free child.* Ft. Lauderdale, FL: Consumer Press.
Ullman, J. R., & Ullman, R. (1996). *Ritalin free kids.* Rockin, CA: Prime Publishing.
For further resources, refer to the entry on **Attention Deficit Disorder.**

Rorschach

This is a personality test developed by the Swiss psychiatrist Hermann Rorschach. It consists of ten cards, each of which contains a symmetric inkblot (some in color, some in black and white). The test consists of showing the patient each inkblot, one at a time, and asking, "What might this be?" By analyzing the manner in which the patient responds to the inkblot in terms of content as well as the factors that contributed to each response, the clinician derives theories about the patient's personality and psychological functioning. **Psychodynamic** in theoretical orientation, the basic premise behind administration of the Rorschach is that by having a person respond to ambiguous stimuli (with a minimum amount of structure) both conscious and unconscious aspects of his or her personality will be revealed.

Rumination Disorder

Rumination disorder is characterized by the intentional and pleasurable regurgitation of food. This is typically followed by reingestion and reswallowing or spitting out of the same food. There appears to be a self-stimulatory quality to the behavior with the child manifesting an obvious sense of satisfaction and psychological involvement in the activity. No visible upset is shown by the child, but rather to the contrary, clinical and empirical reports indicate an observable sense of pleasure and contentment during and following the entire sequence. Rumination disorder does not usually occur in infants under 3 months of age (unless some **Developmental Disorder** is present) and tends to resolve itself by 3 or 4 years of age.

The rumination disorder behavior pattern is entirely self-induced. An observer may see the child actually insert objects into his or her mouth to induce the regurgitating, or there may be no overt inducing activity. Should the behavioral cycle be somehow interrupted by another individual's presence, the child will temporarily cease the activity and will resume the rumination cycle as soon as the other individual leaves.

Treatment approaches for rumination disorder center around improving the relationship between the infant and the primary caretaker as well as selective reinforcing of nonrumination behavior. Instructing the caretaker in performing reinforcing behaviors (e.g., cuddling, hugging, talking, playing) around mealtime is often a primary treatment intervention. Combining such methods with selective ignoring of the rumination behavior or putting the infant down when the rumination behavior begins are also examples of utilizing **Contingency Management** as a means of treating this disorder. Oftentimes **Parent Training** is incorporated into the treatment regimen. When parents react less dramatically to the child's ruminating behaviors, the child is naturally less likely to perceive parental reaction as reinforcing. In addition, parent training for this disorder also entails the teaching of better feeding and general caretaking skills.

S Schizophrenia–Systems Orientation

Schizophrenia

Schizophrenia in young people will usually present in one of three ways: (1) **Acute** onset not involving **Premorbid** signs or symptoms, (2) a gradual deterioration in functioning, and (3) worsening of preexisting symptoms. Older children manifest the gradual onset more frequently than do younger children. In prepubertal children, typical premorbid symptoms include ritualistic or stereotyped behavior, problems with attention span, impairment of language or cognitive function, and symptoms of **Conduct Disorders.**

It appears as if, in children aged 9 and younger, schizophrenia tends to have an *episodic progressive* course, with a combination of continuous and intermittent symptoms. Onset tends to be subacute, with the schizophrenic symptoms appearing at the same time as certain personality abnormalities. These children manifest some **Obsessive** and **Phobic** traits along with some motor and speech pathologies. Delusions and hallucinations are relatively rare during this stage, and symptoms tend to be acute.

From age 10 through 12 years, schizophrenic symptoms are said to assume a *continuous sluggish* course. The symptoms develop gradually, without any indications of clear exacerbation or remission. Most noticeable at this time is a change in the child's self-perception, accompanied by paranoid delusions that take a *continuous progressive* course.

Similar to that seen in adults, the major symptoms of schizophrenia in children and adolescents can be divided into five major categories: **Hallucinations, Delusions,** thought process disorders, disorders of **Affect,** and motor symptoms.

Hallucinations: Please refer to this entry for detailed description.

Delusions: Please refer to this entry for detailed description.

Thought process disorders: This refers to symptoms that affect the manner in which the child or adolescent makes connection between components of thought. Several different types of thought process disorders are evident in adults with schizophrenia, but, those reported in young people are somewhat more limited in range. Three specific disorders of thought process are typical among child and adolescent sufferers of schizophrenia: **Loose Associations, Thought Blocking,** and **Poverty of Content.**

Affect: Affective symptoms characteristic of children and adolescents with schizophrenia include **Blunted Affect, Flat Affect, Incongruent Affect,** spontaneous giggling, and explosive rages of varying intensity.

Motor symptoms: Movement-related symptoms of childhood schizophrenia include **Catatonia,** ritualistic or stereotyped movements, stilted movements, and/or bizarre facial gestures.

Professional Treatment

Both psychotherapy and drug treatment interventions are used in the treatment of schizophrenic disorders, but the literature on the treatment of schizophrenia in children and adolescents is very sparse. Whereas most of the psychotherapy for schizophrenic young people take place in an inpatient setting, **Psychoanalytic, Cognitive Behavioral,** and **Behavioral** approaches have all been used with varying levels of efficacy.

The **Neuroleptic** or **Antipsychotic** medications are considered to be the treatment of first choice in the schizophrenic disorders of childhood and adolescence. They are often necessary to stabilize the patient so that he or she can benefit from psychotherapeutic treatment. Nonetheless, these interventions are not as effective in children as they are in adults. Generally, antipsychotic medications have some positive effects on the positive symptoms of the disorder, with typical dosage schedules beginning with divided doses three or four times per day, moving to twice per day after the optimal dose is determined.

Among the most commonly prescribed neuroleptic medications for schizophrenic children are:

Thorazine	**(Chlorpromazine)**	approved for children over age 5
Thioridazine	**(Mellaril)**	approved for children over age 2
Trifluoperazine	**(Stelazine)**	approved for children over age 6
Haloperidol	**(Haldol)**	approved for children over age 3
Thiothixene	**(Navane)**	approved for children over age 12
Fluphenazine	**(Prolixin)**	approved for children over age 12
Loxipine succinate	**(Loxitane)**	approved for children over age 16

As with adults, the issue of side effects of the antipsychotic medications is crucial to consider. The major side effects are classified into three categories:

Agranulocytosis: Appears early on in treatment and is marked by symptoms of infection.

Cognitive: Involve sedation that tends to lessen as the patient becomes more accustomed to the medication.

Extrapyramidal Side Effects: Are more common with high-potency neuroleptics; refer to entry on extrapyramidal side effects for more information.

SUPPLEMENTAL RESOURCES

Holley, T. E. (1997). *My mother's keeper: A daughter's memoir of growing up in the shadow of schizophrenia.* New York: William Morrow.

Jeffries, J. J., Plummer, E., Seeman, M. U., & Thorton, J. F. (1990). *Living and working with schizophrenia.* Fort Erie, Ontario: Magpie.

Lyden, J. (1997). *Daughter of the Queen of Sheba.* Boston: Houghton Mifflin.

Marsh, D. T. (1998). *How to cope with mental illness in your family.* Fort Erie, Ontario: Magpie.

Mueser, K., & Gingerich, S. (1994). *Coping with schizophrenia: A guide for families.* Oakland, CA: New Harbinger.

School Phobia

School phobia is a specific **Phobic Disorder** in which the target of the phobic response is that of attending school. The symptoms of school phobia are similar to most of the other specific phobias in that they involve an anxiety and fear directed toward school that is unrealistic with respect to the actual danger involved. Further, because of the intensity of the anxiety feelings, the child engages in avoidance behavior, which is behaviorally manifested as not attending school, as would be appropriate.

As with other phobic disorders, the longer the child engages in the avoidance behavior, the more difficult it is to eliminate it. Thus, the first and foremost goal of treatment of a child with school phobia is that of getting him or her back to school as quickly as possible. The actual treatment modalities utilized to accomplish this goal are similar in nature to those used in treating other phobias. However, in cases of school phobia, parental involvement as well as involvement of school personnel becomes more central.

SUPPLEMENTAL RESOURCES

McEwan, E. (1998). *When kids say no to school.* Wheaton, IL: H. Shaw.

Serafino, E. P. (1986). *The fears of childhood: A guide to recognizing and reducing fearful states in children.* New York: Human Science Press.

Siegel, C. J. (1991). *Children with school phobia.* York, PA: William Gladden Foundation.

School Psychologist

A school psychologist is a certified professional, usually with a master's degree, who typically is found working in elementary and secondary schools performing various psychological functions. Depending upon the nature of the school with respect to economic resources, each school can have several school psychologists, whereas, in less fortunate situations, a single school psychologist needs to share his or her time with multiple schools. Again, varying quite often as a function of the resources of the school (and, therefore, the amount of time the school psychologist has available), the school psychologist's function varies considerably.

As this is an area of specific expertise, most school psychologists spend a considerable amount of their time performing intellectual assessments. These are in no way limited to the standard **IQ** tests, and range to incorporate tests for learning disabilities, various learning styles/preferences—eventually extending to include the development of individualized academic programs. Similarly, it is not at all uncommon for the testing performed by the school psychologist to include behavioral assessments for students whose behavior has exhibited some drastic change—again, with recommendations to the teaching team in terms of optimal ways to approach the specific child.

This is by no means meant to imply that school psychologists are limited by their expertise to the performing of evaluations and assessments. Many school psychologists perform individual, group, and family therapy for students in their school. These interventions could be precipitated by some specific difficulty a single student is experiencing, or by a general psychological issue that has become problematic for the school. In yet other situations, the school psychologist is called upon (or opts) to intervene in a proactive manner in an attempt to minimize the chances of psychological problems developing. In addition, it is not at all uncommon for school psychologists to provide inservice training to other school personnel on various topics of psychological interest.

Whereas virtually all school psychologists are involved in academic evaluations to some degree, the extent to which they perform other tasks depends upon the needs of the specific school at any given time, as well as the available resources. In most situations, testing assumes a priority, as state and national laws require such assessments so that every student is exposed to the optimal learning environment to meet his or her needs. **Individual Psychotherapy, Group Therapy, Family Therapy** and other such psychological services are performed to varying degrees depending upon the school, its needs, its resources, and the professional inclination/**Theoretical Orientation** of the specific school psychologist.

School Refusal Behavior

Although often appearing to be behaviorally similar to **School Phobia,** school refusal behavior does not involve the intense anxiety that is so characteristic of cases of school phobia. Rather, children who manifest signs of school refusal manifest extreme resistance to attending school as scheduled, but anxiety is not the primary underlying mechanism. For that reason, school refusal behavior requires the determination of the reasons behind the child's not attending school in order for appropriate treatment to be employed. Once that underlying dynamic is identified, it can be addressed and then the **Secondary** issues around the school behavior become easier (or even unnecessary) to treat.

SUPPLEMENTARY RESOURCES

McEwan, E. (1998). *When kids say no to school.* Wheaton, IL: H. Shaw.

Secondary

The term "secondary" is an adjective used to describe a symptom, group of symptoms, or an entire disorder to indicate that what is observed is a result of another psychopathology or disease process. For example, if the school difficulties resulting from a child's **Attention Deficit Disorder** are causing the child to be clinically depressed, it is said that the depressive symptoms are secondary to the attention deficit disorder. Similarly, if a preteen's **School Phobia** is resulting in the adolescent becoming socially isolated, it is said that the social isolation is secondary to the school phobia.

As a means of contrast, refer to the entry **Primary.**

Selective Serotonin Reuptake Inhibitors (SSRIs)

This is a relatively new group of **Antidepressants** that work by increasing the levels of the **Neurotransmitter** *serotonin* in the person's system. The theoretical basis to their usage centers around the fact that it is believed that low levels of serotonin are **Etiologically** responsible for various disorders. Thus, a drug that increases the amount of serotonin in a person's system would be anticipated to be curative. Although technically classified as antidepressants, the selective serotonin reuptake inhibitors have been also used for the treatment of **Obsessive-Compulsive Disorder,** various other **Anxiety Disorders, Attention Deficit Disorder,** and tic disorders. Although many are prescribed for younger adolescents and children, none of the SSRIs has been approved for children under the age of 16.

Included among the drugs in this classification are **Fluvoxamine Maleate (Luvox), Fluoxetine** hydrochloride **(Prozac), Sertraline** hydrochloride **(Zoloft), Paroxetine Hydrochloride (Paxil)** and celexa (Citalopram).

SUPPLEMENTAL RESOURCES

Gorman, J. M. (1997). *The essential guide to psychiatric drugs.* New York: St. Martin's Press.
Norden, M. J. (1996). *Beyond Prozac.* New York: HarperCollins.
Werry, J. S., & Aman, M. G. (1993). *Practitioner's guide to psychoactive drugs for children and adolescents.* New York: Plenum.

Separation Anxiety Disorder

Separation anxiety disorder is the only anxiety disorder listed in the *DSM-IV* as being exclusive to childhood and adolescence. This disorder is characterized by anxious distress precipitated by separation from key (usually parental) figures. The distress often leads to a resistance to being apart from these key figures. When separation occurs, the child will typically manifest anxiety via **Tantrum Behavior,** insistence on resumption of contact with the parent, an inability to pursue expected activities, and/or somatic symptoms. Children who have separation anxiety disorder often have persistent unrealistic worries about harm or disaster occurring to the key figures and/or an almost phobic level of fear that they will be kidnaped, murdered, or in some other fashion violently removed from the key figure. Such children often have trouble sleeping alone, and experience **Nightmares** and **Night Terrors.** They require repeated reassurance of the presence of the attachment figure, and may find reasons for unusually frequent contact to reassure him or her of the attachment figure being available.

If a parent is concerned that his or her child may be manifesting some of the symptoms of separation anxiety disorder, it is crucial that the developmental stage of the child be taken into account. Indeed, at certain developmental stages, it is appropriate for a child to manifest anxiety upon separation from a key attachment figure. For example, a 3-year-old who cries intensely when left with a baby-sitter for the first time should not be diagnosed with this disorder, in contrast to an 8-year-old who cries similarly every time his mother leaves the home.

Statistics hover around 3% as the generally accepted figure for incidence of separation anxiety disorder in the general population. Some studies report that more girls than boys suffer from this disorder, others do not support such a finding. Symptom presentation tends to vary according to the age of the child, with young children (ages 5 through 8) and adolescents showing the greater number of symptoms. There is even a difference in the content of the associated worries with children ages 5 through 8 worrying about catastrophic events befalling the attachment figures; children ages 9 to 12 having more symptoms of withdrawal, apathy, and poor concentration; and adolescents showing more somatically oriented complaints interspersed with **School Refusal.**

Theories regarding the **Etiology** of separation anxiety disorder are both psychological and biological in nature. The majority of theories around etiology of separation anxiety disorder, however, focus on the more psychosocial aspects. Specifically, these psychosocially based theories can be divided into those which focus on **Psychodynamic** factors, sociological factors, and **Cognitive Behavioral** factors.

> *Psychodynamic:* Contemporary psychodynamic theories of separation anxiety disorder focus on attachment issues as well as difficulties with separation and **Individuation.**

> *Sociological:* These theories focus on the child's relationship with the parents. Theories of **Parent-Induced Anxious Attachment** come into play here as well. Family trauma may also play a factor in separation anxiety disorder, with children who have experienced traumatic separation being likely to manifest such symptoms.

> *Cognitive behavioral:* The cognitive behavioral explanation of separation anxiety disorder focuses on maladaptive thought patterns as well as unhealthy interpretation of environmental stimuli. The child's misperceptions of what is transpiring around him or her induce anxiety as the children interpret harmless stimuli as threatening.

Professional Treatment

In most cases of separation anxiety disorder symptoms, the issue as to whether to seek treatment tends to be a rather clear one. Once this disorder reaches clinical proportions, the child's anxiety upon separation from the parental or key figure becomes a barrier to effective day-to-day functioning. In addition to the adults in the environment being aware of the pathology of the situation, most of the time the child himself or herself is also aware as the anxiety experienced is quite intense, and its behavioral aspects clearly differentiate the child from his or her peers.

Although psychopharmacological treatment is employed in some severe cases, for the most part separation anxiety disorder is treated by psychotherapeutic interventions. Whereas some clinicians work with the child individually, because of the nature of the disorder the more effective treatments tend to involve the parents to at least some degree.

Most of these psychological interventions commonly utilize principles of **Behavior Therapy** as the major intervention. Therapy will usually involve gradual exposure to separation experiences coupled with interventions involving **Reciprocal Inhibition, Differential Reinforcement (DRO),** cognitive behavior therapy, or some combination of these. In order for these treatments to be at all successful, the clinician must develop a trusting relationship with the child. It is best for the therapist to convey an awareness of the difficulties entailed in complying with the therapeutic procedures, but to firmly focus on the necessity of compliance. To the extent to which it is developmentally appropriate, the rationale behind all therapeutic procedures should be explained to the child, and the child should be empowered with as much control as possible throughout the treatment process, especially during the behavioral work.

Questions to Ask the Clinician

Since separation anxiety disorder is one of the more common disorders presented for professional treatment, most clinicians who work with children have considerable experience in treating it. Nonetheless, the parent should ensure that the clinician is indeed experienced in treating this disorder, and is able to articulate a reasonable treatment plan along which he or she is planning to proceed. In most cases, the treatment for separation anxiety disorder should utilize the methods described above, and if this is not how the clinician plans on addressing the symptoms, he or she should have a rationale for the use of alternative methods. Finally, as alluded to above, because of the nature of the symptoms, the parents or key figures should be directly involved in the treatment.

Sertraline

This is the generic or trade name for the antidepressant drug **Zoloft.** Please refer to that entry for a description.

Serzone

Serzone is classified as one of the "new generation" **Antidepressants,** although not one of the **Selective Serotonin Reuptake Inhibitors.** It is a relatively new drug, and, is still being investigated in terms of what other disorders (besides depression) it may potentially be useful in treating. It has only been approved for usage in adults, and, in such cases, dosages between 300 mg and 500 mg per day seem to be the most effective.

Sexual Abuse

The concept of sexual abuse of children is one that has gained a heightened degree of awareness over the past few years. While the term *sexual abuse* is now used to describe a wide range of behaviors, it is best to conceptualize sexual abuse as being defined as any behavior that is inappropriately sexual in nature and is performed in such a way that a child (or adolescent) is the recipient. The issue of whether the behavior is mutually consensual certainly is relevant in terms of whether violence or coercion of any type was present, however a lack of active resistance by the child is not sufficient to rule out the categorization of an interaction as abusive.

Despite the increased clinical sophistication in this area, it remains difficult at times to make a definitive diagnosis of childhood sexual abuse. Figures estimate that anywhere from 2% to 8% of allegations of sexual abuse are false, with an even higher percentage that cannot be substantiated (Kaplan & Sadock, 1996). Of course, this difficulty is in no way to be used as an excuse to dismiss symptoms or to not further investigate them.

Current assessment methods for the sexual abuse of children are wide in their range, many of them dependent upon the developmental age of the child. The use of **Anatomically Correct Dolls,** clinical evaluation of a child's play activity or fantasy content, as well as an awareness of the child/adolescent's psychological level all provide data that are potentially useful in diagnostic situations. Whereas the following symptoms are certainly not to be considered sufficient evidence to diagnose child sexual abuse, children who have been victims of abuse are known to manifest one or more of the following characteristics:

Enuresis: Children who have been toilet trained sufficiently for a long period of time will begin to wet the bed at night and/or have accidents during the day.

Nightmares/Night Terrors: Victims of child sexual abuse may begin to have nightmares or night terrors. This may occur in individuals who have never had nightmares or night terrors previously, or they may increase in frequency and intensity for those individuals who have experienced them previously.

Sexual acting out: The child/adolescent may be observed to be more sexually preoccupied. Behaviorally, this may manifest itself via increased frequency of masturbation, sexual aggression, and/or sexual play with peers, as well as sexual themes in play and fantasy.

Psychopathology: Childhood victims of sexual abuse can show symptoms characteristic of any of the major diagnostic categories. Most frequent, however, are symptoms of the **Anxiety Disorders,** and depression.

Suspicion or actual confirmation that one's child has been involved in a sexually abusive relationship is traumatizing to the parents as well as the child. Whereas medical and legal intervention is usually sought virtually automatically, the psychological component of the necessary postabuse interventions can be overlooked. Issues of shame, denial, and simply wanting to believe that "everything will be all right" all combine to result in a situation wherein it can seem easier not to seek therapy for the child so as "not to bring it up again…he/she has been through enough," and so forth. While exaggerating the severity of a situation or creating a problem where indeed there is not one is certainly not recommended, it is advised that, in most cases of sexual abuse, the child be evaluated for psychological ramifications. The aforementioned factors along with anxiety, guilt, and embarrassment all encourage the child to mask any symptoms and give the impression that everything is okay. If such is indeed the case, a professional evaluation will not alter the status quo. However, if the child is suffering some psychological consequences as a result of the abuse (which is the case more often than not), the professional intervention would be both necessary and helpful.

SUPPLEMENTAL RESOURCES

Bean, B., & Bennett, S. (1993). *The me nobody knows: A guide for teen survivors.* New York: Lexington Books.

Davis, L. (1990). *The courage to heal workbook.* New York: Harper & Row.

Engel, B. (1995). *Families in recovery: Working to heal the damage of child sexual abuse.* Los Angeles: Lowell House.

Ennis, G., & Black, J. (1997). *It's not okay anymore—Your personal guide to ending abuse, taking charge and loving yourself.* Oakland, CA: New Harbinger Press.

Girard, L. W. (1984). *My body is private.* Morton Grove, IL: Albert Whitman.

Hunter, M. (1990). *Abused boys: The neglected victims of sexual abuse.* New York: Ballantine Books.

Maltz, W. (1992). *The sexual healing journey.* New York: HarperCollins.

Sexual Exploration/Touching

Refer to the entry **Masturbation.**

Sexual Orientation

Sexual orientation refers to an individual's preference in terms of sexual partner. More specifically, sexual orientation refers to whether a person prefers to be sexually engaged with a person of his or her own gender, a person of the opposite gender, or if indeed there is no preference. It is sexual orientation that forms the basis of whether a person is classified (or classifies himself or herself as heterosexual (preferring sexual activities with a person of the opposite sex), homosexual (preferring sexual activities with a person of the same sex), or bisexual (not having a specific gender preference in terms of sexual partner).

It should be noted, however, that, for many people, their actual sexual preferences and their sexual behavior are not entirely consistent. Some individuals, for example, have strong homosexual preferences, but because of social and cultural factors choose to function within a heterosexual lifestyle. The source of sexual orientation has not yet been determined conclusively—with many people believing it to be primarily biological, and others feeling it is more environmentally determined.

Sexually Transmitted Diseases (STDs)

Sexually transmitted diseases are those diseases that are spread and contracted via sexual contact. Statistics report that twelve million people in the United States are newly infected with STDs every year, and over half of these are younger than age 25. The majority of these diseases are either viral or bacterial, and could be either prevented or treated appropriately with sufficient knowledge. However, since many young people have shame, embarrassment, and anxiety about sexual activity to begin with, and since many of these young people engage in sexual activity with a somewhat limited knowledge base, sexually active adolescents and teenagers are particularly vulnerable to contracting—as well as not receiving proper treatment for—sexually transmitted diseases.

Included among the most common sexually transmitted diseases affecting adolescents and teenagers are:

Pelvic inflammatory disease (PID): A bacterial disorder that affects the uterus, pelvis, ovaries, or fallopian tubes (or some combination of these); 75% of cases of PID occur in women under the age of 25; scarring of fallopian tubes due to PID can result in infertility (especially likely after more than one occurrence of the disorder).

Gonorrhea: A bacterial infection affecting males and females; for males, the primary symptom is a thick penile discharge along with pain upon urination; women can also manifest a discharge or can be asymptomatic; can be responsive to treatment with penicillin although penicillin-resistant strains have developed.

Chlamydia: Most common bacterial STD in the United States; highest rate of chlamydia is among the teenaged population; normally responds to antibiotics; in men, symptoms include a watery penile discharge; in women, symptoms include urinary pain, pelvic discomfort, or no symptoms at all.

Herpes simplex virus (HSV): Viral infection that has the capability of reoccurring once it infects a person; first outbreak is usually the worst (looking like a cluster of blisters) with the virus capable of being transmitted even when no blisters are visible.

SUPPLEMENTAL RESOURCES

DeMoya, A., DeMoya, D., Lewis, M. E., & Lewis, H. R. (1983). *Sex and health: A practical guide to sexual medicine.* New York: Stein and Day.

Masters, W. H., Johnson, V. E., & Kolodny, R. C. (1986). *Sex and human loving.* New York: Little, Brown.

Shyness

Shyness, in and of itself, should not be considered a problem in a child or adolescent. Indeed, it is a normal variant along the continuum of personality introversion/extroversion, and can often change dramatically with development. In other words, a relatively outgoing child can become rather shy in the early school years, and then return to his or her more outgoing state in adolescence. In some cases, shyness is more of a problem for the parents than it is for the child himself or herself, whereas in other situations, it is the parents who actually promote the shyness by reinforcing the withdrawn behavior.

As with any behavioral characteristic, extremes can indicate psychopathology. There is a large difference in the implications of a child who is simply a bit slow in getting used to people or opening up to strangers, versus the child who will not venture from behind his parent's leg when in a public place. When the degree of shyness is sufficiently intense to interfere with the child or adolescent's ability to function adequately in his or her social, academic, or home and personal life, then the shyness needs to be conceptualized somewhat differently. Similarly, when a child or adolescent manifests a dramatic change in the degree of shyness he or she exhibits, there is a greater likelihood that the shyness is indicative of some deeper problem In such situations, what appears as shyness is likely to actually be a symptom of some more severe disorder requiring professional intervention. **Depression,** the various **Anxiety Disorders, Post-Traumatic Stress Disorder, Acute Stress Disorder,** along with situations in which the child is a victim of **Physical** or **Sexual Abuse** are all disorders in which shyness can manifest itself to a severe degree as a primary symptom. In such situations the parent should attempt to evaluate what, if any, other symptoms are being shown by the child in an attempt to determine the basis of the extreme shy behavior, and whether professional treatment is indicated.

Smoking

The dangers of cigarette smoking are well known to virtually every child from the time he or she is able to read or watch television. This message is further reinforced in formalized classes (such as health, science, etc.) and in their schoolwork. Thus, when a child or adolescent decides to smoke, it is unlikely to be a function of a paucity of information regarding the health risks of the behavior. As a result, when parental figures confront their offspring regarding a newly developed smoking habit, messages about potential health risks would be redundant. Rather, if a parent wants to exert any impact on his or her offspring who recently decided to begin smoking, the underlying dynamic of the behavior needs to be addressed. In the majority of cases, then, the smoking behavior is actually a means of indicating difficulties with one or more fundamental issues.

What is *really* going on when a young person begins to smoke? Possible answers to this question are listed below:

> *Sophistication:* For many individuals, there is a connotation of sophistication and maturity associated with smoking behavior. Young people who are feeling insecure about self-image, and about being perceived by others as a child, may begin smoking as a means of attempting to project a more adultlike image.

> *Rebellion:* Feeling relatively safe in assuming that beginning to smoke will cause some distress in parents, teachers, and other authority figures, smoking serves as a manner of rebellion. This can be a simple attempt at expressing anger, or a manner of indicating rebellion against established rules and norms.

> *Peer impact:* In some adolescent and preteen social circles, smoking is viewed as a badge of honor, an indication of belonging. Young people who feel insecure about their popularity will take up the smoking habit to either fit in, or acquire status among peers.

> *Attention seeking:* Some young people smoke in an attempt to gain attention from parents, teachers, or other authority figures. Perceiving that they are unable to get attention for positive behavior, they utilize smoking as a means of becoming the focus of their parents' attention.

In the majority of cases, one or more of the above issues are relevant to a young person's beginning the habit of smoking, and an average amount of parental awareness and observation can identify the specifics. It is these dynamics that must first be addressed directly so that the young person does not need to utilize smoking as a more indirect means to get substantive psychological needs met.

Social Phobia

Also referred to as *social anxiety* disorder, social phobia is a specific phobia in which the person has anxiety regarding being judged by others in a negative way. Specifically, the socially phobic individual tends to avoid any situation in which he or she perceives the chance of embarrassment as a result of being viewed by other people as stupid, mentally ill, incompetent, or anxious. As with other phobias, in an attempt to avoid experiencing the anxiety associated with this fear, the person will avoid any and all situations in which he or she perceives there is a chance of this anxiety occurring. In children, a diagnosis of social phobia cannot be applied if the child manifests such symptoms only relative to his or her interactions with adults, and if the symptoms do not persist beyond 6 months.

It is noteworthy that social phobia is not the equivalent of stage fright, **Shyness,** or general performance anxiety. These three conditions are considered to be relatively common, normal, and not indicative of pathology. Again, as with cases of other **Anxiety Disorders,** specifically **Phobias,** professional treatment is not indicated unless the fear, anxiety, and avoidance demonstrated is beyond that which would be expected for a child at the specific developmental level, and unless the resulting impairment is sufficiently severe to impact on the child or adolescent's day-to-day functioning.

SUPPLEMENTAL RESOURCES

Heimberg, R. G., Liebowitz, M. R., Hope, D. A., & Schneier, F. R. (1995). *Social phobia: Diagnosis, assessment and treatment.* New York: Guilford Press.
Marshall, R. (1994). *Social phobia.* New York: Basic Books.

Somatic Preoccupation

Somatic preoccupation refers to an unrealistic focus on one's own physiological and bodily processes and functioning. This syndrome can occur under various situations: (1) when a person is suffering from or has in the past suffered from a serious illness; (2) when a (young) person has been exposed to an inordinate amount of physical illness in his or her life; (3) when an individual suffers from various psychological disorders, and rather than acknowledge the psychopathology, explains the symptoms in terms of physiological processes; and (4) in cases of *somatization disorder* (multiple somatic complaints for which the person receives interventions of various severity and necessity).

When a child or adolescent shows signs of somatic preoccupation, the first step is to have the child participate in a thorough medical examination. This is crucial in order to rule out any possible physiological basis for the young person's complaints. Once it is determined that there is no physical basis for the persistent focus on his or her body, the source of this somatic preoccupation needs to be determined. Whereas there are certainly cases in which such cases of somatic preoccupation can be addressed within the family, in most cases professional intervention is required to identify the underlying dynamics and to resolve the issues.

Somatoform Disorders

This is a classification of disorders in the newest edition of the *DSM* (*DSM-IV*) which include those disorders that have as their primary symptom the presence of one or more physical symptoms not explainable by the presence of any diagnosable physical/medical illness. Diagnoses included within this classification are as follows: *somatization disorder* (multiple physical complaints that continue over several years), *undifferentiated somatoform disorder* (multiple physical complaints lasting for at least six months—not as severe as somatization disorder), *conversion disorder* (unexplained physical symptoms that seem to be directly associated with identifiable psychological factors), *pain disorder* (pain without a definable physical explanation that seems to be exacerbated by psychological factors), *hypochondriasis* (insistence upon, and almost obsession with, the idea that one has a serious physical illness—usually precipitated by minor physical symptoms), **Body Dysmorphic Disorder,** and *somatoform disorder not otherwise specified* (a diagnosis used for somatoform disorders that do not meet the clinical criteria for any of the above diagnoses).

Spanking

Over the past several years, spanking has become one of the most controversial issues in child psychology. Although it used to be the case that spanking a child was practically a natural part of adequate parental discipline, some experts have become quite vocal in questioning the merits of spanking, even going so far as to conceptualize it as being detrimental. Indeed, several European countries have made physical punishment of children illegal, and currently some states in the United States are considering the same type of legislation.

Proponents of spanking insist that it is not the same thing as **Physical Abuse,** and that there are certain situations in which spanking is required. These people believe that, when spanking is applied in a nonabusive fashion, it conveys a strong message to the child, is brief and to the point, and can curtail undesirable behavior in a way that verbal interventions cannot. Most proponents of spanking were themselves spanked as children, and they emphasize that most adults were as well. Their ultimate conclusion, then, is that since the large majority of people are basically psychologically intact, spanking is not in and of itself a detrimental practice. Finally, proponents of spanking feel that spanking is an essential component of adequate parental discipline.

Those individuals who oppose spanking as a disciplinary measure focus primarily on the psychological aspects of the behavior. Opponents to spanking purport that, since spanking is a physically aggressive behavior, it models physical aggression to the child—specifically physical aggression against someone less physically powerful. (A common example is the parent who spanks the son for punching his younger sister because hitting is bad.) This argument is taken one step further in that opponents of spanking postulate that, although in most cases serious physical injury is not the intent, it is not uncommon for a spanking to go awry and for the parent to lose control and actually injure the child. A second argument against spanking revolves around the fact that the opponents believe that spanking develops resentment and anger in the child. People opposed to spanking also point to the fact that the very act teaches the child that anger and frustration (the typical mood of the parent when he or she spanks) are to be expressed by hitting. Yet another argument put forth against spanking is that it is psychologically demeaning, insulting, and anxiety provoking for the child. Spanking opponents claim that these negative feelings do not disappear immediately after the episode of spanking is over, thus creating a high risk of psychological consequences. Finally, largely because of the aforementioned reasons, opponents of spanking claim that, in general, punishment of bad behavior is not as effective as reinforcement of good behavior, and, further that even within the realm of punishment, spanking is essentially ineffective and often even detrimental.

SUPPLEMENTAL RESOURCES

Crary, E. (1993). *Without spanking or spoiling*. Seattle, WA: Parenting Press.
Dreikurs, R., & Cassell, P. (1974). *Discipline without tears*. New York: Penguin Books.
Hyman, I. A. (1997). *The case against spanking*. San Francisco: Jossey-Bass.
Peters, R. (1997). *Don't be afraid to discipline*. New York: Golden Books.

State Trait Anxiety Inventory for Children

This is an instrument developed in 1973 and designed to assess the presence of pathological anxiety (and therefore to diagnose **Anxiety Disorders)** in children. The State Trait Anxiety Inventory for Children is an objective self-report measure that asks the child to respond to the questions asked in terms of how he or she is feeling at the present time as well as how he or she tends to feel in general.

Stelazine

Stelazine is an **Antipsychotic** drug, also marketed under the generic label as **Trifluoperazine.** It is approved as a medication for children aged 6 years and older, specifically for the treatment of **Psychotic** symptoms and **Generalized Anxiety Disorder** (in the latter case, only when other medications have not been effective). Available in 1 mg, 2 mg, 5 mg, and 10 mg tablets as well as in concentrate and injectable forms, initial dosage for younger children tends to be 1 mg once or twice daily, with a gradual increase (possibly up to 15 mg) as indicated.

SUPPLEMENTAL RESOURCES

Gorman, J. M. (1997). *The essential guide to psychiatric drugs.* New York: St. Martin's Press.

Maxmen, J., & Ward, N. (1996). *Psychoactive drugs: Fast facts.* New York: Norton.

Rosenberg, D. R., Holttum, J., & Gershon, S. (1994). *Textbook of pharmacotherapy for child and adolescent disorders.* New York: Brunner/Mazel.

Werry, J. S., & Aman, M. G. (1993). *Practitioner's guide to psychoactive drugs for children and adolescents.* New York: Plenum.

Stimulants

Of all the psychopharmacological treatments for psychopathology in children and adolescents, stimulants are by far the most frequently used. Currently, stimulants are used most often in child/adolescent treatment for cases of **Attention Deficit Disorder** as they are relatively effective in increasing attention span and decreasing hyperactivity in these children. Stimulant medications are also prescribed as adjunct treatment for inattention and hyperactivity in children and adolescents suffering from **Conduct Disorder, Oppositional Defiant Disorder, Mental Retardation,** and the **Pervasive Developmental Disorders.** Stimulant medications most commonly used in these situations include **Methylphenidate (Ritalin)** for children aged 6 and older, **Pemoline (Cylert)** for children aged 6 and older, and dextroamphetamine sulfate (**Dexedrine**) for children aged 3 and older. All of these drugs are metabolized partially by the liver and then excreted via the kidneys.

Many of the side effects associated with stimulant treatment will typically disappear within 14 to 21 days. Dosage-related side effects include abdominal pain, weight loss, irritability, mild **Dysphoria,** and **Anorexia.** More serious side effects of stimulants include stunted growth, slowed weight gain, **Psychotic** symptoms, **Manic** symptoms, cardiovascular problems, and the aggravation or inducement of tics. The most common side effect of stimulant medication is **Insomnia,** which is reported to occur in over half of the children who are taking Ritalin for attention deficit disorder.

SUPPLEMENTAL RESOURCES

Gorman, J. M. (1997). *The essential guide to psychiatric drugs.* New York: St. Martin's Press.

Johnston, H. (1990). *Stimulants and hyperactive children: A guide.* Lithium Information Center, University of Wisconsin, Department of Psychiatry.

Maxmen, J., & Ward, N. (1996). *Psychotropic drugs: Fast facts.* New York: Norton.

Rosenberg, D. R., Holttum, J., & Gershon, S. (1994). *Textbook of pharmacotherapy for child and adolescent psychiatric disorders.* New York: Brunner/Mazel.

Werry, J. S., & Aman, M. G. (1993). *Practitioner's guide to psychoactive drugs for children and adolescents.* New York: Plenum.

Stuttering

Stuttering is one of the disorders classified in the current edition of the *DSM* (American Psychiatric Association, 1994) under the category of "Disorders Usu-

ally First Diagnosed in Infancy, Childhood, or Adolescence." Primarily characterized by problems producing smooth, fluid speech, the *DSM-IV* describes
stuttering as being typified by one or more of the following symptoms occurring
on a frequent basis:

1. repetition of sounds and syllables
2. prolongation of certain sounds
3. interjections
4. pauses within a word
5. filled or unfilled pauses in speech
6. substituting of words that are easier to pronounce to avoid problem words
7. words pronounced with an excess of physical tension
8. repetition of monosyllabic whole words. (p. 65)

Stuttering is more common in younger children and significantly less
common once the child reaches adolescence. Onset of stuttering tends to be between the ages of 2 and 7 years of age—with two peak ages of onset: one between
the ages of 2½ and 3 years old and another between 5 and 7 years old. Stuttering
usually begins with barely noticeable problems, then, over the period of months,
becomes more intense. Studies indicate that most cases of stuttering are over by
the age of 16 or so, with over half of the cases recovering spontaneously without
any formalized treatment (American Psychiatric Association, 1994).

The clinical literature defines four phases in the development of stuttering,
many seemingly a function of developmental level:

Phase 1: Preschool aged children stuttering mostly when upset or excited; usually there are extended periods of normal, fluid speech.

Phase 2: Elementary school–aged children who tend to stutter primarily
when attempting to pronounce nouns, verbs, and other major parts of
speech; unlike phase 1, there are few if any periods of normal speech.

Phase 3: Occurring in late childhood and early adolescence, stuttering
intensity or presence largely a function of environmental situations
that elicit anxiety.

Phase 4: The stuttering pattern seen in late adolescence and adulthood
in which the individual has a significant anticipation and anxiety
around the possibility of stuttering.

SUPPLEMENTAL RESOURCES

Treiber, P. M. (1993). *Keys to dealing with stuttering.* New York: Barrons.

Swearing

Children swearing or using profanity in their day-to-day speech is not an uncommon phenomenon, especially in the middle school and adolescent years. Such

behavior tends to be especially prevalent in families and homes in which other people use such language. It is interesting, however, that the underlying dynamics behind the use of such language vary greatly. In cases of families in which such language is used as a matter of course, the child is often modeling the behavior of others around him. Further, in those cases in which it is the older members of the family who utilize such language, the child's swearing is often a means of identifying with the more mature in the family, and, therefore, feeling more adultlike.

More often than not, however, the child or adolescent's engaging in swearing behavior is considered extremely aversive to those around him or her. Further, the more intense the adult reaction to the swearing behavior, the more **Reinforcing** it is to the child. Such is the case because much of the impetus behind the use of such language revolves around the sense of rebellion against authority combined with shocking those in the immediate environment. Engaging in behaviors considered by the "rest of the world" to be forbidden or somehow bad has a considerable amount of appeal to young people, especially as they approach adolescence (see the entry on **Adolescent Rebellion).**

Therefore, as with most other forms of negative behavior (especially that performed with somewhat of a rebellious character), parental reaction is crucial in determining the extent to which the behavior can be modified. Whereas it's perfectly appropriate for parents to convey their disapproval with the child's swearing, this disapproval is best conveyed in a matter-of-fact manner, with as little dramatic emotion as possible. The young person should be informed that such behavior will not be tolerated, and that there will be consequences for engaging in it. Needless to say, it is very important that the parents develop realistic consequences with which they will be able to consistently follow through, and it is also helpful for the parents not to engage in the swearing behavior themselves!

Systematic Desensitization

Systematic desensitization is a **Behavioral** procedure, used most frequently in the treatment of **Phobias** and other **Anxiety Disorders.** Based upon the principles of **Reciprocal Inhibition,** systematic desensitization involves exposing the individual to anxiety-provoking stimuli (either in reality or via imagery) when the person is in a relaxed state so that the person's conditioned response of associating anxiety with the stimulus becomes eliminated and replaced with the new association of relaxation with the formerly anxiety-producing stimuli. The steps typically employed in a systematic desensitization procedure are as follows:

- Training the patient in the relaxation response.
- Constructing a hierarchy of anxiety-producing situations relevant to the specific target object or behavior.
- Exposing the patient to the items on the hierarchy one by one, beginning with the one that is the least anxiety provoking and working the way up the list, while the patient is in a relaxed state; if at any time during the process

the patient becomes anxious, the procedure ceases until the patient resumes the relaxed status.

- The entire list of items on the hierarchy is addressed until the patient is able to maintain an association of the previously anxiety-producing object with relaxation.

Systems Orientation

The systems orientation focuses on the entire family within a therapeutic framework, and is often applied to the psychopathology of childhood and adolescence. Utilizing systems theory, no single individual in a family is labeled as the identified patient, or as suffering from disorder. Rather, the entire family is conceptualized as the patient, even though one individual may represent or manifest the pathology of the entire family system.

Often incorporating other approaches, systems theory examines the family's system in terms of its **Psychodynamics, Behavioral** patterns, **Attachment** issues, and certain biological factors in an attempt to explain the manifest pathology. In addition, systems theory often goes beyond the overt symptoms and probes into deeper dynamics to explore the interactions between family members. Relationships between the parental figures, the siblings, each parent and each child, as well as members of the extended family are all examined.

Further, systems perspectives postulate that all systems, including families, tend to maintain a certain balance or *homeostasis;* that is, they tend to maintain the status quo. Healthy families, however, can change to accommodate the physical, social, and cultural development of family members without a great deal of turmoil. According to systems theory, the ability of the family to withstand disruptions and to be flexible enough to integrate changes into the current system determines its relative health or pathology.

T Tantrum Behavior–Trifluoperazine

Tantrum Behavior

In preschoolers (and sometimes in older children as well), tantrum behavior is manifested to varying degrees. For some children it merely involves crying a bit louder than usual, while in other children, the behavior actually escalates to throwing oneself on the floor, throwing objects, and lashing out at others in the environment. Whereas most children experiment with some form of tantrum behavior at some point in their lives, it is the reactions of the parents that determine whether the tantruming is a one- or two-time occurrence, or if it escalates to a major behavioral problem.

As with any other form of behavior, children (and adults, too, for that matter) engage in those behaviors they find to be **Reinforcing.** In other words, if engaging in a given behavior is perceived by the child to get his or her needs met, it is likely that the child will continue behaving in such a manner. Thus, the key to eliminating tantrum behavior is to determine what needs the child is attempting to get met or is actually getting met from the tantruming, and then to adjust the parental reaction accordingly. Most commonly, the child perceives tantruming to be effective in getting his or her own way, getting the attention of parents or others around him or her, and/or conveying frustration and/or anger with a given situation. Keeping these basic principles in mind, it is intuitive that among the worst things for a parent to do in response to temper tantrum behavior are

Giving in to the child to quiet him down: Understandably, a common reaction from a parent is to give the child what he wants to stop the obnoxious and often embarrassing behavior. Unfortunately, this gives the child the message that the tantrum behavior is so aversive to the parents (which may indeed be so, by the way) that they will do anything possible to get it to cease. Once the child recognizes that fact, he or she realizes that parental response is within his or her control—not a good thing.

Parent getting extremely upset: Such behavior conveys to the child that he or she has control over parental emotional well-being. If the child perceives that the tantruming behavior bothers the parent more than it bothers the child, the tantrum becomes a useful tool to manipulate his or her environment.

296

Engage in a rational discussion with respect to the issue at hand: When the child is involved in a temper tantrum, the parent should refuse to interact with him or her or discuss the matter of conflict at all. Rather, the parent should indicate to the child that the issue will not be discussed when the child is in this state, and once he/she calms down, the issue can be addressed.

In simplistic terms, the parent best reacts to a child's temper tantrum in a manner that conveys disapproval and the fact that this behavior is unacceptable. However, it is crucial that this be done in a manner that does not reinforce the child in any way. Depending, of course, upon the underlying motivation behind the child's tantrum, the parent should react in a matter-of-fact, unemotional manner, and, after the fact, explain to the child that there are indeed alternative, more effective ways to convey his message.

Tardive Dyskinesia

One of the most common and most aversive side effects of **Antipsychotic** or neuroleptic medication is tardive dyskinesia—abnormal, involuntary movements in one or more parts of the body. Symptoms can appear anywhere from days to even years after initiating treatment with an antipsychotic medication. According to the American Psychiatric Association Task Force on Tardive Dyskinesia (1992), there are four characteristics to the syndrome:

1. Contrary to what one would expect, symptoms of tardive dyskinesia will lessen with an increase in dosage of the antipsychotic drug, and will intensify by decreasing the dosage of the drug.
2. Anticholinergic medication will not improve the symptoms and may even make them worse.
3. Tardive dyskinesia symptoms may be worsened by emotional stress.
4. When the person is asleep, the tardive dyskinesia symptoms cease.

Unfortunately, there is no established treatment for tardive dyskinesia. However, a certain percentage of cases spontaneously remit. It is noteworthy, that some of the newer atypical antipsychotic drugs (e.g., **Clozaril**) have little incidence of this syndrome as a side effect.

Tegretol

Although tegretol is officially classified as an anti-seizure medication, it has been used as a treatment for several psychiatric/psychological disorders in adults and is being investigated for treatment of various psychopathologies in children and adolescents. Included among the potential clinical indications for the use of tegretol in young people are the following: **Bipolar Disorder,** depressive disorders, **Attention Deficit Hyperactivity Disorder, Conduct Disorders,** various behavioral acting out problems, sleep terror disorder, and **Enuresis.**

Terrible Twos

Much like the developmental stage of adolescence, the time between the ages of 1½ and 3 years tends to have negative associations with respect to behavioral problems. Specifically, the lore depicts this time as a period of never ending power struggles, **Temper Tantrums,** yelling, toilet training struggles, **Crying,** and whining. Whereas all of these behaviors may very well be components of this stage of parenting, the actual percentage of parenting time spent coping with such behaviors is certainly variable from situation to situation. Again, as with all of the other developmental stages and aspects of parenting, much of this variance is a function of the manner in which the interactions are handled.

First and foremost, it must be acknowledged (and accepted) that between approximately 18 and 30 months, the child is attempting to assert himself or herself as a more independent being. Part of this assertion, by definition, involves challenging parental authority, and more generic testing of limits. Simple recognition of this fact allows the parents to be prepared for what is ahead, to understand the underlying dynamics of the child's acting out behavior, and to be better able to cope with it in a successful fashion. At the risk of oversimplifying the situation, there are three basic premises, which, if followed, can make this developmental stage much easier on both parents and children:

> *Choose your battles:* Although somewhat cliché, this phrase is especially relevant to young children at this stage of life. Although it is in no way encouraged to let your child have his or her way consistently (i.e, to avoid ugly scenes), it is however advised that parents decide what is important and what isn't. In order for a child to mature, he or she needs to have the experience of *successfully* moving away from parental authority. However, if every such move is turned into a battle, such successful movement cannot occur. Thus, it is incumbent upon the parents to recognize certain situations as being acceptable and feasible for the child to "test his or her wings" successfully and then to allow him or her to do so.

> *Avoid power struggles:* There is a clear limit to the extent one can reason with a child of this developmental level. As a result, oftentimes parental restrictions at this stage result in a two-way verbal argument, seemingly with the younger person winning out. Such power struggles are to be avoided whenever possible, because if the situation is such that the parent feels it is important enough to set limits, a power struggle only gives the misimpression that the issue is negotiable (and capable of being won by arguing).

Interact at an appropriate level: Keep in mind that no matter how much trouble a child of this age gives a parent, he or she is still a child of this age! Thus, when interacting with the child, work to ensure that the interactions are appropriate to the child's developmental and cognitive level. For example, to sit and reason with a two year old about the relative advantages and disadvantages of a certain behavior from a philosophical standpoint would be rather meaningless to most children of that age. In addition, interacting with the child on a level inconsistent with his or her understanding also proves frustrating for the child as well. Remember, however, that it is just as fruitless to underestimate a child's ability to comprehend as it is to overestimate.

SUPPLEMENTAL RESOURCES

Please refer to listings under **Oppositional Defiant Disorder.**

Theoretical Orientation/Perspective

A clinician's theoretical orientation or perspective defines the manner in which he or she conceptualizes psychopathology, and, in turn, determines the manner in which treatment is approached. Generally speaking, theoretical perspectives can be classified as follows: **Psychoanalytic** perspectives, **Behavioral** approaches, interpersonal approaches, and **Cognitive Behavioral** approaches. In reality, however, each of these approaches has a considerable amount of overlap with the others when they are actually applied, and the theoretical boundaries separating these approaches are quite blurred in clinical practice. Further, the majority of clinicians use a combination of the various approaches in their work, largely a function of the characteristics of the diagnosis as well as of the specific patient.

Therapeutic Modality

Therapeutic modalities used to treat young people with psychological/psychiatric problems are either primarily *psychopharmacological* or *biological* (drug therapies) or primarily psychotherapeutic (psychotherapy) in nature. Choice of the type of modality employed is a function of the therapeutic orientation of the clinician, the preferences of the patient (and his or her parents), as well as the symptoms being targeted for treatment. The therapeutic modality is defined as to whether the actual intervention takes the form of drugs or some type of talk therapy.

Within the modality of psychotherapy, the actual format utilized is yet another classification. The four major formats utilized in the treatment of the psychiatric/psychological disorders of childhood and adolescence are (1) **Individual Psychotherapy,** (2) **Family Therapy,** (3) **Group Therapy,** (4) **Parent Training.** Detailed descriptions of each of these modalities can be found in the individual entries.

Therapist: Preparing the Child for the First Visit

The manner in which a young child reacts to his or her first visit to a therapist is largely a function of his or her preparation by the parents. During the childhood years, children look to the parents for guidance as to how to react to a new experience. If the child senses from the parental figure that the new experience is something about which he or she should be anxious, that is how the first visit will be approached. Whereas there is certainly an amount of anxiety that is associated with any new experience, there are things that the parents can do to minimize the nervous feelings associated with the first visit.

Pay attention to semantics: If the therapist whom the child is seeing has a doctoral degree, make sure that the child knows that he or she is not going to be physically examined, prodded, or given an injection. Explain to the child that this person is a "different kind of doctor" who helps people by talking to them and playing with them.

Explain the reason for the visit: Within the boundaries of the child's understanding, provide an explanation to the child as to why he or she is consulting the therapist. Even if the explanation needs to be simplified considerably ("this doctor will talk to you and play with you so that you will feel better," or "you know how you have trouble with wetting the bed at night—well, this doctor will help you stop that"), some type of explanation needs to be provided.

Monitor parental fears/anxieties: Parents should do their best to present a positive confidence regarding the appointments with the therapist. As indicated above, children can be exquisitely sensitive to their parents' feelings, and if the parents approach the therapy in a matter-of-fact, calm manner, the child will internalize the message that this is a positive thing.

Pre visit communication from the therapist: In most situations, the therapist (and the parents) prefer to have an initial session without the child being present. During that session, see if the therapist would be willing to somehow communicate with the child prior to first meeting with him or her. This can be in the form of an introductory phone call or a letter, whichever seems more appropriate for the specific situation. Such a communication can do wonders in assuaging anxiety by answering questions and initiating development of clinical rapport prior to the first face-to-face contact with the child.

SUPPLEMENTAL RESOURCES

Galvin, M. (1987). *Ignatius finds help.* New York: Magination Press.

Galvin, M. (1988). *Robby really transforms: A story about grown-ups helping children.* New York: Magination Press.

Therapist: What to Expect on the First Visit

The first visit to a therapist with your child or adolescent is bound to be an emotionally stressful experience for all concerned—you, your child/adolescent, and (perhaps to some extent) the therapist himself or herself. Despite the myriad of emotions running rampant during this initial appointment, it is important that the probability be maximized that this first session is indeed productive. More specifically, the major goal of this first meeting should be the elimination of excessive anxiety, specifically the three following types:

> Anxiety regarding meeting a new professional: A certain amount of anxiety when meeting a new person, especially a treating professional, is natural and healthy. However, by the end of the session, the interaction between you, your child, and the therapist should have been such that a good portion of this anxiety is eliminated. The therapist should have been able to create an environment wherein all involved should be feeling more or less comfortable and relaxed.

> Anxiety regarding the therapeutic process: Whether this is the child/adolescent's first time in therapy, it is likely that it is the first time working with the current clinician. Thus, since every clinician operates somewhat differently, there is bound to be some anxiety in terms of how the actual therapy sessions are going to proceed. Therapeutic modality (i.e., whether individual or family, the degree of directiveness, the amount of confrontation, etc.) varies considerably from clinician to to clinician, from patient to patient and, therefore by situation. It is perfectly acceptable to ask the clinician to explain to you and your child/adolescent how it is anticipated that the therapy sessions will proceed. Specifically, the clinician should be able to provide some idea as to the following aspects:
>
> - who will be participating in the therapy sessions
> - frequency of the appointments
> - modality of therapy that is going to be used and what it will involve
> - length of the therapy sessions
> - approximation as to how long the therapy will last

Anxiety regarding the symptoms: Yet another component contributing to the anxieties around the initial therapy session consists of fears as to the severity, implications, and prognosis for the presenting symptoms. At the first therapy sessions, individuals have concerns regarding what the symptoms are indicative of, whether they can be cured, and in what time frame. Oftentimes, people are assured when they receive an official diagnosis in that it implies that there is indeed a framework within which the symptoms can be conceptualized. This also allows a meaningful discussion of norms and trends for the specific diagnosis in terms of typical clinical course, prognosis, as well as various treatment modalities. All of these issues should be addressed at the first session.

In addition to obtaining information from the therapist, the initial session also involves the clinician obtaining information from the child/adolescent and (most of the time) the parents. As a matter of fact, this initial meeting with the therapist is often viewed primarily as an information/data gathering session for all concerned. In order to help the therapist formulate the optimal treatment plan and goals, it is important that the therapist be provided with the most complete information possible. Although more detailed examples are provided in the entries describing individual diagnostic categories, listed below are some general areas of information which should be accessible in order to provide to the clinician as thorough a description of the presenting complaint as possible:

- Precise description of the nature of the presenting complaint
- When the symptoms were first noticed
- What was transpiring in the child/adolescent's life and in the family at the time of symptom onset
- Any changes in symptom severity, frequency, and/or character since onset
- The reaction of family members, schoolmates, parents, teachers, and others in the child/adolescent's immediate environment to the symptoms

Keep in mind that the initial therapy session is an information-gathering session for child/adolescent, parent, and clinician. It is during this session that the clinician is to decide if he or she has the clinical expertise in this particular area and is therefore the appropriate person to treat the child/adolescent in question. Further, it is during this initial session that the child/adolescent and family members need to make some (at least preliminary) decision as to whether they choose to work with the particular clinician on the current issues. In addition to overall competence in treating the presenting symptoms, the following also need to be taken into account in making this decision:

- Comfort level in talking with the clinician, especially regarding presenting symptoms
- Feeling of being understood and listened to by the clinician
- Agreement with clinician's tentative treatment plan
- Financial demands associated with treatment
- Location, overall appearance, and comfort of office and surroundings
- Feeling liked by the clinician (more importantly, not feeling rejected)

SUPPLEMENTARY RESOURCES

Bush, R. (1995). *A parent's guide to child therapy.* Northvale, NJ: Jason Aronson.

Thioridazine

This is the generic name for the **Antipsychotic** drug known as **Mellaril.**

Thiothixene

This is the generic name for the **Antipsychotic (Neuroleptic)** drug marketed as **Navane.**

Thorazine

This is the trade name for the generic **Antipsychotic (Neuroleptic)** drug **Chlorpromazine.**

Thought Blocking

Thought blocking refers to a process in which a person literally blocks in the middle of a thought, sentence, phrase, or even word. To the listener, it appears as if the person has entered a brief trance in the middle of the conversation. Interestingly enough, in this disorder of thought (most commonly associated with **Schizophrenia**), following the episode of thought blocking, the person does not remember the gist of the conversation in which he or she was involved prior to the thought blocking incident, nor does he or she remember the actual thought blocking itself.

Thought Stopping

This is a technique utilized in the early years of **Cognitive Behavior Therapy,** but now used less frequently. Using the cognitive behavior therapy principle that it is people's maladaptive thoughts that are at the root of their pathology, this procedure involved having the therapist initially shout "STOP" when the patient indicated that he or she was having an unhealthy thought. The process then evolves to the patient performing his or her own thought stopping regimen, either quietly to oneself, or imaging the therapist's shouting voice. The goal behind this procedure would be that of developing a **Conditioned Response** between the unpleasant shout and the maladaptive thinking (thereby eventually eliminating the pathological thought patterns).

Thumb Sucking

It is interesting to note that the sucking of one's thumb is probably one of the most natural habits in which a child can engage, literally so. Indeed, all infants are born with a reflexive (and necessary) ability to suck. Specifically with respect to the sucking of the thumb, it has been indicated that some babies even engage in this behavior prior to birth. Parents seem to have problems with thumb sucking behavior, however, when it continues beyond the age at which they believe it should cease. This is indeed the parents' problem, as studies indicate that almost half of children between the ages of 3 and 4 suck the thumb, 15% of 5 year olds do, and 6% of 6 year olds do.

Is thumb sucking problematic? Technically the answer is no, as the only physical problem it can cause is problems with the child's bite. However, thumb sucking can indeed be problematic from a psychological standpoint when the child begins to experience shame and embarrassment about the behavior. The child's peers may taunt him or her as looking like a baby; to varying degrees, parents may express their own displeasure with the behavior; and the child may feel self-conscious as a result of his or her own awareness of the reactions of others.

As a result, numerous suggestions have been proposed in terms of how to stop a child from sucking his or her thumb. Most of them involve some sort of aversive-tasting substance being placed on the thumb in an attempt to punish the child for sucking, and to eventually diminish the behavior. More humane **Behavior Therapies** are also used in which the child is **Reinforced** for certain periods in which he or she is free from thumb sucking behavior. Despite the seemingly rational qualities to these approaches, oftentimes thumb sucking behavior falls into the category in which less is more with respect to intervention. In time, barring any other intervening psychopathologies or underlying factors, the child will stop the thumb sucking behavior. This is true whether some behavioral approach is employed, or whether the child is left alone to let nature take its course. Keeping this fact in mind, it is often more detrimental to the child to attempt to employ some behavioral strategy (in that it only brings more attention to the situation, thereby embarrassing the child further), and it certainly does very little (if anything) to stop the behavior. A key exception to this less is more strategy is the situation in which the child requests help from the parent in stopping the behavior. In these cases, working with the child in a nonpunitive fashion to help stop the thumb sucking, while consistently reassuring him or her that it will eventually stop by itself anyway, is usually the optimal approach.

Tofranil

This is the trade name of the **Tricyclic Antidepressant** generically referred to as **Imipramine.** Please refer to that entry.

Tomboyism

Refer to the entry **Gender Identity Disorder.**

Tourette's Disorder

Tourette's disorder was first formally documented by Gilles de la Tourette in the late 1800s. Now, it is classified as one of the tic disorders usually first diagnosed in infancy, childhood, or adolescence. According to the *DSM-IV*, in order for Tourette's disorder to be diagnosed, the individual needs to exhibit one or more vocal tics as well as multiple motor tics. (It should be noted, however, that the motor and vocal tics do not need to be present at the same time.) With respect to frequency, the tics tend to occur several times per day for a period of more than 1 year, with a tic-free period never lasting more than three consecutive months (American Psychiatric Association, 1994).

Although symptoms of Tourette's have been reported to occur as young as 1 year of age, the most common age of onset is somewhere around 7 years. While most of the clinical literature report Tourette's being three times more prevalent in boys than in girls, the general consensus is that this gender discrepancy is more a function of reporting artifact than real frequency. In either case, the actual overall frequency of occurrence is estimated to be small—estimated as affecting four to five individuals per 10,000. Symptoms of Tourette's disorder often do not occur in isolation and are often accompanied by attentional problems (which tend to precede the onset of Tourette's symptoms), obsessive and compulsive symptoms (which tend to follow the onset of Tourette's symptoms), **Personality Disorders,** and general impulsivity.

Simple motor tics commonly exhibited in cases of Tourette's disorder include head jerking, facial grimacing, and/or eyeblinking while the simple vocal tics tend to include sniffing, grunting, throat clearing, barking, tongue protrusion, snorting, and/or coughing. It is these simple manifestation of the motor and vocal tics that are the first to appear in cases of Tourette's. Then, as the disorder progresses, the tics become more complex—with the complex motor tics involving hitting oneself, deep knee bends, squatting, and twirling when walking and/or jumping, and common complex vocal tics involving repeating the words of others and self as well as uttering of vulgarity or swear words. In approximately 50% of cases of Tourette's, the vocal tics include some type of profanity. In some situations, **Group Therapy** and/or **Individual Psychotherapy** are employed—not so much as an intervention to lessen the symptoms of Tourette's, but rather to provide the child/adolescent with coping mechanisms/skills to deal with the interpersonal and psychological ramifications of the disorder.

Although considered to be primarily an **Organic** disorder (with respect to **Etiology**), treatment for Tourette's consists of both pharmacological and **Behavioral** treatment approaches. Behavioral treatments are employed to help the patient control his or her tic behavior and tend to involve self-monitoring and other interventions typically used to modify habits and impulse control symptoms. The psychophramacological interventions most commonly used involve **Haldol.** Although it is typically employed in low dosages, it is problematic in that this drug is not approved for use in children younger than 3 years of age. When **Haldol** is not effective, *pimodine (orap)* or *clonidine* is sometimes tried. Those children who suffer from Tourette's disorder as well as **Attention Deficit Disorder** are sometimes prescribed **Desipramine** to address the symptoms of both disorders.

SUPPLEMENTARY RESOURCES

Dornbush, M. P., & Pruitt, S. K. (1998). *Teaching the tiger: A handbook for individuals involved in the education of students with attention deficit disorders, Tourette syndrome or obsessive compulsive disorder.* Duarte, CA: Hope Press.

Haerle, T. (1992). *Children with Tourette's syndrome: A parent's guide.* Bethesda, MD: Woodbine House.

Tricyclic Antidepressant(s)

Tricyclic antidepressants comprise a group of medications used to treat various psychological/psychiatric disorders in children, in adolescents, as well as in adults. Included among the disorders for which tricyclic antidepressants are clinically indicated for children are depression, **Enuresis,** and **Attention Deficit Disorder,** as well as other disorders currently being investigated (**School Phobia, Obsessive-Compulsive Disorder, Panic Disorder, Phobias, Bulimia, Anorexia, Borderline Personality Disorder, Post-Traumatic Stress Disorder,** and trichotillomania). It is important to note, however, that whereas this class of medication has long been considered to be the first line of treatment for adult depression, there are studies that question whether the tricyclics are actually any better than **Placebo** in the treatment of childhood depression. The major tricyclic antidepressants used when treating children and adolescents include **Desipramine, Imipramine, Nortriptyline, Amitriptyline,** and clomipramine.

Regular monitoring of serum blood level and overall condition is crucial with all of the tricyclic antidepressant medications, especially when they are being use with young people. The possible side effects of the drugs in this age group are numerous, ranging from those affecting cardiac functioning to psychosis, mania, confusion, sleep disorders, tremors, skin conditions, tics, to the most severe—that of sudden cardiac death. Thus, tricyclic antidepressants are not to be used with children who have had any history of cardiovascular problems.

Because young people metabolize tricyclic antidepressants so rapidly, some children/adolescents exhibit flulike symptoms of withdrawal when they are on a one dose per day regimen. Thus, it is recommended that the young person have daily dosages divided to prevent this *cholinergic overdrive* phenomenon. Similarly, when a decision is made to discontinue a treatment regimen of tricyclics, it is recommended that there be a tapering (over a 10- to 14-day period) rather than an abrupt discontinuation of the medication.

In sum, tricyclic antidepressants are metabolized, and, therefore, function differently in children from the way they do in adults. The drugs are absorbed more quickly and as a result have an increased risk of toxicity and dangers associated with large doses. Nonetheless, however, tricyclic antidepressants typically take 10 to 14 days (at a therapeutic level) for effects to be noticeable, with full effects not occurring until 4 to 6 weeks.

Trifluoperazine

This is the brand name of the **Antipsychotic (Neuroleptic)** drug **Stelazine.**

U Urine Alarm Training

Urine Alarm Training

Urine alarm training is one of the components frequently used in the behavioral treatment of **Enuresis** (specifically nocturnal enuresis). Originating as the "bell and pad technique," it involves a mechanism whereby some form of alarm goes off once a certain amount of moisture has penetrated the child's bed. Thus, as soon as the child begins to urinate in his or her bed, he or she is awakened. This is designed to serve a dual purpose: First, it awakens the child so he or she can go to the bathroom to urinate. Second, the aversiveness of being woken creates a classical conditioning paradigm in which urinating in bed and the alarm become associated, thereby reducing the likelihood of subsequent incidents of the child urinating in bed.

V Valium

Valium

Valium is one of the drugs in the group benzodiazepines, a drug which is approved for use in children as young as six months of age. The typical dosage ranges from 1–2½ mg. administered 3 to 4 times per day. Although it is technically classified as an *antianxiety* drug, because of the multiple side effects of the benzodiazepines, it is seldom prescribed for young people with **Anxiety Disorders.** Rather, when Valium is prescribed for children or adolescents, it is more often for symptoms of **Enuresis** (when **Imipramine** proves to be ineffective), and less commonly for symptoms of sleep disorders. Again, however, it is important to note that Valium is not commonly prescribed for young people, predominantly because of its potential side effects and addictive potential.

W Wechsler Intelligence Tests

Wechsler Intelligence Tests

These are a set of tests designed to assess "intelligence" or cognitive abilities. There are three different versions of the Wechsler tests, each designed to test a different age group:

Wechsler Preschool and Primary Intelligence Scales–Revised: Designed for children up to age six years.

Wechsler Intelligence Scales for Children–III: Designed for children aged 6 to 16 years.

Wechsler Adult Intelligence Scale–III: Designed for individuals aged 16 years and older.

Each Wechsler test is composed of several scales, each assessing different aspects of intellectual functioning. Scoring results in three IQ scores: the Verbal IQ (a measure of verbal abilities), the Performance IQ (a measure of nonverbal abilities), and the Full Scale IQ (a global measure combining the above two scores).

Z Zoloft

Zoloft

Zoloft is one of the newer antidepressants in the classification of **Selective Serotonin Reuptake Inhibitors.** Although technically classified as an antidepressant, it is used in adults as a treatment for **Obsessive-Compulsive Disorder, Panic Disorder,** trichotillomania (compulsive hair pulling), and cases of major depression. For adults, dosages of Zoloft typically begin around 50 mg with potential increases up to 200 mg per day. The medication is typically administered once per day (either in the morning or in the evening) without any specific concern as to mealtimes.

With respect to children and adolescents, Zoloft has not been proven to be an effective treatment for any disorder (including **Depression**) by any controlled research. Any use of Zoloft with young people is to be considered experimental therefore requiring careful monitoring. Current data report that a 6- to 8-week trial is required prior to determining effectiveness, with any dosages exceeding 100 mg per day to be divided over two administrations. While Zoloft is utilized in the treatment of depression young people as described above, its use for any other psychological/psychiatric disorder in children and adolescents is not recommended at this time.

REFERENCES

Achenbach, T. M., & Edelbrock, C. S. (1982). *Manual for the child behavior checklist and child behavior profile.* Burlington, VT: Child Psychiatry, University of Vermont.

Alcoholics Anonymous. (1990). Comments on AA's triennial surveys. New York: Alcoholics Anonymous World Services.

American Psychiatric Association. (1992). *Report from American Psychiatric Task Force on Tardive dyskinesia.* Washington, DC: Author.

American Psychiatric Association. (1994). *Diagnostic and statistical manual-IV (DSM-IV).* Washington, DC: Author.

Barlow, D. H., & Durand, V. M. (1995). *Abnormal psychology: An integrative approach.* Pacific Grove, CA: Brooks/Cole.

Brems, C. (1993). *A comprehensive guide to child psychotherapy.* Boston: Allyn & Bacon.

Dawson, G., & Castile, P. (1992). Autism. In C. E. Walker & W. C. Roberts (Eds.), *Handbook of clinical child psychology* (2nd ed.). New York: Wiley.

Dulcan, M. K., & Popper, C. W. (1991). *Concise guide to child and adolescent psychiatry.* Washington, DC: American Psychiatric Press.

Erikson, E. (1994). In C. Schaefer & H. Kaduson (Eds.), *The quotable play therapist.* Northvale, NJ: Jason Aronson.

Green, W. H. (1995). *Child and adolescent clinical psychopharmacology.* Baltimore: Williams & Wilkins.

Jacobs, J. (1971). *Adolescent suicide.* New York: Wiley.

Kaplan, H. I., & Sadock, B. J. (1993). *Pocket handbook of psychiatric drug treatment.* Baltimore: Williams & Wilkins.

Kaplan, H. I., & Sadock, B. J. (1996). *Concise textbook of clinical psychiatry.* Baltimore: Williams & Wilkins.

Liden, C. B., Zalenski, J. R., & Newman, R. L. (1989). *Pay attention: Answers to common questions about the diagnosis and treatment of attention deficit disorder.* Monroeville, PA: Transect Health Systems.

Marcus, L. M., & Schopler, E. (1991). Parents as co-therapists with autistic children. In C. E. Schaefer & J. M. Briesmeister (Eds.), *Handbook of parent training.* New York: Wiley.

Martin, C. A., & Colbert, K. K. (1997). *Parenting: A life span perspective.* New York: McGraw-Hill.

Maxmen, J. S. (1996). *Psychotropic drugs: Fast facts.* New York: W. W. Norton.

Nathan, P. E. (1993). Alcoholism: Psychopathology, etiology, and treatment. In P. B. Sutker & H. E. Adams (Eds.), *Comprehensive handbook of psychopathology* (pp. 451–476). New York: Plenum Press.

National Institute on Drug Abuse. (1989). *1988 national household survey on drug abuse.* Bethesda, MD: National Institute on Drug Abuse.

Offer, D., & Boxer, A. M. (1991). Normal adolescent development: Empirical research findings. In M. Lewis (Ed.), *Child and adolescent psychiatry: A comprehensive textbook.* Baltimore, MD: Williams and Wilkins.

O'Leary, K. D. (1984). The image of behavior therapy: It's time to take a stand. *Behavior Therapy, 15,* 219–233.

Pelham, W. E., & Hinshaw, S. P. (1992). Behavioral intervention for attention deficit–hyperactivity disorder. In S. M. Tuyrner, K. S. Calhoun, & H. E. Adams (Eds.), *Handbook of clinical behavior therapy* (2nd ed.). New York: Wiley.

Powers, S, W., & Rickard, H. C. (1992). Behavior therapy with children. In C. E. Walker & M. C. Roberts (Eds.), *Handbook of clinical child psychology* (2nd ed.). New York: Wiley.

Ritvo, E. R., & Freeman, B. J. (1978). National Society for Autistic Children definition of autism. *Journal of Autism and Developmental Disorders, 8,* 162–167.

Rosenberg, D. R., Wright, B. A., & Gershon, S. (1992). Depression in the elderly, *Dementia, 3,* 157–173.

Schneidman, E. S. (1986). A psychological approach to suicide. In G. R. Vandenbos & B. K. Bryant (Eds.), *Cataclysms, crises and catastrophes: Psychology in action.* Washington, DC: American Psychological Association.

Sheras, P. L. (1992). Depression and suicide in adolescence. In C. E. Walker & M. C. Roberts (Eds.), *Handbook of clinical child psychology* (4th ed.). New York: Wiley.

Silver, L. B., & Silver, B. J. (1983). Clinical practice of child psychiatry: A survey. *Journal of the American Academy of Child Psychiatry, 22,* 573–579.

Spitz, R. A. (1946). Anaclitic depression. *Psychoanalytic study of the child,* Vol. 2. New York: International Universities Press.

Stoller, R. J. (1975). *Sex and gender.* London: Hugarth Press.

Strecker, E. A., & Ebaugh, F. G. (1935). *Practical clinical psychiatry for students and practitioners* (4th ed.). Philadelphia: P. Blakiston's Son & Co., Inc.

Szymanski, L. S., & Kaplan, L. C. (1991). Mental retardation. In J. M. Wiener (Ed.), *Textbook of child and adolescent psychiatry.* Washington, DC: American Psychiatric Press.

Weiner, I. B. (1992). *Psychological disturbances in adolescence* (2nd ed.). New York: Wiley.

Zarb, J. M. (1992). *Cognitive-behavioral assessment and therapy with adolescents.* New York: Brunner/Mazel.

Zucker, K. J., & Green, R. (1991). Gender identity and psychosexual disorders. In J. M. Wiener (Ed.), *Textbook of child and adolescent psychiatry.* Washington, DC: American Psychiatric Association.

INDEX

Bandura, A., 218
baseline, 70, 83
bedtime problems, 70–71
bedtime rituals, 71, 72–73, 232
Behavior Assessment System for Children
(BASC), 73
behavior therapy, 58, 66, 74–76, 162, 177, 178, 192,
216, 221, 258, 262, 271
Bellevue index of depression, 103
benzodiazepenes, 31
beta blockers, 59
Bill W., 27
binge, 40, 92–93
biochemical, 66, 158
biofeedback, 76
bipolar disorder, 21, 76, 77, 204, 209
bipolar I disorder, 76–77
bipolar II disorder, 77, 122
birth of a sibling, 78–80
bisexuality, 80
biting, 80–81
blanket carrying, 81–82
Bleuler, E., 170
blunted affect, 82–83, 223, 278
body dysmorphic disorder, 83–87
body noises, 87–88
borderline personality disorder, 89–91, 247, 306
boundaries, 9, 68, 117
Bowlby, John, 53, 92
bradykinesia, 92
Brief Psychiatric Rating Scale for Children, 92,
103
Briquet's syndrome, 92
Broca's aphasia, 47
bruxism, 92
bulimia, 92–94, 134, 204, 219, 306
bullies, 94–97
burping, 97
buspirone, 46

catalepsy, 98
catatonia, 98
catatonic excitement, 98
catatonic posturing, 98
catatonic rigidity, 98
catatonic schizophrenia, 98–99, 152
catatonic stupor, 98
central aphasia, 47
Chambless, Diane, 25

checking compulsions, 231, 233
child abuse, 116, 251–252
Child Behavior Checklist, 99–100, 103
Childhood Anxiety Sensitivity Index, 100
Childhood Assessment Schedule, 99
Childhood Autism Rating Scale, 65
childhood depression, 100–104, 122, 219, 260, 306
Childhood Depression Inventory, 105
childhood disintegrative disorder, 105–106
Children's Depression Rating Scale, 103
Children's Manifest Anxiety Scale, 106
chlamydia, 287
chlorpromazine, 106, 278, 303
cholinergic overdrive, 306
chronological age, 197, 270
classical conditioning, 74, 249, 308
cleaning compulsions, 233
clinical interview, 103, 141
clinical psychologist, 108
clomipramine, 156, 306
clonidine, 306
Clozapine, 108
clozaril, 43, 108, 109, 297
Cluster A, 247
Cluster B, 247
Cluster C, 247
cognitive behavior therapy, 74, 109–110, 193, 244,
249, 258, 303
command hallucinations, 61–62
communication disorder, 110
communication of intention, 15
comorbidity, 6, 111
compulsions, 111–112, 229, 232–234
conduct disorder, 43, 44, 54, 73, 105, 109, 112–115,
199, 209, 239, 277, 292
conduction aphasia, 47
confidentiality, 115–116, 263
congruent affect, 18
conjoint therapy, 117
contagion effect, 17
contingency management, 75, 117–118, 272, 276
continuous progressive course, 277
continuous reinforcement, 256
continuous sluggish course, 277
contraception, 13
copycat suicide, 17
cortisol, 136
counselor, 262
cross dressing, 118–120, 174